DYNAMICS OF INDIA'S IMPORTS

DYNAMICS OF INDIA'S IMPORTS

By

Ms. Meenu

B.Sc.,(Hons.) (Economics)
M.Sc., (Hons.) (Economics)
Ph.D (Economics)

&

Dr. (Ms.) Neena Malhotra

M.Sc., (Hons.) (Economics)
Ph.D (Economics)
Associate Professor
Punjab School of Economics
Guru Nanak Dev University
Amritsar (Punjab)
(India)

NEW DELHI-110 002

Published by:
Tilak Wasan

DISCOVERY PUBLISHING HOUSE PVT. LTD.
4831/24, Prahlad Street, Ansari Road
Darya Ganj, New Delhi-110002 (India)
Phone : +91-11-23279245, 43764432
Fax : +91-11-23253475
E-mail : parul.wasan@gmail.com
discoverypublishinghouse@gmail.com
info@discoverypublishinggroup.com
web : www.discoverypublishinggroup.com

***First Edition:* 2011**
ISBN: 978-81-8356-886-9

Dynamics of India's Imports

Printed at:
Shree Balaji Art Press
Delhi

Preface

In today's globalized and liberalized world, foreign trade again emerged as a powerful engine of growth. Benefits of trade like providing material means indispensable for development, dissemination of technological knowledge, international movement of capital goods and stabalisation of domestic prices are well-established in economic theory. Apart from these, productivity and efficiency gains and encouragement of positive externalities are important especially for developing countries.

Trade in itself is a growth factor and benefits both importing and exporting countries. The imports and exports both play an important role in the development process of a country. Imports are important for both developed and developing countries as no country can be fully self-sufficient. For a developing country, imports are of crucial importance for extending productive capacity at a fast rate. Besides, imports bring with them new taste, new technology and new ideas.

India's foreign trade prior to Independence was typical of a colonial and agricultural economy, mainly trading with Britain and other Commonwealth countries. However, after Independence, the desire for development changed the composition of India's trade drastically. With this India's imports also changed significantly due to growing requirements of industrial, infrastructure and export sectors. Apart from these, international oil price fluctuations and changing trade policy regimes also affected India's import growth and structure. The process of trade liberalization in

India actually started in mid 80s, but it got big boost after 1991, when new economic reforms were initiated. The import policy reforms during 1990s especially after the formation of WTO included abolition of quantitative restrictions and reduction of other tariff and non-tariff barriers. Import liberalization helped to boost export as well as other sectors of Indian economy. The structure of India's imports has changed towards high technology intensive and export-oriented products, though import dependence in case of essential imports and petroleum products imports continues to be high.

Thus, present import policy of India is in sync with overall liberal economic policies, with the main objectives of promoting industrial production and productivity, exports, foreign direct investment, technology development and integration of Indian economy with changing international economic order.

Against this backdrop, this book is a comprehensive study of India's imports sector during the period 1986-87 to 2005-06. The book analyses the growth pattern and structure of India's imports. It studies the determinants of aggregate imports as well as of major categories of imports. The demand for imports is influenced by many factors, including size, growth pattern of population, relative prices, rate of capital formation, growth rate of GNP and growth of export earnings. This book estimates import demand functions for India's total imports as well as for some of its major categories and derives important policy recommendations related to import demand determinants. The relationship between import and growth can be investigated with the help of causality analysis. The book analyses causal relationship for total imports and also for some of the major categories of imports with GDP at factor cost. Apart from income variable, the causality analysis has been extended to cover the impact of domestic production on major categories of imports. In case of machinery imports, causality has been tested with gross domestic capital formation as well. The import policy of India has changed from time to time according to changing economic conditions, domestic requirements and international changes. The book analyses in detail the changing import policy regimes especially during post-1985 period. An attempt has been made to analyse the impact of changing import policy on growth and structure of India's imports. The book gives indepth analysis of various theoretical issues related to the role of imports in economic development. The book also reviews a large number of empirical studies relating to various aspects of the present study.

We would like to acknowledge those whose assistance and contribution has made this book possible. So many people have contributed to and influenced us during our work that we can not list them all and must ask for forgiveness of those we omit.

We duly acknowledge the services of the staff at Bhai Gurdas Library, Guru Nanak Dev University, Amritsar, Departmental library, Punjab School of Economics, Guru Nanak Dev University, Amritsar and Ratan Tata Library, Delhi School of Economics, New Delhi. We are extremely thankful to Sr. Sukhdev Singh and Sr. Surinder Singh from computer department and Mr. Vishal (programmer in computer lab of Punjab School of Economics), Guru Nanak Dev University, Amritsar, who rendered extensive support in analyzing statistical data.

We are deeply indebted to M/s Discovery Publishing House, New Delhi, for bringing out this work in a record time. We thank the writers and researchers who made this task easy and gave a benchmark to proceed further in the field of research.

Meenu

Neena Malhotra

Contents

CHAPTER 1

Introduction

Development in all the societies must have at least following three objectives :

(*i*) to increase the availability and widen the distribution of basic life sustaining goods,

(*ii*) to raise the level of living and

(*iii*) to expand the range of social and economic choices (Todaro, 1981).

Meier (1973) defined economic development as the process whereby real per capita income of a country increases over a long period of time subject to the condition that number of people living below the absolute poverty line does not increase and distribution of income does not become more unequal. We can also define the economic development as the process whereby people of country or region utilize the resources available to bring about a sustained increase in per capita production of goods and services.

The objectives of economic development may vary from country to country. The advanced countries have already achieved the basic requirements for economic development. Their real problem is of maintaining the development rate already attained. The under-developed countries, have yet to create the basic requirements of economic development. Thus the creation of social, political, ideological and psychological environment propitious to economic development will be a vital part of the process of development (Nag, 1962). The concept of sustainable development used by World Commission on Environment (Brundtland Commission) in 1987, has added new dimension to the process of development. The sustainable development is defined as "meeting the needs of present generation without compromising the needs of future generation."

The economic development implies the process of raising productivity in all sectors of economy and this, in turn is a function of the level of technology which requires capital formation. The accelerated rate of growth of capital formation cannot meet through domestic sources alone. Thus, foreign exchange resources for meeting the need of essential imported capital goods are an important input atleast during the early stages of economic development. The basic argument of two gap model is that most developing countries face either shortage of domestic savings to match investment opportunities or a shortage of foreign exchange to finance needed imports of capital and intermediate goods.

The saving gap shows that domestic savings are inadequate to support the level of growth, which could be permitted given the sufficiency of the import purchasing power of the economy and the level of other resources. The foreign exchange gap explains that import purchasing power conferred by the value of exports plus capital transfers may be inadequate to support the level of growth permitted by the level of domestic savings. If saving gap is dominant, this would indicate that the country is operating at full employment and is not using all of its foreign exchange earnings. Such country is said to have a shortage of productive resources to carry out additional investment project, but may have enough foreign exchange to purchase additional capital goods from abroad. If foreign exchange gap is binding, then country is having excess productive resources (mostly labour), and all available foreign exchange is being used for imports. The existence of complementary domestic resources would permit them to undertake new projects if they had the external finance to import new capital goods and associated technical assistance. Foreign aid can therefore play a critical role in overcoming the foreign exchange constraint and raising the real rate of economic growth. A surplus of imports over the exports financed by foreign borrowings allows a country to spend more than it produces or to invest more than it saves.

Most of the developing countries fall into foreign exchange constrained category. The policy implications of these gaps show that as long as one resource constraint is dominant, there will be resource waste. If foreign exchange is the dominant constraint, unused domestic resources must be used to earn more foreign exchange and/or raise the productivity of imports. If domestic saving is the dominant constraint, then foreign exchange must be used to augment domestic savings and/or raise the productivity of domestic resources (Thirlwall, 2003).

The trade has potential for raising the welfare of nations by solving the foreign exchange constraint faced by a country. The availability of foreign exchange can be used to break out the small saving-small growth vicious circle by less developed economy. The economy also uses foreign exchange to import either capital or consumer goods, while devoting domestic resources to the production of capital goods. In either case, investment and hence growth can be increased without cutting consumption. Thus foreign exchange can be used to supplement savings, which are typically quite inadequate in LDCs (Basu, 1998).

In the development process of a developing economy, international trade is an activity of strategic importance. The importance of foreign trade varies from country to country. The dependence on foreign trade is high for smaller countries endowed with less variety of resources. On the contrary, large countries having a wide geographical area and possessing a great variety of natural resources are relatively less dependent on external trade.

The study of relationship between trade and economic development has received greater attention during past few decades. The economists such as Prebisch, Mydral, Singer, Emmunnel, Nurkse and others have suggested an inward-oriented approach for development of developing countries, where trade has limited role to play. Whereas, economists such as J.N. Bhagwati, Kruger, Chenery, Bela Blassa and others have strongly recommended the export-led growth strategy through liberalization and globalization principle for the development of developing countries (Manjappa and Hegde, 1998). For the development of a country, the classical and neo-classical economists attached so much importance to international trade that they regarded it as "an engine of economic growth". Haberler argued that international trade has made a tremendous contribution to the development of LDC's in the 19th and 20th centuries and expected a big contribution in the future, if it is allowed proceed freely. He argued that hundred percent free trade policy is not required and that marginal interference with free trade may speed up the development. Cairncross remarks that foreign trade provides the urge to develop the knowledge and experience that makes development possible and the means to accomplish it. Being deficient in capital goods and material, UDC's are able to quicken their pace of development by importing these goods from developed countries.

The gain from trade is the difference between things that are obtained and value of things that are given up. The gains from trade can be divided into static and dynamic gains. Static gains accrue from international specialization according to comparative advantage. Dynamic gains result from the impact of trade on production possibilities at large. The static gains mainly resulted from the division of labour with given (or autonomously changing) production functions. This enables every country to specialize and to export those things that it can produce cheaper in exchange for what others can provide at a lower cost. The static gains from trade are same as from trade creation that accrue with the establishment of custom unions, when high cost suppliers are replaced by lower cost suppliers as tariffs are reduced. The formation of custom unions or regional trading agreements between countries is based on the doctrine of comparative cost advantage. The contribution of international trade solely by static gains from trade is just like underrating the importance of trade. The indirect or dynamic benefits of trade are:

1. Trade provides material means (capital goods, machinery and raw and semi-finished material) indispensable for economic development.
2. Trade is the mean and vehicle for the dissemination of technological knowledge, the transmission of ideas, for the importation of know how, skills, managerial talents and entrepreneurship.
3. Trade is also the vehicle for the international movement of capital especially from the developed to the under developed countries.
4. Free international trade is the best antimonopoly policy and the best guarantee for the maintenance of a healthy degree of free competition (Meier, 1984; Thirlwall, 2003).

Some other benefits of trade are as follows:

1. Trade is an important stimulator of economic growth. It enlarges a country's consumption capacities, increases world output, and provides access to scarce resources and worldwide markets for products without which poor countries would be unable to grow.
2. Trade tends to promote greater international and domestic equality by equalizing factor prices, raising real incomes of trading countries, and making efficient use of each nation's and world resource endowments.
3. Trade helps countries to achieve development by promoting and rewarding those sectors of economy where individual countries posses a comparative advantages whether in terms of labour efficiency or factors endowments (Todaro, 2007).

So, more trade encourages investment which confers externalities on an economy, particularly if the investment goods come from abroad. Larger volume of output due to more trade, creates greater scope for specialization, leading to learning by doing. Moreover, trade leads to technology transfer and the prospect of faster total productivity growth.

Thus, the foreign trade plays an important role in a country's economic development. It is well-established fact that the trade and commerce are not just the sum of exports and imports, they add a growth factor that benefits exporting and importing countries. If the resource base of a country is limited, it has no alternative but to attach greater importance to its foreign trade for ensuring a respectable standard of living of its people. But even for a country with adequate resources, the role of foreign trade may become highly significant, if its development plans are of a character requiring resources not available at all or available only in limited quantities. Besides international trade open market oppourtunities which allows factor specialization. Because different countries are differently endowed therefore they can help each other through trade to attain the common goal of socio-economic development.

Foreign trade of any country changes as a result of two competing set of forces. On the one hand, those that induce growth of domestic output and on the other those those induce growth of exports and imports (Sodersten and Reed, 1994). In addition to this, specialization due to technological opportunities, which improves industrial production, is also possible through freer trade. Trade makes production more profitable because firm buys in what they cannot produce themselves. This will help the firms to satisfy their customers or they can afford to supply their specialities to other firms (Meyer, 1978).

Historically, the pattern of foreign trade of most of LDCs is usually characterized by former colonial trade relationships. The former colonies used to export the primary commodities and raw materials to the imperial countries and import from them the finished products. For a long time LDCs were chiefly net exporters of primary products and net importers of industrial goods. Dependence is a conditioning situation in which the economies of one group of countries are conditioned by the development and expansion of others. Colonialism was an extreme form of dependence, which leads to unequal exchange relations between rich and poor countries, where poor are dependent on rich for capital and technology for their industrial sector. The other forms of dependence include financial-industrial dependence and technology-industrial dependence. A. Emmanuel has analysed that increasing inequality between nations is rooted in an unequal exchange that tends to increase over time, so that poor nation become poorer and the rich ones richer.

However, dependency theories fail to explain rapid growth experienced by many countries following liberal trade policies like India, China, other countries of South Asia and Latin America. The actual experience of developing countries pursuing nationalist industrial policies has mostly been negative. The classical examples are India and China, which after pursuing inwardly directed development policies for a long time experienced stagnant growth and ultimately decided to substantially open their economies. At the other extreme there are economies like Taiwan and South Korea, which mostly emphasized export sector, grew very strongly. As a matter of fact, in the late 1970's there was a form of neo classical free market counter revolution (Thirlwall, 2003; Meier, 1984; Todaro, 2007).

In 1950s and 1960s, most of the developing countries followed inward looking or import substitution policies for economic growth. Since, the mid 1970s most of the developing countries considerably shifted towards the export promotion strategy (Shirazi and Manap, 2004). In an outward looking strategy, trade and industrial policies neither discriminate between production for the domestic market and exports, nor between purchase of domestic goods and foreign goods. In an inward looking strategy there is a bias of trade and industrial policies in favour of domestic production as against foreign trade, the import restriction policy is adopted by countries which are eager to encourage exports and to solve foreign exchange problem. The outward orientation in contrast to inward orientation is an open strategy. It links the domestic economy to the world economy, encourages competition and innovation and thereby promotes economic efficiency (Cherunilam, 1999).

The import substitution in early stages of industrialization is suited to the non durable consumption goods such as footwear, clothing, leather and wood goods etc, because of relatively little protection is required. After this for maintenance of high growth rates, the import substitution of intermediate goods such as steel and producer durable required, where relatively high rates of protection are required. These high rates act as a tax on exports by keeping cost and exchange rate high. Further, this shifts the distribution of income in favour of higher income groups with high propensity to import, which worsen the balance of payments. Import substitution may also encourage capital intensive activities, which further worsen unemployment. Trade pessimists advocate the greater protection, more inward looking strategies and greater import substitution. They focused on the limited growth of world demand for primary exports, secular deterioration in terms of trade for primary producing nations and the rise of new protectionism against the exports of LDC manufactured and processed agricultural goods.

In any viable long run strategy, the promotion of primary or secondary exports of LDCs, has been considered as a major ingredient. Export promotion needs provision of credit, insurance and transport facilities, tax concessions to exporters and also stable prices of exportable goods. Trade optimists advocate the free trade, outward looking development and export promotion policies. They argued that free trade promotes competition, improves resource allocation and economies of scale in areas where LDCs have a comparative advantage. It helps in lowering cost of production by raising factor productivity through generating pressures for increased efficiencies, product improvement and technical change. In addition to this free trade encourages investment and saving, attracts foreign capital and expertise, generates foreign exchange, improves resource allocation through more equal access to scarce resources and enables LDCs to take advantage of reforms under WTO (Thirlwall, 2003; Todaro, 2007).

A developing economy has to adopt a dynamic trade policy to promote its economic development for various reasons, which also includes international trade relationships. It lays down policy parameters and guidelines for different categories of tradables in a country's trade basket (Mukerjee, 1998; Dikshit, 2002). A trade policy which allows country to take part in international trade with minimum of interference is a liberal trade policy. A trade policy which intended to influence the trade policies of other countries is strategic trade policy. With changes in the trade policies of the country due to changes in the domestic economy as well as in the economies of other countries, the commodity composition of trade and direction of trade, also undergo changes over time (Pal, 2007).

The imports and exports both play an important role in the development process of a country. The goods that enter into a country in the form of purchases from other countries are called imports. The goods leave the country's frontier as sales are called exports. In economics, an import is any good or service brought into one country from another country in a legitimate fashion, typically for use in trade. Imported goods or services are provided to domestic consumer by foreign producers. An import in the receiving country is an export to the sending country. Imports of goods normally require involvement of customs authorization in both the country of import and the country of export and are often subject to import quotas, tariffs and trade agreements. If exports lead to an increase in national income of developing country it also leads to higher level of imports. As Mathur (2003), pointed out that rise in exports leads to an increase in national income and through that a rise in consumption and investment. Higher investment leads to more capacity creation in domestic and export industries which ultimately leads to higher level of imports.

For a developed country, imports provide production inputs, increased investment opportunities and international goodwill. For a developing country, imports fulfil the needs of development, maintenance of essential supplies and inflation control etc. Imports play an important role for economy which decides to embark on a programme of development to extend its productive capacity at a fast rate. Imports create new tastes and stimulate new energies for work and new willingness to make the best use of available resources, so that extra income may become available to buy the new goods (Lewis, 1978). Furthermore, the competitive pressures exerted by imports prevent the emergence of welfare-reducing domestic monopolies and induce domestic producers to improve quality and reduce costs (Lal and Rajapatirana, 1987). Imports are the reverse of comparative cost advantage principle, that is, we import those products in which we have comparative disadvantage (Adiseshiah, 1986).

In the initial stages of economic development, an underdeveloped country needs imports of machinery and equipment which can not be produced in initial stages of development at home. Such imports which help to create new and enlarged capacity in some lines of production are called developmental imports. Secondly, industrialization process at home requires imports of raw material and intermediate goods. These imports help to utilize the capacity created in the country. Such imports which are made in order to make a full use of productive capacity are called maintenance imports. Thus both developmental as well as maintenance imports are important for a developing economy. For developing economies, these imports set limits to the extent of industrialization which can be carried out in a given period. Besides these imports, a developing economy also requires to import consumer goods which are in short supply during the period of industrialization. Such imports are anti-inflationary because they reduce the scarcity of consumer goods.

Thus economic growth normally necessitates larger imports. This is due to increased investment needs arising out of larger money income while increased imports of capital goods and industrial materials are direct result of industrialization. A larger volume of imports is also needed due to increasing incomes, rise in standard of living and consumption habits of the people (Singh, 1971).

The composition of imports depends upon the size of the country, the availability of the resources and also on the pattern of income distribution. Import requirements of any country are mainly determined by relative prices, national income, domestic production, natural calamity, gross domestic capital formation, trade policy and self sufficiency of industrial sector. According to Mathur (2003), volume of imports required for the development is determined by five variables. These are: (*a*) import content of investment, (*b*) techniques of production required for development, (*c*) export earnings, (*d*) foreign exchange reserves and (*e*) foreign aid flow. Besides these size, composition and growth rate of population, level and growth of rate of GNP, tastes and preference of consumer, availability of substitutes to important import items etc are also important variables are also important variables (Kutty, 2001).

The capacity to import of a country largely depends upon the export performance of the country. The large demand for imports in developing countries does not become satisfied fully due to limited export growth, and because foreign exchange earnings from merchandise exports are used to finance both merchandise imports and international services. However, the performance of exports depends on many factors along with availability of imported raw materials. One of the main reasons of export stagnation in Indian economy was non availability of adequate and cheap imported raw materials for exporters. This was due to restrictive trade policy (Sathe, 1997; Afxentiou and Serletis, 2000).

Thus, increased imports are one of the main conditions, which should be fulfilled at the initial stages of economic development. It is now accepted that imports have a developmental role to play and the attitude towards imports should not be one of discriminate restrictions but one of import management for a rational and development inducing import structure (Adiseshiah, 1986). Moreover, availability of imports reduces the risk element in developing new products as imports find out market for new products and give an idea to domestic producers about what is possible to sell in the country. In other words, the development of domestic industries may first require the free entry of imports, and when necessary market settles up, the infant industries will be set up, possibly with the help of protection (Corden, 1974). In addition to this, imports make productivity increases possible through imported ideas and capital goods embodying the new technologies. New technologies, however, require a learning process both to master them and to adapt them to the local conditions (Goldin and Reinert, 2007).

For increasing imports in a developing country, liberalization policy plays an important role. The liberalization policy is expected to improve the allocation of resources, leads to greater efficiency, expands output and accelerates economy's growth. Without liberalization, industries will remain in bad shape due to lack of access to raw material, capital goods and components and parts at lowest world prices (Bhalla, 2004). The economic development is transmitted from advanced to latecomer economies through movement of capital and technology. Globalization accelerated this transmission by creating greater economic integration among the nations of world. While globalization is facilitated and influenced by technological developments such as modern information and communications technology, the process is mainly enabled by rapid liberalization of finance, trade and investment.

Trade liberalization is the most effective anti monopoly tool for goods and requires little complexity of laws, regulation and control (Harylyshyn and Tarr, 1991). Broadly trade liberalization can take one of the two forms-changes in prices (lower tariff, for instance), and changes in the form of intervention (such as shift to tariffs from import quotas). According to Bhattacharya (1993), liberalization of trade may be introduced in various ways:

1. Liberalization of exports and imports through tariff restructuring and export incentives.
2. Trade is also liberalized through variation in exchange rates or altering the exchange control systems.
3. Introduction of partial or full convertibility of the domestic currency also introduces trade liberalization.
4. Conditions may be created to liberalize technology imports and invite multinationals to invest through rate restructuring.

Freeing up trade in goods and services, currencies and capital not only improves the efficiency of national resource use and consumer welfare at a point in time but also contributes to economic growth. A direct consequence of liberalization will be an expanded demand for inputs due to increased industrialization. An indirect consequence would be increased demand for food imports by newly industrializing countries (Mathur, 2003). The substantial trade liberalization has been accompanied by a devaluation of the exchange rate in many programs of IMF or the World Bank. The effects of devaluation will depend on the price elasticity of import demand. If import demand is inelastic, devaluation will result in higher value of imports in local currency. It will increase revenues at any given level of tariffs. If import demand is elastic, there will be reverse effect.

Import liberalization is one of the components of package of structural adjustment reforms. It was argued that import liberalization may actually reduce the growth rate of output if the increased import intensities are not matched by higher import capacity. It is also pointed out that import liberalization stabilizes prices by reducing excess demand in economy if domestic supply of import substitutes is insufficient. It also improves trade balance with efficiency gain in the export sector. To promote exports and thus raise export earnings, import liberalization plays an important role. It firstly reduces excess demand, stabilizes prices and secondly, increases technological innovation, which promotes export sector. Import liberalization as a part of structural adjustment and stabilization policies in the developing countries is expected to generate an improved GDP growth, stabilize domestic prices and narrow down the trade deficit for the domestic economy via export competitiveness. Finally export expansions are also expected with import liberalization (Das, 2000; Bhattacharya, 1993).

The India's foreign trade prior to Independence was typical of a colonial and agricultural economy, mainly trading with Britain and other Commonwealth countries. The composition of trade of a country primarily depends upon level of development and the structure of the economy. The composition of India's foreign trade has experienced a drastic change since Independence, the positions of many commodities which were earlier imported and exported in large quantities, are now occupied by some new items of imports and exports. India, like any other under-developed country was mainly an exporter of primary commodities and an importer of manufactured industries products. But over the time with development, the structure of trade has undergone significant changes. Now India imports capital goods, raw materials, equipments and technical know how for facilitating industrialization. The export sector has also diversified and includes many manufactured industrial goods thereby raising the country's capacity to import. Higher export earnings facilitate the availability of such imported inputs, which are needed for industrial growth, and to broaden the industrial base. For improving export capacity also, technical know how is needed which further increases imports. Thus, it is a continuing process whereby one sector pushing the other.

Since Independence, India also followed inward looking policy to protect domestic industries from foreign competition through various devices such as tariffs, quotas, restrictions, import licensing and other discretionary control. As a result, the cost and quality structure of Indian products was not able to survive in global market. Restricted imports resulted in an uncompetitive domestic industrial structure. However, from mid-1980s onwards, import restrictions were removed and the process of trade liberalization and opening up of the Indian economy was initiated. Under the new economic policy of 1991, the government has brought revolutionary changes to liberalize the Indian economy, which aims at freeing the industry, tertiary and foreign trade sectors from various suffocating controls and restrictions (Mukundan and Manaka, 2005; Sharma and Singh, 2000). The trade policy measures announced in 1991 mark the beginning of new era in India's foreign trade and its performance improved significantly during recent years.

The two components of liberalization are external liberalization and internal liberalization. The internal liberalization mainly includes reducing the domestic barriers to entry, while external liberalization includes liberalization of import regime for exporters, extension of fiscal and monetary concessions etc. The import liberalization makes available the much needed capital goods and raw materials to the exporters and domestic industries. This led to major departure from protectionist trade policies and now India is an open economy and not only its exports are rising but imports are also increasing due to various developmental, industrial and infrastructural requirements.

India's imports have always exceeded exports due to various reasons:

1. Imports increased because of requirements of capital goods, defence equipment, petroleum products, raw material, edible oils and occasionally foodgrains.

2. Rapid industrialization necessasitated increasing imports of machinery and equipments, raw materials etc.

3. To control inflationary pressure within the country through increased imports and supply of price sensitive goods.

4. Policy of liberal imports on the pretext of export promotion, resulting in increase of not only essential imports but also non essential imports.
5. Policy of import liberalization pursued during 1985-86 and thereafter.
6. Periodic increase in international crude oil prices constitutes the single biggest factor for boosting imports of crude petroleum, oil and lubricant.
7. Imports also show an increase due to natural calamities which take place in country.

The structure of India's imports has also undergone complete change with changing structure of Indian economy, international oil prices and also due to changing trade policy regimes. From few decades now petroleum, oil and lubricants have dominated our imports. These imports increased substantially due to heavy demand and insufficiency of oil production in India. Moreover, these imports are of essential nature and also helpful in developmental efforts. Besides this, capital goods and other intermediary goods for export and domestic industries have emerged as key items of imports in 1990s (Bhasin, 2005 and Mathur, 2003). These imports are high due to development of exports and industrial sectors. The imports of pearls, precious and semi precious stones, metals and articles are high due to their direct link with India's large and rising exports of gems and jewellery.

India's policies towards progressive opening up of the economy since the early 1990s were undertaken with the objectives of improving the overall productivity, competitiveness and efficiency of the economy in order to attain a higher growth profile (Kapila and Kapila, 2004). The policies of opening up of Indian economy, undertaken during 1990s mainly included reduction in tariffs and phasing out quantitative restrictions. Thus, import liberalization, in conjunction with external sector reforms, strengthened the external sector of India. This has moved the structure of India's imports towards higher technology intensive and export-oriented products during 1990s, further it helped to change the growth pattern of Indian economy.

Many empirical studies concluded that openness to trade has a positive impact on the growth of GDP of an economy. Further, the import expenditure which is a part of consumption and investment expenditure of a country in aggregate depends on aggregate gross GDP of a country. Thus, with the increase in income of a country, the imports expenditure also increases due to increased exports. In case of India exports growth not only derives import growth but it is also import driven. As the Indian economy liberalized, imports increased and then exports also increased. With more liberalization and openness of the economy, there is more efficient allocation of resources through specialization and efficient exploitation of comparative advantage. Thus many studies conclude that liberalizing imports, both for domestic sector and external sector facilitate export growth which is vital for the growth of the economy (Nandi and Kumar, 2005 and Bajpai and Sachs, 1997).

Trade policy is an important part of policy programmes of a country. It helps to manage the value, composition and direction of the imports and exports. In India, the import policy changed from time to time according to changing economic conditions and domestic requirements. During post-Independence period, the government followed restrictive trade polices through judicious use of import licensing, import quotes, import duties and in extreme cases even banning imports of specific goods. The protectionist policies continued till mid-80s, even during this regime, imports were liberalized from time to time due to domestic requirements. But proper liberalization phase started only after 1990. Thus, imports were liberalized on different points of time for various purposes, i.e., for rapid industrialization, for promoting capacity utilization, export promotion, for improving efficiency, productivity and growth of domestic production and also for facilitating technological upgradation in different sectors of the economy etc. Some major trade policy reforms during 1991 consist of:

1. Quantitative restrictions on imports have been abolished.
2. Import duties which used to be as high as 400% on some items, have been drastically reduced and peak level of duty has been brought down to 25%.
3. Rationalization and simplification of procedures has been undertaken.
4. Number of items subject to export restrictions has been drastically reduced.
5. Exchange rate of rupee *vis-à-vis* major currencies has become more or less market determined (Tripathi, 2005).

India categorized imports of items under five heads: - the prohibited list, the special import license (SIL) list, the restricted list, the canalized list and the free list. At present number of imports lists has come down to three which includes the prohibited list, special list and free list. The prohibited list contains only a few products prohibited on the grounds of religious and cultural sensitivity. The special list includes bulk agricultural commodities, urea, petroleum products, consumer products etc. The free list includes rest of the items. Imports of these freed items attract high tariffs with bound rates (Kalirajan, 2003). Liberalization, openness, transparency and globalization are important aspects of India's trade policy in reform years. Quantitative restrictions on imports have been removed on 1st April, 2001, and India is now market friendly economy in the global competitive market.

The most powerful agency for regulating world trade is World Trade Organisation (WTO) came into effect on 1st January, 1995, with all assets and liabilities of GATT transferred to former. The WTO is only international body dealing with the rules of trade between nations and is directed by Ministerial Conference which meets at least once every two years. The WTO is based on the principles of non-discrimination, free trade and promotion of fair competition among the member countries. Under the Trade Policy Review Mechanism of WTO, the trade policies of all the members are subject to periodic review. India is also a founder member of WTO. Under the Trade Policy Review Mechanism of the WTO, the trade policy of India is subject to review every four years. The second trade policy review of India took place in April 1998. India's economic reforms and trade liberalization policies contributed to a dramatic increase in its economic growth in the mid-1990. Larger flows of inward foreign investment and increased international trade helped India to achieve annual average growth rates of 7 percent from 1993 to 1996. Economic growth slowed, however, in 1997 and, according to a WTO Secretariat report on India's trade policies and practices, India should continue liberalizing its trade and investment regime to ensure strong and stable economic growth. The third trade policy review, practices and measures took place in June 2002. The report concludes that India's economic reforms have resulted in strong economic growth throughout the 1990's (Pal, 2007; Mathur, 2006). The fourth trade policy review of India by trade policy review body of WTO took place in May 2007. The report notes that if India's high rates of economic growth are to be sustained reforms need to be deepened, in particular to address infrastructure bottlenecks such as transport and electricity, which continue to constrain growth. In addition, further structural reforms will be required in agriculture, to address the sector's relatively low productivity and the problems faced by marginal farmers. Continued structural reforms, the report notes, together with greater investment in physical and human capital would also help to generate much needed productive employment for new entrants to the labour force.

India's trade policy was quite complex until the beginning of 1990s. There were various categories of importers, import licenses and ways of importing. As India's import requirement changed along with structural changes. India's trade policy adjusted with liberalized trade regimes. For this, trade policy reforms were initiated in early 1990s. These were geared towards import liberalization through reduction in import tariffs, a phased elimination of quantitative restrictions on imports, import facilities to exporters to provide incentives for exports etc. Thus, India's imports policy is in consonance with overall liberal economic policies with main objectives of promoting industrial production and productivity, export competitiveness, foreign direct investment, technology development and above all integration of Indian economy with changing international economic order.

Globally trade is emerging as a powerful engine of economic growth and development where imports, along with exports form the basis of international trade. In India imports are primarily demand determined, and are also very sensitive to changes in average tariffs and aggregate import demand is expected to be strongly driven by domestic growth rates.

Objectives of the Study

The present study attempts to analyze the dynamic changes in India's Imports. The study analyses the growth, structure, determinants, causal behaviour of imports and also import policy in India. The main objectives of the study are as follows:

1. To study the pattern of growth of India's total imports and its categories during the study period.
2. To study the structural changes in India's imports during the study period.
3. To study the impact of liberalization on growth and structure of India's imports during the study period.
4. To analyze the determinants of India's imports at aggregate and disaggregate levels.
5. To study the import-growth causality for total imports and also for some of its major categories.
6. To study the changing import policy regimes and their impact on India's imports.
7. To derive the policy implications.

Plan of the Study

The study comprises of nine chapters including present one. Chapter 2 reviews the various studies related to the topic. Chapter 3 discusses the data sources and methodology used in the study. Chapter 4 deals with growth of India's imports. Chapter 5 gives the detailed analysis of structure of India's imports and its various categories. Chapter 6 discusses the determinants of India's total imports and also for its major categories. Chapter 7 made an attempt to study the causal behaviour of total imports and its major categories. Chapter 8 discusses the import policy in India. Chapter 9 provides the summary and policy recommendations of the study.

CHAPTER

2

Review of Literature

The present chapter is devoted to the review of empirical studies related to the topic, conducted at national and international level. The chapter is divided into three sections. The section I consists of general studies, section II consists of studies related to the determinants or import demand functions and section III covers the studies based on the causality analysis.

SECTION I

General studies relating to various aspects of imports and development, trade and trade policy etc.

Dutta (1968) studies the trends in India's long-term import capacity for the three plan periods covering 1950-51 to 1965-66. According to Dutta, India's import capacity exclusive of official loans and grants received from abroad is 7.1 per cent, 30.5 per cent and 46.1 per cent for three plan periods respectively. The same for over all plan periods is 30.8 per cent. The inclusion of other capital movements raised the level of import capacity to 92.90 per cent for over all period. The position improved further with the inclusion of official loans and grants. Thus, over other capital movements official loans and grants accounted for an improvement in import capacity to the extent of 4.9 per cent in First Plan, 19.1 per cent in Second Plan, 44.2 per cent in the Third Plan and 25.5 per cent for overall Plan period.

Arora (1977) examines the Indo-Ghanaian trade, by identifying problems and suggesting export prospects for selected Indian products. India's exports to Ghana are valued at Rs. 1.81 crore (1975-76), which contributed 0.4 per cent of total imports into Ghana. Study gives an idea about the commodities under which India can push up substantially its exports to Ghana due to likely upsurge of industrial activity in country. The study period is 1971-72 to 1974-75. Major Indian products exported to Ghana comprise engineering goods, textiles, chemicals and jute manufactures. In 1975-76, these four products groups accounted for 86.1 per cent of India's total exports to Ghana. India's main item of imports from Ghana is pearls, precious and semi-precious stones, which accounted for 86.2 per cent of total during 1975-76. Besides this, India also imported cocoa and industrial diamonds from Ghana in 1975-76. The study discusses that items of auto and auto parts, agricultural machinery and implements, bicycle and parts, diesel engines and parts, electric power and switchgears, medicinal and pharmaceutical products, pigments, paints and varnishes and rubber tires and tubes have greater export prospects for India to Ghana. Because all these items, are exported to Ghana in larger amounts by other countries than India.

Obstfeld (1980) studies the macro-economic effects of an increase in the price of an imported intermediate production input. The analysis includes a small open economy with a floating exchange rate and endogenous terms of trade, in which saving depends on residents (variable) rate of time preference. The conclusion indicates that when the price elasticity of demand for intermediates is near to zero, a surplus on current account, not a deficit, is almost certain to arise. High substitutability between domestic and foreign finished goods leads to sharper exchange rate depreciation in the long run than would otherwise be the case. Only when there is a significant degree of substitution between imported materials and domestically available factors and between finished imports and exports, it is possible for a current deficit and spot depreciation to occur simultaneously in response to a materials price shock. A key feature of the model is that prices are perfectly flexible, and so, free to share the burden of adjustment with the exchange rate.

Pitre (1981) studies the trends in India's imports over the period 1960-61 to 1974-75. The study has constructed time series of India's merchandise imports for assessing trends in real terms and classified imports into major economic categories to view changes in composition of imports. According to pitre, it is quantity of imports which is relevant. For this purpose, he constructed a quantity index at an aggregate level, for which he expressed the quantities in different years in common units (i.e., rupee, by multiplying them with base year prices). The base year chosen is 1960-61 and these prices are used as weights for the construction of index. To view the changes in the composition of imports in terms of economic categories, all the imports have been classified into three major heads viz., (1) consumption goods, (2) intermediate goods and (3) unclassified, with further breakdown into food, cereals and edible products, finished goods, iron and steel, non-ferrous metals, total metals, raw materials and intermediates. According to results, index of total imports shows an increase of 21 per cent. This growth is marked by some fluctuations. The first phase, which lasted till 1967-68, is characterized by steady increase in imports, while in the subsequent period the imports show a great deal of fluctuations. Imports under food and live animals recorded more than 100 per cent increase between 1960-61 and 1966-67, after this import started falling steeply. Imports under manufactured goods accounted for about 30 per cent of the total import bill. Till 1970-71, a trend of general decline is observed. Among other commodity groups, those under mineral fuel, lubricants and related products, animal and vegetable oil and fats, chemicals increased in varying magnitudes. Spectacular increase in fertilizer imports is also observed. According to economic subcategories, imports under intermediate goods reached at peak in 1972-73. It was higher by 55 per cent. During last two years of study period imports under this category showed a decline. The index of imports under consumer goods stood at higher level than corresponding indices for intermediate and capital goods.

Derosa and Goldstein (1981) present estimates of the effect of changes in import competition on the domestic pricing behaviour of U.S. manufacturing industries. The study period is 1972-76. The changes in import competition are measured by changes in import penetration. The import penetration is defined as the ratio of the value of imports to the value of domestic shipments. All this is under the assumptions of constant domestic factor costs and constant market demand conditions. The Ordinary Least Square and Two-stage Least Squares techniques are applied. The results show that increase in import penetration restrain the inflation rate in U.S. manufacturing sector. So, import penetration affects not only profit rates but price behavior also in expected direction. Results also confirm that import discipline is stronger in higher concentrated industries than less concentrated ones. The effect of import penetration on domestic price changes is small as compared to effect of unit cost changes and excess demand conditions. These effects are considerably larger when the two stage least square method is used and when import penetration is measured in value terms.

Sau (1983) studies the implications of the IMF's structural adjustment programme for India. The Sixth Five Year Plan (1980-85) is used as the point of reference. It can be presumed that the sixth plan incorporates the policy stances of the government of India as it was just prior to the commencement of secret negotiations with the IMF for the massive loan. To adjust the deficit in the balance of payments, Structural Adjustment Programme (SAP) calls for greater import liberalization, in the name of efficiency, modernization, and long-term growth. At the same time, it advises for export promotion also. This liberalization leads to more imports to boost efficiency and exports, more exports to pay for those imports, and so on. And all this would entail a greater inflow of foreign capital, which will further aggravate the situation. Thus the Sixth Plan strategy of import restrain broke down under the pressure of the IMF loan and the import pushed growth strategy is the most noteworthy feature of the IMF structural adjustment programme for India. It only accentuated the vicious circle of imports. During Sixth Plan there is sluggishness of food grains production due to several reasons. If agriculture stagnates, home market for India's industry cannot expand. The internal market of industry would become less and less profitable, and the compulsion for export promotion would become all the more pressing. It would call for further imports of capital goods and technology to make India's industry competitive in the world market. The vicious circle of import pushed growth would work with a vengeance.

Singh (1984) studies effects of import control on the rate of profit in public sector undertakings, for which the terms of trade effect of import control has been taken into account. The percentage rate of profit in engineering, trading, shipping, i.e., Air India, Indian Airlines, and several other undertakings such as India Oil Corporation of India Ltd., Engineers (India) Ltd., Hindustan Insecticides Ltd., has increasing trends. On the other hand, the percentage rate of loss in Hindustan Steel Ltd., Indian Drugs and Pharmaceuticals, National Mineral Development Corporation etc., has been fluctuating. Since 1973-74 and 1974-75 these undertakings started to run in profit. On the whole, paper concludes that the rate of profit in selected undertakings of public sector (Central Government) is increasing. After studying the trends of rate of profit in public sector in India study concludes that rate of profit is not merely determined by the terms of trade through tariff as well as quota, but other factors such as managerial efficiency, efficiency of workers, utilization of installed capacity, rate of saving and investment, price policy, wage policy and elasticity of demand and supply etc. are also responsible for the rate of profit. Imported inputs also affect the rate of profit to some extent. The inefficiency of workers, lack of experience and acumen, shortage of power supply, scarcity of many essential raw materials, under utilization of installed capacity and unrest in labour force are the reasons given by study, for the poor performance of public sector undertakings. Hence, study concludes that it is not logical to correlate the import restrictions and rate of profit in an industry by terms of trade effect. Moreover, import restrictions through tariff as well as quota has other effects too, i.e. protective effect, consumption and production effect etc., which also affect the rate of profit.

Donnenfeld *et al.* (1985) examine the case where quality controls are imposed by the government upon an industry. This industry consists of a domestic monopoly which is facing competition from the large number of foreign firms. It focuses on the situation where consumers have full information about the quality of domestic goods but only partial information about quality of imported goods. For this a model is developed, according to which foreign firms may enter freely and compete in a specific foreign country, while in the same country a monopolist dominates the import competing industry. Both the average quality and actual quality increased when standard controls are imposed on imports. The monopolist further increases the quality in response to the imposition of quality standard of imports, but he may increase or decrease their price. This leads to decrease in the domestic industry's market share and profitability. Based on this profitability criterion, it is concluded that setting minimum quality standards on imports yields negative protection. It is also concluded that increase in import standards leads to decline in welfare, in case when monopolist's market share is sufficiently large and when monopolist's choice of quality is not too susceptible to competing imported qualities.

AW and Roberts (1985) study the relationship among U.S. imports from the NICs (New Industrializing Countries), imports from developed countries, capital and labour in the production of goods for final demand. The NICs include Hong Kong, Taiwan, South Korea, Singapore, Philippines, Brazil, Mexico and Columbia. The study period is 1960-80. The empirical model based on work by Burgess (1974) is used. A production model is specified in which capital, labour and imports from both developed countries and the NICs are treated as inputs into the production of goods for final demand. The results indicate that U.S. imports from NICs are found to be complements with domestic labour while U.S. imports from developed countries are substitutes for labour. The important implication of this effect resulting from U.S. commercial policies which raise the price of imports from the NICs will lead to reductions in aggregate employment. The results show that despite their increasing importance, the NICs account for a small portion of total U.S. imports and it is only through desegregation of the imports that their distinctive role is noticed. If transportation equipment, automobiles, and consumer goods are classified as final products and food, industrial supplies, and machinery are classified as intermediate products then 59 per cent of total U.S. imports from Canada, Japan and the OECD countries in 1980 are intermediate products. Similarly, 71 per cent of U.S. imports from Latin America and Southeast Asia are intermediate products. The share of intermediate products in imports from Latin America and Southeast Asia is even higher in earlier years. As a result, price reductions on imports from NICs may have more opportunities for downstream impacts which could lead to increases in employment in the aggregate.

Das and Donnenfeld (1987) study the role of trade policies in influencing a foreign monopolist's decision on price, quantity and in particular, the quality of its product. The study uses the model of foreign monopoly which is modified and extended in order to handle quality choice in a convenient fashion. This model is closely related to the approach used by Katrak, Savedberg and Brander and Spencer. The paper concludes that specific tariff increases welfare as it reduces quantity but improves the quality of imports. *Ad volorem* tariff reduces the quality but increases the quantity of imports which leads to reduction in foreign price. The paper also shows that while a specific tariff and quota are equivalent, an *ad valorem* tariff and quota are not. The welfare increases due to specific tariff is higher with variations in quality of imports than without, but welfare changes with quality variation under advalorem duty is lower than without. The study also examines that when home country imposes minimum quality requirements on imported products, then these dominate other forms of protection.

Gonclaves (1987) discusses the experience of Latin America concerning the effect of export expansion and import liberalization on the process of economic growth of the region. The analysis is mostly centred on the period 1970-80. The clustering exercise is undertaken and the variables used for forming the four clusters are population, GDP per capita, the share of agriculture in GDP, the share of industry in GDP, investment ratio, employment in agriculture, employment in industry, elementary school registration and high school registration. Cluster I includes Brazil and Mexico, which are the largest and most industrialized countries of Latin America. Cluster II is composed of Argentina, Chile, Colombia, Costa Rica, Peru and Uruguay. Cluster III is formed by Bolivia, Dominican Republic, Ecuador, El Salvador, Guatemala, Honduras and Paraguay. It consists of least developed economies of the region. Cluster IV consists of panama and Venezuela. Both countries have relatively high trade openness. Based on different clustering exercises, investigation shows that the marginal propensity to import and the import income elasticity are particularly important in determining the values of the multipliers (mainly super multipliers), and the balance of payments constrained output growth rate. The concept of super multiplier is based on the presumption that an expansion of exports allows an increase of other autonomous expenditure through the relaxation of the balance of payments constraint. An increase in exports allows an increase in autonomous private consumption, investment and government expenditures so that induced level of imports is equal to the increase in exports. Indeed, a comparative analysis of the inter-country differences in output growth in Latin America indicates that the capacity to export and the ability to reduce the relevant import ratios are two-key variables in the process of economic growth. An inter-country comparison showed that the values of the multipliers in Latin America are particularly sensitive to the export-output ratio and marginal propensity to import. The study shows that distinct combinations of export-output ratios and marginal propensity to import in economies with very different economic structure may result in similar values for the super-multiplier. The study also indicates that the highest output growth rates among Latin American economies are associated with the lowest import income elasticity and marginal propensity to import.

Kantawala (1988) examines all commodities (at the 7 digit level of RITC group 1965) which are imported by India on bilateral basis. The paper studies whether it benefits India to import on bilateral basis. The period used is 1966 to 1977. The commodities are chemicals, drugs and pharmaceutical, newsprint paper, rock phosphate, raw cotton, arabic gun, asafoetida, fresh and dried fruits, fertilizers, ball roller and taper bearings, seamless pipes and tubes, printing machinery, agricultural machinery, oil prospecting and drilling equipments, textile machinery etc. Out of these industrial raw materials and capital goods are imported from East European countries. While the rest of the commodities, are mainly imported bilaterally from developing countries. Considering the East European countries, paper compares unit value of Indian imports from countries having commodity agreements *vis-à-vis* other countries. The results indicate that unit import price realized on the bilateral agreement basis are higher for majority of commodities falling under the group of chemicals, drugs and pharmaceutical products and non-ferrous metals as compared to other countries of world. Moreover, it is lower for the majority of commodities belonging to fertilizers, rock phosphates, ball roller and taper bearings, printing machines, pumps, textile machineries and other capital goods as compared to the rest of the countries. Results also show that there are certain commodities (fertilizers, rice, fruits, textile machinery and raw cotton) for which India has paid higher price on commodity agreement basis as compared to other countries of the world for majority of years and still it has resulted into advantageous position for India. But there are certain commodities for which India has paid lower price on the commodity agreement basis as compared to other countries of world and still India is loser on the commodity agreement basis during 1966 to 1977. These commodity groups are fertilizers, non-ferrous metals and newsprint papers. There are certain commodities for which unit import price paid by India is higher and lower for equal years on the commodity agreement basis as compared to other countries of the world belonging to thirteen different commodity groups imported by India. Out of these 13 different types of commodity groups, India is in gainful position for leather making machinery, rice, chemicals, non ferrous metals, fruits, textile machinery, ball roller and taper bearings and printing machinery. While for rest of the commodity groups (wood pulp, X-ray generator, asbestos, pumps and natural rubber), India is a loser on the commodity agreement basis as compared to other countries of the world. Thus, paper concludes that India is in a beneficial position, if it imports bilaterally from those countries which have included these commodities in their list of goods to be traded.

Dinopoulos and Kreinin (1989) adopt a general equilibrium two goods and three country approach to compare tariffs, quotas and VERs (Voluntary Export Restrains). The three countries are US, Japan and Europe. The paper assumes that once a VER is negotiated between two countries, the exporting country and third country suppliers do not retaliate. The paper uses the 'offer curve-trade indifference curves' analysis to examine the welfare effects of quotas and VERs. The results differ from those obtained either in partial equilibrium or in two-country framework. Results show that welfare comparison between quota and VER is decomposed into 'revenue' and 'trade substitution' effects, when the importing country's objective is a fixed quantity of imports. The comparison of U.S. import quota with a U.S. VER, limits only Japanese exports and exempts Europe from any restraint. The U.S. welfare is higher under a quota than under an equivalent VER (two country analyses). However, in contrast to two country case the relative effects of two instruments on Japan welfare are indeterminate because of substitution from third country analysis. For Europe (third country) a U.S. VER is preferable to quota.

Bhattacharya (1989) studies import intensity of exports of Indian economy for the period 1973-74 to 1979-80. India adopted a policy of export linked import liberalization since mid seventies. The paper estimates the Index of import intensity of exports of the economy. The value of this index can assess the efficiency with which import linked export policy is working in the economy. Bhattacharya uses Leontiff open static input-output model for calculating the value of direct plus indirect import content per unit of output of any sector. Results show that by and large direct plus indirect import content per unit of output has increased in almost all the sectors, except a few. Thus, export linked import liberalization followed in India led to increase in sectoral import content in large number of sectors.

Lopez and Rodrik (1989) study the impact of trade restrictions of imported inputs on trade balance. The study used the average import composition of large samples of developing countries in Africa, Asia and Latin America over the 1975-85 periods. They consider a model of small open economy which imports intermediate inputs and where all prices are flexible. The economy produces two types of goods, an exportable and a non-tradable (finished) goods. Lopez and Rodrik assume that intermediate imports are not subject to the quantitative restriction and their domestic prices are determined by the border prices plus import tariffs. According to the results, when imports are predominantly intermediate inputs (as they are in most developing countries) import restriction acts as a supply shock to the economy. The paper concludes that net effect of a small tariff remains ambiguous. As it leads to negative income effect in terms of, increased domestic price of imported inputs. This causes fall in employment and real income.

Malhotra and Raikhy (1989) study the Indian experience about the import policy and self reliance. They examine the import substitution experience of the Indian economy during 1960 to 1984-85 and the impact of import policy on the pace of import substitution. Data collected on imports have been re-classified so as to make it comparable with production data. Measurement of import substitution made with the help of chennry's measure where import substitution is defined as difference between actual growth in output over a period of time and growth in output with constant imports availability ratio. During 1960-61 to 1984-85 period as whole, results show positive import substitution in most of the industries except wearing apparel footwear, vegetable and animals oils and fat, iron and steel basic industries, ship building and repair and manufacture of jewellery and related articles. Considerable import substitution is attained in petroleum refineries, pottery, china and earthenware, non-ferrous basic metal industries, machinery except electrical machinery apparatus, appliance and supplies, rail and road equipment and professional and scientific measuring and controlling instruments. Paper discusses that the main reason of import liberalization is encouragement of exports. Due to liberalization policies the growth prospects might not be hampered but the development prospects will be adversely affected. The imports dependence will adversely affect the attainment of self-reliance.

Sastry (1990) studies whether the manufacturing companies in India are self reliant in technology. The data collected from the annual reports of medium and large public limited companies, which have consistently reported foreign exchange earnings during period

1980-81 to 1984-85 have been utilized. Of the five hundred ninety companies, companies reported expenditure on R & D as well as on import of capital goods in 1984-85 are used for the present study. The number of such companies is ninety one and only those companies which belong to manufacturing sector are considered. Companies with the same or similar products are combined and grouped under an industry. There are thirty three such industries and they are further grouped into six major groups. The log linear regression equations are estimated. The R & D expenditure is a dependent variable. The independent variables are imported technology, number of companies in industry, size and royalty and technical fees. The expenditure of R & D is positively related to imported technology. The number of companies in an industry and size has a positive role in the expenditure on R & D. The positive signs of these variables suggest that expenditure on R & D is complementary to the imported technology. This confirms the strategy of 'import and adapt'. The expenditure on royalty and technical fee payments has shown the appropriate sign. The regression equations are separately estimated for the two sets, local companies and substitutable in foreign controlled rupee companies, in both the cases the effect of imported technology has been complementary in nature to R & D.

Datar (1990) studies some special features of large developing economies and then discusses them in the context of India. The arguments discussed in the light of Indian experience for the period 1970-71 to 1988-89. The paper discusses that large sized countries are likely to exhibit a lower degree of openness than smaller sized countries. Most of the imports have no domestic substitutes for them. The price elasticity of developing country exports would be more than the price elasticity of imports. Other features discussed include that initial trade balance is important for the success of devaluation strategy, stage of import liberalization could be initiated after the anticipated beneficial effects of export promotion strategy are stabilized. Export promotion through liberalization of imports should be linked with industrial policy. The degree of openness of Indian economy is low (i.e., export percentage of GNP), it is 3.8 per cent in 1970-71 and increased to 5.9 per cent in 1988-89. The paper studies that cereals, edible oil, petroleum, oil and lubricant (POL), fertilizers and capital goods accounted for 53.6 per cent of total imports in 1970-71, which increased to 52.7 per cent of imports in 1987-88. While relative importance of various components is not clear from the composition of total imports. Paper also concludes that the exchange rate policy seems to be more effective in regard to exports than its effect on imports. This is confirmed by studying effectiveness of expenditure switching policies, which is studied through its effect on real exports/imports. The coefficient of real effective exchange rate (REER) in import function was found to be lower than corresponding coefficient in export function.

Chand and Tewari (1991) study the growth and instability of Indian exports and imports of agricultural commodities for the period 1970 to 1988. For this purpose exponential time trend is fitted to the data on value (in terms of U.S. dollars) of imports and exports using four yearly moving averages of data. Thus, the analysis is based on the quadrennia 1970-73, 1974-77, 1978-81, 1982-85 and 1985-88. The agricultural commodities grouped under agricultural products, forest products, fish and fishery products and agricultural requisites. According to the results, all the items included in the agricultural sector except pulses, sugar and honey and forest product indicated positive growth rates in exports. Among the various items of imports, pulses and sugar and honey show a trend rate of growth which exceeded 50 per cent per annum during the period 1970-88. For most of the agricultural commodities exports showed less instability than the imports. The growth in exports as well as imports of agricultural sector was much lower than the growth in total merchandise imports and exports. The trade of agricultural sector showed a surplus in most of the periods. The exports of fish and fishery products and coffee, tea and cocoa show a remarkable performance. The imports of agricultural commodities pulses, vegetable oils and fertilizer exerted severe strain on India's foreign exchange earnings.

Mani (1991) examines whether the import dependence of Indian industrial sector has increased in post liberalization phase compared to the earlier period. The period 1986-87 to 1988-89 is considered as post liberalization phase. The study includes only manufacturing enterprises in private and public sectors. Mani considers three measures of import dependence. The first measure is Net Foreign Exchange Inflows Rate (NFIR), which is the ratio of net exports to total exports of a specific industry. The second measure is the Import Intensity Rate (IIR), which is the ratio of imports to net value added expressed as percentage. The third measure is Direct Cost of Technology Imports Rate (DCTR), which is the ratio of the sum of royalty, technical fees and dividends to net value added and expressed as percentage. The results show that NFIR has increased by about 23 per cent in the post-liberalization period, which confirms about increased import dependence of the sector. The magnitude of NFIR is much higher in private sector as compared to public sector, while rate of growth is higher in case of public sector. The transport equipment industry recorded the highest growth rate in NFIR. (i.e. risen by 243%). The second measure of import dependence (i.e., IIR) confirms about increased import dependence by 29 per cent in post liberalization measure. The IIR of most of the industry groups has increased. The three industrial groups, cotton and blended textiles, aluminum and basic Industrial chemicals, have registered high growth rates of over 50 per cent. The third measure of DCTR also shows an increase. This measure show the highest increase of 35 per cent in the import dependence. Thus, all three measures of import dependence have shown an increase in post liberalization phase.

Sathe (1993) analyses the dependence of the economy on trade through examining the beneficial impact of exports and imports on domestic production and the structure of the Indian economy. He also studies whether composition of exports and imports of India maximizes the growth rate in the economy. The study has used input-output framework for this purpose. It includes six input output tables (1951-52, 1959, 1963, 1968-69, 1973-74 and 1978-79) at current and constant prices. The analysis extended to eighties in certain aspects by using structural coefficients for the years 1978-79, which have been adjusted for price changes and the foreign trade data for 1983-84 and 1988-89. The results show that forward linkages have greater impact on output than backward linkages and that imports have stimulated the output to a greater degree than the exports. It has been found that linkages of trade have changed mainly due to a change in exports and imports and much less due to technological and allocational changes in the economy. The study also confirms that import substitution has played an important role in changing the structure of the economy as compared to export expansion (become important only after 1973-74). The study also concludes that traditional imports should not be neglected as they have a role to play in the economy due to their linkage effects. The liberalization led to increased imports intensity of exports, has had a favorable impact on the domestic production.

Leela and Raju (1993) examine the trends in the import dependence of the Indian economy on imports of newsprint for the period 1960-61 to 1987-88. The share of imports in the consumption of newsprint is taken as an index of the import dependence of the Indian economy in respect of newsprint, which is a ratio of imports of newsprint to consumption of newsprint. Exponential growth rates are estimated for the variables. The results show that the relative share of import of newsprint in the consumption of newsprint in India declined from 76 per cent in 1960-61 to 46 per cent in 1987-88, i.e., at a rate of 1.48 per cent per annum. This indicates the decline in the import dependence of Indian economy of newsprint imports, this decline is particularly high and significant during the period 1980-81 to 1987-88. The paper also discusses that consumption of newsprint directly depends on GDP. The paper concludes that there is great need to create additional capacity in newsprint industry in India. The main difficulty in expanding capacity of indigenous production of newsprint is the lack of adequate quantities of raw materials. In other words, due to lack of self sufficiency, imports of newsprint continue to play an important role in supplementing the indigenous production of newsprint.

Rao (1996) studies about the import content of various industries, grouped according to use-based classification for the period 1973-74 and 1983-84. The paper also works out, the direct and indirect requirements of imports to support the final consumption expenditure level of primary and non-primary goods for the years 1989-90 to 1991-92. Whole of the analysis take place within the input-output framework. The input-output table presents the data on inter-industry transactions for the economy classified into sixty sectors. These are regrouped into thirty three sectors and further regrouped into six sectors by use based classification. The paper uses the methodology developed by Hazari (1980) to drive the total import requirement for inter-industry use and final consumption of primary and non-primary goods. According to the results, import intensity is very low i.e., less than 5 per cent in majority of the sectors in both 1973-74 and 1983-84. The analysis also indicated that nearly 35-38 per cent of imports were consumed indirectly through inter-industry use and another 15 per cent directly to support the final consumption of primary and non-primary goods. The import content for inter-industry use in meeting the final consumption of primary and non-primary goods has increased during 1983-84 to 1989-90 and then recorded a marginal decline by 1991-92. The estimates of consumption of imports at disaggregated 33-sector level indicate that a relatively large proportion of imports is required by crude, petroleum and natural gas, food, petroleum products, machinery and equipment, transport services, sugar and food products and chemicals as compared to that of other commodity sectors.

Greaney (1996) studies the concept of voluntary import expansion (VIE). A VIE agreement firstly took place between U.S. and Japan. A VIE agreement sets a target level or target market share for import sales in domestic market. For this, Greaney uses Bertrand model of imperfect competition with substitute goods, two countries and two firms. The results show that market share VIEs do not increase competition and reduce prices, even if domestic market is protected by a tariff type barrier. Under quantity competition, a VIE that increases the import market share unambiguously hurts the home firm. With price competing firms, a VIE can benefit the home firm if it increases the import market share by a relatively small margin.

Jha (1997) studies the trade and prospects for inter-regional trade in Asia for 1980s and onwards. The countries included are Japan, People's Republic of china (PRC), Newly Industrializing Economies (Hong Kong, Korea, Singapore and Taipei, China); South East Asia (Indonesia, Philippines and Thailand); South Asia (Bangladesh, India, Pakistan and Sri Lanka). The study shows that for the period of 1980-92 for Asia average rate of growth of merchandise exports (9.6%) is higher than the average rate of growth of merchandise imports (8.1%). Asia's share in world trade rose sharply for the exports and imports. Since mid 80s inter-Asia's trade share of total trade in Asia has been increasing steadily. By the early of 1990s, intra-Asian trade dominated total trade of Asia. Among all Asian Countries, China has the second highest share of intra Asian trade in its total trade, which is next to Indonesia. But Intraregional flows in South Asian (which consists of India also) countries are small in value. This also explained the reasons for rapid intra regional trade growth in Asia. The main reasons were economic complementarity among Asian countries and is closely linked to the dynamic of real output growth in the region trade. Trade liberalization allows direct investment flows and increased imports of machinery. Paper also discusses that future trade liberalization results in changing industrial structure and increased exports in Asia. But policy of protectionism will have adverse implications for the long term growth rates of region. Another reason which contributed to the prosperity and hence to large intra-regional trade and capital flows was regional economic cooperation. The study is optimistic on the future prospects for intra regional trade in Asia.

Mehta (1997) studies the trade policy reforms and their impact on external trade. The data are collected for the period of 1989-90 to 1995-96. Mehta shows that India's trade has increased significantly during post-reform period. The share of India's trade in GDP has increased to more than 24 per cent in 1995-96. During 1990s the higher growth has been recorded in India's exports than in India's imports. To quantify protectionism, Indices of India's Non-tariff Barriers (NTBs) have been calculated for fifty two manufacturing sectors. The Index is found to be on higher side (70% or more) for a group of twelve sectors, while it is comparatively lower (less than 30%) for seventeen sectors. In terms of use based classification, index is highest for primary agro based intermediates (77%) and lowest for other primary intermediates (11%). The semi-finished, finished non-food consumer goods and primary consumer goods reveal the next highest index of NTBs. The capital goods, semi finished and finished intermediate goods have medium levels of NTBs index of protection. A large number of measures for the control of imports have been dismantled. Also a number of quantitative restrictions have been measured by Effective Rate of Protection (ERP) and Nominal Rate of Protection (NRP) for 55 sectors. These are measured for the years 1989-90, 1993-94 and 1995-96. The ERP and NRP estimates are based on two alternate methods: (*a*) scheduled tariff rates and (*b*) estimates based on collection of import duties. Results show that average NRP and ERP have declined for all three years in case of both the methods. The collection rates are lower than the schedule rates, the average NRP and ERP based on collection rates are also lower. The coefficients of variation (for ERP and NRP) showed increasing trends.

Sathe (1997) examines the export intensities of a sample of Indian industries and import intensity of their exports. He also examines Net Foreign Exchange Inflow Rate (NFIR) and Direct Cost of Technology Imports (DCTR). The study period is 1989-90 to 1992-93. The sample consists of 1521 manufacturing companies, aggregated into 96 industries and four sectors. It is concluded that import intensity of exports has declined (from 10.9% in 1989-90 to 8.9% in 1992-93) for the study period. The share of imported raw material in total raw material consumed has fallen over period. It point towards import substitution. The correlation coefficient between exports and imported raw material consumed by them has declined over study period (from 0.64 to 0.59). The high import intensities are observed in chemical and capital goods industries for the study period. The NFIR has increased for the sample for study period (from 89% to 91%). It is highest for traditional exports and lowest for diamond cutting/trading. The DCTR has also increased slightly for study period (from 1.15 to 1.65). The number of industries spending more than one per cent of their sales on technology imports has also increased over the period.

Lee (1998) analyses the relation between expected exchange rates and import prices of durable goods. It also shows that durability induces inter-temporal substitution in the price of imported durable. It is shown in the context of a duopoly model with linear demand, which is an extension of monopoly model of durables to an international setting with domestic and foreign firms. This paper concludes that expected exchange rates have a significant effect on import prices of durable goods. Results also show that relative import price between durables and non durables increases in response to expected appreciation. The same is the result in case of import price of durables relative to domestic price of durables.

Singh (2001) analyses the balance of trade, exchange rate policies, trade policy regimes and performance of external sector of India. The period covered is from 1950-51 to 1995-96. The main feature of India's trade policy observed by Singh is its continued reliance on relative price factors. This reliance is either through the provision of export incentives and imposition of import tariffs or through devaluation of exchange rate. The import policy is marked by high quantitative and tariff restriction on imports. The study concluded that lack of supply reduces exports and also increases imports to meet growing demand of populated country. For solving this problem, efforts should be made to raise productive capacity. Trade policy reforms of 1990s showed improvements in external sector and observed the need to lay emphasis on supply side factors such as quality output and control of inflation. The share of total trade in GDP is 14.62 per cent during 1950s, it increased to 21.19 per cent during 1990s. The share of imports in GDP is higher than the share of exports in GDP both for 1950s and 1990s.

Dholkia and Kapur (2001) study the economic reforms and trade performance for private corporate sector in India. It is based on data for five hundred fifty seven firms for the period of 1980-81 to 1995-96. The companies are divided into exporting and non-exporting groups. The study fitted linear function on the annual median value of variables. It is expected that with trade liberalization and globalization, import of both the groups (exporting and non-exporting firms) would increase significantly. For examining this, median (average) import intensity (value of ratio of total imports to net sales) is measured. The median (average) raw material import intensity (average of the proportion of imported raw material value to the value of total raw material) is also measured. Both median (average) of overall import intensity and raw material import intensity are higher for exporting companies than for non-exporting companies. Thus, Indian exports from private corporate sectors are more import intensive and also showed dependence of exporting companies on imports. So it is concluded that import liberalisation acts as an important measure of export promotion.

Hargopal (2001) examines external variables from 1980-81 to 1997-98 for India. The study period is divided into pre-liberalization period (1980-81 to 1990-91) and post-liberalization period (1991-92 to 1997-98). The basic economic variables considered are exports, imports, trade deficits, current account deficits, foreign exchange reserves and external debt. Ratio analysis is employed to estimate eleven different ratios. The ratio analysis is applied to study the inter-relationship between above given different variables. The simple and linear growth rates are estimated for external variables. The study shows that imports have grown at faster rate than exports in post liberalization period (in both the forms). The study concludes that trade liberalisation policies have a positive impact on external variables. There is tremendous growth of exports, imports, foreign exchange reserves and a decline in foreign debt. The only negative thing is that of high growth of imports than exports. Thus, it is concluded, after studying various ratios and growth trends that exports have to be increased for reducing the negative impact of increased imports. For this, study suggested for tapping untapped foreign markets and giving the fillip to traditional exports where we have indigenous strength.

Burange (2001) estimates import intensity of Indian manufacturing sector and the different industries over the period of 1978-79 to 1997-98. Attempt is also made to identify the industries which have high import intensity, export intensity and their contribution to foreign exchange earnings. The study uses data of two types. One is from Annual Survey of Industries (ASI), which has been used for estimating import intensity for the years 1978-79, 1983-84, 1989-90, 1993-94 and 1994-95. The other source of data is Centre for Monitoring Indian Economy (CMIE), which have been used to estimate import intensity, export intensity, net foreign exchange inflow rate and import dependence of manufacturing activity in India for the period 1991-92 to 1997-98 (i.e. post-liberalization period). Analysis based on ASI data shows that overall import intensity is fluctuating one, i.e. up to 1983-84 it shows increasing trends but after that import intensity has declined during the years 1993-94. It has again increased in the year 1994-95. In case of use based classification, import intensity of basic goods industries shows rising trend. The capital goods sector recorded first declining and then rising trend and the intermediate goods industries show the mixed trend in import intensity. The consumer goods industries recorded the lowest and declining import intensity. On the basis of input based classification of industries, the agro based industries record the lowest and declining import intensity. The chemical based industries show highest but falling import intensities. Only metal based industries record rising import intensity for given years. Analysis of Annual Survey of Industries (ASI) data also show that import dependence of chemical and chemical products industries on imported raw material is the highest, but it is declining over the period. The rubber, plastic, petroleum and coal products also show a substantial dependence on imported raw materials with rising trend. The import dependence of other manufacturing industries is rising at a faster rate over the years. On the basis of use based classification; intermediate goods industry is relatively more dependent on imported raw materials. The import dependence of capital goods industry recorded a decreasing trend while consumer durable shows an increasing trend. According to input based classification, the agro based industries are least dependent on imported raw material while chemical industries are most dependent. But both show downward trend in import dependence over the period. Only metal based industries showed upward trends over the period of 1978-79 to 1994-95. Analysis based on the sample or CMIE data showed that the chemicals, non-ferrous metals, electronics and miscellaneous products industries have relatively high import intensity during the period of 1991-92 to 1997-98. There is a substantial rise in the import intensity in leather and leather products, electronic and diversified industries. The dependence of industry on imported raw materials is increasing through out the period of post liberalization (1991-92 to 1997-98). Similarly export intensity of manufacturing sector recorded a continuous rise during the period 1991-92 to 1997-98. On the basis of comparison of both export and import intensities of manufacturing sector, export performance of manufacturing sector is found to be very disappointing. Sample data also measures Net Foreign Inflow Rate (NFIR) and show that the net contribution of manufacturing sector to foreign exchange is negative for the period of 1991-92 to 1997-98. There are some industries, which show positive and high NFIR such as beverages and tobacco, textiles, leather and leather products, but all these are from the group of traditional export industries. Even with some exceptions the NFIR of these industries shows downward trends which implies exports are not increasing as compared to import of raw material. This is mainly because of decreasing price competitiveness in international market over the period.

Cuevas (2002) estimates common stochastic trends of real GDP and imports in Venezuela from 1974-2000, by using structural time series model. The real imports trend has an underlying rate of drift of 2.8 per cent annually by contrast, the rate of drift of real GDP is 1.6 per cent annually. This underlines the powerful structural tendency towards increasing imports that characterizes the Venezuelan economy, even at slow rates of GDP growth. The elasticity coefficient associated with real exchange rate has reasonable magnitude (0.4) and has the expected sign. It means 1 percent real appreciation leads to 0.4 per cent increase in imports. The study also estimated common stochastic cycles, which have been found to have approximately 5 and 17 year periods. The GDP elasticity of imports increases with frequency, at the highest frequency, elasticity is 4.55 associated with 5 year cycle. At zero frequency, the elasticity is smaller at 1.71. It means one per cent real GDP growth in the long run is associated with 1.7 per cent real imports growth. The powerful imports responsiveness at the higher cycle frequency is associated with the recurrence of external imbalances in Venezuela.

Nanda and Raikhy (2002) examine the impact of trade liberalization policies on foreign trade (exports and imports). The study period is 1991-92 to 1998-99. To study direction of imports and exports, only those nations which have greater than one per cent share in country's imports and exports in 1998-99, have been included and six groups of exports and five groups of import commodities are discussed. The study estimates annual compound growth rates, geographic concentration index and linear trend analysis for export import share of each country. The linear trend in geographical concentration index for exports and imports are also worked out for the period 1992-93 to 1998-99. The study shows that exports of agriculture and allied products and manufactured groups are on higher side. The export growth has been poor in case of leather and leather manufacture and readymade garments. The exports are concentrated to few nations and importance of developed countries in exports has decreased during study period. The India's imports of cereal preparations, milk and cream, rice, petroleum crude and products, oil seeds and silk raw have shown declining trends. The imports of sugar have been geographically diversified. Results also indicate that imports have increased at higher rates than exports during the study period. The study emphasized that India should make serious efforts to promote exports and geographically diversified, in view of declining importance of developed nations. For this, efforts should be made for better techniques, better management, more efficient use of raw material and avoidance of wastes. The study also suggested that export promotion can be fruitful to trade through selective import liberalization.

Goldar and Anita (2003) evaluate that impact of import liberalization on productivity growth in India. The main objective of the study is to find out how far import liberalization contributed to the better productivity performance of Indian industry in post-reform period. Firstly, paper estimates the TFP growth in India manufacturing and 72-digit industry groups in the period 1981-82 to 1997-98. For this translog index of TFP has been used. The estimated growth rate of TFP show a significant growth in TFP in Indian manufacturing but there is a fall in the rate of TFP in 1990s as compared to the 1980s. The reason is explained in terms of gestation lags. The growth rates of TFP for the years 1981-82 to 1997-98 are pooled for regression analysis. The regression analysis is used for studying the effect of import liberalization and gestations lags on industrial productivity. To capture the effect of gestation lags on productivity, the ratio of investment in fixed assets made in previous two years to the existing fixed capital stock and ratio of investments made in previous two years to investment made in the previous five years are taken as explanatory variables. The variables indicating import liberalization in regression analysis are, effective rate of protection (ERP), real effective exchange rate (REER) and non-tariff barriers (NTBs). Besides these variables two more variables, i.e., growth rate of agricultural output and dummy variable for post liberalisation period, are also included in the equation. The results of regression analysis show that coefficients of variables representing the effect of gestation lags on productivity, are found to be negative and significant at five per cent level. The coefficient of NTBs and REER are found to be positive. There is negative relationship between ERP and TFP, which confirms the productivity enhancing effect of tariff reforms. The coefficient of interaction term (i.e. product of ERP and NTB) is found to be positive and significant. The coefficient of dummy variable is positive, but statistically insignificant. The coefficient of dummy variable is found to be significantly negative, when investment ratio variable and all liberalization related variables are dropped from the equation. The study however does not support that import liberalization has actually resulted in the productivity growth in Indian manufacturing sector. The results rather show lower productivity growth in post-reform period as compared to pre-reform period. Thus, the productivity impact of import liberalization and tariff reduction are partly considered by gestation lags in investment projects. This study incorporates two more variables in the regression equation, i.e., rate of change in capacity utilization and rate of change in man days per employee. It was found that there is strong positive relation between capacity utilization and productivity. On the other hand coefficient of rate of change in man days per employee is not statistically significant.

Virmani (2003) deals with India's external reforms, focuses on nineties because of their wide and deep scope than that of eighties. The paper discusses about macro-economic adjustments undertaken in 1991-1992 to deal with BOP crisis of 1990. The impact of fiscal deficit on the current account deficit is measured by using the data from 1970-71 to 1999-2000. The equation is estimated for this purpose, where ratio of current account deficit (CAD) to GDP dependent upon fiscal deficit of the Central Government (FDC) as a ratio to GDP, 36 country trade weighted real effective exchange rate (REER), and ratio of private investment to GDP (Ipvt). Besides these, the time trend 't' is also taken as independent variable. The results show that every percent point of GDP increase in the fiscal deficit of Central Government resulted in 0.47 per cent of GDP increase in the current account deficit. Results also confirm that in India the exchange rate is powerful instrument of adjustment in the current account deficit. A six percent depreciation of REER is sufficient to counter and nullify the impact of a one percent point increase in the fiscal deficit. The effect of private investment on the current account show that with one per cent point increase in its ratio to GDP resulting in 0.3 per cent point increase in current account deficit. The time trend 't' represents the upward trend in the private saving rate. The paper concludes that liberalisation of the current and the capital account, as a part of external sector reforms, increased the flexibility and resilience of the BOP.

Roy and Pattnaik (2004) examine the feasibility of adopting uniform tariff for India. The paper assumes that government introduces uniform tariff rate of 15 per cent with effect from 1st April, 2004, to assess the revenue impact for fiscal year 2004-05. It also implies that exemptions to all the categories of import are also withdrawn (due to introduction of uniform rate). The study shows that there would not be severe adverse revenue implications due to implementation of a uniform tariff rate at 15 per cent.

Applying uniform rates to defence imports and withdrawal of exemptions would enhance revenue collection by Rs. 50,000 crore. The study concludes that revenue impact is not the critical issue. The important issue is of handling the transitional problem on account of introducing uniform tariff rate and especially removing exemptions to defence and life saving drugs. To handle these transitional problems, study recommends creation of Drug Fund and Defence Fund. The revenue impact of imposing 15 per cent uniform tariff rate in case of life saving drugs and defence imports is also worked out. The results indicate that there will be revenue collection of around Rs. 46,000 crore from defence imports and Rs. 500-700 crore from life saving drugs. These two funds would be revenue neutral in the budget. The proceeds from these funds would be utilized for the primary health (with the help of Drug Fund) and rehabilitation of defence personnel and their families (with the help of Defence Fund). Besides this, study also concludes that it help us to sustain a high level of growth through fuller integration into the world economy and also provide a clear signal to foreign investors that India is a serious liberalizer.

Paul and Ramanathan (2004) examine the overall trade performance of India, deal with cross country comparison, also analyse export performance of industrial sectors. The overall trade performance includes total value of imports and exports for the pre- liberalization (1980-81 to 1990-91) and post-liberalization (1991-92 to 2001-02) periods. The annual average growth rates of exports for two periods are 7.89 per cent and 9.38 per cent respectively. The annual average growth rates of imports for two periods are 4.25 per cent and 10.23 per cent respectively. The yearly growth rates for imports and exports are not uniform, also trade deficit continues to be permanent feature. The paper also deals with cross country comparisons of Indian exports with selected East Asian countries (including China), developing countries as a group and world as a whole for the period 1992-2001. The results show that all East Asian countries (except Indonesia) and developing countries as a group recorded higher growth rates than the rates relating to the world (5.6%). The export growth rate for India is 9.2 per cent and China has recorded maximum growth rate, i.e., 13.5 per cent. The paper examines exports performance of industrial sector in the 1990s. The results show that contribution of exports of manufactured goods in the exports of country is steadily increasing. This increase is largely due to consistently growing exports performance of chemical and allied products sector and engineering goods sector, during post trade liberalization period. The growth in exports performance of small scale industrial sector, both in absolute and relative terms, has not been accentuating, which is totally contrary to expectations.

Siddharthan (2004) studies the impact of liberalization and globalization on the productivity, efficiency and growth of Indian industries. This is a review article and author has discussed six studies on the related subject, the authors of which have been associated with Institute of Economic Growth (IEG). These papers are by Das (2003), Ray (2003), Goldar, Ranganathan and Banga (2003), Siddharthan and Lal (2003), Banga (2003) and Narayanan (2003). These six papers with different methodologies and data sets do not support the hypothesis relating to an increase in productivity/efficiency in Indian industries due to economic liberalization. Major inter-firm differences are found in behaviour relating to technology and growth strategy. This results in productivity and efficiency differences. Some firms have gained due to liberalization and globalization while others have lost. The main gainers are multinational entrepreneurs (MNEs). To compete against these MNEs, domestic firms have adopted a strategy of entering into non-equity strategic alliance with foreign and domestic firms. This results in technology imports against royalty. It is concluded that technology is the main vehicle of growth. The firms with better technologies and having smaller productivity gap in relation to MNEs, have benefited by liberalisation. But firms with old technologies with large productivity gap have lost out.

Santos Paulino and Thirlwall (2004) study the impact of trade liberalization on exports, imports and the balance of payments of twenty two countries. These countries are from different continents that have undergone extensive trade liberalisation since the mid 1970s. The study period is 1972-97. The standard equations are specified for studying different variables. The two different measures of trade liberalisation are used (*a*) export duty and import duty, (*b*) dummy variable applied to year in which trade liberalization is deemed to have taken place in a significant way. The second version is compiled by WTO, World Bank and other bodies. The liberalization dummy also interacted with price and income variables. This study showed that there is inverse relationship between import duty and import growth. The study concludes that more liberalized trade regime has raised import growth more than exports (independently of duty reduction) as compared with pre-liberalization period. The impact of liberalisation on import growth differs considerably between regions. The effect is strongest in Africa and weakest in Latin America. The liberalisation has increased income elasticities by roughly equal amounts for both exports and imports. The price elasticity has increased more for imports than exports.

Sathe and Agarwal (2004) examine the issues related to the opening up of Indian pulses sector. They also study the relationship between production, prices and imports. The study period is 1985-86 to the year 2001-02 most recent data are available. The study shows that pulses market is fairly narrow and has also had a flat rate of growth since 1985. As an importer of pulses, India is among the top three-four countries. The pulses prices are determined purely by demand and supply factors. In volume terms, pulses imports have increased at a rate of 1.29 per cent while the domestic production has increased at 0.33 per cent for period 1985-86 to 2001-02. There is fairly strong and negative relationship between domestic production and imports (with one year lag). The price index is not affected much by imports (both with and without lag).

The increase in imports decreases the prices only with lag and that too weakly at -0.058. Thus the pulses imports have not augmented supply to such an extent that there would be a strong and negative relationship between prices and imports of pulses. Domestic production and price index for pulses are positively related for both year to year and one year lag, but the relationship is weak. The correlation coefficient between domestic production and imports is positive and weak on year to year basis. But it is strong and negative with lagged imports (by one year). Thus if domestic production falls in one year, the imports are expected to increase in next year.

Chand *et al.* Mittal (2004) study the trends and competitiveness of Indian exports and imports of major oilseeds products. The paper also discusses about WTO commitments. The study period is 1980-81 to 2001-02. Total imports of oilseeds have risen sharply during the decade of 1990s and this increase is quite substantial in post WTO period. The study discusses that Indian edible oils do not compete well with imports as domestic prices are higher. Study argues that low world prices of edible oils are due to high levels of protection and agricultural subsidies in developed countries. The Indian oilseeds sector will remain under pressure even as these are properly adjusted. There is consensus that the present level of import dependence is unsustainable. The reason which led to the uncompetitiveness of oil sector are inefficient processing sector and policy of reservation for villages and small industries. The import volume of this commodity has become too large and increase in world price of this politically sensitive commodity will have serious consequences.

Kee *et al.* (2004) estimate import demand elasticities for over 4625 goods (at six digits of harmonized system) in 117 countries. The paper studies the effects of tariffs on GDP through import demand elasticities at a tariff line level that are consistent with GDP maximization. For this purpose, paper modifies Kohli's GDP function approach to estimate import demand elasticities. The imports are considered as inputs of domestic production, for given exogenous world prices, productivity and endowments. According to results, the sample average import demand elasticity is -1.67, while sample median is -1.08. There is wide variation in import demand elasticities across countries and tariff lines. The homogeneous goods have more elastic imports than differentiated goods. The average estimated elasticities decrease as we increase the level of aggregation at which they are estimated. The large countries tend to have more elastic import demand and more developed countries tend to have less elastic import demand. The paper also calculates Trade Restrictiveness Indices (TRIs) and welfare losses associated with the existing tariff structure of 88 countries. Both simple and weighted average tariffs tend to underestimate the distortion imposed by the tariff regime by 30 per cent on average. Thus, distortion is non trivial. The GDP losses are largest in China, Germany, India, Mexico and the United States.

Mathur and Sachdeva (2005) study the trend in simple customs duty rates at six-digit harmonized system level of classification in order to examine custom tariff structure in India during post economic reforms period. It also discusses the changes in import weighted duty rates for these tariff lines. The study period is 1991-92 to 2004-05. It compiled the imports of over five thousand commodities at six digit level brought out by the DGCI&S and mapping it so as to match with six digit tariff lines. The custom duty rates are available up to the year 2004-05 and six digit level imports are available upto 2003-04. The results show that while average tariff duties have been reduced substantially since 1991-92, the overall dispersion across commodities has increased. The import weighted tariffs of all commodities followed a downward trend, but agriculture and allied tariff rates started increasing from 1997-98, despite initial reductions. This increase in agriculture tariff rates is due to removal of quantitative restrictions, decline is recorded in 2004-05 only. There is a concentration of imports from a few items at the six-digit level, with barely fifteen items contributing to half of the imports and realised revenue. It is concluded that based on prevailing duties and rates, the revenue potential is higher than the actual customs collection reportedly due to large number of exemptions. It is suggested that all exemptions should be done away with, so as to make tariff structure more transparent. This would also raise the customs revenue collections and compensate for loss associated with tariff reductions.

Goldar and Aggarwal (2005) examine the effect of post 1991 trade liberalisation on price cost margin (PCMs) in Indian industries for 1980-81 to 1997-98. An econometric model is estimated to explain variations in PCMs, taking tariff and non-tariff barriers separately (i.e., results with tariff and non-tariff barriers). The variables which effect PCMs are import barriers, capital output ratio, dummy variable representing industrial concentration, growth rate of industry, deviation of share of wages and salaries in value added from estimated elasticity of output with respect to labour, dummy variable for post reform period and product of industrial concentration and import barriers. According to results, PCMs are positively related with tariff and non-tariff barriers. The interaction of import barriers, industrial concentration and capital output ratio are positively related with PCMs. There is negative relationship between growth rate of industries and PCMs and also between labour's income share on profitability of industrial firms and PCMs. Thus lowering of tariff and removal of quantitative restrictions on imports of manufactures in 1990s has significant procompetitive effect on Indian industries. These effects are particularly on concentrated industries which tend to reduce the PCM. Results also suggest that there is significant reduction in labour's share in value added in the post reform period (reflecting perhaps a weakening of industrial labour bargaining power).

Rao (2005) examines the productivity effects on Indian auto ancillary industry by studying liberalisation policies of 1984 and 1991. The productivity changes are estimated over 1977-84, 1985-91 and then for 1992-99. The average factor productivities are measured for labour, domestic raw materials, imported raw materials and capital. The averages are in terms of mean and median values. The study estimated translog production function using fixed effects (FE) and generalized method of moment estimator (GMM). The study also estimated average productivity growth rates. Results show that except labour, imported material input is a substitute for all other factors in first period (1977-84). In second period (1985-91) labour is complement of both imported and domestic material inputs. However, in third period (1992-99), labour and imported raw materials are found to be complements whereas labour and domestic materials are found to be substitutes. The study concluded that productivity of all the factors is very variable. It is found that closed regime of the first period favours the smaller firms more whereas the most open regime of the third period favours the bigger firms. This leads to higher growth in productivity for the auto ancillary industry as a whole.

Kaundal (2005) examines the impact of economic reforms on the external sector of India. The study is based on time series secondary data. The study period is 1984-85 to 2003-04. The study period is sub-divided into pre-reform phase (1984-85 to 1990-91), first generation reforms (1991-92 to 1997-98) and the second generation reforms (1998-99 to 2003-04). For this, compound growth rates and instability index, are used. According to the study, the share of exports in the world exports has risen from 0.51 to 0.86 percent in 2002-03. But in overall of study period import share has been higher than export share because reforms improved the openness of the Indian economy *vis-a-vis* other emerging economies. The higher import share show that still resource utilization is larger than the amount of resources generated within the economy. The overall balance and real exchange rate reflects the strengthening of the balance of payment position as a result of external sector reforms. The position of external sector also improved in terms of total exchange reserves, reserves in terms of months of imports, external debt position and foreign investment inflows.

Sarkar and Bhattacharyya (2005) investigate whether or not trade liberalization is stimulating growth in India and Korea. The study uses three indices of liberalization over the period 1956 to 1999 for India and 1956 to 2001 for Korea. The liberalization indices are export/GDP, import/GDP and (export + import)/GDP. So the share of foreign trade in GDP was 16.33 per cent in mid 1950's. It started declining and reached to 8.92 per cent by 1970 due to ISI (import substituting industrialization) and export pessimism. Thereafter, due to rising share of imports and also due to the increased export drive to pay for the rising import bill, it started rising and reached to 16.64 per cent by 1980. The share of India's foreign trade in GDP started rising due to trade liberalization in mid 1980's and accelerated under New Economic Policy in 1990s and reached at 25.24 per cent in 1998, of which 11.98 per cent was the share of exports and 13.27 per cent was the share of imports. Similarly, Koreas share of foreign trade in GDP was 14.67 per cent in mid 1950s, which increased to 37.63 per cent in 1970 due to major policy reforms. Further, it increased to 73.71 per cent by 1980. Finally in the wake of economic crisis in 1997 share increased to 83.47 per cent. To test the trend stationarity with and without structural break, ADF tests and Perron tests are applied, the tests exhibit that all the series have deterministic trend except the export share of Korea. In view of the expected increase in trade openness with the emergence of an export drive that was stimulated by the oil price shock of 1973 to pay for import, the possibility of structural break in the Indian series is explored in 1973. Similarly, the structural break in the Korean series is considered in 1973. The trend analysis reveals that initially trade openness in India declines and grows after 1972, whereas in Korea trade opens at a high rate up to 1972 and decelerates afterwards. For studying the impact of trade openness on growth based on time series data, the linear regression is fitted with time trends. Where, real GDP per capita depends upon the index of trade openness, time trend and error term. Further Autoregressive Distributed Lag approach to cointegration finds no evidence of favourable impact trade liberalization on real growth rates of India and Korea.

SECTION II

Import demand functions conducted at national and international levels

Khan (1974) estimates import and export demand functions for fifteen developing countries. These are Argentina, Brazil, Chile, Colombia, Costa Rica, Ecuador, Ghana, India, Morocco, Pakistan, Peru, Philippines, Sri Lanka, Turkey and Uruguay. These functions are estimated in log form for the period 1951-69 on an annual basis. Equilibrium and disequilibrium equations are estimated by two stage least square method (both for imports and exports). Quantity of imports demanded by the country depends on the ratio of imports prices to domestic prices and domestic real income. Exports quantity is related to the ratio of unit value of exports of country to world price level and real world income. The equilibrium results show that for imports, estimated price elasticities are generally high. This indicates that relative prices have significant effect on the imports of developing countries. Relative price elasticities have negative sign in case of eleven countries (including India). Except for the results of six countries (including India), all of the estimated income elasticities are significantly different from zero at five per cent level and have positive signs. In the disequilibrium estimates of imports, the short run price elasticities are significantly different from zero and have correct signs in equations for six countries. The income elasticities are significantly different from zero at five per cent level and have positive signs in the results for four countries. The coefficient of autocorrelation is significantly different from zero in the estimates for eight countries in case of equilibrium estimates and for six countries in case disequilibrium estimates for imports. The equilibrium export equations show that estimated price elasticities are significantly different from zero at five per cent level and have negative signs in case of nine countries. The income elasticities are positive and significant in case of eight countries. The results of disequilibrium export equation show that short run price elasticities are significant and have correct signs in the equations for six countries (including India). Except for the three countries these price elasticities are also long run equilibrium elasticities for the rest of the countries. The estimated income elasticities are significant and have positive signs in case of two countries only. The coefficient of autocorrelation is significant in case of three countries (equilibrium estimates) and there is no case of positive autocorrelation in case of disequilibrium estimates for exports. On the whole it appears that prices do play an important role in the determination of imports and exports of developing countries. This is indicated by much higher price elasticities of imports and exports, than expected one, and lower income elasticities for both imports and exports. It is also concluded that degree of autocorrelation is greater in the imports equation than export equation. This confirms that restrictions are more important in the determination of imports than exports (as degree of autocorrelation is an indicator of quantitative restriction having been omitted).

Khan and Ross (1975) specify a relatively simple import equation and separate the demand variable into its cyclical and secular components. The resulting equation is estimated for fourteen industrial countries (U.S., Canada, France, Germany, Italy, U.K., Japan, Belgium, Netherlands, Austria, Switzerland, Denmark, Norway and Sweden). The study period is 1960 to 1972 on a semiannual basis. The results show that estimated price elasticity of imports has the expected negative sign at the 10 per cent level in 50 per cent of the countries in the sample. The proportion is greater than obtained by Houthakker and Magee (1969) for the same group of countries on an annual basis for the period 1951-66. Apart from the estimates for U.S. and Belgium estimated current real income elasticities tended to be much greater than the estimates of Houthakker and Magee (1969). Potential real income elasticities are positive and significant in the estimates for the U.S. and the

U.K., while they are negative and significant in the estimates for Canada, France, Japan and Switzerland. In the remaining cases elasticity turned out to be insignificant. The results also show that if exports are assumed to be constant, the U.S. and U.K. would experience a secular deterioration in their trade balance as their imports would increase secularly, while others, such as Canada, France, Japan and Switzerland would experience a secular improvement.

Sundararajan and Thakur (1976) use input-output approach to develop import demand functions in case of Korea. The paper tries to show that input-output approach for estimating import demand functions is better than both the approaches of linear and log linear. For this purpose, study has used three commodity categories, viz., petroleum, machinery and chemicals and also aggregate imports of Korea. Traditional as well as log linear, both approaches give wrong signs, while input output approach gives correct sign for different variables. So paper concludes that while comparing input output approach to traditional and log linear approach, input output approach is preferable. It avoids specification bias and the consequent erroneous coefficients for the variables in import demand function. Results also show that with the use of traditional import functions, the effect of relative price on aggregate import of Korea will be overestimated in case of linear specifications. While it will be underestimated in case of log linear specification. The time trends in aggregate import will be underestimated in case of linear specification, while it is overestimated in case of log linear specifications.

Murray and Ginman (1976) study the specification of functional form of import demand model. According to the authors, various studies used the mathematical specification of the relation of imports to price of import in domestic currency as well as to the price of domestically produced substitutes. Which constraints the influence of the two price variables to be equal in magnitude, but opposite in sign. They conduct a statistical test for the equality of the magnitude of the influence of these two variables. For this unadjusted aggregate data for Canada covering the 58 quarter period beginning with the third quarter of 1950 and ending with the fourth quarter of 1964 is used. Firstly, the traditional import demand function is estimated where quantity of imports depend upon real gross national product, the price of imports and GNP deflator. After the improvements, another equation is estimated where quantity of imports depend upon real gross national product, unit value of import index, wholesale price index and price index of non-traded items. The real income elasticity is approximately one, much lower than in the traditional equation, but more consistent with theoretical expectations for an aggregate income parameters. The import price elasticity is approximately one, this is lower than in the traditional equation. The domestic price elasticity coefficients are very much as expected. The price elasticity with respect to domestically produced import competing products of 2.0 to 2.5 is quite reasonable. Positive price elasticity with respect to non-traded items of 1.25 simply reflects that both imports and non traded items are substitutes. Thus the primary conclusion of this paper is that relative price specification of traditional import demand model is inappropriate for estimating aggregate import demand parameters. Though this same conclusion is not demonstrated for disaggregate models.

Jayaraman (1977) estimates the demand functions for various categories of imports of India. The study shows that aggregate imports are uniformly price inelastic over time whereas income elasticity is not significantly different from zero and elasticity of demand w.r.t. net foreign assets is significant but has a negative sign. The quantity of imports is taken for the period of 1961-72 and depends upon level of real income (GNP), the import price level relative to domestic price level and net foreign assets in current prices. In addition to these, dummy variable is added in order to capture the influence of devaluation. All the equations have theoretically expected signs for the relative price variable. But for mineral fuels and lubricants, relative prices contain positive sign. Only two categories of imports have significant income elasticities i.e., for food and live animals and machinery and transport equipment. Similarly, only two categories have significant elasticities with respect to net foreign assets, i.e., crude materials and misc. manufactured goods.

Khan and Ross (1977) discuss that there is no theoretical presumption regarding the appropriate functional form (linear or log linear) of aggregate import demand equation. So they decided to verify empirically about the appropriate form of the aggregate import demand equations in case of three major trading countries - the United States, Canada and Japan. The linear and log linear equations are estimated through both equilibrium model and dynamic model. The aggregate import demand functions of three countries in case of equilibrium model depends upon ratio of the price of imports to the domestic price level and real gross national product. The dynamic model involves adjustments in import, in which change in imports related to difference between demand for imports in period 't' and actual level of imports in the previous period. For this quarterly data for the period 1960 to 1972 is used. To determine the relevant functional form, the study uses Box-Cox (1964) analysis of transformation. This method allows the data itself to determine the functional form of the relationship instead of having to formulate it in advance. The Box-Cox procedure involves the specification of a general power function that contains both the linear and log linear specifications as special cases. This also involves maximum likelyhood test in both the cases of equilibrium and dynamic equations. Results show that, degree of significance of parameters is about the same between the two specifications in each of the countries and signs are according to the theory (for both equilibrium and dynamic equations). But by using Box-Cox (1964) analysis of transformations it is concluded that log linear form is better than linear form, as price and income elasticities can be directly obtained from log linear regression equation.

Biswas and Ram (1980) estimate a model of food grains import demand by India for the period 1951-75. The model is based on both the likely demand for import by the public at large and decision process of the government based on it. Firstly, traditional import demand function is specified, where quantity demanded depends upon income and relative prices. Traditional import demand function is modified by simple governmental intervention instrument, which is defined as a function of domestic production of foodgrains, opening level of the central stocks of foodgrains and foreign exchange reserves. The dummy variable is also included for the buffer stock years. The comparison of traditional import demand model and its modified version show that later model has higher explanatory power. Results also confirm that coefficient of government stock variable has expected sign and significant at 1 per cent level. Also the signs of income and domestic foodgrain prices are as expected, but their t-statistic are quite low. The effect of import price is virtually zero. The coefficient of foreign exchange reserves suggests that the reserve is not an important consideration. The dummy of the buffer stock years has the expected sign and a moderate but not significant statistic. Thus, the study observed the strong effects of central stock, modest effect of domestic production and extremely small effect of income and world prices.

Boylan *et al.* (1980) present the functional form of import demand equations for three smaller economies of the European Economic Community-Ireland, Denmark and Belgium. The aggregate import is depending on relative prices of imports to domestic prices, and to the level of domestic real income. The study period is 1953 to 1975 and log linear form of regression is used to obtain results. The results show that the parameter estimates for the income variable have the sign expected from theory. The estimated coefficients of the price variable have the expected sign for all three countries and are statistically significant in the case of Ireland and Denmark. There is no autocorrelation for all three countries. The price variable coefficients for Ireland and Denmark are –0.45 and –0.52, respectively, and for income variable for

Ireland, Denmark and Belgium, the values are 1.84, 1.58 and 1.75 respectively.

Grossman (1982) studies the substitutability between imports from developed countries (DC), imports from less developed countries, and home goods in the U.S. market for certain manufactures. Separate import demand equations are estimated for imports from developed countries and from LDCs. These equations are estimated for eleven commodities, which represent both consumer and intermediate goods for which imports constitute a large (growing in many cases) share of the U.S. domestic market, and for which the LDC share in total U.S. imports is significant. The study period is 1968-78. The demand for imports depends upon price of imported good, the price of the similar imports that originate in the alternative supply source (i.e., DC vs LDC), the price of the good produced by the U.S. industry and a real activity variable (captures both cyclical and secular income effects on import demand). The equations include a four quarter lag on import prices and a three quarter lag on the domestic price. The study also includes dock strike effects, which occasionally disrupt the flow of traded goods and dummy variable for each quarter are included to reflect seasonal shifts in the level of the constant term of the regression. The log linear functional form is estimated. The results show that income elasticities of demand for LDC imports are larger than those for DC imports. The results also show that price competitiveness does seem to play an important role in the determination of international trade flows. The import demand elasticities for these disaggregate commodities groups are largely of expected sign, and are of much larger magnitude than those previously found in the literature. This finding indicates an increasingly important role for LDC manufactures in the US market in the future. There is no equal substitutability between developing country products, advanced country products and goods produced domestically for the home market, for the eleven commodities considered. This suggests that the effects of the tariff preference scheme will be seen more through trade creation than trade diversion. It has the important implication that future displacement costs that may result from the growth of manufactured exports by the developing countries to the U.S. are more likely to be concentrated in the US home goods industries than in the export industries of other developed countries. Finally, it suggests that the concern expressed by the trade oriented LDCs over the erosion of their tariff preferences is, in many cases, unwarranted. Results also conclude that set of goods that US imports from the LDCs is largely distinct from those imported from developed countries. In particular, imports from developed countries tend to be "up-market" goods, whereas those supplied by the LDCs are "down market" products and in each case we find that home firms are engaged in the production of both types of goods.

Mohabbat *et al.* (1984) estimate the demand for imports as factor of production for India. The paper also studies the effect of composition of output on demand for imports in India. The study period is 1960-75. The paper uses translog cost function approach. In case of translog specification separability between inputs and outputs is not imposed a priori, but may be specified as hypotheses to be tested. If separability exists between primary factors (capital and labour) and import, then it implies that import demand depends only on import prices, a price index of domestic value added, and an index of aggregate output. Translog specification also helps in obtaining estimates of Allen Elasticities of Substitutions (AES) between primary inputs and imports, and between capital and labour. The paper uses three inputs of labour, imports and capital to produce consumption and investment goods. According to results, the demand for labour is most inelastic, followed by imports and capital services, respectively. The study concludes that in India imported resources are less responsive to import price changes. It means import demand may be heavily dependent upon the needs of economic development. The results also show that changes in the composition of output between consumption and investment goods will not alter the cost-minimizing input mix. Neither linear nor non-linear separability between imports and between capital and labour exists. It is also found that capital services and imports and capital services and labour, are substitutes. The substitutability between former pair is greater than later one. However, imports and labour do not show a significant degree of substitutability.

Gafar (1984) studies the impact of devaluation with the help of traditional import demand function of Jamaica. The study period is 1954-72. The demand for imports is assumed to be dependent on domestic real income and the ratio of import prices to domestic prices (i.e., assuming some degree of substitutability between imports and domestic goods). The dummy variable is also included to account the effect of 1967 devaluation on the demand for imports. The value is zero for pre-devaluation period (1954-67) and one for post-devaluation period (1968-72). The empirical results indicate that the income variable is positive and statistically significant, while the estimated price parameter is negative (except beverages) but not significant in some cases at the five per cent (one tail) level. The dummy variable is statistically insignificant at the five per cent (two-tail) level. In those cases where results are significant, the import substitution process pursued under incentives, legislation law is partly responsible. Experimentation with the chow test also produces results which are statistically insignificant. According to Gafar, while econometric result indicates about little impact of devaluation on the demand for imports, it is incorrect to conclude that devaluation is failure unless we take into account the magnitude of appropriate elasticities and domestic monetary and fiscal policies pursued after devaluation. The estimates of the price and income elasticities computed at point of sample means, together with the average percentage share of imports for 1954-72. The value of the weighted aggregate price elasticity is absolutely greater than 0.5 implying that the Johnson-Heien rule of thumb for a successful devaluation is satisfied. Thus the econometric results indicate that devaluation did not affect the demand for imports significantly. The continued deterioration in the balance of payments subsequent to devaluation may be partly due to the expansionary policy. The paper suggests that exchange rate policies should be accompanied with the appropriate policy mix to achieve internal and external balance.

Arize (1986) investigates the price responsiveness of export and import demand and supply in eight developing countries. The countries are Ivory Coast, Tunisia, Morocco, Kenya, Upper Volta, Zambia, Mauritius and Malawai. The annual data are used for the period 1960 to 1982. The countries are selected due to availability of data on relevant variables and these countries are at similar developmental stages. The log linear equations are estimated and Two-stage Least Squares estimates are given. There are four import demand equations and two import supply equations. The real quantity of imports of a country is dependent on the ratio of unit value of imports to domestic price level, real gross domestic product of country, quantity obtained by fitting a linear time trend to the logarithm of real output deviations about the trend income (capacity utilization), world real income, world price level and imports in previous year. Similarly, there are four equations for export demand and one equation for export supply. The real quantity of exports of a country is dependent upon unit value of exports, world real income, world price level and exports in previous year. As per the results for the supply and demand for exports except Upper Volta, the estimated supply price elasticity is statistically different from zero at ninety percent level of confidence. The trend income variable is significantly positive in Tunisia, Kenya, Mauritius and Malawai. The capacity utilization variable is significantly positive in Ivory Coast, Zambia, Mauritius and Malawi. The domestic price variable is positive and significant in case four countries. The coefficient of lagged export supply is positive and significantly different from zero in case of six of eight countries. The estimated demand price elasticity is statistically different from zero at ninety percent level of confidence in case of Morocco, Upper Volta, and Malawi. The trend or potential income is statistically significant in Tunisia, Kenya and Malawi. In Zambia, the world income carries a positive sign and statistically significant, and negative and significant in case of Mauritius. The short-run price elasticities are significantly different from zero and have the correct signs in import demand equations in case of six countries. The trend of income elasticities is significant in case of five countries. The capacity utilization is significant in case of four countries. The results of import supply equations give significant coefficient for lagged import price variable (suggesting that the supply behaviour is more appropriately specified with price and not quantity). This is not the case in Malawi, where supply quantity equation is statistically stable and supply price equation is not.

Kabir (1988) constructs import demand and export demand models to estimate the effect of exchange rate changes on the demand for imports and exports of Bangladesh. Study also estimates the relevant elasticities. Usually exchange rates are introduced indirectly specified by expressing the prices in common currency units. In this paper, exchange rate variable is directly specified. The demand functions are specified in a traditional multiplicative way and estimated in transformed log linear form. Demand for imports is assumed to be dependent upon income in the importing country, price of import substitutes, foreign currency price of imported goods, the exchange rate, international reserves and foreign aid. Similarly, quantity of exports depends upon weighted average of real income of the country's trading partner, relative price index, export weighted local currency price of exports and nominal effective exchange rate. For estimation, ordinary least squares (OLS) method is used and some equations are re-estimated due to presence of first order autocorrelation by using cochrane-orcutt (CORC) technique. All equations are estimated for the period of 1973-83. The results show that income elasticity of import demand for Bangladesh has the expected positive sign. The relative price elasticity is negative. The foreign currency reserves and foreign aid, both have expected signs. Import demand model shows that exchange rate and foreign aid variables are the most significant variables. The influence of income and international reserves is also considerable whereas influence of price is negligible. Income elasticity for exports has expected positive sign and less than unity. The estimated relative price elasticity for exports bears negative sign and it is significantly greater than unity. Separating the relative price variable into two components, (the world export price and Bangladesh's export price) yields more information. It shows that variations in world price would affect the quantity of exports demanded from Bangladesh, whereas variations in Bangladesh's own exports prices would not have any major impact. The separate specification of the exchange rate reveals significantly elastic influence of exchange rate on export volume.

Lopez and Thomas (1988) study the import-GDP relationship in the context of Africa's financing constraints. It focuses on Africa and on selected countries involving significant policy changes, these countries are Coast d' Ivoire, Ghana, Kenya, Madagascar, Nigeria, Tanzania, Zaire and Zambia in the quantitative analysis, as well as Ethopia and Zimbabwe in some of the discussions. Paper also examines broader issues regarding import projections. The study period taken is 1965 to 1986. The income elasticity of demand for imports for the African countries is more than one. The price elasticity is more than minus one. Thus, the partial measured impact of income and of relative price changes on imports over the long term has been more than proportionate. The estimates also indicate significant country differences in their income and price effects. According to the study, the actual import may be the result of changes in foreign exchange availability which is reflected in widespread quantitative restrictions. The composite elasticity of price, income and quantitative restrictions has been for above one during 1970s, but highly variable in 1980s given reductions in imports and GDP. The import GDP ratio for Africa and eight countries is about 24 per cent in 1965-81. Import GDP ratio has hardly changed during 1982-86 compared to 1965-81, in group of countries undergoing structural adjustment, it has actually declined in eight African countries, a significant increase has occurred only in Asian developing countries and Asia's average is 17 per cent. In some of the African countries production is more dependent on imports as compared to the developing countries. The smaller country sizes and less diversity in structure are the reasons of higher import ratios in Africa. These trends indicate for special attention to the financing requirements for imports needed for growth. The paper also noted that secular decline in agriculture's share of GDP would increase the import content of production. The higher is agriculture's share in GDP and the lower is the share of agricultural imported inputs in total imported inputs (as in Tanzania and Ghana), the greater will be the reduction in import growth from accelerated agricultural growth. It is also indicated that in many cases restructuring of industries to achieve greater efficiency would be associated with a lowering of import dependency. At the same time, different types of imports might be needed to rehabilitate and redirect the industry as in Tanzania or increased imports might be needed to replace and modernize outdated capital equipment as in Zimbabwe. The role of absorption as a determinant of imports is also examined. While for some of the countries, adjustments of the level of absorption is feasible, this may also be a limited avenue for achieving further reductions in import-GDP coefficients. The results show biggest change in the composition of absorption rather than the level of absorption can be especially significant in increasing the flexibility of overall import dependence. Further, paper also explored the role of exchange rate and import reforms in affecting import dependency. The negative effect on imports of real devaluation varies substantially among the countries. The degree of currency overvaluation is also vastly different, based on one index of the real exchange rate, considerable depriciation can be seen during 1984-86 in most cases, although there is still some appreciation compared to 1980 level in Tanzania and hardly any change in Kenya and Nigeria.

Moran (1988) studies the import demand model by adding traditional variables, prices and income, to international reserves and foreign capital inflows. Moran considers foreign exchange constraints as important as price and income for determining import demand model. For this purpose, two theoretical models were discussed. The traditional model, i.e., A Benchmark model, and it is later extended to include foreign exchange constraint, i.e., A Hemphill Model. The empirical estimation of import models is conducted using pooled cross section time series for 21 developing countries for the period of 1970-83. Here estimates are presented for four country groups (low income countries, major exporter of manufactures, non fuel primary commodity exporters, and oil exporters as well as for all developing countries). The first model includes two sets of explanatory variables, i.e., relative prices and domestic output; and foreign exchange receipts and international reserves. The reduced form of estimates of this model produced long-run foreign exchange elasticities that ranged between 0.5 and 0.8. The price elasticities are ranged between –0.3 and –0.1, and income elasticities ranged between 0.2 and 0.4. This general import model contains as special cases of the models normally adopted in the estimation of import equations - the Benchmark and Hemphill models. The general model dominates strongly the Benchmark model in all the four country groups. It also dominates Hemphill model in two of four country groups and in estimates for all developing countries. Here real import price is assumed to be exogenous. The second import model assumed that import volumes and import prices are both endogenous. This model includes two independent structural equations an infinitely inelastic import, supply curve and a normal downward sloping demand curve. In first equation supply curve do not respond to changes in domestic output because it is infinitely inelastic, so import volumes depend only on foreign exchange receipts and international reserves. For second equation, the long run price and income elasticity estimates of import demand for each of four country groups are estimated using both

Ordinary Least Squares (OLS) and Two-stage Least Squares (2SLS). In all the cases, the 2SLS estimates – which use foreign exchange receipts and international reserves, are much higher in absolute value than the OLS estimates. Thus, while price and income effects are important in analyzing the import behaviour in developing countries, foreign exchange constraints also play a critical role in determining the imports. Hence paper concludes that import models that neglect either of these effects will yield biased estimates for developing country imports.

Faini *et al.* (1988) organise the study with objectives of identification of stable parameters in the description of import behaviour and analysis of structural and policy determinants of parameters themselves. For these objectives, they have relied on three different but complementary approaches. In first approach, traditional import demand function relating imports to relative price and domestic output are estimated for 50 countries. Traditional import demand equations work well when import controls are relatively stable over time, but it is difficult to determine, if this is the case. The second approach takes into account the import of foreign exchange constraint. This approach applied to the countries for which a statistically satisfactory import demand equation could not be identified using first approach. The third approach relied on direct incorporation of quantitative restrictions or import controls. The main results show that measured income elasitcities in developing countries are generally higher than one. The relative price elasticities are mostly inelastic but significantly affect demand for imports. Results also show that less restrictive trade regime is associated with higher responsiveness of imports to economic incentives. Paper concludes that the econometric evidence that does not allow for the impact of import controls cannot be used reliably to assess the effect of devaluation on the trade balance. Indeed, if devaluation is combined with a liberalization of trade regime, its effect on import demand will be more pronounced than the available evidence would suggest.

Costa (1988) studies India's balance of commodity trade for 15 year period 1970-71 to 1984-85. The paper discusses about determinants of exports, imports and net barter terms of trade. The quantum of exports is dependent upon weighted index of real GDP of eleven countries, real effective exchange rate including export incentives and dummy variable. The dummy variable indicate a structural shift in the export function over 1982-83 through 1984-85. The quantum of imports is dependent upon GNP at factor cost, ratio of unit of imports to wholesale price index and dummy variable for import liberalization. The net barter terms of trade is a function of percentage annual change in GDP (at 1980 prices) of industrial countries, percentage annual change in GDP deflator of industrial countries and Rupee SDR rate. The functional relationships are estimated through OLS method. The results show that the quantity of exports doubled over the study period. The quantity of imports is stable for first seven years, thereafter, there is steep climb. India's net barter terms of trade fell sharply to its lowest level for the period, in 1980-81. It is only in the terminal years, when oil prices are depressed, inflation rates decreased and growth picked up in the industrial countries that India's terms of trade moved up. For exports, coefficients of real income and crude petroleum export dummy are positive. The exports are negatively related with real effective exchange rate. In case of imports, dummy variable and real income have positive coefficients, whereas imports are negatively related with relative prices. India's net barter terms of trade increased from the base level to its peak for the study period. It is positively associated with growth of real income of industrial countries, and negatively with both inflation rates in industrial countries and exchange rate in India. Several policy implications are given by the analysis of paper. First, world economic growth is extremely important for India's net barter terms of trade and exports - both quantum and value. Secondly, since the country's exports are also assisted by falling real effective exchange rates, it is necessary that this competitive edge is not eroded by high inflation in the home economy relative to the industrial economies. Thus, exchange rate policy must ensure, in the interest of satisfactory export performance that no appreciation in the real effective exchange rate is allowed to take place. Thirdly, import substitution in respect of food grains is achieved in India, it must be extended to include other imports. In the interest of this objective, it is necessary to monitor more closely the imports of the country. Finally, it needs to be recognized that import intensive growth in an unfavourable world economic development (low growth and high incidence of protectionist policies) leads to low growth in country's volume of exports, a depressed levels of net barter terms of trade, and then to large trade and payments deficits. Alternatively, adopt a developmental approach, which more emphasized to produce agriculture exportable as well as import competing goods-housing, health and education through a more stable domestic economy. It not only expand exports, lower import dependence and trade deficits, but also put less strains on resources while allowing for higher growth, and lead to more equitable distribution of income and improve living standards for the people.

Siddharthan (1989) studies the impact of import liberalization on export intensities in case of the Indian private corporate sector. The study estimates export functions for sample consisting of cross section of industries for three years before and after liberalization and compare their performance. For pre liberalization period (1982-83 to 1984-85) export functions fitted for nineteen sectors (manufacturing industries). The number of observations for the pooled cross section time series sample is fifty seven. Similarly, for the years 1985-86 to 1987-88, twenty one manufacturing sectors are considered. The sample size for the post liberalization period is sixty three. The variables considered for export functions are ratio of import of raw materials to total raw materials used (MRAW), import of spares to total spares used (MSP), import of machinery to value added (MK), technology imports as seen by ratio of royalty, technical fee and other payments to sales turnover (MT) and dividends in foreign exchange to total dividends indicating changes in foreign equity holdings (FS). The ratios are averages of two periods (pre-and post-liberalization). In analyzing the inter industry differences in export intensities both before and after liberalization, in addition to import liberalization variables, other variables denoting capital sales ratio (KSR), size of the firm in the industry measured in terms of sales turnover (SIZE) and value added to sales ratio (VS). The linear and log linear forms are measured. The results indicate that in case of linear form, the variables KSR, VS and FS are significant in pre-liberalization period while the variables KSR, MRAW and MSP are found to be significant in case of post-liberalization period. In case of log linear form, the variables MSP, VS, FS and SIZE are found to be significant during pre-liberalization period, while the variables KSR, MSP, MT, VS and SIZE are found to be significant during post-liberalization period. Thus the results indicate that impact of liberalization policies on export performance among large firms is at best mixed. There is almost immediate impact of liberalization policies on the import intensities and for large number of products the import intensities of many items increased substantially immediately after 1985 and stay at that high level.

Sundararajan and Bhole (1989) provide an estimate of import demand function for developing countries such as India. They also test the hypothesis of whether conventional functional forms are significantly different from the generalized functional form. The demand for imports is function of domestic real income, the ratio of import prices to domestic prices and foreign exchange reserves. For estimation three forms are used, namely, linear, log linear (conventional function forms) and generalized form. The study period is 1960-61 to 1982-83. The seven categories of commodities are taken into account to estimate generalized functional form. Taking the results obtained from conventional functional form as starting point, Box-Cox (1964) power transform and the procedure discussed in Sundararajan and Bhole (1988) is applied. The equilibrium estimates show that the income elasticity has expected sign and varies significantly from moderate to high at one or five per cent level, respectively. The price elasticities are found to be low in four of the seven cases which confirm about price inelastic demand for imports. The foreign reserves are significant in six out of seven cases. The disequilibrium results show that the income elasticities are again consistently elastic and significantly different from zero at five or one per cent level, respectively. The short run price elasticity is negative and significantly inelastic in three, moderate in one and elastic in three, of the total seven cases. The estimated foreign reserves are positive and significant in all the categories of the demand for imports. As the estimates derived from the generalized functional from cannot be interpreted directly, the elasticities are derived from the generalized functional form (GFF). The derived elasticities are in turn compared with the direct elasticities of the conventional functional form (CFF). The study concludes that elasticities derived from GFF are different from those of CFF (with the help of likelihood ratio test) and CFFs like linear and/or log linear are not free from functional misspecification and do not fit in the import demand function.

Virmani (1991) estimates the aggregate export and import functions for India for the period 1970-71 to 1985-86. The paper shows that exports are function of exchange rate, prices of Indian exports, income, rate of export subsidy, prices of non exported goods and other supply factors (such as rainfall or capacity utilization). Similarly, imports are function of price of imports (as measured by unit value Index of imports), prices of non-exported commodities, income and other factors. The results show that 10 per cent depreciation would lead to a 15 per cent to 19 per cent increase in foreign currency value of manufactured exports and an 8.4 per cent increase in manufactured imports. From the same depreciation the fall in primary imports would be 4.2 per cent, while primary exports may not change significantly. So price effects are found to be large and significant in both export demand and import demand functions for manufactured goods, while they are smaller for primary exports and imports demand functions. Domestic inflation has a particularly strong effect on both manufactured and primary imports. In case of export growth of world income and trade affects both manufactured and primary exports. Domestic demand for manufacture is also found to affect the manufactured export price. The rainfall is negatively related to export price, while capacity utilization is not found to have a significant effect. Manufactured imports strongly respond to growth in GDP from agriculture. The rainfall has an independent effect on primary imports.

Aksoy and Tang (1992) study the major changes in policies and their impact on manufacturing imports, exports and output in case of India. The study period is 1970-71 to 1987-88. The structural function is estimated for manufactured export which consists of both supply and demand factors. The manufactured exports depend upon manufactured export weighted REER adjusted by export incentives, reserves in months of imports and manufacturing GDP. Import of capital goods are modelled as function of relative import to domestic prices of capital goods before taxes, gross fixed investment in machinery and import duty on capital goods. Here all the coefficients are significant. The price elasticity is 0.8 and the demand elasticity is 1.16. Import duty has a significant negative effect on capital goods imports, with an elasticity of around 0.6. The imports of intermediate goods are function of relative import to domestic price of intermediate goods before taxes, import duty on intermediate goods and manufacturing GDP. The short run price elasticity for intermediate goods imports is 1.5, the long run price elasticity is 2.1 and the demand elasticity is 1.5. The elasticity of import duty is around 1.5. The paper concludes that foreign trade has contracted relative to domestic output due to increase in relative prices of imports to domestic output due to increasing tariffs, large real devaluations (especially after 1986), and rapidly expanding domestic demand that has increased the attractiveness of the domestic market relative to exporting.

Patra and Rangan (1992) study the structure of India's imports for the period 1970-71 to 1988-89. The paper estimates import demand functions for total imports and also for various categories of imports. The categories of imports taken in this study are decided by the availability of disaggregate indices. The quantum of total imports and imports of individual commodities is dependent upon gross domestic product at factor cost (GDPFC), unit value of imports (UVI), domestic wholesale price (PD), domestic production (DP) and real foreign assets (FAP). The import demand functions are estimated both in linear and double log forms. The double log functional form is found to have a better fit than the linear form except in case of dyeing, tanning and colouring materials and transport equipment where a linear form gives better results. The overall aggregate price and income elasticity of demand for imports are found to be –0.42 and 1.57 respectively. After correcting for bias involved in estimates based on aggregate imports only, aggregate weighted price and income elasticities of demand for imports calculated turned out to be –0.60 and 1.44 respectively. All the categories of imports have significant and positive income elasticity except in the case of edible oils, fruits, vegetables, iron and steel and paper, paper board and manufactures thereof. Negative income elasticity is obtained in respect of iron and steel, fruits and vegetables and paper, paper board and manufactures, however it is found to be insignificant. The imports of beverages and tobacco, fruits and vegetables, pulp and waste paper, dyeing, tanning and colouring materials, textiles yarn, fabric etc, iron and steel and electrical machinery are found to be significantly price elastic. Except iron and steel, these commodities are also significantly income elastic. Commodities like paper, paper board and manufactures, transport equipment and professional and scientific instruments were price inelastic. All elasticities have the expected negative sign. In case of edible oils, paper, paper board and manufacture thereof and capital goods, real net foreign exchange reserves variable is a significant factor in explaining the behaviour of import demand.

The domestic production was significant only in case of beverages and tobacco, petroleum crude and electrical machinery. The dummy variable used as a proxy for import liberalization is found to be significant only in respect of iron and steel, transport equipment and professional and scientific instruments as well as in aggregate imports.

Hossain (1995) estimates the trade elasticities of disaggregated commodities for Bangladesh and also calculates the trade balance elasticity to know the situation of trade balance. The paper uses the annual time series data for the period 1975 to 1994. The import demand and export supply functions are estimated. The first order autoregressive distributive lag (ADL) model is used for both import demand and export supply functions. The imports of Bangladesh depend upon production capacity, foreign exchange reserves, price of imports and price of domestic goods. The exports of Bangladesh depend upon price of exports, price of exportable goods in domestic markets and output capacity. Both import demand and export supply functions are estimated by using Error Correction Modelling (ECM) procedure which involves only a linear transformation of the Autoregressive Distributed Lag (ADL) formulation with variables in differences. The results show that Bangladesh import demand is relatively price elastic (–1.50) and export supply is inelastic (0.97) in aggregate products. The elasticities of import demand for all product categories are greater than unity except that for cotton, whereas export supply elasticities of most individual products are found to be less than unity. The lowest import demand elasticity is 1.03 for iron and steel (a construction material) and highest is 12.16 for manufacture fertilizers (an agricultural input). It is also observed that in most of the cases, the foreign exchange reserves do not have any significant influence. As against this export supply elasticities of most of individual products are found to be less than unity. The textiles and clothing has the lowest elasticity of supply (0.77), whereas for manufacturing sector it is greater than unity (1.53). Hossain discusses that trade balance elasticity of 2.05, shows that one per cent devaluation will improve the trade balance by 2.05 per cent of import value. As import demand is price elastic and export supply is price inelastic so devaluation in Bangladesh improves trade balance only by reducing imports. The paper also suggests that Bangladesh needs implementation of the policies for structural reforms (in addition to the policy of adjustment of exchange rate) so as to diversify its export base and reduce cost of production.

Verma (1997) studies the India's international trade in services and broad determinants of services for imports and exports. The estimated functions of exports and imports of services involved the impact of factors determining their behaviour. This study considers the period from beginning of sixties till eighties. The services are classified into transport, travel, insurance, capital services and professional, technical and other services. The annual rate of real imports of transport, travel and professional, technical and other services varies between thre per cent and six per cent. But the annual rate of real imports of insurance and capital services hardly recorded any growth. The annual rate of real exports of travel, capital services and professional, technical and other services varies between 11 per cent and 15 per cent. But the annual rate of real exports for both transport and insurance is 3.4 per cent. Results show that travel, transport and professional technical and other services receipts are raising faster than their payments. The receipts of insurance and investment have been rising, while payments have been sluggish. According to results, travel receipts are mainly dependent on expansion of tourist facilities in country and travel payments are affected by growth of domestic income. Transportation receipts are dependent on merchandise exports from country and its payments are mainly for import of foreign merchandise. The insurance receipts are dependent generally on exports of merchandise, while its payments are mainly affected by foreign exchange availability. The receipts of capital services are mainly dependent on growth of world economy whereas its payments mainly depend on growth of domestic industrial economy. The professional, technical and other services receipts abroad are mainly dependent on development of the expertise in the country, and their payments have been determined by growth of domestic economic activity. The foreign exchange availability has also affected the demand for these services. The government policy has directly determined utilization of these services.

Emran *et al.* (1997) critically review the available price and income elasticity estimates of aggregate imports of Bangladesh. The studies discussed are of Nguyen and Bhuyan (1977), Kabir (1988), Shilpi (1990), Bayes *et al.* (1995), Hossain (1995) and Emran and Shilpi (1996, 1997). All these studies except of Emran and Shilpi, uses Ordinary Least Square (OLS) technique for the estimation of import equation. All these studies did not test for order of integration of the data and for existence of cointegration among the variables. Therefore, it is simply not clear whether or not the estimated relation suffers from the problem of spurious regression. All these studies also not included theoretically consistent treatment of foreign exchange constraints (except Kabir). As against this, study by Emran and Shilpi use cointegration technique to estimate price and income elasticity of aggregate imports of Bangladesh. It also discusses aggregate imports under foreign exchange rationing. Thus, reliable estimates suggested by paper are –0.6 (price elasticity) and 1.6 (income elasticity), which are from the study by Emran and Shilpi (1996). These estimates derived from a theoretically consistent model and appropriate econometric technique. The price elasticity is higher than all other available estimates. The study period is 1973-93, which is also longest among all the available studies.

Kutty (2001) build an import demand model for analyzing the pattern of imports of coffee in various countries, to which India exports coffee. The countries considered are U.S.A., U.K., Australia, Belgium, Canada, France, Germany, Italy, Japan, the Netherlands, Spain, Sweden and Switzerland. The secondary data sources are used for the period of 1978 to 1997. The import volume of coffee depends upon real prices of coffee in U.S. dollar, real GDP in U.S. dollar, population and relative prices i.e., ratio of coffee prices to tea prices. As countries considered are developed and coffee imports constituting an insignificant share in their total imports, the foreign exchange variable has been deliberately excluded from the model. The multiple regression equations with and without log specifications have been estimated. The coffee drinking is inversely related to coffee prices in U.K., Belgium, Canada, Sweden, Netherlands, Italy and Switzerland and positively related in case of France. The coffee drinking is positively related to income in case of four countries. The coefficient of population is greater than zero in case of seven countries and it is because of spread of coffee drinking habit. In remaining countries coefficient of population is lower than zero due to shift in consumer preferences from coffee to other beverages. The relative prices are positively related to coffee drinking in case of U.K. and the Netherlands (i.e., preference of coffee over tea). The relative prices and coffee drinking habit are inversely related in remaining countries.

Rao and Nagabhushanam (2001) describe the nature of traditional demand for precious metals in India, and estimate the elasticities of demand for imports of non-monetary gold, non-monetary silver and merchandise for the period 1901 to 1913. The period has been chosen as it seemed to be quite free from any structural changes in the Indian economy. For this purpose linear static econometric model is estimated. The model contains three linear equations in three endogenous variables namely, demands for imports of non-monetary gold (Dg), demand of imports of non-monetary silver (Ds) and demand for imports of merchandise (Di). These linear equations were estimated by the inverse transformation from the least square estimates of the corresponding reduced system. The demand elasticities of endogenous variables with respect to each of the exogenous ones are simultaneously estimated from the structural equations. The exogenous variables are national income (N), price of gold (Pg), price of silver (Ps) and price of imports (Pi). The results show that gold has the highest income elasticity relative to silver and merchandise. The income elasticity of demand for silver imports is negative. The reasons given include that the true value is small, though positive, and there may be sampling errors. It is also supposed that with rise in income, people regard silver as an inferior commodity. The price elasticities of demand for imports of gold, or silver, or merchandise are negative (as an increase in price of any of these items reducing the demand for it). The cross price elasticities of gold and silver are both positive, which confirms that they are substitutes for each other.

Tang (2002) studies the stability of aggregate import demand function in India. The study has estimated the responsiveness of import demand with respect to real income and relative prices in long run. It covered the period of 1970-1999 (annual data). The quantity of imports is a function of real GDP and relative prices. The log linear model is specified and multivariate maximum likelihood estimation procedure is used. The results show that presence of cointegration relationship among the variables reveals that aggregate import demand function for India is stable. The estimated long-term model revealed that India's aggregate import behaviour is income elastic (1.427), but price in elastic (0.339).

Dash (2005), studies the import demand function for India using the yearly time series data for the period 1975 to 2003. The co integration and error correction techniques are used to measure the impact of GDP, import price, foreign exchange reserves and price of domestically produced goods on aggregate import demand. The aggregate import volume is co-integrated with India's import prices, prices of domestically produced goods, foreign exchange reserves and GDP. The import demand is largely explained by price of domestically produced goods, GDP, lag of import and foreign exchange reserves.

Dutta and Ahmed (2006) study the behaviour of Indian aggregate imports during the period 1971 to 1995. For this co integration, error correction modelling approaches are used. The real quantity of merchandise imports has been assumed to be dependent upon relative prices, GDP and dummy variable to capture the effect of liberalization. The aggregate import volume is found to be co-integrated with relative import price and real GDP. In the estimated error correction model, all considered variables emerged as important determinants of the import demand function of India. The aggregate import volume is found to be price inelastic. The import demand is largely explained by real GDP. There is little effect of import liberalization policy on aggregate import volume

Kalyoncu (2006) determines whether there exists a long-run relationship between Turkey's aggregate import volume and its major determinants. The study uses for period of 1994-2001. The import demand function for Turkey is estimated by using log linear specification. The imports depend upon the relative prices (ratio of import price index to consumer price index) and real GNP. The paper conducted the Augmented Dickey-Fuller (ADF) and Phillips-Perron (PP) Unit Root tests. These tests confirm no stationary for all the three variables. However, first differencing of all the variables shows stationary under the tests. The co-integration tests are conducted by using Engle-Granger's (EG) Residual-based ADF test and Johansen-Juselius (JJ) method. The results of co-integration tests support the proposition that in Turkey, there exists a stable long-run relationship of aggregate import demand with its major determinants. The Error Correction Model is also estimated, where relative prices and real GNP (lagged six months) have emerged as important determinants of the import demand function for Turkey. The coefficient of error correction term is –0.28. The results suggest that imports are sensitive to relative import price changes (–1.07). The value of income elasticity of demand for imports is –0.88 (lagged six months). Thus, price elasticities of demand for imports is greater than income elasticites.

Nkang *et al*., (2007) study the major determinants of rice (which is one of the widely grown and consumed cereal crops in Nigeria)

import demand in Nigeria. The study uses macro level data from 1970 to 2002. The paper uses multiple regression model with cointegration and error correction testing framework. The quantity of imported rice is assumed to be dependent upon domestic price of production, total import value, population estimate, consumer price index, GDP at current factor cost, trade weighted exchange rate, external reserves, lagged import demand and SAP (structural adjustment programme) dummy. The study adopted Engel and Granger (1987) two step procedure in cointegration and to carry out Unit Root Test for checking stationarity, the Dickey-Fuller (DF) and Augmented Dickey-Fuller (ADF) tests are used. The results confirm the existence of a long run equilibrium relationship between quantity of rice imports and domestic production of rice, external reserves and import value. These variables remarkably shaped rice import behaviour in Nigeria during the study period. The estimates show that all the explanatory variables have the expected signs and are statistically significant at one per cent except the coefficient of domestic rice production variable (significant at 10 per cent level). The elasticity of domestic rice production is inelastic (–0.138). Which indicates that a policy directed towards reducing imports of rice by increasing production may not achieve its goal in short run. The short run elasticity of external foreign exchange reserves (1.297) is greater than unity. A reduction in rice imports would conserve external reserves. The short run elasticity of import value (0.447) is very much less than unity. This means that reduction in rice imports in short run may not be achieved through the reduction in total import value.

SECTION III

Causality analysis conducted at national and international levels

Mallick (1992) studies the causality between India's export growth and industrial development by using techniques of co integration and error correction modeling over the period 1950-51 to 1990-91. The industrial development is measured in terms of growth in Net Domestic Product (NDP) in manufacturing. The Augment Dickey Fuller, Phillips-Perron and Bayesian tests for Unit Root are used for two variables, i.e., export growth and industrial development. The results are presented both for level data and log of level data. The results show the existence of strong co-integration and Granger feedback between industrial output and exports growth. The causation from exports growth to growth in industrial manufacturing suggests about export led growth strategy. The exports not only promote the growth of national income but also lead to structural transformation in India.. The Granger causation running from industrial manufacturing growth to export growth implies that development of manufacturing industries may be prerequisite for India to expand their exports. Further the error correction models provide consistent evidence of unidirectional causation running from industrial output to exports growth in the case of logarithms (irrespective of differences in lag), whereas the reverse is the situation in case of original level data (for differing lag length).

Mallick (1996) studies causation between exports and economic growth for the period 1950-51 to 1991-92. The co integration and error correction models are applied to examine the nature of causation. The study illustrates how an additional source of temporal causality between exports and economic growth can be captured by including the error correction term in the standard Granger causality test. The results show the existence of strong co integration and Granger feedback between income and exports growth. Further the error correction models provide consistent evidence of unidirectional causation running from income growth to exports growth.

Tijani and Ajobo (1999) examine the causal relationship between productivity and agricultural exports in Nigeria over the period 1961-1992. The data are using unit root test, co integration and Granger causality test. The coefficient of the variables of the output function are estimated and used to compute the value of total factor productivity (TFP). The study indicates that agricultural exports cause productivity. The study suggests the opening of economy to stimulate Nigerian farmers to grow new crops and increase production of indigenous ones for foreign markets. This must have forced the domestic farms to improve productivity, both quantity and quality wise in order to stay competitive.

Afxentiou and Serletis (2000) examine possible causality relations between the growth of GNP and exports, as well as between that of GNP and imports. The study uses time series analysis covering a sample of 50 developing countries over a period of 1970-1993. The fifteen countries are from sub-sharan Africa, three from South Asia and the Pacific, nineteen from Latin America and Caribbean and seven from Middle East and North America. The statistical properties of data pretaining to three variables (imports, exports and GNP) checked for stationarity through Unit Root test. The cointegration is applied to examine long run equilibrium relation, which also ensure that the causality test do not produce spurious results. In addition to this, volatility models are used to display the impact of fluctuations in the variables to show importance of variability of time series. The results did not support the hypothesis that export growth led to GNP growth in a Granger sense (Indonesia and Osman are the exceptions). Similarly for imports, only Pakistan is found to exhibit causality from import growth to GNP. When volatility was introduced in causality analysis, anticipated export growth volatility was found to be associated with GNP growth only in the case of Indonesia at the five per cent level. The unanticipated export growth volatility is found to be causally related to GNP growth in South Africa only, at 10 per cent level. Whereas for both (anticipated and unanticipated), export growth causality is marginally more evident in six cases mainly at 10 per cent level. Similarly, when volatility is introduced in causality for imports, then anticipated import growth volatility is found at 5 per cent level leads to GNP growth in Granger sense in Indonesia.

The 10 per cent level anticipated and non-anticipated import growth volatility is leading to growth again in Pakistan, South Africa, Tanzania and Venezuala. On the whole, irrespective of geographical location or level of development, export growth and much less import growth does not causally affect per capita GNP growth. The study states that international trade plays a minor role in the process of development but rather that the main development forces are derived from domestic sources.

Krishnamoorthy and Reddy (2002) examine the relationship between export (import) growth and export (import) instability using India's foreign trade data in terms of rupees and dollars. The study uses the period 1980-81 to 1990-91 as pre-liberalization period and period of years 1991-92 to 2001-02, is used as post-liberalization period. The causality between export (and import) growth and instability is analysed using Granger's method of causality without error correcting term. Instability is measured in terms of Linear Trend Instability (LTI) and Exponential Trend Instability (ETI) Indices. The growth rates of exports and imports in terms of dollar (6.22% and 4.24% respectively) are much lower than the growth rates (16.4% and 12.4%) of exports and imports in terms of Indian rupees during pre-liberalisation period. This implies that there is substantial amount of depreciation of rupee *vis-à-vis* United States dollar during period of pre-liberalisation. In the post-liberalisation period the growth rates for exports in terms of both rupees and dollars (16.56% and 9.56% respectively) are lower than that of imports (17.97% and 10.91% respectively). The instability in both rupee and dollar terms, is negatively related with growth for both exports and imports, in terms of LTI as well as in terms of ETI. The reason for this inverse relationship is lower growth in exports and imports which might be due to high and frequent fluctuation in exports and imports. Once fluctuations in trade get stabilized there will be higher growth in exports and imports. The study also conducted Granger Causality test between growth and instability of exports and imports in India for the period of 1949-50 to 2001-

02. Paper concludes that there is no significant cause and effect relationship between growth and instability in either direction.

Alam and Butt (2002) empirically investigate the causal issues between energy consumption and economic growth along with capital and labour in Pakistan for the period 1960 to 1998. The techniques of co-integration, error correction modeling and Granger causality test are used in the study. The total energy consumption is specified to depend on gross national product, total labour force and gross fixed capital formation. The study finds that energy consumption, economic growth, capital and labour are cointegrated. So all considered explanatory variables follow a long run equilibrium relationship in case of Pakistan. The paper also confirms about causality between energy consumption to economic growth in Pakistan in the short run as well as in the long run. The capital formation Granger causes energy consumption both in the short run and in the long run and there is no causality found from labour to economic growth in Pakistan in short run. Labour is found Granger causes to energy consumption and economic growth only in long run, but causality from capital to economic growth is found in long run as well as in short run. The paper concludes that the key ingredient for growth in energy consumption is the growth in capital accumulation. While, labour force participation and capital accumulation are important factors for economic growth. Therefore Pakistan should adopt such economic growth policies that expand job opportunities in the country.

Fatima *et al.* (2003) examine the differentials of Total Factor productivity (TFP) growth in Pakistan. The major determinants to TFP growth are human capital employed and openness to trade liberalization. The other two determinants are physical capital and labour employed. This study uses unit root and co-integration and Error correction method (ECM) to estimate long run relationship and causality among the variables under considerations. The study has estimated the trend rate of TFP for Pakistan. The results show that TFP growth for Pakistan is mostly positive, it became negative only for some years. TFP growth in Pakistan is significantly related to openness of trade. But due to high taxation, government intervention and regulation of domestic companies, it did not result in higher TFP growth. The TFP in Pakistan has been also found to be depending on quality of labour force, i.e., on its human capital. Study shows that better work force leads to increase in aggregate productivity in Pakistan. The stock of physical capital and labour employed also influence TFP growth of Pakistan, but in long run. The study suggests that the improvements in productivity can be achieved, through importing more efficient and modern machinery (increasing physical capital stock) and through the employment of better or more productive skilled workers (human capital stock). All this is possible by openness of trade. Results also support the hypothesis that trade orientation (openness to trade) does cause the growth in total factor productivity.

Shirazi and Manap (2004) attempt to reinvestigate the exports and economic growth nexus in Pakistan for the period 1960-2003. For testing the long run relationship among the variables the real output (GDP), real exports and real imports, co-integration techniques of Johnson and Johnson and Juselius have been used. To check the directions of causality among these variables, the study uses Granger causality test based on Toda and Yamamoto (1995). The results strongly support a long run relationship among the three variables. The paper finds feedback effect between imports and output. Though exports causes output growth, but converse is not true. There is no significant causality between exports and imports. The paper suggested that Pakistan may continue with the imports of necessary raw material for value addition and needed technology to expand capacity and improve productivity. It may pay full attention to boost up the exports.

Nandi and Kumar (2005) examine the inter relationship between exports and imports in the context of liberalization of Indian economy. The paper explores that whether import growth causes the growth of exports or *vice versa*. This aspect is examined with the help of econometric framework, i.e., causality between exports and imports of India. To understand the pattern of exports and imports of India, different tests of unit root, co-integration and Granger Causality are conducted. The study uses the quarterly exports and imports data for the period of 1987(Q_1) to 2002(Q_3). Unit Root test shows that level of data has a unit root, so the time series are not stationary. Therefore, first difference data is used which has no unit root. The results of co integration show strong evidence of integration between exports and imports. This means that first differencing data series are also found to be cointegrated, integrating a long term stable equilibrium relationship between exports and imports data series. Granger causality test show that the growth of imports appears to cause the export growth in Granger sense. On the other hand there is no reverse causation from exports to imports. Thus findings from causality tests support the conclusion that it is import growth that causes the export growth. Study suggests that increased openness of Indian economy increases imports, which ensures more efficient allocation of resources through specialization and efficient exploitation of comparative advantage.

Chang *et al.* (2005) examine the long run relationship among exports, imports and output in United States from 1971 to 2001. The paper also examines temporal (Granger) causality among these variables, by using cointegration and vector autoregression. For this purpose quarterly data on real gross domestic product, exports and imports for US are used. Data are seasonally adjusted and transformed to log form. Using ADF tests, it is found that all series are stationary and are integrated of order 1, I (1). The Error Correction Model (ECM) is used to test for inter-temporal causality. It is concluded that three variables are co integrated. Bi-directional feedback is found in between output and imports, and between exports and imports. There is causality from output to exports, but inverse is not true. The argument that an increase in exports itself will cause economic growth in the U.S. is apparently tenuous.

CHAPTER

Data Base and Methodology

This chapter has been devoted to explain the database and methodology used in the present study entitled "Dynamics of India's Imports". The study was based on secondary data and examined the pattern of growth, structure, determinants and import-growth causality in India. Besides, this study also examined the import policy of India.

The pattern of growth of India's total imports and its categories/sub-categories was examined for the period from 1986-87 to 2005-06, both at current prices and constant prices. The structure of India's imports was also analysed for the period from 1986-87 to 2005-06 (at current prices and constant prices). The determinants of India's total imports and also for some of its major categories were studied for the period from 1986-87 to 2003-04. The imports-growth causality in India with the help of total imports and also some of its major categories was measured for the period from 1974-75 to 2003-04. The details of data sources are given below:

1. *Annual Statements and Monthly Statistics of Foreign Trade of India*, Directorate General of Foreign Trade of

India, Ministry of Commerce, Government of India (various issues).

2. *Economic Survey*, Government of India, (various issues).
3. *Report on Currency and Finance*, Reserve Bank of India, (various issues).
4. Centre for Monitoring Indian Economy (CMIE) Pvt. Ltd., Mumbai, (various issues).
5. *Annual Survey of industries (factory sectors),* Central Statistical Organization, Government of India, (various issues).

The data for total imports and also for its categories/sub-categories were collected at current prices. The data were deflated by using common base, i.e. 1993-94, for studying growth and structure of imports of India. The data for determinants and causality were also deflated by using appropriate deflators with base year 1993-94.

Methodology

Data taken from various sources analysed by calculating growth rates, percentages, regression equations etc., with the help of appropriate method. The methodology used for various types of analysis is explained below:

(a) Growth Rates of Imports : In order to study the growth pattern of Indian imports and its categories/sub-categories, the annual average growth rates were worked out. The growth rates have been calculated by fitting the exponential function of the type.

$$Y_t = ab^t e^u$$

Transforming the above equation into linear form:

$$\log y_t = \log a + t \log b + u \log e$$

Where, Y_t = value of dependent variable in the year t

t = trend variable

u = disturbance term

a and b = constants

For the estimated value of regression coefficient 'b' the compound growth rate 'r' was calculated as following

$$r\ (\%) = (\hat{b} - 1) \times 100$$

Where, $\hat{b}$ = estimated value of b

The growth rates were calculated for whole of the study period (1986-87 to 2005-06) and also for some of the sub periods (1986-87 to 1990-91, 1991-92 to 1995-96, 1996-97 to 2000-01, 2001-02 to 2005-06, 1990-91 to 1999-2000, 1996-97 to 2005-06), both at current as well as at constant prices with the base year 1993-94. For deflation, Unit Value Indices with base year 1993-94 were used. As we don't have the series of Unit Value Indices (UVI) with common base of 1993-94 throughout, so base was shifted by using base shifting method of index numbers.

(b) Structure of Imports : For analyzing the structure, the share of various categories/sub categories in total imports was calculated in the form of percentages. The shares of various categories and sub categories measured both at current as well as constant prices (base year 1993-94) at all points of time during 1986-87 to 2005-06. However for the discussion the points of time considered were 1986-87, 1990-91, 1996-97, 2000-01 and 2005-06.

(c) Regression Analysis for Determinants of Imports : For studying the determinants of India's total imports and for some of its major categories (agricultural imports, products of chemical or allied industries imports, base metals and articles of base metals imports, machinery and their parts imports, textiles and articles of textiles imports, mineral products imports and pearls precious and semiprecious stones, metals and articles imports), the regression equations were estimated for the period from 1986-87 to 2003-04. The regression analysis could not be extended beyond 2003-04 due to non availability of data on price indices and domestic production. The determinants taken at aggregate level for total imports were Relative Prices (RP), which was the ratio of Unit Value Indices to Wholesale Price Indices (UVI/WPI), Gross Domestic Product at Factor Cost (GDPFC) as income measure, Foreign Exchange Reserves (FR) as measure of capacity to import and a dummy variable (Dum) was included to capture the impact of liberalization policies. The value of dummy variable was '0' for 1986-87 to 1990-91 and '1' for 1991-92 to 2003-04. In addition to this, the Domestic production (DP) variable was also considered in case of all major categories of imports except for the mineral products imports and pearls, precious, and semi precious stones, metals and articles imports due to non availability of comparable data. The variable of Gross Domestic Capital Formation (GDCF) was also considered as one of the determinants in case of machinery and their parts imports. The export in previous year (Exp_{t-1}) variable was also taken as determinant in case of imports of pearls, precious and semi precious stones, metals and articles.

The data used for different variables were at constant prices except the category of pearls, precious and semi precious stones, metals and articles imports as no appropriate price deflator for this particular category of imports was available. The import demand functions were measured (at aggregate and disaggregate level), both in linear as well as in double log forms. Further, the linear and double log forms were estimated, both with and without dummy variable. Thus, determinants of total imports and its major categories were explained with the help of four models, i.e.,

(1) linear form without dummy variable,

(2) linear form with dummy variable,

(3) double log form without dummy variable, and

(4) double log form with dummy variable.

Specifications of Import Demand Function (Linear Form and Double Log Form)

(1) TI = f (GDPFC, RP, FR)

TI = f (GDPFC, RP, FR, Dum)

Where, TI = Total Imports

GDPFC = Gross Domestic Product at Factor Cost

RP = Relative Prices

FR = Foreign Reserves

Dum = Dummy Variable

(2) AI = f (GDPFC, RP, DP, FR)

AI = f (GDPFC, RP, DP, FR, Dum)

Where, AI = Agricultural Imports

GDPFC = Gross Domestic Product at Factor Cost

RP = Relative Prices

DP = Domestic Production

FR = Foreign Reserves

Dum = Dummy Variable

(3) CI = f (GDPFC, RP, DP, FR)

CI = f (GDPFC, RP, DP, FR, Dum)

Where, CI = Products of Chemical or Allied Industries Imports

GDPFC = Gross Domestic Product at Factor Cost

RP = Relative Prices

DP = Domestic Production

FR = Foreign Reserves

Dum = Dummy Variable

(4) BI = f (GDPFC, RP, DP, FR)

BI = f (GDPFC, RP, DP, FR, Dum)

Where, BI = Base Metals and Articles of Base Metals Imports

GDPFC = Gross Domestic Product at Factor Cost

RP = Relative Prices

DP = Domestic Production

FR = Foreign Reserves

Dum = Dummy Variable

(5)	MhI	= f (GDPFC, RP, DP, FR, GDCF)
	MhI	= f (GDPFC, RP, DP, FR, GDCF, Dum)
Where,	MhI	= Machinery and their Parts Imports
	GDPFC	= Gross Domestic Product at Factor Cost
	RP	= Relative Prices
	DP	= Domestic Production
	FR	= Foreign Reserves
	GDCF	= Gross Domestic Capital Formation
	Dum	= Dummy Variable
(6)	TxI	= f (GDPFC, RP, DP, FR)
	TxI	= f (GDPFC, RP, DP, FR, Dum)
Where,	TxI	= Textiles and Textiles Articles Imports
	GDPFC	= Gross Domestic Product at Factor Cost
	RP	= Relative Prices
	DP	= Domestic Production
	FR	= Foreign Reserves
	Dum	= Dummy Variable
(7)	MnI	= f (GDPFC, RP, DP, FR)
	MnI	= f (GDPFC, RP, DP, FR, Dum)
Where,	MnI	= Mineral Products Imports
	GDPFC	= Gross Domestic Product at Factor Cost
	RP	= Relative Prices
	FR	= Foreign Reserves
	Dum	= Dummy Variable
(8)	PI	= f (GDPFC, FR, Exp_{t-1})
	PI	= f (GDPFC, FR, Exp_{t-1}, Dum)
Where,	PI	= Pearls, Precious and Semi Precious Stones, Metals and Articles

GDPFC = Gross Domestic Product at Factor Cost

FR = Foreign Reserves

Exp_{t-1} = Exports in Previous Year

For statistical significance of estimates, t-values, R^2, $\bar{R}^2$, F-ratio and D-W statistics were analysed.

(d) Causality Analysis : For studying the import-growth causality with the help of India's total imports and some of its major categories the period considered was 1974-75 to 2003-04 and Granger causality test has been applied. This test procedure assumes that the information relevant to the prediction of respective variables is contained solely in the time series data on the variables. We have studied the causal relationship in the following cases:

1. Total imports (TI) and Gross Domestic Product at Factor Cost (GDPFC).
2. Agricultural Imports (AI) and Gross Domestic Product at Factor Cost (GDPFC).
3. Products of Chemical or Allied Industries Imports (CI) and Gross Domestic Product at Factor Cost (GDPFC).
4. Products of Chemical or Allied industries Imports (CI) and Domestic Production (DP).
5. Base Metals and Articles of Base Metals Imports (BI) and Gross Domestic Product at Factor Cost (GDPFC).
6. Base Metals and Articles of Base Metals Imports (BI) and Domestic Production (DP).
7. Machinery and their Parts Imports (MhI) and Gross Domestic Product at Factor Cost (GDPFC).
8. Machinery and their Parts Imports (MhI) and Domestic Production (DP).
9. Machinery and their Parts Imports (MhI) and Gross Domestic Capital Formation (GDCF).
10. Textiles and Textiles Articles imports (TxI) and Gross Domestic Product at Factor Cost (GDPFC).

11. Textiles and Textiles Articles Imports (TxI) and Domestic production (DP).
12. Mineral Products Imports (MnI) and Gross Domestic product at Factor Cost (GDPFC).
13. Pearls, Precious and Semi Precious Stones, Metals and Articles Imports (PI) and Gross Domestic Product at Factor Cost (GDPFC).

Granger test for causality presupposes the stationarity in the data. The unit root test is used for checking stationarity of the data. This test has been performed as follows:

1. The following regression has been estimated:

   $\Delta Y_t = A_1 + A_2 t + A_3 Y_{t-1} + U_t$

   Δ = first difference operator,

   t = trend variable and

   Y_{t-1} = one period lagged value of Y.
2. The null hypothesis (Ho) is that A_3 is zero, which is a coefficient of Y_{t-1} or time series is non-stationary. This is a unit root hypothesis.
3. In order to calculate the values for Dickey-Fuller (DF) test, there are two approaches as follows:

   $DF_\tau = \hat{A}_3 - 1/S.E\ (\hat{A}_3)$

   or

   $DF_\gamma = T\ (\hat{A}_3 - 1)$

   Where $\hat{A}_3$ is estimated coefficient of Y_{t-1},

   T is time period of study,

   S.E. $(\hat{A}_3)$ is standard error of A_3.
4. The computed values of DF_τ and DF_γ have been compared with their critical values. If the computed values are greater than the critical values then we reject null hypothesis (Ho) and conclude that time series is stationary (Gujrati, 2004 and Greene, 2003). In Granger causality test, $\bar{R}^2$ was used

for finding out appropriate number of lags i.e., we will consider a particular lag if $\bar{R}^2$ improves by adding it in regression equation. The results of causality analysis were calculated both with single lag and double lag as $\bar{R}^2$ was almost same in both the lags, only in few cases it slightly improved. After this, the value of F statistic was calculated for all possible directions of causality, which helps us to decide about the type of causation existing in the given variables. After confirming the stationarity in data, further steps involved in implementing Granger causality test are as follows:

For example to study whether Y causes X or X causes Y, we have to consider following equations:

$$(A) \quad Y_t = \sum_{i=1}^{n} \alpha_i y_{t-i} + u_{1t}$$

$$(A_1) \quad Y_t = \sum_{i=1}^{n} \alpha_i y_{t-i} + \sum_{j=1}^{n} \beta_j x_{t-j} + u_{2t}$$

$$(B) \quad X_t = \sum_{i=1}^{n} \lambda_i x_{t-i} + u_{3t}$$

$$(B_1) \quad X_t = \sum_{i=1}^{n} \lambda_i y_{t-i} + \sum_{j=1}^{n} \delta_j x_{t-j} + u_{4t}$$

Equations (A) and (A_1) help us to find out whether X causes Y or not. Similarly equations (B) and (B_1) give the results whether Y causes X or not. Following are the steps involved in this process:

1. Firstly, regress current values of Y on all lagged Y terms and by not including the lagged X variables in this regression. This is a restricted regression, from which we obtain restricted residual sum of squares (RSS_r).
2. Now run regression A_1, where current values of Y regressed on all lagged values of Y terms and also on all lagged values of X terms. This is unrestricted regression,

which provides us with unrestricted residual sum of squares (RSS_{ur}).

3. Set the null hypothesis, Ho: $\Sigma\beta j = 0$, i.e., lagged X terms do not belong to the regression.
4. To test this hypothesis we apply the F-test i.e.

$$(C)\ F = \frac{RSS_r - RSS_{ur}/m}{RSS_{ur}/(n-k)}$$

Which follows F-test with 'm' and 'n-k' d.f. where m is number of lagged X terms and k is number of parameters. estimated in unrestricted regression.

5. If computed F value is greater than the tabulated or critical F value at chosen level of significance, we reject the null hypothesis, in which case lagged X terms belong to the regression or X causes Y. Step 1 to 5 can be repeated to test the models (B) and (B_1), i.e., whether Y causes X (Gujrati, 2004; Nandi and Kumar, 2005).
6. For measuring the causal relationships, following regression equations have been estimated in different cases:

1. Total imports (TI) and Gross Domestic Product at Factor Cost (GDPFC)

(*i*) GDPFC → TI

(*a*) Single Lag

$TI = \alpha_0 + \alpha_1\ TI_{(t-1)} + U_{1t}$

$TI = \alpha_0 + \alpha_1\ TI_{(t-1)} + \beta_1\ GDPFC_{(t-1)} + U_{2t}$

(*b*) Double Lag

$TI = \alpha_0 + \alpha_1\ TI_{(t-1)} + \alpha_2\ TI_{(t-2)} + U_{1t}$

$TI = \alpha_0 + \alpha_1\ TI_{(t-1)} + \alpha_2\ TI_{(t-2)} + \beta_1\ GDPFC_{(t-1)} + \beta_2\ GDPFC_{(t-2)} + U_{2t}$

(*ii*) TI → GDPFC

(*a*) Single Lag

$GDPFC = \lambda_0 + \lambda_1\ GDPFC_{(t-1)} + U_{3t}$

$GDPFC = \lambda_0 + \lambda_1\ GDPFC_{(t-1)} + \delta_1\ TI_{(t-1)} + U_{4t}$

(*b*) Double Lag

$$GDPFC = \lambda_0 + \lambda_1 \text{ GDPFC}_{(t-1)} + \lambda_2 \text{ GDPFC}_{(t-2)} + U_{3t}$$

$$GDPFC = \lambda_0 + \lambda_1 \text{ GDPFC}_{(t-1)} + \lambda_2 \text{ GDPFC}_{(t-2)} + \delta_1 \text{ TI}_{(t-1)} + \delta_2 \text{ TI}_{(t-2)} + U_{4t}$$

(2) Agricultural imports (AI) and Gross Domestic Product at Factor Cost (GDPFC)

(*i*) GDPFC → AI

(*a*) Single Lag

$$AI = \alpha_0 + \alpha_1 \text{ AI}_{(t-1)} + U_{1t}$$

$$AI = \alpha_0 + \alpha_1 \text{ AI}_{(t-1)} + \beta_1 \text{ GDPFC}_{(t-1)} + U_{2t}$$

(*b*) Double Lag

$$AI = \alpha_0 + \alpha_1 \text{ AI}_{(t-1)} + \alpha_2 \text{ AI}_{(t-2)} + U_{1t}$$

$$AI = \alpha_0 + \alpha_1 \text{ AI}_{(t-1)} + \alpha_2 \text{ AI}_{(t-2)} + \beta_1 \text{ GDPFC}_{(t-1)} + \beta_2 \text{ GDPFC}_{(t-2)} + U_{2t}$$

(*ii*) AI → GDPFC

(*a*) Single Lag

$$GDPFC = \lambda_0 + \lambda_1 \text{ GDPFC}_{(t-1)} + U_{3t}$$

$$GDPFC = \lambda_0 + \lambda_1 \text{ GDPFC}_{(t-I)} + \delta_1 \text{ AI}_{(t-1)} + U_{4t}$$

(*b*) Double Lag

$$GDPFC = \lambda_0 + \lambda_1 \text{ GDPFC}_{(t-1)} + \lambda_2 \text{ GDPFC}_{(t-2)} + U_{3t}$$

$$GDPFC = \lambda_0 + \lambda_1 \text{ GDPFC}_{(t-1)} + \lambda_2 \text{ GDPFC}_{(t-2)} + \delta_1 \text{AI}_{(t-1)} + \delta_2 \text{ AI}_{(t-2)} + U_{4t}$$

(3) Products of Chemical or Allied Industries Imports (CI) and Gross Domestic Product at Factor Cost (GDPFC)

(*i*) GDPFC → CI

(*a*) Single Lag

$$CI = \alpha_0 + \alpha_1 \text{ CI}_{(t-1)} + U_{1t}$$

$$CI = \alpha_0 + \alpha_1 \text{ CI}_{(t-1)} + \beta_1 \text{ GDPFC}_{(t-1)} + U_{2t}$$

(*b*) Double Lag

$$CI = \alpha_0 + \alpha_1\ CI_{(t-1)} + \alpha_2\ CI_{(t-2)} + U_{1t}$$

$$CI = \alpha_0 + \alpha_1\ CI_{(t-1)} + \alpha_2\ CI_{(t-2)} + \beta_1\ GDPFC_{(t-1)} + \beta_2\ GDPFC_{(t-2)} + U_{2t}$$

(*ii*) CI → GDPFC

(*a*) Single Lag

$$GDPFC = \lambda_0 + \lambda_1\ GDPFC_{(t-1)} + U_{3t}$$

$$GDPFC = \lambda_0 + \lambda_1\ GDPFC_{(t-I)} + \delta_1\ TI_{(t-1)} + U_{4t}$$

(*b*) Double Lag

$$GDPFC = \lambda_0 + \lambda_1\ GDPFC_{(t-1)} + \lambda_2\ GDPFC_{(t-2)} + U_{3t}$$

$$GDPFC = \lambda_0 + \lambda_1\ GDPFC_{(t-1)} + \lambda_2\ GDPFC_{(t-2)} + \delta_1\ CI_{(t-1)} + \delta_2\ CI_{(t-2)} + U_{4t}$$

(4) Products of Chemical or Allied Industries Imports (CI) and Domestic Production (DP)

(*i*) DP → CI

(*a*) Single Lag

$$CI = \alpha_0 + \alpha_1\ CI_{(t-1)} + U_{1t}$$

$$CI = \alpha_0 + \alpha_1\ CI_{(t-1)} + \beta_1\ DP_{(t-1)} + U_{2t}$$

(*b*) Double Lag

$$CI = \alpha_0 + \alpha_1\ CI_{(t-1)} + \alpha_2\ CI_{(t-2)} + U_{1t}$$

$$CI = \alpha_0 + \alpha_1\ CI_{(t-1)} + \alpha_2\ CI_{(t-2)} + \beta_1\ DP_{(t-1)} + \beta_2\ DP_{(t-2)} + U_{2t}$$

(*ii*) CI → DP

(*a*) Single Lag

$$DP = \lambda_0 + \lambda_1\ DP_{(t-1)} + U_{3t}$$

$$DP = \lambda_0 + \lambda_1\ DP_{(t-1)} + \delta_1\ CI_{(t-1)} + U_{4t}$$

(*b*) Double Lag

$$DP = \lambda_0 + \lambda_1\ DP_{(t-1)} + \lambda_2\ DP_{(t-2)} + U_{3t}$$

$$DP = \lambda_0 + \lambda_1\ DP_{(t-1)} + \lambda_2\ DP_{(t-2)} + \delta_1\ CI_{(t-1)} + \delta_2\ CI_{(t-2)} + U_{4t}$$

(5) Base Metals and Articles of Base Metals Imports (BI) and Gross Domestic Product at Factors Cost (GDPFC)

***(i)* GDPFC → BI**

(*a*) Single Lag

$$BI = \alpha_0 + \alpha_1 BI_{(t-1)} + U_{1t}$$

$$BI = \alpha_0 + \alpha_1 BI_{(t-1)} + \beta_1 GDPFC_{(t-1)} + U_{2t}$$

(*b*) Double Lag

$$BI = \alpha_0 + \alpha_1 BI_{(t-1)} + \alpha_2 BI_{(t-2)} + U_{1t}$$

$$BI = \alpha_0 + \alpha_1 BI_{(t-1)} + \alpha_2 BI_{(t-2)} + \beta_1 GDPFC_{(t-1)} + \beta_2 GDPFC_{(t-2)} + U_{2t}$$

***(ii)* BI → GDPFC**

(*a*) Single Lag

$$GDPFC = \lambda_0 + \lambda_1 GDPFC_{(t-1)} + U_{3t}$$

$$GDPFC = \lambda_0 + \lambda_1 GDPFC_{(t-1)} + \delta_1 BI_{(t-1)} + U_{4t}$$

(*b*) Double Lag

$$GDPFC = \lambda_0 + \lambda_1 GDPFC_{(t-1)} + \lambda_2 GDPFC_{(t-2)} + U_{3t}$$

$$GDPFC = \lambda_0 + \lambda_1 GDPFC_{(t-1)} + \lambda_2 GDPFC_{(t-2)} + \delta_1 BI_{(t-1)} + \delta_2 BI_{(t-2)} + U_{4t}$$

(6) Base Metals and Articles of Base Metals Imports (BI) and Domestic Production (DP)

***(i)* DP → BI**

(*a*) Single Lag

$$BI = \alpha_0 + \alpha_1 BI_{(t-1)} + U_{1t}$$

$$BI = \alpha_0 + \alpha_1 BI_{(t-1)} + \beta_1 DP_{(t-1)} + U_{2t}$$

(*b*) Double Lag

$$BI = \alpha_0 + \alpha_1 BI_{(t-1)} + \alpha_2 BI_{(t-2)} + U_{1t}$$

$$BI = \alpha_0 + \alpha_1 BI_{(t-1)} + \alpha_2 BI_{(t-2)} + \beta_1 DP_{(t-1)} + \beta_2 DP_{(t-2)} + U_{2t}$$

***(ii)* BI → DP**

(*a*) Single Lag

$$DP = \lambda_0 + \lambda_1 DP_{(t-1)} + U_{3t}$$

$$DP = \lambda_0 + \lambda_1 DP_{(t-1)} + \delta_1 BI_{(t-1)} + U_{4t}$$

(*b*) Double Lag

$$DP = \lambda_0 + \lambda_1 DP_{(t-1)} + \lambda_2 DP_{(t-2)} + U_{3t}$$

$$DP = \lambda_0 + \lambda_1 DP_{(t-1)} + \lambda_2 DP_{(t-2)} + \delta_1 BI_{(t-1)} + \delta_2 BI_{(t-2)} + U_{4t}$$

(7) Machinery and their Parts Imports (MhI) and Gross Domestic Product at Factors Cost (GDPFC)

(*i*) GDPFC → MhI

(*a*) Single Lag

$$MhI = \alpha_0 + \alpha_1 MhI_{(t-1)} + U_{1t}$$

$$MhI = \alpha_0 + \alpha_1 MhI_{(t-1)} + \beta_1 GDPFC_{(t-1)} + U_{2t}$$

(*b*) Double Lag

$$MhI = \alpha_0 + \alpha_1 MhI_{(t-1)} + \alpha_2 MhI_{(t-2)} + U_{1t}$$

$$MhI = \alpha_0 + \alpha_1 MhI_{(t-1)} + \alpha_2 MhI_{(t-2)} + \beta_1 GDPFC_{(t-1)} + \beta_2 GDPFC_{(t-2)} + U_{2t}$$

(*ii*) MhI → GDPFC

(*a*) Single Lag

$$GDPFC = \lambda_0 + \lambda_1 GDPFC_{(t-1)} + U_{3t}$$

$$GDPFC = \lambda_0 + \lambda_1 GDPFC_{(t-1)} + \delta_1 MhI_{(t-1)} + U_{4t}$$

(*b*) Double Lag

$$GDPFC = \lambda_0 + \lambda_1 GDPFC_{(t-1)} + \lambda_2 GDPFC_{(t-2)} + U_{3t}$$

$$GDPFC = \lambda_0 + \lambda_1 GDPFC_{(t-1)} + \lambda_2 GDPFC_{(t-2)} + \delta_1 MhI_{(t-1)} + \delta_2 MhI_{(t-2)} + U_{4t}$$

(8) Machinery and their Parts Imports (MhI) and Domestic Production (DP)

(*i*) DP → MhI

(*a*) Single Lag

$$MhI = \alpha_0 + \alpha_1 MhI_{(t-1)} + U_{1t}$$

$$MhI = \alpha_0 + \alpha_1 MhI_{(t-1)} + \beta_1 DP_{(t-1)} + U_{2t}$$

(*b*) Double Lag

$$MhI = \alpha_0 + \alpha_1 MhI_{(t-1)} + \alpha_2 MhI_{(t-2)} + U_{1t}$$

$$MhI = \alpha_0 + \alpha_1 MhI_{(t-1)} + \alpha_2 MhI_{(t-2)} + \beta_1 DP_{(t-1)} + \beta_2 DP_{(t-2)} + U_{2t}$$

(*ii*) MhI → DP

(*a*) Single Lag

$$DP = \lambda_0 + \lambda_1 DP_{(t-1)} + U_{3t}$$

$$DP = \lambda_0 + \lambda_1 DP_{(t-I)} + \delta_1 MhI_{(t-1)} + U_{4t}$$

(*b*) Double Lag

$$DP = \lambda_0 + \lambda_1 DP_{(t-1)} + \lambda_2 DP_{(t-2)} + U_{3t}$$

$$DP = \lambda_0 + \lambda_1 DP_{(t-1)} + \lambda_2 DP_{(t-2)} + \delta_1 MhI_{(t-1)} + \delta_2 MhI_{(t-2)} + U_{4t}$$

(9) Machinery and their Parts Imports (MhI) and Gross Domestic Capital Formation (GDCF)

(*i*) GDCF → MhI

(*a*) Single Lag

$$MhI = \alpha_0 + \alpha_1 MhI_{(t-1)} + U_{1t}$$

$$MhI = \alpha_0 + \alpha_1 MhI_{(t-1)} + \beta_1 GDCF_{(t-1)} + U_{2t}$$

(*b*) Double Lag

$$MhI = \alpha_0 + \alpha_1 MhI_{(t-1)} + \alpha_2 MhI_{(t-2)} + U_{1t}$$

$$MhI = \alpha_0 + \alpha_1 MhI_{(t-1)} + \alpha_2 MhI_{(t-2)} + \beta_1 GDCF_{(t-1)} + \beta_2 GDCF_{(t-2)} + U_{2t}$$

(*ii*) MhI → GDCF

(*a*) Single Lag

$$GDCF = \lambda_0 + \lambda_1 GDCF_{(t-1)} + U_{3t}$$

$$GDCF = \lambda_0 + \lambda_1 GDCF_{(t-I)} + \delta_1 MhI_{(t-1)} + U_{4t}$$

(*b*) Double Lag

$$GDCF = \lambda_0 + \lambda_1 GDCF_{(t-1)} + \lambda_2 GDCF_{(t-2)} + U_{3t}$$

$$GDCF = \lambda_0 + \lambda_1 GDCF_{(t-1)} + \lambda_2 GDCF_{(t-2)} + \delta_1 MhI_{(t-1)} + \delta_2 MhI_{(t-2)} + U_{4t}$$

(10) Textile and Textile articles Imports (TxI) and Gross Domestic Product at Factor Cost (GDPFC)

(*i*) GDPFC → TxI

(*a*) Single Lag

$$TxI = \alpha_0 + \alpha_1 TxI_{(t-1)} + U_{1t}$$

$$TxI = \alpha_0 + \alpha_1 TxI_{(t-1)} + \beta_1 GDPFC_{(t-1)} + U_{2t}$$

(*b*) Double Lag

$$TxI = \alpha_0 + \alpha_1\ TxI_{(t-1)} + \alpha_2\ TxI_{(t-2)} + U_{1t}$$

$$TxI = \alpha_0 + \alpha_1\ TxI_{(t-1)} + \alpha_2\ TxI_{(t-2)} + \beta_1\ GDPFC_{(t-1)} + \beta_2\ GDPFC_{(t-2)} + U_{2t}$$

(*ii*) TxI → GDPFC

(*a*) Single Lag

$$GDPFC = \lambda_0 + \lambda_1\ GDPFC_{(t-1)} + U_{3t}$$

$$GDPFC = \lambda_0 + \lambda_1\ GDPFC_{(t-1)} + \delta_1\ TxI_{(t-1)} + U_{4t}$$

(*b*) Double Lag

$$GDPFC = \lambda_0 + \lambda_1\ GDPFC_{(t-1)} + \lambda_2\ GDPFC_{(t-2)} + U_{3t}$$

$$GDPFC = \lambda_0 + \lambda_1\ GDPFC_{(t-1)} + \lambda_2\ GDPFC_{(t-2)} + \delta_1\ TxI_{(t-1)} + \delta_2\ TxI_{(t-2)} + U_{4t}$$

(11) Textile and Textile articles Imports (TxI) and Domestic Production (DP).

(*i*) DP → TxI

(*a*) Single Lag

$$TxI = \alpha_0 + \alpha_1\ TxI_{(t-1)} + U_{1t}$$

$$TxI = \alpha_0 + \alpha_1\ TxI_{(t-1)} + \beta_1\ DP_{(t-1)} + U_{2t}$$

(*b*) Double Lag

$$TxI = \alpha_0 + \alpha_1\ TxI_{(t-1)} + \alpha_2\ TxI_{(t-2)} + U_{1t}$$

$$TxI = \alpha_0 + \alpha_1\ TxI_{(t-1)} + \alpha_2\ TxI_{(t-2)} + \beta_1\ DP_{(t-1)} + \beta_2\ DP_{(t-2)} + U_{2t}$$

(*ii*) TxI → DP

(*a*) Single Lag

$$DP = \lambda_0 + \lambda_1\ DP_{(t-1)} + U_{3t}$$

$$DP = \lambda_0 + \lambda_1\ DP_{(t-1)} + \delta_1\ TxI_{(t-1)} + U_{4t}$$

(*b*) Double Lag

$$DP = \lambda_0 + \lambda_1\ DP_{(t-1)} + \lambda_2\ DP_{(t-2)} + U_{3t}$$

$$DP = \lambda_0 + \lambda_1\ DP_{(t-1)} + \lambda_2\ DP_{(t-2)} + \delta_1\ TxI_{(t-1)} + \delta_2\ TxI_{(t-2)} + U_{4t}$$

(12) Mineral Products Imports (MnI) and Gross Domestic Product at Factor Cost (GDPFC)

(i) GDPFC → MnI

(a) Single Lag

$$MnI = \alpha_0 + \alpha_1 \, MnI_{(t-1)} + U_{1t}$$

$$MnI = \alpha_0 + \alpha_1 \, MnI_{(t-1)} + \beta_1 \, GDPFC_{(t-1)} + U_{2t}$$

(b) Double Lag

$$MnI = \alpha_0 + \alpha_1 \, MnI_{(t-1)} + \alpha_2 \, MnI_{(t-2)} + U_{1t}$$

$$MnI = \alpha_0 + \alpha_1 \, MnI_{(t-1)} + \alpha_2 \, MnI_{(t-2)} + \beta_1 \, GDPFC_{(t-1)} + \beta_2 \, GDPFC_{(t-2)} + U_{2t}$$

(ii) MnI → GDPFC

(a) Single Lag

$$GDPFC = \lambda_0 + \lambda_1 \, GDPFC_{(t-1)} + U_{3t}$$

$$GDPFC = \lambda_0 + \lambda_1 \, GDPFC_{(t-1)} + \delta_1 \, MnI_{(t-1)} + U_{4t}$$

(b) Double Lag

$$GDPFC = \lambda_0 + \lambda_1 \, GDPFC_{(t-1)} + \lambda_2 \, GDPFC_{(t-2)} + U_{3t}$$

$$GDPFC = \lambda_0 + \lambda_1 \, GDPFC_{(t-1)} + \lambda_2 \, GDPFC_{(t-2)} + \delta_1 \, MnI_{(t-1)} + \delta_2 \, MnI_{(t-2)} + U_{4t}$$

(13) Pearls, Precious and Semi-Precious Stones, Metals and Articles Imports (PI) and Gross Domestic Product at Factor Cost (GDPFC)

(i) GDPFC → PI

(a) Single Lag

$$PI = \alpha_0 + \alpha_1 \, PI_{(t-1)} + U_{1t}$$

$$PI = \alpha_0 + \alpha_1 \, PI_{(t-1)} + \beta_1 \, GDPFC_{(t-1)} + U_{2t}$$

(b) Double Lag

$$PI = \alpha_0 + \alpha_1 \, PI_{(t-1)} + \alpha_2 \, PI_{(t-2)} + U_{1t}$$

$$PI = \alpha_0 + \alpha_1 \, PI_{(t-1)} + \alpha_2 \, CI_{(t-2)} + \beta_1 \, GDPFC_{(t-1)} + \beta_2 \, GDPFC_{(t-2)} + U_{2t}$$

***(ii)* PI → GDPFC**

(a) Single Lag

$$GDPFC = \lambda_0 + \lambda_1\ GDPFC_{(t-1)} + U_{3t}$$

$$GDPFC = \lambda_0 + \lambda_1\ GDPFC_{(t-I)} + \delta_1\ PI_{(t-1)} + U_{4t}$$

(b) Double Lag

$$GDPFC = \lambda_0 + \lambda_1\ GDPFC_{(t-I)} + \lambda_2\ GDPFC_{(t-2)} + U_{3t}$$

$$GDPFC = \lambda_0 + \lambda_1\ GDPFC_{(t-I)} + \lambda_2\ GDPFC_{(t-2)} + \delta_1\ PI_{(t-1)} + \delta_2\ PI_{(t-2)} + U_{4\,t}$$

Limitations of Database

Overall the results of study depend upon the accuracy of data, the nature of the study was such that secondary data were used. We could not extend the time period beyond 2003-04 for measurement of determinants and causality for India's total imports and also for some of its major categories, due to non availability of data on some of the variables. In case of pearls, precious and semi precious stones, metals and articles imports, no appropriate deflator could be found. For analysis of growth rates and structure, a proxy deflator was used, but however in case of determinants and causality analysis, study preferred to use current price data, as use of proxy deflator was making the series non stationary in case of pearls, precious and semi precious stones imports.

CHAPTER

4

Growth of India's Imports

The liberalization policies since 1990s gave a boost to Indian economy, which led to fast growth of imports for the purpose of industrialisation as well as for export promotion. The period 1980 onwards is a very crucial period for the Indian economy due to vast changes in International economic order as well as domestic policy regimes (Sau, 1983; Patra and Rangan, 1992).

A developing country needs imports of machinery and equipment which can not be produced at home in initial stages of economic development. Such imports, which help to create new capacity in production, are called developmental imports. The imports which help to properly utilize the capacity created in the country are called maintenance imports. Besides, these imports, a developing economy also requires to import consumer goods as these imports are anti-inflationary and they reduce the scarcity of consumer goods in domestic market. Thus, for a developing country like India, on one hand the imports fulfil the needs of development, maintenance of essential supplies and inflation control and on other imports also provide production inputs, increase investment opportunities and international goodwill. Moreover, the higher investment taking place in different sectors, creating more capacity in export and domestic industries, again leads to higher level of imports. Structure of India's imports has changed over time as a result of changing structure of Indian economy, trade policy changes and international oil prices. As development proceeds, the raw material exports generally decline because their demand increases at home to meet the requirements of growing domestic industries. Consequently, a developing economy is required to find new commodities and new markets in which it can sell its manufactures and when export earnings increase then industrial production as well as imports increase and further broaden the industrial base of the economy and its growth.

The policies of opening up of Indian economy, undertaken during 90s, mainly included reduction in tariffs and phasing out of quantitative restrictions. Thus, import liberalization, in conjunction with external sector reforms, strengthened the external sector of India.

With the above mentioned background the present chapter provides a thorough analysis of the growth rates of India's total imports and its various categories. The study period taken for this purpose was 1986-87 to 2005-06. The growth rates were estimated for the whole of the study period and also for sub-periods, i.e., 1986-87 to 1990-91, 1991-92 to 1995-96, 1996-97 to 2000-01, 2001-02 to 2005-06, 1991-92 to 1999-2000 and 1996-97 to 2005-06.

These growth rates were estimated both at current and constant prices. The period 1990-91 to 1995-96 showed the immediate impact of liberalization, while the sub periods of 1996-97 to 2000-01 and 2001-02 to 2005-06 reveal more stable picture of import growth pattern in post liberalisation era. Tables 4.1 and 4.2 give the annual average growth rates for the study period and also for sub-periods, both at current and constant prices respectively.

Growth of Total Imports

At current prices, total imports of India have grown at the rate of 19.15 per cent for whole of the study period 1986-87 to 2005-06.

Table 4.1 : Annual Average Growth Rates of India's Imports at Current Prices

Sl.No.	Categories	Period						
		1986-87 to 2005-06	1990-91 to 1999-2000	1996-97 to 2005-06	1986-87 to 1990-91	1991-92 to 1995-96	1996-97 to 2000-01	2001-02 to 2005-06
1	2	3	4	5	6	7	8	9
1.	Live animals : animal products	9.86	31.06	12.16	-28.63	26.34	38.98	8.20
2.	Vegetable products	15.15	19.88	10.13	20.65	21.62	0.13	8.17
	(*a*) Edible vegetable and certain roots and tubers	13.74	8.20	17.54	16.97	26.25	-20.50	-7.68
	(*b*) Edible fruits and nuts: peel of citrus fruits or melons	19.26	23.20	10.59	16.23	31.73	12.22	29.49
	(*c*) Cereals	-11.32	44.36	-48.61	48.58	-36.40	-38.73	67.62
	(*d*) Coffee, tea, mate and spices	24.76	32.68	25.10	-8.68	18.86	31.11	14.22
	(*e*) Oil seeds and oleaginous fruits: misc. grams seeds & fruits: industries or med	19.16	19.09	23.21	4.44	19.62	32.28	26.64
	(*f*) Lac: gums, resins and other veg. sabs and extracts	13.75	14.32	9.09	26.00	23.61	3.39	16.73
3.	Animal or vegetable fats and oils and their cleavage products: animal or vegetable waxes	23.65	52.48	14.63	-23.03	67.10	29.15	9.95
4.	Prepared foodstuffs, beverages and tobacco	14.33	27.20	12.01	-11.96	54.67	11.15	41.76

(Contd.)

Table 4.1—Contd.

1	2	3	4	5	6	7	8	9
5.	Mineral products	22.14	17.39	21.37	36.07	16.74	20.41	30.45
	(*a*) Salt, sulphur, earths and stone, plastering materials lime and cement	10.00	9.06	9.25	21.36	9.80	14.16	18.11
	(*b*) Ores, slag and ash	25.91	23.55	30.86	32.02	44.42	28.08	34.96
	(*c*) Mineral fuels, min. oil and products: bituminous substances: min waxes	22.70	17.71	21.51	37.72	16.75	20.48	30.57
6.	Products of the chemical or allied industries	16.86	15.76	13.81	25.42	25.78	3.66	23.76
	(*a*) Inorganic Chemicals	16.53	19.50	9.60	16.09	7.84	11.62	17.08
	(*b*) Organic Chemicals	19.29	21.61	14.31	32.23	42.85	1.07	27.96
	(*c*) Fertilizers	11.71	13.91	4.60	37.80	25.94	0.38	40.05
	(*d*) Misc. Chemical Products	21.00	26.76	15.03	14.96	21.78	11.58	20.87
7.	Plastic and rubber	15.23	14.97	14.99	25.79	25.10	3.69	29.85
	(*a*) Plastic and articles thereof	14.73	13.91	15.00	28.05	23.00	2.42	31.74
	(*b*) Rubber and articles thereof	16.82	18.61	14.86	18.86	33.42	7.11	24.37
8.	Hides and skins: leather products, furskins and article thereof	22.57	16.36	12.84	84.22	25.30	14.61	9.43
9.	Wood, cork and article thereof, manuf. of plaiting material: basket-ware wicker work	18.00	20.08	15.48	35.12	17.47	21.28	18.10
	(*a*) Wood and articles of wood : wood charcoal	18.07	20.15	15.52	35.07	17.44	21.36	18.11

10.	Paper and paper board and article thereof	16.00	19.48	11.86	17.31	30.52	8.27	18.17
	(*a*) Pulp of wood or of other material : waste and scrap of paper and paperboard	13.75	14.92	12.73	16.24	30.89	9.91	15.74
	(*b*) Paper and paper board: articles of paper pulp, of paper and paper board	16.34	21.64	8.76	19.25	31.82	3.15	18.96
11.	Textile and Textile articles	19.76	20.75	18.31	25.71	41.84	19.21	12.74
	(*a*) Silk	18.77	11.01	24.52	28.61	17.48	19.97	21.95
	(*b*) Wool, fine or coarse animal hair	11.66	11.95	8.15	24.01	23.35	-9.47	12.93
	(*c*) Cotton	28.87	34.35	32.55	32.09	84.03	88.96	-1.35
	(*d*) Man-made filaments	18.96	16.56	24.83	34.09	41.91	34.20	11.76
12.	Foot wear, headgear, umbrellas: prepared feather and articles thereof	17.52	17.54	13.73	22.29	33.76	10.59	35.55
13.	Stone, cement and similar material: ceramic products, glass and glassware	17.88	16.74	21.57	18.69	23.96	16.48	29.59
	(*a*) Particles of stone, plaster, cement, asbestos, mica or similar materials	21.05	16.52	24.27	26.59	24.44	15.45	34.87
	(*b*) Ceramic products	19.19	15.75	24.38	15.44	19.19	11.70	40.77
	(*c*) Glass and glassware	16.35	17.33	18.78	18.86	26.71	19.41	21.24

(Contd.)

Table 4.1—Contd.

1	2	3	4	5	6	7	8	9
14.	Pearls, precious or semi-precious stones, metals and articles thereof: imitation jewellery and coins	24.36	30.50	19.45	28.51	15.25	33.47	22.75
15.	Base metals and articles of base metals	12.59	13.12	13.39	19.42	26.55	-4.99	39.65
	(*a*) Iron and steel	11.70	10.18	16.00	20.11	25.25	-4.80	50.33
	(*b*) Articles of iron and steel	11.82	13.16	13.67	5.11	15.40	-3.99	36.03
	(*c*) Copper and articles thereof	9.83	10.75	1.75	43.53	28.31	-21.10	36.97
	(*d*) Aluminium and articles thereof	19.53	34.79	14.17	-5.32	84.39	-0.52	25.02
16.	Machinery and their parts, electrical and electronic equipments, parts thereof	22.96	22.13	20.32	40.01	38.79	9.87	33.20
	(*a*) Nuclear reactors, boilers, machinery and mechanical appliances, parts thereof	17.76	21.51	15.48	9.77	38.26	5.13	32.06
	(*b*) Elec. mach. and equip and parts thereof: sound and TV recorder and reproducers and parts thereof	21.94	23.32	28.43	13.96	39.88	20.13	34.76
17.	Transport equipments	19.17	16.45	26.49	24.60	45.53	-1.45	59.68
	(*a*) Railway/tramway locomotives truck etc., equipment and parts thereof	9.27	8.28	8.88	31.31	-5.02	-14.69	72.45
	(*b*) Road vehicles and parts	14.04	17.86	10.52	9.08	32.57	-4.48	36.38
	(*c*) Aircraft, spacecraft and parts	19.76	8.61	36.54	42.93	91.88	-18.23	85.66
	(*d*) Ship, boat and floating structure	27.66	26.23	33.99	12.71	17.95	21.17	49.90

18.	Instrument and appratus: clocks and watches: parts and accessories thereof	17.80	18.18	18.46	24.36	22.94	19.81	19.80
	(*a*) Optical measuring, medical and similar instruments and parts thereof	18.13	18.21	18.75	25.94	23.14	20.27	19.62
19.	Arms and Ammunitions: parts & Accessories thereof	21.09	39.83	18.99	-16.85	19.96	5.77	0.51
20.	Misc. manufactured articles	27.18	30.15	25.71	28.31	41.36	25.85	33.11
21.	Work of art, collectors pieces and antiques	35.80	22.63	46.02	64.16	30.97	-1.06	88.10
22.	Project goods: some special uses	3.20	10.77	-12.75	11.52	22.55	-17.80	8.44
23.	Misc. goods	21.81	12.48	22.22	37.25	25.24	12.78	49.13
	Total Imports	19.15	20.19	17.63	22.08	25.02	14.46	28.45

Source: Author's Calculations.

Table 4.2 : Annual Average Growth Rates of India's Imports at Constant Prices

Sl.No.	Categories	Period						
		1986-87 to 2005-06	1990-91 to 1999-2000	1996-97 to 2005-06	1986-87 to 1990-91	1991-92 to 1995-96	1996-97 to 2000-01	2001-02 to 2005-06
1	2	3	4	5	6	7	8	9
1.	Live animals : animal products	2.30	26.22	9.59	-41.44	30.46	30.30	17.95
2.	Vegetable products	7.37	13.49	6.28	6.45	9.97	-0.29	-10.23
	(*a*) Edible vegetable and certain roots and tubers	5.72	2.44	14.72	3.21	14.15	-20.83	-27.20
	(*b*) Edible fruits and nuts: peel of citrus fruits or melons	11.36	16.64	5.81	2.56	19.11	11.75	14.92
	(*c*) Cereals	-19.32	37.23	-63.38	51.21	-48.58	-41.15	13.90
	(*d*) Coffee, tea, mate and spices	17.06	26.26	7.28	0.57	28.55	-2.49	32.72
	(*e*) Oil seeds and oleaginous fruits: misc. grams seeds & fruits: industries or med	5.66	25.29	106.89	-89.57	-46.37	47.24	204.55
	(*f*) Lac: gums, resins and other veg. sabs and extracts	-4.20	26.65	89.41	-81.22	-55.49	-9.69	146.20
3.	Animal or vegetable fats and oils and their cleavage products: animal or vegetable waxes	12.17	30.82	15.83	-30.92	44.54	32.40	31.37

4.	Prepared foodstuffs, beverages and tobacco	5.44	17.66	11.04	-30.07	42.23	17.64	33.67
5.	Mineral products	9.55	10.86	5.18	8.96	11.40	4.68	8.39
	(*a*) Salt, sulphur, earths and stone, plastering materials lime and cement	4.29	3.58	12.19	-1.07	13.31	17.27	14.50
	(*b*) Ores, slag and ash	18.89	17.34	33.80	7.60	49.05	31.58	24.40
	(*c*) Mineral fuels, min. oil and products: bituminous substances: min waxes	10.09	10.94	5.32	10.28	4.35	4.74	8.58
6.	Products of the chemical or allied industries	8.89	8.35	7.58	-2.55	12.18	1.86	20.86
	(*a*) Inorganic Chemicals	6.27	7.39	5.51	3.67	-7.47	6.24	8.53
	(*b*) Organic Chemicals	15.66	29.83	2.79	3.81	41.18	21.35	27.60
	(*c*) Fertilizers	2.74	5.91	-7.08	-1.86	16.89	-4.22	12.07
	(*d*) Misc. Chemical Products	12.99	18.65	9.62	-10.68	8.61	9.65	19.13
7.	Plastic and rubber	7.43	9.64	7.94	5.45	17.04	-2.56	20.51
	(*a*) Plastic and articles thereof	6.78	8.63	7.39	7.79	15.08	-3.75	20.22
	(*b*) Rubber and articles thereof	9.34	13.11	9.44	-0.35	24.83	0.64	21.26
8.	Hides and skins: leather products, furskins and article thereof	23.63	32.59	-3.11	62.16	48.06	25.11	-21.75
9.	Wood, cork and article thereof, manuf. of plaiting material: basketware wicker work	18.24	36.77	-0.90	18.94	39.79	32.39	-12.73
	(*a*) Wood and articles of wood : wood charcoal	18.31	36.85	-0.85	18.90	39.75	32.48	-12.71

(Contd.)

Table 4.2—Contd.

1	2	3	4	5	6	7	8	9
10.	Paper and paper board and article thereof	7.91	11.41	9.39	-5.39	13.29	3.16	18.84
	(*a*) Pulp of wood or of other material : waste and scrap of paper and paperboard	5.43	6.27	8.29	-3.87	7.40	0.40	11.83
	(*b*) Paper and paper board: articles of paper pulp, of paper and paper board	8.35	13.43	5.77	-3.83	14.41	-1.71	19.49
11.	Textile and Textile articles	14.83	16.50	19.87	15.18	33.54	22.10	7.68
	(*a*) Silk	13.38	7.11	25.67	17.84	10.60	22.89	17.36
	(*b*) Wool, fine or coarse animal hair	6.94	8.02	8.32	13.63	16.13	-7.27	12.42
	(*c*) Cotton	24.50	29.64	40.75	21.04	73.26	93.55	-4.44
	(*d*) Man-made filaments	13.86	12.47	28.05	22.86	33.60	37.46	7.41
12.	Footwear, headgear, umbrellas: prepared feather and articles thereof	17.01	33.09	-5.86	10.03	59.18	20.72	-7.46
13.	Stone, cement and similar material: ceramic products, glass and glassware	9.26	18.09	15.33	-8.21	8.92	2.62	38.66
	(*a*) Articles of stone, plaster, cement, asbestos, mica or similar materials	12.36	17.87	18.25	-2.11	9.34	1.71	49.95
	(*b*) Ceramic products	10.21	17.09	17.07	-10.73	4.73	-1.59	52.64
	(*c*) Glass and glassware	7.99	18.68	13.13	-8.08	11.34	5.19	27.00
14.	Pearls, precious or semi-precious stones, metals and articles thereof: imitation jewellery and coins	17.06	24.45	17.37	9.59	9.56	31.74	16.79

15.	Base metals and articles of base metals	3.86	5.06	4.81	1.16	13.88	-6.90	17.03
	(*a*) Iron and steel	-1.43	0.80	-0.01	-6.70	13.92	-9.06	20.87
	(*b*) Articles of iron and steel	0.51	3.53	4.82	-18.35	4.97	-8.29	24.83
	(*c*) Copper and articles thereof	2.32	7.26	-5.35	9.71	18.00	-14.98	2.02
	(*d*) Aluminium and articles thereof	9.78	24.11	6.30	-24.27	59.91	-7.65	10.93
16.	Machinery and their parts, electrical and electronic equipments, parts thereof	16.56	14.73	14.09	34.11	46.93	5.22	17.61
	(*a*) Nuclear reactors, boilers, machinery and mechanical appliances, parts thereof	58.84	11.50	13.26	34.24	43.93	7.11	23.62
	(*b*) Elec. mach. and equip and parts thereof: sound and TV recorder and eproducers and parts thereof	14.99	15.59	6.73	33.29	38.10	3.79	-0.04
17.	Transport equipments	8.10	5.86	18.59	3.29	18.00	5.76	40.19
	(*a*) Railway/tramway locomotives truck etc., equipment and parts thereof	-0.43	-1.56	2.57	8.85	-22.99	-8.43	86.59
	(*b*) Road vehicles and parts	4.43	7.14	5.40	-9.57	7.47	2.51	27.54
	(*c*) Aircraft, spacecraft and parts	7.73	-1.25	25.04	18.48	55.58	-12.23	57.48
	(*d*) Ship, boat and floating structure	16.30	14.76	29.22	-6.56	-4.35	30.05	37.40

(Contd.)

Table 4.2—Contd.

1	2	3	4	5	6	7	8	9
18.	Instrument and appratus: clocks and watches: parts and accessories thereof	20.95	37.22	18.27	-5.22	23.78	60.89	-11.58
	(*a*) Optical measuring, medical and similar instruments and parts thereof	18.63	37.17	-1.70	16.62	48.59	30.68	-15.94
19.	Arms and Ammunitions: parts & Accessories thereof	22.78	59.34	9.40	-26.82	42.61	15.44	-0.37
20.	Misc. manufactured articles	27.13	48.25	6.67	12.95	68.22	37.38	-6.34
21.	Work of art, collectors pieces and antiques	33.20	39.80	11.12	53.63	56.41	8.02	-11.34
	Project goods: some special uses	3.52	26.16	-28.90	-1.82	45.84	-10.27	-29.80
23.	Misc. goods	21.20	28.12	1.42	20.82	49.03	23.12	6.50
	Total Imports	10.44	14.31	8.86	3.33	22.10	8.86	14.43

Source: Author's Calculations.

The growth rate for the sub-period 1986-87 to 1990-91 was 22.08 per cent, which increased to 25.02 per cent for the sub period of 1991-92 to 1995-96. Total imports grew at the rate of 14.46 per cent for the sub period of 1996-97 to 2000-01, which doubled for next sub-period of 2001-02 to 2005-06, i.e., 28.45 per cent. The growth rate registered for the decade of 1990-91 to 1999-2000 was 20.19 per cent. The growth rate for the decade of 1996-97 to 2005-06 was 17.63 per cent.

At constant prices (1993-94 base year), total imports grew at the rate of 10.44 per cent for whole of the study period 1986-87 to 2005-06. The growth rate was 3.33 per cent for the first sub period of 1986-87 to 1990-91. Further, the growth rate increased to 22.10 per cent for the sub period 1991-92 to 1995-96, but again declined to 8.86 per cent for the sub period of 1996-97 to 2000-01. In next sub period 2001-02 to 2005-06, the growth rate again increased to 14.43 per cent. The growth rate was 14.31 per cent for the decade of 90's, i.e., 1990-91 to 1999-2000. The growth rate for the period 1996-97 to 2005-06 was 8.86 per cent.

The growth rates for total imports were high except for the sub period 1986-87 to 1990-91 (at constant prices). At current prices, the highest growth rate for total imports was for the sub period 2001-02 to 2005-06 and lowest rate was for the sub period 1996-97 to 2000-01. At constant prices, the highest growth rate was during 1991-92 to 1995-96 and the lowest growth rate was for the sub period 1986-87 to 1990-91. Being major categories, the import of petroleum, oil and lubricants and capital goods, inflated our import bill in first sub period 1986-87 to 1990-91. Besides this, increased imports of essential commodities due to drought of 1987, growing pressure of domestic demand due to increased real income and also Gulf crisis of 1990-91, were significant factors which caused the Indian imports to rise.

Further, all these factors accompanied with the policies of liberalisation as a part of economic reforms 1991 and reduction in custom duties, led to higher growth rate of imports during the sub-period 1991-92 to 1995-96. Moreover, the diversification of industrial structure, build up of additional industrial capacity and larger use of imported inputs by the industrial sector led to increased imports, which reflected the smart recovery in industrial production. This was also confirmed by a notably high growth rate registered for non oil imports while petroleum, oil and lubricants registered only a marginal increase. Imports have also responded to the replacement of quantitative restrictions by tariffs in liberalised trade regime (Government of India, 1994-95 and RBI, 1994-95).

The growth rate for imports declined for the sub period 1996-97 to 2000-01, due to sharp reduction in International oil prices in 1997-98. The other factors like East-Asian crisis of 1997 and Russian economic crisis of 1998, adversely affected Indian exports, which indirectly resulted into slowdown of Indian imports.

Total imports again showed upward trend during the sub period 2000-01 to 2005-06, mainly because of higher oil imports and oil prices and pick up in industrial activity. The growth was contributed by robust increases in imports of food and allied products (mainly edible oils), capital goods, raw materials and intermediate goods and consumer goods (Government of India, 2003-04). In 2004-05, the larger imports filled the gap between growing demand and stagnant domestic crude oil production. The lower tariffs, a cheaper U.S. dollar, a buoyant manufacturing sector and higher export growth boosted non oil imports particularly capital goods, intermediates, raw materials and imports needed for exports. Growth of imports of capital goods reflected the higher domestic investment and firming up of manufacturing growth. The increased imports also indicated the economy's growing absorptive capacity of imports (Government of India, 2005-06).

Categorywise Analysis of Growth Rates

On the whole, we have twenty three broad categories of imports some of which are further divided into sub-categories.

Live Animal: Animal Products

At current prices, the imports of this category grew at the rate of 9.86 per cent during whole of the study. The growth rate for the sub period 1986-87 to 1990-91 was highly negative, i.e., -28.63 per cent, which sharply increased to 26.34 per cent for the next sub period 1991-92 to 1995-96 and further increased to 38.98 per cent for the sub period 1996-97 to 2000-01. The growth rate declined to 8.20 per cent for the last sub period 2001-02 to 2005-06. The growth rate for the decade of 1990-91 to 1999-2000 was 31.06 per cent. The growth rate for the decade of 1996-97 to 2005-06 was 12.16 per cent.

At constant prices, the growth rate for this category during whole of the study period was 2.30 per cent. The growth rate was exceptionally negative for the sub period 1986-87 to 1990-91, i.e., -41.44 per cent. There was marginal difference in the growth rates for the sub periods of 1991-92 to 1995-96 and 1996-97 to 2000-01 i.e., 30.46 per cent and 30.30 per cent respectively. But the growth rate declined to 17.95 per cent for the sub period 2001-02 to 2005-06. The growth rate was 26.22 per cent for the decade of 1990-91 to 1999-2000. The growth rate was 9.59 per cent for the decade of 1996-97 to 2005-06.

Thus, the growth rates for the imports of live animals and animal products were fluctuating one. The growth rate was negative for the sub period of 1986-87 to 1990-91 (both at current as well as constant prices). At current prices, the imports of this category have grown at highest rate for the sub period 1996-97 to 2000-01, the period which gives lagged impact of liberalisation. At constant prices, the growth rate was highest for the sub period 1991-92 to 1995-96.

Vegetable Products

At current prices, the imports of this category grew at the rate of 15.15 per cent for the study period 1986-87 to 2005-06. The growth rate for the sub period 1986-87 to 1990-91 was 20.65 per cent, which increased to 21.62 per cent for the sub period 1991-92 to 1995-96. The growth rate sharply declined to 0.13 per cent for the sub period 1996-97 to 2000-01, but it again increased to 8.17 per cent for the sub period of 2001-02 to 2005-06. The growth rate for the decade of 1990-91 to 1999-2000 was 19.88 per cent. The growth rate was 10.13 per cent for the decade of 1996-97 to 2005-06.

At constant prices, imports grew at the rate of 7.37 per cent during whole of the study period. The growth rate for the sub-period 1986-87 to 1990-91 was 6.45 per cent, which increased to 9.97 per cent for the sub period 1991-92 to 1995-96. The growth rates for the sub periods 1996-97 to 2000-01 and 2001-02 to 2005-06 were negative, i.e. -0.29 per cent and -10.23 per cent respectively. The imports of vegetables products grew at the rate of 13.49 per cent for the decade of 1990-91 to 1999-2000. The growth rate for the decade of 1996-97 to 2005-06 was 6.28 per cent.

The imports of this category have grown at the high rates during 1986-87 to 1990-91 and 1991-92 to 1995-96 as compared to the sub periods 1996-97 to 2000-01 and 2001-02 to 2005-06 (both at current as well as constant prices). The highest rate was during sub period of 1991-92 to 1995-96 (at current prices and constant prices). The lowest rate at current prices was during 1996-97 to 2000-01. The growth rates were negative during 1996-97 to 2000-01 and 2001-02 to 2005-06 (at constant prices). It also confirmed about stronger immediate impact (1991-92 to 1995-96) of liberalisation policies.

Edible Vegetables and certain Roots and Tubers

At current prices, the growth rate for whole of the study period was 13.74 per cent. The growth rate was 16.97 per cent for the sub period 1986-87 to 1990-91, which increased to 26.25 per cent for the sub period 1991-92 to 1995-96. The growth rates for the sub periods 1996-97 to 2000-01 and 2001-02 to 2005-06 were negative i.e., -20.50 per cent and -7.68 per cent respectively. The growth rate for this sub category was 8.20 per cent for the decade of 1990-91 to 1999-2000. The growth rate for the sub period 1996-97 to 2005-06 was 17.54 per cent.

At constant prices, the growth rate of edible vegetables imports was 5.72 per cent during whole of the study period. The growth rate for the sub period of 1986-87 to 1990-91 was 3.21 per cent and further increased to 14.15 per cent for the sub period of 1991-92 to 1995-96. The growth rates were negative for the sub periods 1996-97 to 2000-01 and 2001-02 to 2005-06 i.e., -20.83 per cent and -27.20 per cent respectively. The growth rate for the decade of 1990-91 to 1999-2000 was 2.44 per cent. The growth rate for the decade of 1996-97 to 2005-06 was 14.72 per cent.

The imports of this sub category of vegetable products grew at higher rate during first two sub periods (1986-87 to1990-91 and 1991-92 to 1995-96) as compared to last two sub periods (1996-97 to 2000-01 and 2001-02 to 2005-06). The growth rates were highest for the sub period 1991-92 to 1995-96 (both at current as well as constant prices). The growth rates experienced during sub periods 1996-97 to 2000-01 and 2001-02 to 2005-06, were negative (current and constant prices). The immediate impact (1991-92 to 1995-96) of liberalisation policies was much stronger in case of current prices.

Edible fruits and Nuts: Peel of Citrus Fruits or Melons

At current prices, the growth rate for whole of the study period was 19.26 per cent. The growth rate for the sub period 1986-87 to 1990-91 was 16.23 per cent, which increased to 31.73 per cent (almost doubled) for the sub period 1991-92 to 1995-96. The growth rate for the sub period 1996-97 to 2000-01 declined to 12.22 per cent, but it again increased to 29.49 per cent for the sub period 2001-02 to 2005-06. The growth rate for the decade of 1990-91 to 1999-2000 was 23.20 per cent. The growth rate for the decade of 1996-97 to 2005-06 was 10.59 per cent.

At constant prices, the growth rate for the imports of edible fruits and nuts for whole of the study period was 11.36 per cent. The growth rate for the sub-period 1986-87 to 1990-91 was 2.56 per cent, which sharply increased to 19.11 per cent for the sub-period 1991-92 to 1995-96. The growth rate declined to 11.75 per cent for the sub period 1996-97 to 2000-01, but it again increased to 14.92 per cent for the sub period 2001-02 to 2005-06. The growth rate for the decade of 1990-91 to 1999-2000 was 16.64 per cent. The growth rate of imports of this sub category for the decade of 1996-97 to 2005-06 was 5.81 per cent.

The imports of this sub category grew at fluctuating rates throughout the study period. The growth rate for the sub period 1991-92 to 1995-96 was highest one (both at current as well as constant prices). The lowest growth rate was for the sub period 1996-97 to 2000-01 at current prices. The growth rate was lowest one during 1986-87 to 1990-91 at constant prices. Here again immediate impact (1991-92 to 1995-96) of liberalisation policies was stronger than lagged impact (1996-97 to 2005-06).

Cereals

At current prices, the growth rate for cereal imports for whole of the study period was negative, i.e. -11.32 per cent. The growth rate for the sub-period 1986-87 to 1990-91 was 48.58 per cent, opposite to this it experienced a marked fall in next sub-period 1991-92 to 1995-96, i.e. -36.40 per cent. The growth was negative for the sub period 1996-97 to 2000-01, i.e. -38.73 per cent as well, but it abruptly increased to 67.62 per cent for the sub period 2001-02 to 2005-06. The growth rate for the decade of 1990-91 to 1999-2000 was 44.36 per cent. The growth rate for the decade of 1996-97 to 2005-06 was -48.69 per cent.

At constant prices, the growth rate for whole of the study period 1986-87 to 2005-06 was negative, i.e., -19.32 per cent. The growth rate for the sub period 1986-87 to 1990-91 was highly positive i.e., 51.21 per cent, but growth rate was highly negative for the next sub period 1991-92 to 1995-96, i.e., -48.58 per cent. Further, the growth was again negative for the sub period 1996-97 to 2000-01, i.e., -41.15 per cent, which abruptly increased to 13.90 per cent for the sub period 2001-02 to 2005-06. The growth rate for the decade of 1990-91 to 1999-2000 was 37.23 per cent. The growth rate for the decade of 1996-97 to 2005-06 was -63.38 per cent.

India is self-sufficient in foodgrains and same is reflected in growth rates of imports of cereals. The category of cereal imports is a minor category within the foodgrains category of imports. The growth rate of this sub-category was negative for the study period taken as a whole. At current prices, the growth rate was highest one for the sub period 2000-01 to 2005-06. At constant prices, the highest growth rate was for the sub period 1986-87 to 1990-91.

Overall there are high fluctuations in the growth rates experienced by this sub category.

Coffee, Tea, Mate and Spices

At current prices, the growth rate for this sub category for the study period 1986-87 to 2005-06 was 24.76 per cent. The growth rate for the sub period 1986-87 to 1990-91 was negative, i.e., – 8.68 per cent, which sharply increased to 18.86 per cent for the sub period 1991-92 to 1995-96 and further increased to 31.11 per cent for the sub period 1996-97 to 2000-01. The growth rate declined to 14.22 per cent for the sub period 2001-02 to 2005-06. The growth rate for the decade of 1990-91 to 1999-2000 was 32.68 per cent. The growth rate for the decade of 1996-97 to 2005-06 was 25.10 per cent.

At constant prices, the growth rate of imports of coffee, tea, mate and spices for whole of the study period was 17.06 per cent. The growth rate for the sub period 1986-87 to 1990-91 was 0.57 per cent, which sharply increased to 28.55 per cent for the sub period 1991-92 to 1995-96. The growth rate was negative for the sub period 1996-97 to 2000-01 i.e., -2.49 per cent, but it abruptly increased to 32.72 per cent for the sub period 2001-02 to 2005-06. The growth rate for the decade of 1990-91 to 1999-2000 was 26.26 per cent. The growth rate for the decade of 1996-97 to 2005-06 was 7.28 per cent.

The growth rates indicate high fluctuations in imports of this sub category of vegetable products. At current prices, the highest growth rate was for the sub period 1996-97 to 2000-01, whereas growth rate during 1986-87 to 1990-91 was negative. At constant prices, the highest growth rate was for the sub period 2001-02 to 2005-06, whereas growth rate was negative during 1996-97 to 2000-01. In case of current prices, lagged impact (1996-97 to 2005-06) was stronger while in case of constant prices immediate impact (1991-92 to 1995-96) of liberalisation policies was stronger.

Oil seeds and Oleaginous Fruits: Miscellaneous Grains, Seeds and Fruits: Industrial or Medicinal Plants: Straw and Fodder

At current prices, the imports of this sub category of vegetable products have grown at the rate of 19.16 per cent for whole of the study period. The growth rate for the sub period 1986-87 to 1990-91 was 4.44 per cent, which increased to 19.62 per cent for the sub period 1991-92 to 1995-96 and further increased to 32.28 per cent for the sub period 1996-97 to 2000-01. But the growth rate declined to 26.64 per cent for the sub period 2001-02 to 2005-06. The growth rate for the decade of 1990-91 to 1999-2000 was 19.09 per cent. The growth rate during 1996-97 to 2005-06 was 23.21 per cent.

At constant prices, these imports grew at the rate of 5.66 per cent for whole of the study period. The growth rates for the sub periods of 1986-87 to 1990-91 and 1991-92 to 1995-96 were highly negative, i.e., -89.57 per cent and -46.37 per cent respectively. But the growth rate sharply increased to 47.24 per cent for the sub-period 1996-97 to 2000-01 and further to 204.55 per cent for the sub period 2001-02 to 2005-06. The growth rate for the decade of 1990-91 to 1999-2000 was 25.29 per cent. The imports of this sub category grew at the rate of 106.89 per cent during 1996-97 to 2005-06.

The growth rates for this sub category had increased during post-liberalization period. This indicated stronger lagged impact (1996-97 to 2005-06) as compared to immediate impact (1990-91 to 1995-96) of liberalisation policies. However, this sub category experienced wide fluctuations during various sub periods. At current prices, the growth rate was highest during 1996-97 to 2000-01 and lowest during 1986-87 to 1990-91. At constant prices, the growth rate was highest for the sub period 2001-02 to 2005-06, whereas rates were negative during the sub periods of 1986-87 to 1990-91 and 1991-92 to 1995-96.

Lac: Gums, Resins and other Vegetable Saps and Extracts

At current prices, the growth rate of this sub category of vegetable products imports for the study period was 13.75 per cent. The imports of this sub category registered a growth rate of 26.00 per cent for the sub period 1986-87 to 1990-91. The growth rate declined to 23.61 per cent for the sub-period 1991-92 to 1995-96 and further to 3.39 per cent for the sub-period 1996-97 to 2000-01. But the growth rate for the sub period 2001-02 to 2005-06 increased to 16.73 per cent. The growth rate for the decade of 1990-91 to 1999-2000 was 14.32 per cent. The imports of this sub category grew at the rate of 9.09 per cent during 1996-97 to 2005-06.

At constant prices, the growth rate for whole of the study period 1986-87 to 2005-06 was negative, i.e., - 4.20 per cent. The growth rates for the sub periods 1986-87 to 1990-91 and 1991-92 to 1995-96 were also negative, i.e., -81.22 per cent and -55.49 per cent respectively. Further, the imports again grew at a negative rate of -9.69 per cent for the sub period 1996-97 to 2000-01, but it abruptly increased to 146.20 per cent for the sub period 2001-02 to 2005-06. The growth rate for the decade of 1990-91 to 1999-2000 was 26.65 per cent. The growth rate for the decade of 1996-97 to 2005-06 was 89.41 per cent.

The imports of this sub category had experienced wide fluctuations. At current prices, the highest growth rate was for the sub period 1986-87 to 1990-91 and rate was lowest during 1996-97 to 2000-01. At constant prices, the growth rate for the imports of this sub category of vegetable products was positive only during sub period 2000-01 to 2005-06.

Overall within the category of imports of vegetable products, the sub category of coffee, tea, mate and spices imports had grown at highest rate both at current and constant prices for the study period taken as whole. The imports of cereals registered a negative growth rate for the study period (both at current as well as at constant prices).

Animal or Vegetable Fats and Oils and their Cleavage Products: Animal or Vegetable Waxes

At current prices, the growth rate for whole of the study period 1986-87 to 2005-06 was 23.65 per cent. The growth rate for the sub period 1986-87 to 1990-91 was negative, i.e., -23.03 per cent, which sharply increased to 67.10 per cent for the sub period 1991-

92 to 1995-96. The growth rate for the next sub period 1996-97 to 2000-01 declined to 29.15 per cent and further to 9.95 per cent for the sub period 2001-02 to 2005-06. The growth rate for the decade of 1990-91 to 1999-2000 was 52.48 per cent. The imports of this category grew at the rate of 14.63 per cent during 1996-97 to 2005-06.

At constant prices, the imports of this category have grown at the rate of 12.17 per cent during whole of the study period. The growth rate was negative for the sub period 1986-87 to 1990-91, i.e., -30.92 per cent, but it abruptly increased to 44.54 per cent for the sub period 1991-92 to 1995-96. The growth rate declined to 32.40 per cent for the sub period 1996-97 to 2000-01, and further to 31.37 per cent for the sub period 2001-02 to 2005-06. The growth rate for the decade of 1990-91 to 1999-2000 was 30.82 per cent. The growth rate was 15.83 per cent for the decade of 1996-97 to 2005-06.

The imports of animal or vegetable fats and oils and their cleavage products grew at high rate during the study period. This category includes imports of edible oils also, which is one of the major items of imports within the category of food items imports. The growth rates were negative for the first sub period (1986-87 to 1990-91) both at current prices and constant prices. The highest growth rate was for the sub period 1991-92 to 1995-96 (at current and constant prices). The immediate impact (1991-92 to 1995-96) of liberalisation policies was stronger than the lagged impact (1996-97 to 2005-06).

Prepared Food Stuffs, Beverages and Tobacco

At current prices, the imports of this sub category grew at the rate of 14.33 per cent during whole of the study period. The growth rate for the sub period 1986-87 to 1990-91 was negative, i.e., -11.96 per cent, which sharply increased to 54.67 per cent for the sub period of 1991-92 to 1995-96. The growth rate again declined to 11.15 per cent for the sub period of 1996-97 to 2000-01, but sharply increased to 41.76 per cent for the sub period of 2001-02 to 2005-06. The growth rate for the decade of 1990-91 to 1999-2000 was 27.20 per cent. The imports of this sub category grew at the rate of 12.01 per cent during 1996-97 to 2005-06.

At constant prices, the growth rate of imports of this category for the study period taken as a whole was 5.44 per cent. The imports of this category grew at high negative rate of -30.07 per cent for the sub period 1986-87 to 1990-91. The growth rate abruptly increased to 42.23 per cent for the sub period of 1991-92 to 1995-96, but declined to 17.64 per cent for the sub period 1996-97 to 2000-01. The growth rate again increased to 33.67 per cent for the sub period of 2001-02 to 2005-06. The growth rate for the decade of 1990-91 to 1999-2000 was 17.66 per cent. The growth rate was 11.04 per cent for the decade of 1996-97 to 2005-06.

The growth rate of prepared food stuffs, beverages and tobacco imports, was negative for first sub period 1986-87 to 1990-91 (at current prices and constant prices) and highly fluctuating one for rest of the sub periods. During the sub period 1991-92 to 1995-96, the growth rates were highest at current as well as constant prices. The immediate impact (1991-92 to 1995-96) of liberalisation policies was stronger than the lagged impact (1996-97 to 2005-06).

Mineral Products

At current prices, the growth rate for the imports of mineral products was 22.14 per cent during whole of the study period. The growth rate for the sub-period 1986-87 to 1990-91 was 36.07 per cent, which declined to 16.74 per cent for the sub period of 1991-92 to 1995-96. But the growth rate again increased to 20.41 per cent for the sub-period 1996-97 to 2000-01 and further to 30.45 per cent for the sub-period of 2001-02 to 2005-06. The growth rate for the decade of 1990-91 to 1999-2000 was 17.39 per cent. The imports of this category grew at the rate of 21.37 per cent during 1996-97 to 2005-06.

At constant prices, the growth rate of imports of this category during whole of the study period was 9.55 per cent. The growth rate for the sub period 1986-87 to 1990-91 was 8.96 per cent, which increased to 11.40 per cent for the sub-period of 1991-92 to

1995-96. The growth rate declined to 4.68 per cent for the sub-period 1996-97 to 2000-01, but rate increased to 8.39 per cent for the sub period of 2001-02 to 2005-06. The growth rate registered for the decade of 1990-91 to 1999-2000 was 10.86 per cent. The imports of this category during 1996-97 to 2005-06, grew at the rate of 5.18 per cent.

The category of mineral products imports is a major and dominating category of Indian imports. India has high import dependence in case of this category because of increasing industrial and infrastructural requirements. This led to higher growth of imports of this category. The fall during 1990-91 to 1995-96 might be due to fall in international prices of crude oil. At current prices, the growth rate of this category was highest for the sub period of 1986-87 to 1990-91 and lowest during 1991-92 to 1995-96. At constant prices, the growth rate for the sub period 1991-92 to 1995-96 was highest one and growth rate for the sub period 1996-97 to 2000-01 was lowest one.

Salt, Sulphur, Earths and Stone, Plastering Materials, Lime and Cement

At current prices, the growth rate of imports of this sub category of mineral products for whole of the study period 1986-87 to 2005-06 was 10.00 per cent. The growth rate for the sub period of 1986-87 to 1990-91 was 21.36 per cent, which declined to 9.80 per cent for the sub period of 1991-92 to 1995-96. The growth rate increased to 44.16 per cent for the sub-period 1996-97 to 2000-01, but declined to 18.11 per cent for the sub- period 2000-01 to 2005-06. The growth rate for the decade of 1990-91 to 1999-2000 was 9.06 per cent. The imports of this sub category grew at the rate of 9.25 per cent during 1996-97 to 2005-06.

At constant prices, the growth rate during whole of the study period was 4.29 per cent. The imports of this sub-category of mineral products recorded a negative rate of -1.07 per cent for the sub period 1986-87 to 1990-91. The growth rate abruptly increased to 13.31 per cent for the sub-period 1991-92 to 1995-96 and further to 17.27 per cent for the sub-period 1996-97 to 2000-01. The growth rate declined to 14.50 per cent for the sub period 2001-02 to 2005-06. The growth rate for the period of 1990-91 to 1999-2000 was registered as 3.58 per cent. The growth rate for the imports of this sub category during 1996-97 to 2005-06 was 12.19 per cent.

There was a wide difference between the growth rates at current and constant prices. At current prices, the growth rate was highest for the sub period 1986-87 to 1990-91 and lowest growth rate was recorded during 1996-97 to 2000-01. At constant prices, the imports of this sub category grew at highest rate during 1996-97 to 2000-01, while growth rate was negative for sub period 1986-87 to 1990-91.

Ores, Slag and Ash

At current prices, the imports of this sub category grew at the rate of 25.91 per cent for the study period. The growth rate for the sub period 1986-87 to 1990-91 was 32.02 per cent, which increased to 44.42 per cent for the sub period 1991-92 to 1995-96. The growth rate declined to 28.08 per cent for the sub period 1996-97 to 2000-01, which increased to 34.96 per cent for the sub period 2001-02 to 2005-06. The growth rate for the period of 1990-91 to 1999-2000 was registered as 23.55 per cent. The growth rate for the imports of this sub category during 1996-97 to 2005-06 was 30.86 per cent.

At constant prices, the growth rate during whole of the study period was 18.89 per cent. The growth rate for the sub period of 1986-87 to 1990-91 was 7.60 per cent, which abruptly increased to 49.05 per cent for the sub period of 1991-92 to 1995-96. The growth rate declined to 31.58 per cent for the sub period 1996-97 to 2000-01 and further to 24.40 per cent for the sub period 2001-02 to 2005-06. The growth rate registered for the decade of 1990-91 to 1999-2000 was 17.34 per cent. The imports of this sub category during 1996-97 to 2005-06, grew at the rate of 33.80 per cent.

This sub-category of mineral product imports grew at high and fluctuating rate during the study period. The highest growth rate was for the sub period 1991-92 to 1995-96, both at current as well as constant prices. The lowest growth rate at current prices was for the sub period 1996-97 to 2000-01. At constant prices, the lowest growth rate was for the sub period 1986-87 to 1990-91. The growth rates gave an idea about stronger immediate impact (1991-92 to 1995-96) than lagged impact (1996-97 to 2005-2006) of liberalisation policies.

Mineral Fuels, Mineral Oils and Products: Bituminous Substances, Mineral Waxes

At current prices, the imports of this sub category grew at the rate of 22.70 per cent for whole of the study period. The growth rate registered for the sub period of 1986-87 to 1990-91 was 37.72 per cent, which declined to less than its half, i.e., 16.75 per cent for the sub period 1991-92 to 1995-96. The growth rate increased to 20.48 per cent for the sub period 1996-97 to 2000-01 and further to 30.57 per cent for the sub period 2001-02 to 2005-06. The growth rate for the decade of 1990-91 to 1999-2000 was 17.71 per cent. The imports of this sub category grew at the rate of 21.51 per cent during 1996-97 to 2005-06.

At constant prices, the growth rate for the whole of the study period was 10.09 per cent. The growth rate for the sub period 1986-87 to 1990-91 was 10.28 per cent. The growth rate declined and there was marginal difference between the growth rates for the sub periods 1991-92 to 1995-96 and 1996-97 to 2000-01, i.e., 4.35 per cent and 4.74 per cent respectively. The growth rate doubled and increased to 8.58 per cent for the sub period 2001-02 to 2005-06. The growth rate for the decade of 1990-91 to 1999-2000 was 10.94 per cent. The imports of this sub category grew at the rate of 5.32 per cent during 1996-97 to 2005-06.

The imports of mineral fuel, oils and products grew at high rate for the study period and this sub category is also major contributor within the category of mineral product imports. The highest growth rate both at current as well as constant prices was for the sub period 1986-87 to 1990-91. The lowest growth rate was for the sub period 1991-92 to 1995-96 (at current prices and constant prices). The lagged impact (1996-97 to 2005-06) of liberalisation policies was stronger than the immediate impact (1991-92 to 1995-96) of liberalisation policies.

On the whole, within the category of mineral product imports, the sub category of ores, slag and ash imports grew at highest growth rate for the study period at current prices. While the sub-category of mineral fuels, oils and products grew at highest rates at constant prices. This category of mineral product imports grew at high rates throughout the study period on account of increase in prices of petroleum products internationally, along with heightened demand, limited spare capacity and geopolitical threats to the existing capacity (Govt. of India, 2005-06).

Products of Chemical or Allied Industries

At current prices, the imports of this category grew at the rate of 16.86 per cent. The growth rates for the sub periods 1986-87 to 1990-91 and 1991-92 to 1995-96 were recorded around 25 per cent. But the growth rate abruptly declined to 3.66 per cent for the sub period 1996-97 to 2000-01, which sharply increased to 23.76 per cent for the sub period 2001-02 to 2005-06. The growth rate registered for the decade of 1990-91 to 1999-2000 was 15.76 per cent. The imports of this category during 1996-97 to 2005-06, grew at the rate of 13.81 per cent.

At constant prices, the growth rate for the study period taken as a whole was 8.89 per cent. The growth rate for the sub period 1986-87 to 1990-91 was negative, i.e., -2.55 per cent, which sharply increased to 12.18 per cent for the sub period 1991-92 to 1995-96. The growth rate for the sub period of 1996-97 to 2000-01 declined to 1.86 per cent, which abruptly increased to 20.86 per cent for the sub period 2001-02 to 2005-06. The growth rate for the decade of 1990-91 to 1999-2000 was 8.35 per cent. The imports of this sub category grew at the rate of 7.58 per cent during 1996-97 to 2005-06.

This category of imports had grown at high rate except for the sub period 1996-97 to 2000-01 (at current prices and constant prices) and 1986-87 to 1990-91 (at constant prices). There were wide fluctuations between current price growth rate and constant price growth rate. The immediate impact (1991-92 to 1995-96) of liberalisation policies was stronger one.

Inorganic Chemicals

At current prices, the growth rate of imports of this sub category for the study period was 16.53 per cent. The growth rate for the sub period 1986-87 to 1990-91 was 16.09 per cent, which declined to 7.84 per cent for the sub period 1991-92 to 1995-96. The growth rate increased to 11.62 per cent for the sub period 1996-97 to 2000-01 and further to 17.08 per cent for the sub period 2001-02 to 2005-06. The growth rate for the decade of 1990-91 to 1999-2000 was 19.50 per cent. The imports of this sub category grew at the rate of 9.60 per cent during 1996-97 to 2005-06.

At constant prices, the growth rate of inorganic chemicals imports for the study period was 6.27 per cent. The growth rate for the sub period 1986-87 to 1990-91 was 3.67 per cent, same was negative for the sub period 1991-92 to 1995-96, i.e., -7.47 per cent. The growth rate increased to 6.24 per cent for the sub period 1996-97 to 2000-01 and to 8.53 per cent for the sub period 2001-02 to 2005-06. The growth rate for the decade of 1990-91 to 1999-2000 was 7.39 per cent. The imports of this sub category grew at the rate of 5.51 per cent during 1996-97 to 2005-06.

This sub category of chemicals and allied product imports grew at high rate except for the sub period 1991-92 to 1995-96 (at current prices and constant prices). The highest growth rate was recorded for sub period of 1996-97 to 2000-01 (at current and constant prices). The lagged impact (1996-97 to 2005-06) of liberalisation policies was stronger one both at current as well as constant prices.

Organic Chemicals

At current prices, the growth rate for whole of the study period was 19.29 per cent. The imports of this sub category grew at the rate of 32.23 per cent for the sub period 1986-87 to 1990-91, which increased to 42.85 per cent for the sub period 1991-92 to 1995-96. The growth rate sharply declined to 1.07 per cent for the sub period 1996-97 to 2000-01, but again increased to 27.96 per cent for the sub period 2001-02 to 2005-06. The growth rate for the decade of 1990-91 to 1999-2000 was 21.61 per cent. The imports of this sub category grew at the rate of 14.31 per cent during 1996-97 to 2005-06.

At constant prices, the growth rate of this sub category for the study period was 15.66 per cent. The growth rate for the sub period 1986-87 to 1990-91 was 3.81 per cent, which abruptly increased to 41.18 per cent for the sub period 1991-92 to 1995-96. The growth rate declined to 21.35 per cent for the sub period 1996-97 to 2000-01, but increased to 27.60 per cent for the sub period 2001-02 to 2005-06. The growth rate registered for the decade of 1990-91 to 1999-2000 was 29.83 per cent. The imports of this sub category during 1996-97 to 2005-06, grew at the rate of 2.79 per cent.

The imports of organic chemicals grew at high rate both at current and constant prices. The highest growth rate at current prices was during 1991-92 to 1995-96, the period immediately after liberalisation. The lowest growth rate at current prices was during 1996-97 to 2000-01. Similarly, at constant prices, highest growth was during 1991-92 to 1995-96 and lowest growth was during 1986-87 to 1990-91. The immediate impact (1991-92 to 1995-96) of liberalisation policies was stronger one, in both the cases of current and constant prices.

Fertilizers

At current prices, the growth rate for whole of the study period was 11.71 per cent. The growth rate for the sub period 1986-87 to 1990-91 was 37.80 per cent. The growth rate declined to 25.94 per cent for the sub period 1991-92 to 1995-96 and further declined abruptly to 0.38 per cent for the sub period 1996-97 to 2000-01.But the growth rate increased to 40.05 per cent for the sub period 2001-02 to 2005-06. The growth rate for the period 1990-91 to 1999-2000 was 13.91 per cent. The imports of this sub category during 1996-97 to 2005-06, grew at the rate of 4.60 per cent.

At constant prices, the growth rate for fertilizers imports for the study period taken as a whole was 2.74 per cent. The growth rate for sub period 1986-87 to 1990-91 was negative, i.e., -1.86 per cent, which increased to 16.89 per cent for the sub period 1991-92 to 1995-96. The growth rate was again negative for the sub period

1996-97 to 2000-01, i.e., -4.22 per cent, but it increased to 12.07 per cent for the sub period 2001-02 to 2005-06. The growth rate for the decade of 1990-91 to 1999-2000 was 5.91 per cent. The imports of this sub category grew at the rate of -7.08 per cent during 1996-97 to 2005-06.

The growth rates were high except during 1986-87 to 1990-91 (at constant prices) and 1996-97 to 2000-01 (at current and constant prices). The highest growth rate at current prices was during 2000-01 to 2005-06 and at constant prices during 1991-92 to 1995-96. The growth was negative during 1986-87 to 1990-91 and 1996-97 to 2000-01 at constant prices. Also the immediate impact (1991-92 to 1995-96) of liberalisation policies was stronger one.

Miscellaneous Chemical Products

At current prices, the growth rate for this sub category of chemical and allied industries imports for whole of the study period was 21.00 per cent. The growth rate for the sub period 1986-87 to 1990-91 was 14.96 per cent, which increased to 21.78 per cent for the sub period 1991-92 to 1995-96. The growth rate for the sub period 1996-97 to 2000-01 declined to 11.58 per cent (almost half of previous sub period's rate). But rate again increased to 20.87 per cent for the sub period 2001-02 to 2005-06. The growth rate for the decade of 1990-91 to 1999-2000 was 26.76 per cent. The imports of this sub category grew at the rate of 15.03 per cent during 1996-97 to 2005-06.

At constant prices, the growth rate for whole of the study period 1986-87 to 2005-06 was 12.99 per cent. The growth rate for the sub period 1986-87 to 1990-91 was negative, i.e., -10.68 per cent, which increased to 8.61 per cent for the sub period 1991-92 to 1995-96. The growth rate increased to 9.65 per cent for the next sub period 1996-97 to 2000-01 and further to 19.13 per cent for the sub period 2001-02 to 2005-06. The growth rate registered for the decade of 1990-91 to 1999-2000 was 18.65 per cent. The imports of this sub category during 1996-97 to 2005-06, grew at the rate of 9.62 per cent.

The growth rates of miscellaneous chemical product imports were high except negative growth rate during 1986-87 to 1990-91 at constant prices and an abrupt fall during the sub period 1996-97 to 2000-01 at current prices. The highest growth rate at current prices was during 1991-92 to 1995-96 and at constant prices during 2001-02 to 2005-06. The immediate impact (1991-92 to 1995-96) of liberalisation measures taken was stronger at current prices.

On the whole, the category of chemical and allied industries product imports showed increasing trend except for the sub period 1996-97 to 2000-01 at current prices. Within this category, the sub category of miscellaneous chemical products imports showed highest growth rate for the study period at current prices. While the sub category of organic chemicals imports experienced highest growth rate for the study period at constant prices. Within the category of chemical imports, the sub category of organic chemicals imports experienced highest growth rate during all the sub periods (at constant prices). At current prices, during 1986-87 to 1990-91 and 2001-02 to 2005-06, the sub category of fertilizers imports recorded highest growth rate. During 1991-92 to 1995-96, the sub category of organic chemicals imports had highest growth rate. Further, during 1996-97 to 2000-01, the sub category of inorganic chemicals imports registered highest growth rate. The imports of chemical products were included in the developmental imports which recorded sharp increases during 1994-95 (RBI, 1994-95).

Plastic and Rubber

At current prices, the growth rate for this category of imports during whole of the study period 1986-87 to 2005-06 was 15.23 per cent. The growth rate for the sub period 1986-87 to 1990-91 and 1991-92 to 1995-96 were around 25 per cent, but it abruptly declined to 3.69 per cent for the sub period 1996-97 to 2000-01. The growth rate sharply increased to 29.84 per cent for the sub period 2001-02 to 2005-06. The growth rate for the decade of 1990-91 to 1999-2000 was 14.97 per cent. The growth rate for the decade of 1996-97 to 2005-06 was 14.99 per cent.

At constant prices, the growth rate for whole of the study period was 7.43 per cent. The growth rate for the sub-period 1986-87 to 1990-91 was 5.45 per cent, which abruptly increased to 17.04

per cent for the sub period 1991-92 to 1995-96. The growth rate of plastic and rubber imports for the sub period 1996-97 to 2000-01 was negative i.e., -2.56 per cent, but it again increased to 20.51 per cent for the sub period 2001-02 to 2005-06. The growth rate for the decade of 1990-91 to 1999-2000 was 9.46 per cent. The imports of this category grew at the rate of 7.94 per cent during 1996-97 to 2005-06.

The growth rates for imports of this category were high except an abrupt decline during 1996-97 to 2000-01 (when rate was negative), both at current as well as constant prices. The highest growth rate was for the sub period 2001-02 to 2005-06 (current prices and constant prices). The immediate impact (1991-92 to 1995-96) of liberalisation policies was stronger than lagged impact (1996-97 to 2005-06).

(a) Plastic and Articles thereof

At current prices, the imports of plastic and articles grew at the rate of 14.73 per cent for whole of the study period. The growth rate for the sub period 1986-87 to 1990-91 was 28.05 per cent. The growth rate declined to 23.00 per cent for the sub period 1991-92 to 1995-96, and further declined to 2.42 per cent for the sub period 1996-97 to 2000-01. Further the rate abruptly increased to 31.74 per cent for the sub period 2001-02 to 2005-06. The growth rate for the decade of 1990-91 to 1999-2000 was 13.91 per cent. The imports of this sub category grew at the rate of 15.00 per cent during 1996-97 to 2005-06.

At constant prices, the growth rate during whole of the study period was 6.78 per cent. The growth rate for the sub period 1986-87 to 1990-91 was 7.79 per cent, which almost doubled for the sub period 1991-92 to 1995-96, i.e., 15.08 per cent. The growth rate was negative for the sub period 1996-97 to 2000-01, i.e., -3.75 per cent, but it sharply increased to 20.22 per cent for the sub period 2001-02 to 2005-06. The growth rate for the decade of 1990-91 to 1999-2000 was 8.63 per cent. The growth rate for the decade of 1996-97 to 2005-06 was 7.39 per cent.

The growth rates for this sub category were high except for the sub period 1996-97 to 2000-01 (both at current prices and constant prices). The growth rate was highest during 2001-02 to 2005-06 at current prices and constant prices. The growth rates also indicate about stronger immediate impact (1991-92 to 1995-96) of liberalisation policies.

(b) Rubber and Articles thereof

At current prices, the growth rate of this sub category of plastic and rubber imports during whole of the study period 1986-87 to 2005-06 was 16.82 per cent. The growth rate for the sub period 1986-87 to 1990-91 was 18.86 per cent, which abruptly increased to 33.42 per cent for the sub period 1991-92 to 1995-96. The growth rate declined to 7.11 per cent for the sub period 1996-97 to 2000-01, but it increased to 24.37 per cent (more than tripled) for the sub period 2001-02 to 2005-06. The growth rate for the decade of 1990-91 to 1999-2000 was 18.61 per cent. The growth rate of imports of this sub category for the decade of 1996-97 to 2005-06 was 14.86 per cent.

At constant prices, the growth rate for the study period was 9.34 per cent. The growth rate for the sub period 1986-87 to 1990-91 was negative, i.e., -0.35 per cent, but it sharply increased to 24.83 per cent for the sub period 1991-92 to 1995-96. The growth rate abruptly declined to 0.64 per cent for the sub period 1996-97 to 2000-01, but the rate again sharply increased to 21.26 per cent for the sub period 2001-02 to 2005-06. The growth rate for the decade of 1990-91 to 1999-2000 was 13.11 per cent. The imports of this sub category grew at the rate of 9.44 per cent during 1996-97 to 2005-06.

The growth rates were high and fluctuating for the study period. The growth rate was highest during 1991-92 to 1995-96, at current as well as constant prices. The growth rate was lowest at current prices during 1996-97 to 2000-01. At constant prices, the imports of this sub category grew at negative rate during 1986-87 to 1990-91. The liberalisation measures had experienced stronger immediate impact (1991-92 to 1995-96) as compared to the lagged impact (1996-97 to 2005-06).

Overall results of growth rates for plastic and rubber imports showed lower rates for the sub period 1996-97 to 2000-01. The growth rates for study period showed that rubber and articles imports grew at higher rates as compared to plastic and articles imports.

Hides and Skins: Leather Products, Furskins and Articles thereof

At current prices, the growth rate during whole of the study period 1986-87 to 2005-06 was 22.57 per cent. The growth rate for the sub period 1986-87 to 1990-91 was at very high level, i.e., 84.22 per cent. The growth rate abruptly declined to 25.30 per cent for the sub period 1991-92 to 1995-96 and further to 14.61 per cent for the sub period 1996-97 to 2000-01. The growth rate continued to decline and for the sub period 2001-02 to 2005-06 it was 9.43 per cent. The growth rate registered for the decade of 1990-91 to 1999-2000 was 16.36 per cent. The imports of this category during 1996-97 to 2005-06, grew at the rate of 12.84 per cent.

At constant prices, the growth rate of hides and skins imports for whole of the study period were 23.63 per cent. The growth rate for the sub period 1986-87 to 1990-91 was 62.16 per cent. The growth rate declined to 48.06 per cent for the sub period 1991-92 to 1995-96 and to 25.11 per cent for the sub period 1996-97 to 2000-01. Contrary to this, the growth rate was highly negative, i.e., -21.75 per cent for the sub period 2001-02 to 2005-06. The growth rate for the decade of 1990-91 to 1999-2000 was 32.59 per cent. The growth rate for the decade of 1996-97 to 2005-06 was -3.11 per cent.

The growth rates for this category of imports indicate a declining trend in both the cases of current and constant prices. The growth rate for the sub period 1986-87 to 1990-91 was highest one (at current prices and constant prices). The growth rate was lowest (at current prices) and negative (at constant prices) for the sub period 2001-02 to 2005-06. The growth rates also confirmed about stronger immediate impact (1991-92 to 1995-96) of liberalisation measures.

Wood, Cork and Articles thereof, Manufacture of Plating Materials: Basket ware and Wicker Work

At current prices, the growth rate for the imports of this category registered as 18.00 per cent for whole of the study period. The growth rate for the sub period 1986-87 to 1990-91 was 35.12 per cent, which declined to 17.47 per cent for the sub period 1991-92 to 1995-96. The growth rate registered an increase for the sub period 1996-97 to 2000-01, i.e., 21.28 per cent, which declined to 18.10 per cent for the sub period 2001-02 to 2005-06. The growth rate for the decade of 1990-91 to 1999-2000 was 20.08 per cent. The imports of this category grew at the rate of 15.48 per cent during 1996-97 to 2005-06.

At constant prices, the growth rate for imports of this category for whole of the study period was 18.24 per cent. The growth rate registered for the sub-period 1986-87 to 1990-91 was 18.94 per cent, which doubled and increased to 39.79 per cent for the sub period 1991-92 to 1995-96. The growth rate declined to 32.39 per cent for the sub period 1996-97 to 2000-01 and further negative growth rate was recorded for the sub period 2001-02 to 2005-06, i.e., -12.73 per cent. The growth rate for the decade of 1990-91 to 1999-2000 was 36.77 per cent. The growth rate for the decade of 1996-97 to 2005-06 was -0.90 per cent.

The growth rate for this category of imports was high except during 2001-02 to 2005-06 (at constant prices). At current prices, the highest growth rate was during 1986-87 to 1990-91 and lowest growth rate was for the sub period 1991-92 to 1995-96. At constant prices, the growth rate was highest during 1996-97 to 2000-01 and negative during 2001-02 to 2005-06. The results showed stronger immediate impact of liberalisation policies at constant prices, whereas the lagged impact (1996-97 to 2005-06) at current prices was stronger one.

Wood and Articles of Wood: Wood Charcoal

At current prices, the growth rate during whole of the study period was 18.07 per cent. The growth rate for the sub period 1986-87 to 1990-91 was 35.07 per cent, which declined to 17.44 per cent for the sub period 1991-92 to 1995-96. The growth rate increased to 21.36 per cent for the sub period 1996-97 to 2000-01, but it declined to 18.11 per cent for the sub period 2001-02 to 2005-06. The growth rate registered for the decade of 1990-91 to 1999-2000 was 20.15 per cent. The imports of this sub category during 1996-97 to 2005-06, grew at the rate of 15.52 per cent.

At constant prices, the growth rate of this sub category for whole of the study period was 18.31 per cent. The growth rate for the sub period 1986-87 to 1990-91 was 18.90 per cent, which increased to 39.75 per cent for the sub period 1991-92 to 1995-96. The growth rate declined to 32.48 per cent for the sub period 1996-97 to 2000-01, but it was highly negative, i.e., -12.71 per cent for the sub period 2001-02 to 2005-06. The growth rate for the decade of 1990-91 to 1999-2000 was 36.85 per cent. The growth rate for the decade of 1996-97 to 2005-06 was -0.85 per cent.

The growth rate for this sub category was high except for the sub period 2001-02 to 2005-06 at constant prices. At current prices the highest and lowest growth rates were during 1986-87 to 1990-91 and 1991-92 to 1995-96 respectively. At constant prices, the highest rate was for the sub period 1991-92 to 1995-96 and growth rate was negative during 2001-02 to 2005-06. The liberalisation policies led to higher growth of imports of this sub category during 1991-92 to 1995-96 (immediate impact period) as compared to that of during 1996-97 to 2005-06 (lagged impact period).

Paper and Paper Board and Articles thereof

At current prices, the growth rate of imports of this category for the study period was 16.00 per cent. The growth rate for the sub period 1986-87 to 1990-91 was 17.31 per cent, which abruptly increased to 30.52 per cent for the sub period 1991-92 to 1995-96. The growth rate declined to 8.27 per cent for the sub period 1996-97 to 2000-01, which again increased to 18.17 per cent (i.e. more than double) for the sub period 2001-02 to 2005-06. The growth rate for the decade of 1990-91 to 1999-2000 was 19.48 per cent. The growth rate for imports of this category for the decade of 1996-97 to 2005-06 was 11.86 per cent.

At constant prices, the growth rate recorded for the study period was 7.91 per cent. The growth rate for the sub period 1986-87 to 1990-91 was negative, i.e., -5.39 per cent, which increased to 13.29 per cent for the sub period 1991-92 to 1995-96. But opposite to this, rate again declined to 3.16 per cent for the sub period 1996-97 to 2000-01. The rate for this category of imports sharply increased to 18.84 per cent for the sub period 2001-02 to 2005-06. The growth rate registered for the decade of 1990-91 to 1999-2000 was 11.41 per cent. The imports of this category during 1996-97 to 2005-06, grew at the rate of 9.39 per cent.

There were wide differences between current prices growth rates and constant prices growth rates for the imports of this category. The growth rate was highest during 1991-92 to 1995-96, both at current and constant prices. The lowest growth rate at current prices was for the sub period 1996-97 to 2000-01. At constant prices, the growth rate was negative during 1986-87 to 1990-91 and was at very low level during 1996-97 to 2000-01. The liberalisation policies showed noticeable impact during 1991-92 to 1995-96 (immediate impact period) as compared to sub period 1996-97 to 2005-06 (lagged impact period).

Pulp of Wood or of Other Materials: Waste and Scrap of Paper and Paper Board

At current prices, the growth rate for imports of this sub category during whole of the study period 1986-87 to 2005-06 was 13.75 per cent. The growth rate for the sub period 1986-87 to 1990-91 was 16.24 per cent, which increased to 30.89 per cent for the sub period 1991-92 to 1995-96. But the growth rate abruptly declined to 9.91 per cent for the sub period 1996-97 to 2000-01, which increased to 15.74 per cent for the sub period 2001-02 to 2005-06. The growth rate for the decade of 1990-91 to 1999-2000 was 14.92 per cent. The growth rate for the decade of 1996-97 to 2005-06 was 12.73 per cent.

At constant prices, the growth rate was 5.43 per cent for the study period taken as a whole. The growth rate for the sub period 1986-87 to 1990-91 was negative, i.e., -3.87 per cent, which increased to 7.40 per cent for the sub period 1991-92 to 1995-96. The growth rate declined to its lowest level, i.e., 0.40 per cent for the sub period 1996-97 to 2000-01, but rate again increased to 11.83 per cent for the sub period 2001-02 to 2005-06. The growth rate for the decade of 1990-91 to 1999-2000 was 6.27 per cent. The growth rate for this sub category for the decade of 1996-97 to 2005-06 was 8.29 per cent.

The growth rates for this sub category of paper and paper board and articles imports were fluctuating. At current prices, the highest growth rate was for the sub period 1991-92 to 1995-96 and growth rate for the sub period 1996-97 to 2000-01 was lowest one. At constant prices, the highest rate was during 2001-02 to 2005-06 and growth rate was negative during 1986-87 to 1990-91. The immediate impact (1991-92 to 1995-96) was much stronger than lagged impact (1996-97 to 2005-06) of liberalisation policies, both at current prices and constant prices.

Paper and Paper Board: Articles of Paper Pulp, of Paper and Paper Board

At current prices, the growth rate for whole of the study period was 16.34 per cent. The growth rate for the sub period 1986-87 to 1990-91 was 19.25 per cent, which increased to 31.82 per cent for the sub period 1991-92 to 1995-96. Further, the growth rate declined to 3.15 per cent for the sub period 1996-97 to 2000-01, but again increased to 18.96 per cent for the sub period 2001-02 to 2005-06. The growth rate for the decade of 1990-91 to 1999-2000 was 21.64 per cent. The imports of this sub category grew at the rate of 8.76 per cent during 1996-97 to 2005-06.

At constant prices, the growth rate for this sub category was 8.35 per cent for whole of the study period. The growth rate was negative for the sub period 1986-87 to 1990-91, i.e., -3.83 per cent, which increased to 14.41 per cent for the sub period 1991-92 to 1995-96. Again the negative growth rate was recorded for the sub period 1996-97 to 2000-01, i.e., -1.71 per cent, which sharply increased to 19.49 per cent for the sub period 2001-02 to 2005-06. The growth rate for the decade of 1990-91 to 1999-2000 was 13.43

per cent. The imports of this sub category grew at the rate of 5.77 per cent during 1996-97 to 2005-06.

The growth rates indicated fluctuating trend during the study period. The highest growth rate was during 1991-92 to 1995-96 (both at current as well as constant prices). The lowest growth rate at current prices was during 1996-97 to 2000-01. At constant prices the growth was negative during sub periods of 1986-87 to 1990-91 and 1996-97 to 2000-01. Here again the immediate impact (1990-91 to 1995-96) of liberalisation policies was stronger than its lagged impact (1996-97 to 2000-01).

On the whole, the category of paper imports showed a highly fluctuating trend for the various sub periods. The imports of sub category of paper and paper board had grown at higher rates as compared to the imports of pulp of wood and of other material.

Textile and Textile Articles

At current prices, the growth rate for whole of the study period 1986-87 to 2005-06 was 19.76 per cent. The growth rate was 25.71 per cent for the sub period 1986-87 to 1990-91, which sharply increased to 41.84 per cent for the sub period 1991-92 to 1995-96. The growth rate declined to 19.21 per cent for the sub period 1996-97 to 2000-01, which was almost less than half of previous sub period's growth rate. The growth rate again decelerated to 12.74 per cent for the sub period 2001-02 to 2005-06. The growth rate registered for the decade of 1990-91 to 1999-2000 was 20.75 per cent. The imports of this category during 1996-97 to 2005-06, grew at the rate of 18.31 per cent.

At constant prices, the growth rate for the study period was 14.83 per cent. The growth rate for the sub period 1986-87 to 1990-91 was 15.18 per cent, which increased to 33.54 per cent (i.e., doubled) for the sub period 1991-92 to 1995-96. The growth rate registered a decline for the sub period 1996-97 to 2000-01, i.e., 22.10 per cent which further declined to 7.68 per cent for the sub period 2001-02 to 2005-06. The growth rate registered for the decade of 1990-91 to 1999-2000 was 16.50 per cent. The imports of this category during 1996-97 to 2005-06, grew at the rate of 19.87 per cent.

The growth rates for textiles and textile articles imports were high during study period. The highest growth rate was during sub period 1990-91 to 1995-96, both at current and constant prices. The growth rate was lowest during 2001-02 to 2005-06 (at current prices and constant prices). Relatively stronger immediate impact (1991-92 to 1995-96) of liberalisation policies was observed for this category.

Silk

At current prices, the growth rate during whole of the study period was 18.77 per cent. The growth rate for the sub period 1986-87 to 1990-91 was 28.61 per cent, which declined to 17.48 per cent for the sub period 1991-92 to 1995-96. The growth rate increased to 19.97 per cent for the sub period 1996-97 to 2000-01 and further to 21.95 per cent for the sub period 2001-02 to 2005-06. The growth rate registered for the decade of 1990-91 to 1999-2000 was 11.01 per cent. The imports of this sub category during 1996-97 to 2005-06, grew at the rate of 24.52 per cent.

At constant prices, the growth for this sub category of textile imports was 13.38 per cent. The growth rate for the sub period 1986-87 to 1990-91 was 17.84 per cent, which declined to 10.60 per cent for the sub period 1991-92 to 1995-96. The growth rate increased to 22.89 per cent for the sub period 1996-97 to 2000-01, but declined to 17.36 per cent for the sub period 2001-02 to 2005-06. The growth rate for the decade of 1990-91 to 1999-2000 was 7.11 per cent. The imports of this sub category grew at the rate of 25.67 per cent during 1996-97 to 2005-06.

The growth rates for this sub category of imports textiles and textiles articles were high and fluctuating for the study period. At current prices, the highest growth rate was during 1986-87 to 1990-91 and at constant prices, the highest growth rate was for the sub period 1996-97 to 2000-01. The growth rate was lowest for the sub period 1991-92 to 1995-96 (both at current and constant prices). The lagged impact (1996-97 to 2005-06) was stronger than immediate impact (1991-92 to 1995-96) of liberalisation policies.

Wool, Fine or Coarse Animal Hair

At current prices, the growth rate during whole of the study period 1986-87 to 2005-06 was 11.66 per cent. The growth rate for the sub period 1986-87 to 1990-91 was 24.01 per cent and it declined to 23.35 per cent for the sub period 1991-92 to 1995-96. The growth rate for the sub period 1996-97 to 2000-01 was negative, i.e., -9.47 per cent, which abruptly increased to 12.93 per cent for the sub period 2001-02 to 2005-06. The growth rate for the decade of 1990-91 to 1999-2000 was 11.95 per cent. The imports of this sub category grew at the rate of 8.15 per cent during 1996-97 to 2005-06.

At constant prices, the growth rate for the study period was 6.94 per cent. The growth rate for the sub period 1986-87 to 1990-91 was 13.63 per cent, which increased to 16.13 per cent for the sub period 1991-92 to 1995-96. The growth rate was negative for the sub period 1996-97 to 2000-01, i.e., -7.27 per cent, which increased to 12.42 per cent for the sub period 2001-02 to 2005-06. The growth rate for the decade of 1990-91 to 1999-2000 was 8.02 per cent. The imports of this sub category grew at the rate of 8.32 per cent during 1996-97 to 2005-06.

The imports of this sub category grew at negative rate during 1996-97 to 2000-01 (at current prices and constant prices). The highest growth rates were during 1986-87 to 1990-91 (at current prices) and 1991-92 to 1995-96 (at constant prices). The immediate impact (1991-92 to 1995-96) was stronger than the lagged impact (1996-97 to 2005-06) of liberalisation policies.

Cotton

At current prices, the growth rate was 28.87 per cent for whole of the study period. The growth rate for the sub period 1986-87 to 1990-91 was 32.09 per cent. The growth rate abruptly increased to 84.03 per cent for the sub period 1991-92 to 1995-96 and further to 88.96 per cent for the sub period 1996-97 to 2000-01. But for the sub period 2001-02 to 2005-06, the growth rate was negative, i.e., -1.35 per cent. The growth rate for the decade of 1990-91 to 1999-2000 was 34.35 per cent. The imports of this sub category grew at the rate of 32.55 per cent during 1996-97 to 2005-06.

At constant prices, the growth rate of cotton imports was 24.50 per cent for the study period taken as a whole. The growth rate for the sub period 1986-87 to 1990-91 was 21.04 per cent, which abruptly increased to 73.26 per cent for the sub period 1991-92 to 1995-96. This increase was continued and growth rate increased to 93.53 per cent for the sub period 1996-97 to 2000-01. But suddenly this sub category experienced a negative growth for the sub period 2001-02 to 2005-06, i.e., -4.44 per cent. The growth rate for the decade of 1990-91 to 1999-2000 was 29.64 per cent. The imports of this sub category grew at the rate of 40.75 per cent during 1996-97 to 2005-06.

The results indicated high growth rates for this sub category of textile imports except for the sub period 2001-02 to 2005-06. During this sub period, growth rate was negative both at current and constant prices. The highest growth rate was for the sub period 1996-97 to 2000-01 (at current as well as constant prices). The immediate impact (1991-92 to 1995-96) was stronger than the lagged impact (1996-97 to 2005-06) of liberalisation measures.

Man-Made Filaments

At current prices, the growth rate for whole of the study period 1986-87 to 2005-06 was 18.96 per cent. The growth rate for the sub period 1986-87 to 1990-91 was 34.09 per cent, which increased to 41.91 per cent for the sub period 1991-92 to 1995-96. The growth rate declined to 34.20 per cent for the sub period 1996-97 to 2000-01 and further to 11.76 per cent for the sub period 2001-02 to 2005-06. The growth rate for the decade of 1990-91 to 1999-2000 was 16.56 per cent. The imports of this sub category grew at the rate of 24.83 per cent during 1996-97 to 2005-06.

At constant prices, the growth rate for man made filaments imports for whole of the study period was 13.86 per cent. The growth rate for the sub period 1986-87 to 1990-91 was 22.86 per cent. The growth rate increased to 33.60 per cent for the sub period 1991-92 to 1995-96 and further increased to 37.46 per cent for the sub period 1996-97 to 2000-01. But growth rate declined to 7.41

per cent for the sub period 2001-02 to 2005-06. The growth rate for the decade of 1990-91 to 1999-2000 was 12.47 per cent. The imports of this sub category grew at the rate of 28.05 per cent during 1996-97 to 2005-06.

The growth rates were high for this sub category of textiles imports. At current prices, the highest growth rate was for the sub period 1991-92 to 1995-96, whereas at constant prices the highest growth rate was during 1996-97 to 2000-01. The lowest growth rate was during 2001-02 to 2005-06 (both at current prices and constant prices).

On the whole, within the category of textiles imports, the imports of sub category of cotton grew at highest rate during 1991-92 to 1995-96 and 1996-97 to 2000-01. During the sub period 1986-87 to 1990-91, the sub category of manmade filaments imports grew at highest rate. The imports of silk grew at highest rate during 2001-02 to 2005-06.

Footwear, Headgear, Umbrellas: Prepared Feathers and Articles thereof

At current prices, the growth rate of this category of imports for whole of the study period 1986-87 to 2005-06 was 17.52 per cent. The growth rate for the sub period 1986-87 to 1990-91 was 22.29 per cent, which increased to 33.76 per cent for the sub period 1991-92 to 1995-96. The growth rate for the sub period 1996-97 to 2000-01 declined to 10.59 per cent, which increased to 35.55 per cent for the sub period 2001-02 to 2005-06. The growth rate registered for the decade of 1990-91 to 1999-2000 was 17.54 per cent. The imports of this category, during 1996-97 to 2005-06, grew at the rate of 13.73 per cent.

At constant prices, the growth rate was 17.01 per cent for the study period taken as a whole. The growth rate for the sub period 1986-87 to 1990-91 was 10.03 per cent, which sharply increased to 59.18 per cent for the sub period 1991-92 to 1995-96. But on the contrary growth rate declined to 20.72 per cent and even became negative, i.e., -7.46 per cent for the sub periods 1996-97 to 2000-01 and 2001-02 to 2005-06 respectively. The growth rate for the decade of 1990-91 to 1999-2000 was 33.09 per cent. The imports of this category grew at the rate of -5.86 per cent during 1996-97 to 2005-06.

The growth rates of footwear, headgear, umbrellas etc, imports showed high growth rates with wide fluctuations. At current prices highest growth rate was during 2001-02 to 2005-06, whereas at constant prices growth rate was highest during 1991-92 to 1995-96. The lowest growth rate was for the sub period 1996-97 to 2000-01 (at current prices and constant prices).

Stone, Cement and Similar Material: Ceramic Products, Glass and Glassware

At current prices, the growth rate of this category of imports during whole of the study period was 17.88 per cent. The growth rate for the sub period 1986-87 to 1990-91 was 18.69 per cent, which increased to 23.96 per cent for the sub period 1991-92 to 1995-96. The growth rate declined to 16.48 per cent for the sub period 1996-97 to 2000-01, but again increased to 29.59 per cent for the sub period 2001-02 to 2005-06. The growth rate registered for the decade of 1990-91 to 1999-2000 was 16.74 per cent. The imports of this category during 1996-97 to 2005-06, grew at the rate of 21.57 per cent.

At constant prices, the growth rate was 9.26 per cent during whole of the study period. The growth rate for the sub period 1986-87 to 1990-91 was negative, i.e., -8.21 per cent, which abruptly increased to 8.92 per cent for the sub period 1991-92 to 1995-96. Further, the growth rate declined to 2.62 per cent for the sub period 1996-97 to 2000-01. On the contrary, the growth rate abruptly increased to 38.66 per cent for the sub period 2001-02 to 2005-06. The growth rate for the decade of 1990-91 to 1999-2000 was 18.09 per cent. The imports of this category grew at the rate of 15.33 per cent during 1996-97 to 2005-06.

The growth rates gave an idea about high and fluctuating growth for the imports of stones, cement and similar material. The highest growth rate was for the sub period 2001-02 to 2005-06 at current prices and constant prices. The lowest growth rate at current prices was for the sub period 1996-97 to 2000-01. At constant prices, growth rate was negative for the sub period 1986-87 to 1990-91. There were wide differences between current prices growth rate and constant prices growth rate. The immediate impact (1991-92 to 1995-96) of liberalisation policies was stronger one at current prices, whereas at constant prices lagged impact (1996-97 to 2005-06) was stronger one.

Articles of Stone, Plaster, Cement, Asbestos, Mica or Similar Materials

At current prices, the growth rate of this sub category during whole of the study period 1986-87 to 2005-06 was 21.05 per cent. The growth rate for the sub period 1986-87 to 1990-91 was 26.59 per cent, which declined to 24.44 per cent for the sub period 1991-92 to 1995-96. The growth rate continued to decline and it was 15.45 per cent for the sub period 1996-97 to 2000-01, but it increased to 34.87 per cent for the sub period 2001-02 to 2005-06. The growth rate for the decade of 1990-91 to 1999-2000 was 16.52 per cent. The imports of this sub category grew at the rate of 24.27 per cent during 1996-97 to 2005-06.

At constant prices, the growth rate during whole of the study period was 12.36 per cent. The growth rate was negative for the sub period 1986-87 to 1990-91, i.e., -2.11 per cent, which increased to 9.34 per cent for the sub period 1991-92 to 1995-96. The growth rate again declined to 1.71 per cent for the sub period 1996-97 to 2000-01, which abruptly increased to 49.95 per cent during 2001-02 to 2005-06. The growth rate for the decade of 1990-91 to 1999-2000 was 17.87 per cent. The imports of this sub category grew at the rate of 18.25 per cent during 1996-97 to 2005-06.

The growth rate was fluctuating one and highest rate was for the sub period 2001-02 to 2005-06 at current prices and constant prices. The imports of this sub category grew at lowest rate for the sub period 1986-87 to 1990-91 at constant prices. The growth rate was lowest for the sub period 1996-97 to 2000-01 at current prices.

Ceramic Products

At current prices, the growth rate for this sub category of stone, cement and similar material imports during whole of the study period was 19.19 per cent. The growth rate for the sub period 1986-87 to 1990-91 was 15.44 per cent, which increased to 19.19 per cent for the sub period 1991-92 to 1995-96. Further, the growth rate declined to 11.70 per cent for the sub period 1996-97 to 2000-01, but it sharply increased to 40.77 per cent for the sub period 2001-02 to 2005-06. The growth rate for the decade of 1990-91 to 1999-2000 was 15.75 per cent. The imports of this sub category grew at the rate of 24.38 per cent during 1996-97 to 2005-06.

At constant prices, the growth rate for whole of the study period was 10.21 per cent. The growth rate for the sub period 1986-87 to 1990-91 was negative, i.e., -10.73 per cent, which increased to 4.73 per cent for the sub period 1991-92 to 1995-96. The growth rate was again negative, i.e., -1.59 per cent for the sub period 1996-97 to 2000-01, but it abruptly increased to 52.64 per cent for the sub period 2001-02 to 2005-06. The growth rate for the decade of 1990-91 to 1999-2000 was 17.09 per cent. The imports of this sub category grew at the rate of 17.07 per cent during 1996-97 to 2005-06.

The constant prices growth rates were relatively lower than current prices growth rates for ceramic products imports and this sub category grew at fluctuating rate for the study period. The highest growth rate was for the sub period 2001-02 to 2005-06 (at current prices and constant prices). At current prices, the lowest growth rate was for the sub period 1996-97 to 2000-01. At constant prices, the growth rate was negative for the sub periods 1986-87 to 1990-91 and 1996-97 to 2000-01. The lagged impact (1996-97 to 2005-06) has been found to be stronger than immediate impact (1991-92 to 1995-96) of liberalisation policies.

Glass and Glassware

At current prices, the growth rate for the study period 1986-87 to 2005-06 taken as a whole was 16.35 per cent. The growth rate for the sub period 1986-87 to 1990-91 was 18.86 per cent, which increased to 26.71 per cent for the sub period 1991-92 to 1995-96. The growth rate declined to 19.41 per cent for the sub period 1996-

97 to 2000-01, but increased to 21.24 per cent for the sub period 2001-02 to 2005-06. The growth rate for the decade of 1990-91 to 1999-2000 was 17.33 per cent. The imports of this sub category grew at the rate of 18.78 per cent during 1996-97 to 2005-06.

At constant prices, the growth rate for the study period was 7.99 per cent. The growth rate for the sub period 1986-87 to 1990-91 was negative i.e., -8.08 per cent, which increased to 11.34 per cent for the sub period 1991-92 to 1995-96. The growth rate again declined to 5.19 per cent for the sub period 1996-97 to 2000-01, but increased to 27.00 per cent for the sub period 2001-02 to 2005-06. The growth rate for the decade of 1990-91 to 1999-2000 was 18.68 per cent. The imports of this sub category grew at the rate of 13.13 per cent during 1996-97 to 2005-06.

This sub category of stone, cement and similar material imports also gave an idea about fluctuating trend for the study period. In general the constant prices growth rates were less than current prices growth rates for this sub category. At current prices, the highest growth rate was during 1991-92 to 1995-96 and lowest growth rate was during 1986-87 to 1990-91. At constant prices the growth rate was highest during 2001-02 to 2005-06 and rate was negative during 1986-87 to 1990-91. The immediate impact of liberalisation policies was stronger one at current prices.

In general constant prices growth rates were less than current price growth rates. The category of stone, cement and similar material imports showed highly fluctuating trend. To this trend second sub category of ceramic products imports contributed the most. At constant prices, the growth rate was negative for the category as well as for its sub categories during first sub period (1986-87 to 1990-91). The imports of sub category of glass and glassware grew at highest rate during 1991-92 to 1995-96 and 1996-97 to 2000-01. During the sub period 2001-02 to 2005-06, the sub category of ceramic product imports grew at highest rate.

Pearls, Precious and Semi-Precious Stones, Metals and Articles thereof: Imitation Jewellery and Coins

At current prices, the growth rate registered for this export oriented category of imports for the study period 1986-87 to 2005-06 was 24.36 per cent. The growth rate for the sub period 1986-87 to 1990-91 was 28.51 per cent, which decelerated to 15.25 per cent for the sub period 1991-92 to 1995-96. Further, the growth rate increased to 33.47 per cent (almost doubled) for the sub period 1996-97 to 2000-01, but rate again decelerated to 22.75 per cent for the sub period 2001-02 to 2005-06. The growth rate for the decade of 1990-91 to 1999-2000 was 30.50 per cent. The imports of this category grew at the rate of 19.45 per cent during 1996-97 to 2005-06.

At constant prices, the growth rate for whole of the study period was 17.06 per cent. The growth rates for the sub periods 1986-87 to 1990-91 and 1991-92 to 1995-96 were around 9 per cent. But the rate abruptly increased to 31.74 per cent for the sub period 1996-97 to 2000-01 and declined to 16.79 per cent for the sub period 2001-02 to 2005-06. The growth rate for the decade of 1990-91 to 1999-2000 was 24.45 per cent. The imports of this category grew at the rate of 17.37 per cent during 1996-97 to 2005-06.

Being export related item, the growth rates for pearls, precious and semi precious stones, metals and articles imports were quite higher. Larger imports of this category were required for the growing export industry of reworked precious stones (Sixth Five Year Plan, chapter six). The import compression measures taken by Govt. in 1990-91 led to fall in imports of this category, which in turn resulted into decelerated growth rate for the sub period 1991-92 to 1995-96. The growth rate was highest during 1996-97 to 2000-01, both at current as well as constant prices. The imports of this export oriented category grew at lowest rate during 1991-92 to 1995-96 (current prices and constant prices). The growth rates also confirmed about relatively stronger lagged impact (1996-97 to 2005-06).

Base Metals and Articles of Base Metals

At current prices, the growth rate for this category during whole of the study period 1986-87 to 2005-06 was 12.59 per cent. The growth rate for the sub period 1986-87 to 1990-91 was 19.42 per cent, which increased to 26.55 per cent for the sub period 1991-92 to 1995-96. Further, the growth rate suddenly turned into negative rate i.e., -4.99 per cent for the sub period 1996-97 to 2000-01, but it sharply increased to 39.65 per cent for the sub period 2000-01 to 2005-06. The growth rate for the sub period 1990-91 to 1999-2000 was 13.12 per cent. The imports of this category grew at the rate of 13.29 per cent during 1996-97 to 2005-06.

At constant prices, the growth rate for whole of the study period was 3.86 per cent. The growth rate for the sub period 1986-87 to 1990-91 was 1.16 per cent, which increased to 13.88 per cent for the sub period 1991-92 to 1995-96. But the growth rate for the sub period 1996-97 to 2000-01 was negative, i.e., -6.90 per cent, which again increased to 17.03 per cent for the sub period 2001-02 to 2005-06. The growth rate for the sub period 1990-91 to 1999-2000 was 5.06 per cent. The imports of this category grew at the rate of 4.81 per cent during 1996-97 to 2005-06.

The imports of base metals and articles of base metals had grown at high rates except for the sub period 1986-87 to 1990-91 (at constant prices) and 1996-97 to 2000-01 (at current prices). The highest growth rates were recorded during 2001-02 to 2005-06 (at current prices and constant prices). The growth rate was negative during 1996-97 to 2000-01 (both at current as well as constant prices). The immediate impact (1991-92 to 1995-96) of liberalisation policies was stronger than lagged impact (1996-97 to 2005-06).

Iron and Steel

At current prices, the growth rate of imports of this sub category for whole of the study period 1986-87 to 2005-06 was 11.70 per cent. The growth rate for the sub period 1986-87 to 1990-91 was 20.11 per cent, which increased to 25.25 per cent for the sub period 1991-92 to 1995-96. Suddenly, the growth rate for the sub period 1996-97 to 2000-01 turned into negative rate, i.e., -4.80 per cent, which sharply increased to 50.33 per cent for the sub period 2001-02 to 2005-06. The growth rate for iron and steel imports for the decade of 1990-91 to 1999-2000 was 10.18 per cent. The imports of this sub category grew at the rate of 16.00 per cent during 1996-97 to 2005-06.

At constant prices, the growth rate for imports of iron and steel for the study period taken as a whole was negative, i.e., -1.43 per cent. The growth rate for the sub period 1986-87 to 1990-91 was again negative one, i.e., -6.70 per cent, which abruptly increased to 13.92 per cent for the sub period 1991-92 to 1995-96. But the growth rate sharply declined and was highly negative, i.e., -9.06 per cent for the sub period 1996-97 to 2000-01. Further, the growth rate sharply increased to 20.87 per cent for the sub period 2001-02 to 2005-06. The growth rate of imports of this sub category for the decade of 1990-91 to 1999-2000 was 0.80 per cent. The imports of this sub category grew at the rate of -0.01 per cent during 1996-97 to 2005-06.

The imports of this sub category grew at fluctuating rate. The highest growth rate was for the sub period 2001-02 to 2005-06 (at current prices and constant prices). The growth rate was negative for the sub periods 1996-97 to 2000-01 (at current prices and constant prices) and 1986-87 to 1990-91 (at constant prices). The growth rates at constant prices were much lower than growth rates at current prices.

Articles of Iron and Steel

At current prices, the growth rate for this sub category during whole of the study period was 11.82 per cent. The growth rate for the sub period 1986-87 to 1990-91 was 5.11 per cent, which increased to 15.40 per cent for the sub period 1991-92 to 1995-96. But it abruptly declined and was negative, i.e., -3.99 per cent for the sub period 1996-97 to 2000-01. Further, the growth rate sharply increased to 36.03 per cent for the sub period 2001-02 to 2005-06. The growth rate registered for imports of this sub category for the decade of 1990-91 to 1999-2000 was 13.16 per cent. The imports of this sub category during 1996-97 to 2005-06, grew at the rate of 13.67 per cent.

At constant prices, the growth rate for the study period taken as a whole was 0.51 per cent. The growth rate for the sub period 1986-87 to 1990-91 was negative one i.e., -18.35 per cent, which increased to 4.97 per cent for the sub period 1991-92 to 1995-96. The growth rate was again negative for the sub period 1996-97 to 2000-01, i.e., -8.29 per cent, which abruptly increased to 24.83 per cent for the sub period of 2001-02 to 2005-06. The growth rate registered for the decade of 1990-91 to 1999-2000 was 3.53 per cent. The imports of this sub category during 1996-97 to 2005-06, grew at the rate of 4.82 per cent.

This sub category of base metals and articles of base metals imports gave the same trends as of Iron and steel sub category. The imports of this sub category had grown at highest rate during 2001-02 to 2005-06 (at current prices and constant prices). The growth was negative during 1986-87 to 1990-91 (at constant prices) and 1996-97 to 2000-01 (at current prices and constant prices). The constant prices growth rates were much lower than the current prices growth rates.

Copper and Articles thereof

At current prices, the growth rate during whole of the study period 1986-87 to 2005-06 was 9.83 per cent. The growth rate for the sub period 1986-87 to 1990-91 was 43.53 per cent, which declined to 28.31 per cent for the sub period 1991-92 to 1995-96. The growth rate was highly negative for the sub period 1996-97 to 2000-01, i.e., -21.10, which abruptly increased to 36.97 per cent for the sub period 2001-02 to 2005-06. The growth rate for the decade of 1990-91 to 1999-2000 was 10.75 per cent. The imports of this sub category grew at the rate of 1.75 per cent during 1996-97 to 2005-06.

At constant prices, the growth rate for imports of copper and articles for whole of the study period was 2.32 per cent. The growth rate for the sub period 1986-87 to 1990-91 was 9.71 per cent, which doubled for the sub period 1991-92 to 1995-96, i.e., 18.00 per cent. The growth rate for the sub period 1996-97 to 2000-01 was negative, i.e., -14.98 per cent, which increased to 2.02 per cent for the sub period 2001-02 to 2005-06. The growth rate of imports of this sub category for the decade of 1990-91 to 1999-2000 was 7.26 per cent. The imports of this sub category grew at the rate of -5.35 per cent during 1996-97 to 2005-06.

For this sub category of base metals and articles of base metals imports, growth rate was highly negative during 1996-97 to 2000-01 (both at current and constant prices). The highest growth rate was during 1986-87 to 1990-91 at current prices. The growth rate was highest during 1991-92 to 1995-96 at constant prices. Here liberalisation policies showed stronger immediate impact (1991-92 to 1995-96) on imports of this sub category. The constant prices growth rates were much lower than the current prices growth rates.

Aluminium and Articles thereof

At current prices, the growth rate for the study period 1986-87 to 2005-06 was 19.53 per cent. The growth rate for the sub period 1986-87 to 1990-91 was negative, i.e., -5.32 per cent, which abruptly increased to 84.39 per cent for the sub period 1991-92 to 1995-96. The growth rate was again negative for the sub period 1996-97 to 2000-01, i.e., -0.52 per cent, but increased to 25.02 per cent for the sub period 2001-02 to 2005-06. The growth rate of imports of aluminium and articles for the decade of 1990-91 to 1999-2000 was 34.79 per cent. The imports of this sub category grew at the rate of 14.17 per cent during 1996-97 to 2005-06.

At constant prices, the growth rate for whole of the study period was 9.78 per cent. The growth rate for the sub-period 1986-87 to 1990-91 was highly negative, i.e., -24.27 per cent, and rate increased abruptly to 59.91 per cent for the sub period 1991-92 to 1995-96. Further, the growth rate was again negative for the sub period 1996-97 to 2000-01, i.e., -7.65 per cent, which increased to 10.93 per cent for the sub period 2001-02 to 2005-06. The growth rate for the decade of 1990-91 to 1999-2000 was 24.11 per cent. The imports of this sub category grew at the rate of 6.30 per cent during 1996-97 to 2005-06.

The imports of aluminium and articles grew at fluctuating rate. The growth rates were negative during 1986-87 to 1990-91 and

1996-97 to 2000-01, whereas the rates were highly positive during 1991-92 to 1995-96 and positive during 2001-02 to 2005-06 (both at current as well as constant prices). The immediate impact (1991-92 to 1995-96) was much stronger than lagged impact (1996-97 to 2005-06).

On the whole, the category of base metals and articles of base metals imports had grown at high rates during the sub periods 1991-92 to 1995-96 and 2001-02 to 2005-06, which also gave an idea about the stronger immediate impact of liberalisation policies. The growth rates were negative for all sub categories during the sub period 1996-97 to 2000-01. The sub category of the aluminium and articles imports experienced highest rate for the study period, both at current as well as constant prices, which highlighted less domestic production but high domestic demand for this particular sub category.

Machinery and their parts, Electrical and Electronic Equipments, Parts thereof

At current prices, the growth rate for imports of this category for whole of the study period 1986-87 to 2005-06 was 22.96 per cent. The imports of this category have grown at the rate of 40.01 per cent for the sub period 1986-87 to 1990-91. The growth rate declined to 38.79 per cent for the sub period 1991-92 to 1995-96 and further to 9.87 per cent for the sub period 1996-97 to 2000-01. But the growth rate again increased to 33.20 per cent for the sub period 2001-02 to 2005-06. The growth rate of imports of this category for the decade of 1990-91 to 1999-2000 was 22.13 per cent. The imports of this category grew at the rate of 20.32 per cent during 1996-97 to 2005-06.

At constant prices, the growth rate during whole of the study period was 16.56 per cent. The growth rate for the sub period 1986-87 to 1990-91 was 34.11 per cent, which increased to 46.93 per cent for the sub period 1991-92 to 1995-96. The growth rate abruptly declined to 5.22 per cent for the sub period 1996-97 to 2000-01, which again increased to 17.61 per cent for the sub period 2001-02 to 2005-06. The growth rate for the decade of 1990-91 to 1999-2000 was 14.73 per cent. The imports of this category grew at the rate of 14.09 per cent during 1996-97 to 2005-06.

The category of machinery and their parts imports falls under capital goods imports and it grew at high rate for the study period. At current prices, the growth rate was highest for the sub period 1986-87 to 1990-91. At constant prices, the highest growth rate was during 1991-92 to 1995-96. The growth rate was lowest one for the sub period 1996-97 to 2000-01, both at current prices and constant prices. The immediate impact (1990-91 to 1995-96) of liberalisation policies experienced by this category was relatively stronger one. Being a part of capital goods the imports of this category facilitated industrial activity in the country.

Nuclear Reactors, Boilers, Machinery and Mechanical Appliances Parts thereof

At current prices, the growth rate of this sub category for the study period 1986-87 to 2005-06 was 17.76 per cent. The growth rate for the sub period 1986-87 to 1990-91 was 9.77 per cent, which increased to 38.26 per cent for the sub period 1991-92 to 1995-96. The growth rate again declined to 5.13 per cent for the sub period 1996-97 to 2000-01, which increased to 32.06 per cent for thc sub period 2001-02 to 2005-06. The growth rate for the decade of 1990-91 to 1999-2000 was 21.51 per cent. The imports of this sub category grew at the rate of 15.48 per cent during 1996-97 to 2005-06.

At constant prices, the growth rate for whole the study period was at very high level, i.e., 58.84 per cent. The growth rate for the sub period 1986-87 to 1990-91 was 34.24 per cent, which increased to 43.93 per cent for the sub period 1991-92 to 1995-96. The growth rate declined to 7.11 per cent for the sub period 1996-97 to 2000-01, but it again increased to 23.62 per cent for the sub period 2001-02 to 2005-06. The growth rate for the decade of 1990-91 to 1999-2000 was 11.50 per cent. The imports of this sub category grew at the rate of 13.26 per cent during 1996-97 to 2005-06.

The growth rates of this sub category were high and fluctuating. The lowest growth rate was for the sub period 1996-97 to 2000-01 (at current prices and constant prices). Both at current prices and constant prices, the highest growth rate was during 1991-92 to

1995-96. The immediate impact (1991-92 to 1995-96) of liberalisation policies was stronger one.

Electrical Machinery and Equipments and Parts thereof: Sound and TV Recorders and Reproducers and Parts thereof

At current prices, the growth rate for this sub category for whole of the study period was 21.94 per cent. The growth rate for the sub period 1986-87 to 1990-91 was 13.96 per cent which tripled for the sub period 1991-92 to 1995-96, i.e., 39.88 per cent. The growth rate declined to 20.13 per cent for the sub period 1996-97 to 2000-01, which increased to 34.76 per cent for the sub period 2001-02 to 2005-06. The growth rate for the decade of 1990-91 to 1999-2000 was 23.32 per cent. The imports of this sub category grew at the rate of 28.43 per cent during 1996-97 to 2005-06.

At constant prices, the growth rate for the imports of this sub category during whole of the study period was 14.94 per cent. The growth rate for the sub period 1986-87 to 1990-91 was 33.29 per cent, which increased to 38.10 per cent for the sub period 1991-92 to 1995-96. The growth rate declined to 3.79 per cent and further to -0.04 per cent for the sub periods 1996-97 to 2000-01 and 2001-02 to 2005-06 respectively. The growth rate for the decade of 1990-91 to 1999-2000 was 15.59 per cent. The imports of this sub category grew at the rate of 6.73 per cent for the decade of 1996-97 to 2005-06.

The growth rates were highest for the sub period 1991-92 to 1995-96 both at current and constant prices. The growth rate was lowest for the sub period 1986-87 to 1990-91 at current prices, while it was negative for last sub period (2001-02 to 2005-06) at constant prices. The immediate impact was stronger than lagged impact of liberalisation policies both at current as well as constant prices.

On the whole, the higher growth rates were recorded for the category of machinery imports during study period, which also confirms about increased industrial activity in India. The sub categories of nuclear boiler machine etc. imports and electrical machinery and equipments and parts imports had grown at highest rates during 1991-92 to 1995-96, both at current and constant prices.

Transport Equipment

At current prices, the imports of this category grew at the rate 19.17 per cent during whole of the study period. The growth rate for the sub period 1986-87 to 1990-91 was 24.60 per cent, which almost doubled for the next sub period 1990-91 to 1995-96, i.e., 45.53 per cent. But the growth rate was negative, i.e., -1.45 per cent for the sub period 1996-97 to 2000-01, which abruptly increased to 59.68 per cent for the sub period 2001-02 to 2005-06. The growth rate for the decade of 1990-91 to 1999-2000 was 16.45 per cent. The imports of this category grew at the rate of 26.49 per cent during 1996-97 to 2005-06.

At constant prices, the growth rate for transport equipments imports for the study period was 8.10 per cent. The growth rate for the sub period 1986-87 to 1990-91 was 3.29 per cent, which increased to 18.00 per cent for the sub period 1991-92 to 1995-96. The growth rate declined to 5.76 per cent for the sub period 1996-97 to 2000-01, but it abruptly increased to 40.19 per cent for the sub period 2001-02 to 2005-06. The growth rate for the decade of 1990-91 to 1999-2000 was 5.86 per cent. The imports of this category grew at the rate of 18.59 per cent during 1996-97 to 2005-06.

The imports of transport equipments grew at high rates except for the sub periods 1986-87 to 1990-91 (at constant prices) and 1996-97 to 2000-01 (at current prices and constant prices). The constant prices growth rates were relatively lower and growth rate was highest during 2001-02 to 2005-06, both at current as well as constant prices. The growth rate was negative for the sub period 1996-97 to 2000-01 at current prices. The lowest growth rate at constant prices was during 1986-87 to 1990-91. The stronger immediate impact of liberalisation policies was observed for this category of imports (at current prices), whereas lagged impact was relatively stronger at constant prices.

Railway/Tramway Locomotives, Truck etc., Equipment and Parts thereof

At current prices the growth rate for whole of the study period 1986-87 to 2005-06 was 9.27 per cent. The growth rate for the sub period 1986-87 to 1990-91 was 31.31 per cent, which was negative, i.e., -5.02 per cent for the sub period 1991-92 to 1995-96. The growth rate continued to be negative, i.e., -14.69 per cent for the sub period 1996-97 to 2000-01, but abruptly increased to 72.45 per cent for the sub period 2001-02 to 2005-06. The growth rate for the decade of 1990-91 to 1999-2000 was 8.28 per cent. The imports of this sub category grew at the rate of 8.88 per cent during 1996-97 to 2005-06.

At constant prices, the growth rate for the study period was negative one i.e., -0.43 per cent. The growth rate for the sub period 1986-87 to 1990-91 was 8.85 per cent. The rate was highly negative, i.e., - 22.99 per cent for the sub period 1991-92 to 1995-96 and -8.43 per cent for the sub period 1996-97 to 2000-01. But rate abruptly increased to 86.59 per cent for the sub period 2001-02 to 2005-06. The growth rate of imports of this sub category for the decade of 1990-91 to 1999-2000 was -1.56 per cent. The imports of this sub category grew at the rate of 2.57 per cent during 1996-97 to 2005-06.

The growth rates showed high fluctuations in imports of this category. The growth rate was highest during 2001-02 to 2005-06 (current and constant prices). The growth rates for railway/ tramway, locomotives, truck etc. imports were negative for the sub periods 1991-92 to 1995-96 and 1996-97 to 2000-01, both at constant as well as current prices. There was an abrupt rise during the last sub period 2001-02 to 2005-06.

Road Vehicles and Parts

At current prices, the growth rates for the study period taken as a whole was 14.04 per cent. The growth rate for the sub period 1986-87 to 1990-91 was 9.08 per cent, which increased to 32.57 per cent for the sub period 1991-92 to 1995-96. The growth rate experienced by the sub period 1996-97 to 2000-01 was negative, i.e., -4.48 per cent, but it sharply increased to 36.38 per cent for the sub period 2001-02 to 2005-06. The growth rate for the decade of 1990-91 to 1999-2000 was 17.86 per cent. The imports of this sub category grew at the rate of 10.52 per cent during 1996-97 to 2005-06.

At constant prices, the growth rate for road vehicles and parts imports was 4.43 per cent for whole of the study period. The growth rate for the sub-period 1986-87 to 1990-91 was negative, i.e., -9.57 per cent, which sharply increased to 7.47 per cent for the sub period 1991-92 to 1995-96. Further, the growth rate declined to 2.51 per cent for the sub period 1996-97 to 2000-01, but it increased to 27.54 per cent for the sub period 2001-02 to 2005-06. The growth rate for imports of this sub category for the decade of 1990-91 to 1999-2000 was 7.14 per cent. The imports of this sub category grew at the rate of 5.40 per cent during 1996-97 to 2005-06.

The growth of the imports of road vehicles and parts imports experienced wide fluctuations. The growth rate was highest for the sub period 2001-02 to 2005-06, both at current and constant prices. The imports of this sub category grew at negative rate during 1996-97 to 2000-01 (at current prices) and 1986-87 to 1990-91 (at constant prices). The lagged impact (1996-97 to 2005-06) of liberalisation policies was much stronger at current prices.

Aircraft, Spacecraft and the Parts

At current prices, the growth rate of imports of this sub category during whole of the study period taken as a whole was 19.76 per cent. The growth rate for the sub period 1986-87 to 1990-91 was 42.93 per cent, which abruptly increased to 91.88 per cent (almost more than double) for the sub period 1991-92 to 1995-96. But suddenly the growth rate for the sub period 1996-97 to 2000-01 turned into negative rate, i.e., -18.23 per cent, which again increased to 85.66 per cent for the sub period 2001-02 to 2005-06. The growth rate for the decade of 1990-91 to 1999-2000 was 8.61 per cent. The imports of this sub category grew at the rate of 36.54 per cent during 1996-97 to 2005-06.

At constant prices, the growth rate of this sub category was 7.73 per cent for the study period taken as a whole. The growth rate for the sub period 1986-87 to 1990-91 was 18.48 per cent, which increased to 55.58 per cent (almost tripled) for the sub period 1991-92 to 1995-96. The growth rate was negative, i.e., -12.23 per cent for the sub period 1996-97 to 2000-01, which again increased to 57.48 per cent for the sub period 2001-02 to 2005-06. The growth rate for the decade of 1990-91 to 1999-2000 was -1.25 per cent. The imports of this sub category grew at the rate of 25.04 per cent during 1996-97 to 2005-06.

The growth rates for this sub category of transport equipments imports were at high level except for the sub period 1996-97 to 2000-01. At current prices, the growth rate was highest for the sub period 1991-92 to 1995-96, whereas at constant prices, the growth rate was highest for the sub period 2001-02 to 2005-06. The immediate impact (1991-92 to 1995-96) of liberalisation policies was relatively stronger one.

Ship, Boat and Floating Structure

At current prices, the growth rate of this sub category was 27.66 per cent for the study period 1986-87 to 2005-06. The growth rate for the sub period 1986-87 to 1990-91 was 12.71 per cent, which increased to 17.95 per cent for the sub period 1991-92 to 1995-96. The growth rates increased to 21.17 per cent and further to 49.90 per cent for the sub periods 1996-97 to 2000-01 and 2001-02 to 2005-06 respectively. The growth rate for the decade of 1990-91 to 1999-2000 was 26.23 per cent. The imports of this sub category grew at the rate of 33.99 per cent during 1996-97 to 2005-06.

At constant prices, the growth rate was 16.30 per cent for the study period. The growth rates for the sub periods 1986-87 to 1990-91 and 1991-92 to 1995-96 were negative, i.e., -6.56 per cent and -4.35 per cent respectively. But the growth rate sharply increased to 30.05 per cent for the sub period 1996-97 to 2000-01 and further to 37.40 per cent for the sub period 2001-02 to 2005-06. The growth rate for the decade of 1990-91 to 1999-2000 was 8.28 per cent. The imports of this sub category grew at the rate of 8.88 per cent during 1996-97 to 2005-06.

The imports of ship, boat and floating structure grew at high rates and increasing except for the sub periods 1986-87 to 1990-91 and 1991-92 to 1995-96 (at constant prices). The growth rates for these sub periods were negative. The highest growth rate was recorded during 2001-02 to 2005-06, both at current prices and constant prices. The lowest growth rate at current prices was for the sub period 1986-87 to 1990-91. The lagged impact of liberalisation policies was quite stronger than their immediate impact (1991-92 to 1995-96).

The growth rates for imports of transport equipments gave mixed results because we had both highly positive and negative rates. The period after mid 90's witnessed the increased rates, this might be due to increased demand for infrastructure with in the country. During the sub periods 1986-87 to 1990-91 and 1991-92 to 1995-96, within the category of transport equipments imports, the growth rate for the sub category of aircraft, spacecraft and parts was highest (current prices and constant prices). During 1996-97 to 2000-01, the sub category of ship boat and floating structure imports had grown at highest rate (current prices and constant prices). During 2001-02 to 2005-06, the sub categories of aircraft, spacecraft and parts imports (at current prices) and railway/tramway, locomotives, trucks imports (at constant prices) had grown at highest rate.

Instrument and Apparatus: Clocks and Watches: Parts and Accessories thereof

At current prices, the growth rate for the study period 1986-87 to 2005-06 was 17.80 per cent. The growth rate for the sub period 1986-87 to 1990-91 was 24.36 per cent, which declined to 22.94 per cent for the sub period 1991-92 to 1995-96. The growth rate for the sub period 1996-97 to 2000-01 declined to 19.81 per cent, which was marginally different from the growth rate for the sub period 2001-02 to 2005-06, i.e., 19.80 per cent. The growth rate for the decade of 1990-91 to 1999-2000 was 18.18 per cent. The imports of this category grew at the rate of 18.46 per cent during 1996-97 to 2005-06.

At constant prices, the growth rate for this category for the study period was 20.95 per cent. The growth rate for the sub period 1986-87 to 1990-91 was negative i.e., -5.22 per cent. The growth rate increased to 23.78 per cent for the sub period 1991-92 to 1995-96 and further increased to 60.69 per cent for the sub period 1996-97 to 2000-01. But rate was negative for the sub period 2001-02 to 2005-06, i.e., -11.58 per cent. The growth rate of imports of this category for the decade of 1990-91 to 1999-2000 was 37.22 per cent. The imports of this category grew at the rate of 18.27 per cent during 1996-97 to 2005-06.

The imports of this category grew at high rates except for the sub periods 1986-87 to 1990-91 and 2001-02 to 2005-06 (at constant prices). The growth rates were negative during these sub periods. At current prices, the growth rate was highest for the sub period 1986-87 to 1990-91 and lowest during 2001-02 to 2005-06. At constant prices, the growth rate was highest during 1996-97 to 2000-01. The immediate impact (1991-92 to 1995-96) was stronger than the lagged impact (1996-97 to 2005-06).

Optical Measuring, Medical and Similar Instruments and Parts thereof

At current prices, the growth rate for whole of the study period was 18.13 per cent. The growth rate for the sub period 1986-87 to 1990-91 was 25.94 per cent, which decelerated to 23.14 per cent for the sub period 1991-92 to 1995-96. The growth rate declined to 20.27 per cent and further to 19.62 per cent for the sub periods 1996-97 to 2000-01 and 2001-02 to 2005-06 respectively. The growth rate for imports of this sub category for the decade of 1990-91 to 1999-2000 was 18.21 per cent. The imports of this sub category grew at the rate of 18.75 per cent during 1996-97 to 2005-06.

At constant prices, the growth rate registered for the imports of this sub category for whole of the study period was 18.63 per cent. The growth rate for the sub period 1986-87 to 1990-91 was 16.62 per cent, which abruptly increased to 48.59 per cent (almost tripled) for the sub period 1991-92 to 1995-96. But the rate declined to 30.68 per cent for the sub period 1996-97 to 2000-01, and was negative, i.e., -15.94 per cent for the sub period 2001-02 to 2005-06. The growth rate for the decade of 1990-91 to 1999-2000 was 37.17 per cent. The imports of this sub category grew at the rate of -1.70 per cent during 1996-97 to 2005-06.

The growth rates for imports of this sub category were high except during 2001-02 to 2005-06 (at constant prices). At current prices, the highest growth rate was during 1986-87 to 1990-91 and lowest rate was during 2001-02 to 2005-06. At constant prices, the highest growth rate was for the sub period 1991-92 to 1995-96 and growth rate was negative during 2001-02 to 2005-06. The immediate impact (1991-92 to 1995-96) of liberalisation policies was stronger one.

The growth rates for the category of instruments and apparatus showed high fluctuations at constant prices, while some stability was observed in case of current prices.

Arms and Ammunition: Parts and Accessories thereof

The imports of this category grew at the rate of 21.09 per cent for the study period 1986-87 to 2005-06 at current prices. The growth rate for the sub period 1986-87 to 1990-91 was negative, i.e., -16.85 per cent, which increased to 19.96 per cent for the sub period 1991-92 to 1995-96. The growth rate decelerated to 5.77 per cent and further to 0.51 per cent for the sub periods 1996-97 to 2000-01 and 2001-02 to 2005-06 respectively. The growth rate registered for the decade of 1990-91 to 1999-2000 was 39.83 per cent. The imports of this category during 1996-97 to 2005-06, grew at the rate of 18.99 per cent.

At constant prices, the growth rate of imports of this category for whole of the study period was 22.78 per cent. The rates recorded for the sub period 1986-87 to 1990-91 was negative, i.e., -26.82 per cent, which abruptly increased to 42.61 per cent for the sub period 1991-92 to 1995-96. But growth rate declined to 15.44 per cent and further it became negligible for the sub periods 1996-97 to 2000-01 and 2001-02 to 2005-06 respectively. The growth rate registered for the decade of 1990-91 to 1999-2000 was 59.34 per cent. The imports of this category during 1996-97 to 2005-06, grew at the rate of 9.40 per cent.

The growth for category of arms and ammunition imports was fluctuating one. The highest growth rate was for the sub period 1991-92 to 1995-96 (at current prices and constant prices). The growth rates were negative and at very low level during 1986-87 to 1990-91 and 2001-02 to 2005-06 (both at current prices as well as constant prices). The immediate impact (1991-92 to 1995-96) was stronger one both at current and constant prices.

Miscellaneous Manufactured Articles

At current prices, the growth rate for this category of imports for the study period 1986-87 to 2005-06 was 27.18 per cent. The imports of this category have grown at the rate of 28.31 per cent for the sub period 1986-87 to 1990-91, which increased to 41.36 per cent for the sub period 1991-92 to 1995-96. The rate declined to 25.85 per cent for the sub period 1996-97 to 2000-01, but it again increased to 33.11 per cent for the sub period 2001-02 to 2005-06. The growth rate for the decade of 1990-91 to 1999-2000 was 30.15 per cent. The imports of this category grew at the rate of 25.71 per cent during 1996-97 to 2005-06.

At constant prices, the growth rate for this category of imports for whole of the study period was 27.13 per cent. The growth rate for the sub period 1986-87 to 1990-91 was 12.95 per cent, which sharply increased to 68.22 per cent for the sub period 1991-92 to 1995-96. The growth rate declined to 37.38 per cent and was negative, i.e., -6.34 per cent for the sub periods 1996-97 to 2000-01 and 2001-02 to 2005-06 respectively. The growth rate for the decade of 1990-91 to 1999-2000 was 48.25 per cent. The imports of this category grew at the rate of 6.67 per cent during 1996-97 to 2005-06.

For the category of miscellaneous manufactured articles imports, the growth rates were high except for the sub period 2001-02 to 2005-06 (at constant prices). The highest growth rate was during 1991-92 to 1995-96 (both at current prices and constant prices). The growth rate was lowest during 1996-97 to 2000-01 at current prices. The liberalisation measures had stronger immediate impact (1991-92 to 1995-96) on the imports of this category.

Work of Art, Collectors Pieces and Antiques

At current prices, the growth rate of this category of imports was 35.38 per cent for the study period taken as a whole. The growth rate for the sub period 1986-87 to 1990-91 was 64.16 per cent. The rate declined to 30.97 per cent for the sub period 1991-92 to 1995-96 and further it was negative, i.e., -1.06 per cent for the sub period 1996-97 to 2000-01. The growth rate abruptly increased to 88.10 per cent for the sub period 2001-02 to 2005-06. The growth rate registered for the decade of 1990-91 to 1999-2000 was 22.63 per cent. The imports of this category during 1996-97 to 2005-06, grew at the rate of 46.02 per cent. At constant prices, the growth rate for this category for whole of the study period was 33.20 per cent. The growth rate for the sub period 1986-87 to 1990-91 was 53.63 per cent, which increased to 56.41 per cent for the sub period 1991-92 to 1995-96. But it declined to 8.02 per cent and was negative, i.e., -11.34 per cent for the sub periods 1996-97 to 2000-01 and 2001-02 to 2005-06 respectively. The growth rate for the decade of 1990-91 to 1999-2000 was 39.80 per cent. The imports of this category grew at the rate of 11.12 per cent during 1996-97 to 2005-06.

The growth rates for the category of work of art, collector pieces and antiques imports, were high except negative rate for the sub periods 1996-97 to 2000-01 (at current prices) and 2001-02 to 2005-06 (at constant prices). At current prices, the growth rate was highest for the sub period 2001-02 to 2005-06 whereas at constant prices, the highest growth rate was during 1991-92 to 1995-96. The immediate impact (1991-92 to 1995-96) of liberalisation policies was relatively stronger as compared to lagged impact (1996-97 to 2005-06).

Project Goods: Some Special Uses

At current prices, the imports of this category have grown at the rate of 3.20 per cent for whole of the study period. The growth rate for the sub period 1986-87 to 1990-91 was 11.52 per cent, which increased to 22.55 per cent (almost doubled) for the sub period 1991-92 to 1995-96. But the growth rate of this category was negative, i.e., -17.80 per cent for the sub period 1996-97 to 2000-01, which increased to 8.44 per cent for the sub period 2001-02 to 2005-06. The growth rate of imports of this category for the decade of 1990-91 to 1999-2000 was 10.77 per cent. The imports of this category grew at the rate of -12.75 per cent during 1996-97 to 2005-06.

At constant prices, the growth rate of imports of project goods for the study period was 3.52 per cent. The growth rate for the sub period 1986-87 to 1990-91 was negative, i.e., -1.82 per cent, which abruptly increased to 45.84 per cent for the sub period 1991-92 to 1995-96. Further the growth rates were again negative, i.e., -10.27 per cent and -29.80 per cent for the sub periods 1996-97 to 2000-01 and 2001-02 to 2005-06 respectively. The growth rate for the decade of 1990-91 to 1999-2000 was 26.16 per cent. The imports of this category grew at the rate of -28.90 per cent during 1996-97 to 2005-06.

The growth rate for project goods imports were fluctuating for the study period. The highest growth rate was for the sub period 1991-92 to 1995-96 (at current prices and constant prices). At current prices, the growth rate was negative during sub period of 1996-97 to 2000-01. At constant prices, the growth rates were negative except during 1991-92 to 1995-96 (when rate was highly positive). The immediate impact (1991-92 to 1995-96) was very much stronger than lagged impact (1996-97 to 2005-06) of liberalisation policies.

Miscellaneous Goods

At current prices, the growth rate of imports of this category during whole of the study period was 21.81 per cent. The growth rate for the sub period 1986-87 to 1990-91 was 37.25 per cent, which declined to 25.24 per cent for the sub period 1991-92 to 1995-96. Further, growth rate again declined to 12.78 per cent for the sub period 1996-97 to 2000-01, but it increased to 49.13 per cent (almost four times) for the sub period 2001-02 to 2005-06. The growth rate for the decade of 1990-91 to 1999-2000 was 12.48 per cent. The imports of this category grew at the rate of 22.22 per cent during 1996-97 to 2005-06.

At constant prices, the growth rate for the study period taken as a whole was 21.20 per cent. The growth rate for the sub period 1986-87 to 1990-91 was 20.82 per cent, which sharply increased to 49.03 per cent for the sub period 1991-92 to 1995-96. The growth rates declined to 23.12 per cent and further to 6.50 per cent for the sub periods 1996-97 to 2001-02 and 2001-02 to 2005-06 respectively. The growth rate for the decade of 1990-91 to 1999-2000 was 28.12 per cent. The imports of this category grew at the rate of 1.42 per cent during 1996-97 to 2005-06.

At current prices, the highest growth rate was during 2001-02 to 2005-06 and lowest rate was during 1996-97 to 2000-01. At constant prices, the growth rate was highest during 1991-92 to 1995-96 and lowest during 2001-02 to 2005-06. The immediate impact (1991-92 to 1995-96) of liberalisation policies was stronger than the lagged impact (1996-97 to 2005-06) for this category of imports.

Growth rates of Indian imports and its various categories for whole of the study period give mixed results. At current price, aggregate imports grew at the rate of 19.15 per cent and at constant prices total imports grew at the rate of 10.44 per cent for the study period taken as a whole. At current prices, the imports of categories of animal or vegetable fats and oils, mineral products, hides and skins, pearls, precious and semi precious stones, machinery and their parts, arms and ammunitions, misc. manufactured products, work of arts, collector pieces and antiques and misc. goods grew at the rate, which was more than 20 per cent during the study period. The categories which grew between the rates of 15 per cent to 20 per cent were vegetable products, prepared food stuffs and beverages, products of chemical or allied industries, plastic and rubber articles, wood, cork and articles, paper and paper board, textile and textile articles, foot wears, headgears, umbrellas, stone, cement and ceramic products, transport equipments and instrumental apparatus. The rest of the categories grew at the rate which was less than 15 per cent for the study period.

Similarly, at constant prices, the categories of hides and skins, instrumental apparatus, arms and ammunition, misc. manufactured articles, project goods and work of art, collector pieces and antiques, grew at the rate which was more than 20 per cent. The categories which grew at the rate of 15 per cent to 20 per cent were wood, cork and articles, textile and textile articles, machinery and their parts, pearls, precious and semi precious stones. The category of mineral products, animal and vegetables oils and fats, products of chemical and allied industries, stone, cement and ceramic products, transport equipments, grew around 10 per cent rate for the study period. The categories of live animal and animal products, base metal and articles of base metals and project goods have grown at less than five per cent rate for the study period.

Growth rates for the sub period 1991-92 to 1995-96 give an immediate impact of liberalisation policies, whereas growth rates for the sub period of 1996-97 to 2005-06 presented the lagged impact of liberalisation policies during post 1990 period. The immediate impact of liberalisation policies was relatively stronger for total imports and also for most of the categories (both at current prices and constant prices). At current prices, the immediate impact was stronger for most of the categories except for the categories of imports of mineral products, pearls, precious and semi precious stones, metals and articles and work of art, collector pieces and antiques. At constant prices, except the categories of imports of stone, cement and similar material, pearls, precious and semi-precious stones, metals and articles and transport equipments, all other categories experienced stronger immediate impact as compared to lagged impact of liberalisation policies.

Under the group of capital goods imports, the machinery and their parts imports and project goods imports grew at higher rate during immediate impact (1991-92 to 1995-96) period, both at current prices and constant prices. The imports of transport equipments grew at higher rate during immediate impact period at current prices, whereas at constant prices the lagged impact (1996-97 to 2005-06) was stronger one. For export oriented imports of pearls, precious and semi-precious stones, metals and articles, the lagged impact period experienced higher growth rate. Under the group of industry oriented goods, the immediate impact was relatively stronger for the imports of chemical and allied industries and base metals and articles of base metals, both at current prices and constant prices. Within the imports of food items, the category of animal or vegetable fats and oils (includes edible oils) imports grew at higher rate during immediate impact (1991-92 to 1995-96) period, both at current prices and constant prices. The category of mineral products imports showed stronger lagged impact (1996-97 to 2005-06) at current prices, whereas the immediate impact (1991-92 to 1995-96) was stronger one at constant prices.

Another point to be noted down was about slower growth during sub period 1996-97 to 2000-01 for most of the categories. This was due to slowdown in Indian economy mainly because of East Asian crisis of 1997 and Russian Economic crisis of 1998. It adversely affected the Indian exports, which indirectly resulted into slowdown of Indian imports. The other factor contributed to this was sharp reduction in international oil prices in 1997-98.

Thus, the increased imports of pearls, precious and semi precious stones, machinery and their parts, mineral products and transport equipment gave an idea about increased import of exports related items, capital goods, petroleum products and infrastructure related items in total Indian imports respectively.

CHAPTER

Structure of India's Imports

The study of composition of foreign trade of a country enables us to analyse the structural changes taking place in the economy, similarly the study of composition of imports of a country enables us to analyse the structural shifts taking place in the imports of the economy. The composition of imports mainly depends upon the size of the country, the availability of resources and also on the pattern of income distribution and nature of trade policy.

In developing countries, imports of capital goods including machinery, electrical machinery and electronic goods, transport equipments and project goods are bound to increase due to industrialization. Besides these, a large volume of imports is also necessasitated by increasing incomes, rise in standard of living and consumption habits of people (Singh, 1971). The volume of imports required for development is broadly determined by five variables. These are:

(*a*) import content of investment,

(*b*) techniques of production required for development,

(*c*) export earnings,

(d) foreign exchange reserves and

(*e*) foreign aid flow (Mathur, 2003).

The structure of India's imports has also undergone a significant change with growth and changing structure of Indian economy and also due to changing policy regimes. The desire for rapid industrialization necessitated large imports of machinery, capital equipment, transport equipment and project goods. While, before Independence, manufactured commodities predominated in our imports, for a few decades now, petroleum, oil and lubricants have dominated our imports. Besides this, capital goods and other intermediary goods for export purposes have emerged as key items of imports in 1990s (Bhasin, 2005). The imports of consumer goods and food grains have been usually allowed only when they are required to meet domestic shortages and they are broadly high during the year succeeding the bad crop year. The imports of capital goods like machinery equipment have constituted an important category of imports throughout the post independence period. Imports of capital goods increased at a fast rate during the decade of 90s because of introduction of advanced technology to meet international competition, increased flow of FDI and relaxed import duties. As growth process moved, shortages or scarcities of intermediate goods leads to growing importance of these commodities (Dhingra, 2003).

Before analyzing the structure of Indian imports, it is pertinent to study the general pattern of Indian foreign trade and the change therein over time. For this purpose we have considered India's imports, exports, trade balance, share of foreign trade in GDP, share of imports in GDP, share of exports in GDP, percentage of change in imports, percentage of change in exports and ratio of imports to exports. The share of foreign trade of India in its GDP increased continuously for the study period (1986-87 to 2005-06) except for some of the years. The share of foreign trade in GDP was 11.47 per cent for the year 1986-87, which increased to 21.14 per cent for the year 1995-96 and further to 34.35 per cent for the year 2005-06. The share of foreign trade increased continuously for the years 1986-87 to 1995-96, after this it stabilized around 20 per cent up to the year 1999 to 2000, but again increased for the rest of the years.

The share of imports and exports in GDP indicates the degree of openness of the economy in regard to trade activity. The share of imports in GDP was higher than the share of exports in GDP for all the years of study period. The difference between the share of imports and exports in GDP fluctuated from one per cent to three per cent for most of the years (1986-87 to 2003-04), but for rest of the years the difference was larger one. The share of imports in GDP was 6.38 per cent and for exports it was 3.96 per cent for the year 1986-87. The share of imports in GDP increased to 10.29 per cent whereas of exports increased to 8.92 per cent for the year 1995-96. Further the share again increased to 20.90 per cent of imports in GDP and to 13.86 per cent of exports in GDP. The proportion of imports in GDP was higher than the proportion of exports in GDP for all the years of study period. There was an increase in proportion of exports in GDP for the study period but it was less than the proportion of imports in GDP, thereby reflecting the import dependence of Indian economy.

The imports of India for the study period have been continuously increasing with negative trade balance. The total imports were Rs. 20096 crs, whereas total exports were Rs. 12452 crs for the year 1986-87. Both imports and exports increased to Rs. 122678 crs and Rs. 106352 crs respectively, for the year 1995-96. For the year 2005-06, the imports increased to Rs. 660408 crs and the exports increased to Rs. 456418 crs. The higher imports as compared to exports for all the years of study period resulted into negative trade balance. The negative trade balance also gave an idea about dependence on imports of Indian economy.

The percentage of change in imports was 2.23 per cent whereas the same for exports was 14.29 per cent for the year 1986-87. The percentage of change in imports increased abruptly to 36.35 per cent and percentage of change in exports doubled, i.e., 28.64 per cent for the year 1995-96. Further the percentage of change in imports and of change in exports, both declined to 31.80 per cent and 21.60 per cent respectively for the year 2005-06. The percentage of change in imports was higher than percentage of change in exports for the years 1990-91, 1992-93, 1994-95 to 1999-2000, 2001-02 and 2003-04 to 2005-06. Further, we have considered the ratio of imports to exports which was higher than hundred for all the years of study period. It again indicated about higher imports as compared to exports of Indian economy. This ratio in terms of percentage was 161.38 per cent for the year 1986-87, but declined to 115.35 per cent for the year 1995-96. The ratio again increased to 144.69 per cent for the year 2005-06.

On the whole, the higher share of imports in GDP, negative trade balance, higher import-export ratio and fluctuating percentage of change in imports and exports strongly reflect the dependence of Indian economy on imports. The structure of Indian imports basically include the imports of petroleum products, capital goods, export oriented items and industrial raw materials. The higher international prices, increase in industrial activity due to growing investments and growing consumer demand, for promotion of exports and also for enhancement of infrastructural facilities, are some of the main reasons which led to increased imports of the above mentioned categories.

Categorywise Analysis of Structure of Imports

The changes in structure of Indian imports have been analyzed by measuring the share of various categories of imports in India's total imports (both at current and constant prices) during the study period 1986-87 to 2005-2006.

Live Animals: Animal Products

This is a minor category of imports, which witnessed wide fluctuations for the study period, as it consisted of minor imports. At current prices, this category of imports experienced a share of 0.16 per cent (Rs. 32.42 crs) for the year 1986-87, which declined to 0.02 per cent (Rs. 9.22 crs) for the year 1990-91. Further the share increased to 0.09 per cent (Rs. 117.05 crs) for the year 1995-96, but it again declined to 0.06 per cent (Rs. 146.40 crs) during the year 2000-01. The share continued to decline and it was 0.03 per cent (Rs. 204.99 crs) for the year 2005-06. The highest share was for the year 1987-88, i.e., 0.66 per cent (Rs. 148.50 crs) and lowest share was 0.02 per cent (Rs 9.22 crs) for the year 1990-91. After the year 1988-89, the share was continued to be less than 0.10 per cent except for the year 1999-2000. In value terms, imports of this category showed fluctuating trend, highest value was for the year 1999-2000, whereas lowest was for the year 1990-91 and in the same year the share of this category was also lowest (in percentage) in total imports. The share of this category in total imports was less than 0.5 per cent throughout the study period except for the year 1987-88.

At constant prices, this category experienced the share of 0.19 per cent (Rs. 91.63 crs) for the year 1986-87, which declined to 0.02 per cent (Rs. 14.05 crs.) for the year 1990-91. The share again increased to 0.18 per cent (Rs 215.87 crs) for the year 1995-96, which declined to 0.08 per cent (Rs. 128.28 crs) for the year 2000-01. The share further declined to 0.03 per cent (Rs 122.36 crs) for the year 2005-06. The highest share was for the year 1987-88, i.e., 1.53 per cent (Rs. 698.49 crs) and lowest was for the year 1990-91, i.e., 0.02 per cent (Rs 14.05 crs). In value terms, also this category showed fluctuating pattern, in some years the value was high whereas it was at very low level for some of the years.

Thus, the imports of live animals: animal products had fluctuated share in total imports, both at constant as well as current prices. This category of imports is minor one with share less than 0.5 per cent (except for the year 1987-88) for the whole the study period.

Vegetable Products

This category further is sub divided into edible vegetables and certain roots and tubers, edible fruits and nuts peel of citrus fruits or melons, cereals, coffee, tea, mate and spices, oil seeds and oleaginous fruits, miscellaneous grains, seeds and fruit, lac; gums, resins and other vegetable sobs and extracts.

The imports of this category at the current prices, recorded the share of 2.38 per cent (Rs. 478.68 crs) for year 1986-87. The share declined to 2.15 per cent (Rs. 929.59 crs) for the year 1990-91 and to 1.68 per cent (Rs. 2062.88 crs) for the year 1995-96. The share continued to decline and it was 1.24 per cent (Rs. 2871.32 crs) for the year 2000-01 and to 1.18 per cent (Rs. 7815.47 crs) for the year 2005-06. The share was highest for the year 1988-89, i.e., 4.68 per cent (Rs. 1322.42 crs) and it was lowest for the year 2005-06, i.e., 1.18 per cent (Rs 7815.47 crs). The share of this category in total imports was between 1 per cent and 2 per cent for all the years of the study period except for the year 1988-89 (the same is the year for highest share also). In value terms, the imports of this category fluctuated upto the year 2000-01, thereafter showed rising trend. However, the share of this category had declined during post 2000-01 period.

The sub-category of edible vegetables experienced more than one per cent share for first three years of study period (1986-87 to 1988-89). After this, the share was less than one per cent for all the years except for the years 2001-02 and 2002-03. The sub-category of edible fruits and nuts recorded the share between 0.40 per cent and 0.90 per cent except for the year 1994-95 when it was 1.11 per cent (Rs. 1004.73 crs). The sub category of cereals, showed share of more than 0.5 per cent for the years 1988-89, 1992-93, 1997-98 and 1998-99.

At constant prices, the share of vegetable products imports in total imports was 3.20 per cent (Rs. 1517.21 crs) for the year 1986-87, which slightly increased to 3.32 per cent (Rs. 1751.62 crs) for the year 1990-91. The share experienced a decline for the year 1995-96, i.e., 1.40 per cent (Rs 1603.10 crs). The share again increased to 1.69 per cent (Rs.2633.99 crs) for the year 2000-01, but declined to 1.10 per cent (Rs. 4008.86 crs) for the year 2005-06. The highest share was for the year 1988-89, i.e., 6.60 per cent (Rs.3276.56 crs) and lowest share was for the year 2005-06, i.e., 1.10 per cent (Rs. 4008.86 crs). The share of this category in total imports fluctuated between one per cent and 3.6 per cent for all the years of the study period except for the year 1988-89. In value terms, the imports of this category fluctuated upto the year 2000-01, thereafter, declined continuously. The sub categories of edible vegetables and edible fruits contributed more as compared to other sub categories for all the years of study period, both in terms of value as well as percentage.

Animal or Vegetable Fats and Oils and their Cleavage Products: Animal or Vegetable Waxes

This category comprises of animal or vegetable fats and oils and their cleavage products. The major import item under this category is that of edible oils. India is a leading importer of vegetable oil and world's fourth largest vegetable oil economy, due to slow growth of domestic output as compared to the demand (*World Import News*, 2007). At current prices, the share of this category in total imports was 3.33 per cent (Rs. 670.88 crs), for the year 1986-87, which abruptly decreased to 0.84 per cent (Rs. 364.26 crs) for the year 1990-91. Further, the share increased to 2.07 per cent (Rs 2550.23 crs) during the year 1995-96 and to 2.80 per cent (Rs 6467.15 crs) during the year 2000-01. The share of this category in total imports declined to 1.53 per cent (Rs. 10151.70 crs) for the year 2005-06. The highest share was for the year 1987-88, i.e., 4.56 per cent (Rs. 1016.48 crs.) and the lowest share was for the year 1992-93, i.e., 0.45 per cent (Rs. 286.99 crs). The share of this category was more than two per cent for all the years of study period except for the years 1989-90 to 1994-95, out of which the share was even more than four per cent for the years 1987-88 and 1998-99. The value of this category also indicated toward increased imports of animal or vegetable fats and oils and their cleavage products as this is an important agricultural import category, in case of which India is having high import dependence.

At constant prices, the share of this category in total imports was 5.30 per cent (Rs.2382.38 crs) for the year 1986-87 ,which declined to 1.62 per cent (Rs. 855.07 crs) for the year 1990-91.

The share further declined to 1.52 per cent (Rs. 1741.12 crs) for the year 1995-96,which increased to 4.29 per cent (Rs. 6654.81 crs) for the year 2000-01. The share again declined to 1.95 per cent (Rs. 7136.52 crs) for the year 2005-06. The highest share of this category in total imports was for the year 1987-88, i.e., 6.54 per cent (Rs. 2976.51 crs) and lowest share was for the year 1992-93, i.e., 0.41 per cent (Rs. 258.75 crs). The share of this category was more than three per cent for years 1986-87 to 1988-89, while it was less than two per cent for the years 1989-90 to 1997-98 and for rest of the years the share was more than two per cent. In value terms, there were wide fluctuations in imports of this category. In certain years imports were very high due to shortfall in domestic production of edible oils of this category within the country.

Prepared Foodstuff, Beverages and Tobacco

The share of this category fluctuated highly throughout the study period. At current prices, the share of this category in total imports was 1.40 per cent (Rs. 283.15 crs) for year 1986-87, which declined to 0.40 per cent (Rs. 172.90 crs) for the year 1990-91. The share increased to 0.53 per cent (Rs. 658.14 crs) for year 1995-96, which again declined to 0.28 per cent (Rs. 659.35 crs) for the year 2000-01. The share of this category in total imports was 0.41 per cent (Rs 2707.69 crs) for the year 2005-06. The highest share was recorded for the year 1994-95, i.e., 3.09 per cent (Rs. 2783.44 crs), whereas lowest share was 0.27 per cent (Rs. 982.41 crs) for the year of 2003-04. The share remained more than 0.30 per cent for all years of the study period except for the years 2000-01 and 2003-04. In value terms, imports of this category increased continuously for the years 1986-87 to 1994-95 (except for the year 1990 91) and showed fluctuating pattern for the rest of the study period.

At constant prices, the share of prepared foodstuffs, beverages and tobacco imports was 3.10 per cent (Rs. 1470.14 crs) for the year 1986-87. The share abruptly declined to 0.61 per cent (Rs. 323.23 crs) for the year 1990-91 and remained at same level for the year 1995-96 (in value terms, i.e., Rs. 702.31 crs). The share of this category in total imports further declined to 0.42 per cent (Rs. 656.31 crs) for the year 2000-01, which again increased to 0.61 per cent (Rs. 2247.97 crs) for the year 2005-06. The highest share of this category was for the year 1994-95, i.e., 3.48 per cent (Rs. 3151.53 crs) and lowest was for the year 1996-97, i.e., 0.38 per cent (Rs. 442.11 crs). The share of this category in total imports remained less than 1.5 per cent for all the years of study period except for the years 1986-87, 1987-88 and 1994-95. For these years, the share of prepared foodstuffs, beverages and tobacco imports was higher than 2 per cent. In value terms, the imports of this category were low and fluctuating one, except for some of the years when imports were at very high level (1994-95, 2004-05 and 2005-06).

Mineral Products

The category of mineral products is further sub divided into salt sulphur, earths and stone, plastering materials lime and cement, ores, slag and ash and mineral fuels, mineral oils and products, bituminous substances, mineral waxes. The third sub category mainly consisted of petroleum, oil and lubricant and this category witnessed highest share in total imports for all the years of study period.

At current prices, the share of mineral products imports remained more than 20 per cent for all the years of study period except the years 1986-87 and 1988-89. These imports accounted for 17.46 per cent (Rs. 3509.97 crs) of total imports for the year 1986-87, which increased to 29.65 per cent (Rs. 12,807.21 crs) for the year 1990-91. The share declined to 25.37 per cent (Rs. 31,124.59 crs) for the year 1995-96, which increased to its highest level, i.e., 36.15 per cent (Rs. 83,480.64 crs) for the year 2000-01. The share of this category in total imports decreased slightly to 35.27 per cent (Rs. 2,32,951.08 crs) for the year 2005-06. The lowest share of this category in total imports was for the year 1986-87, i.e., 17.46 per cent (Rs. 3509.97 crs) and highest share was for the year 2000-01, i.e., 36.15 per cent (Rs. 83,480.64

crs). For the years 1990-91 to 1997-98, the share of imports of this category was more than 25 per cent in total imports. However, during 1998-99 the share of this category declined to 20 per cent (Rs. 36,346.18 crs). After 1998-99, share remained at the level which was more than 30 per cent for rest of the years of study period.

The imports of sub category mineral fuels, mineral oils and products contributed highly and accounted for the largest share in total imports. The share of this sub category was 15.03 per cent (Rs. 3021.81 crs) for the year 1986-87 at current prices, which abruptly increased to 27.29 per cent (Rs. 11,788.39 crs) for the year 1990-91. The share was 23.66 per cent (Rs. 24,037.26 crs) for the year 1995-96, which increased to its highest level, i.e., 34.71 per cent (Rs. 80,153.92 crs) for the year 2000-01. The share slightly declined, i.e., 33.77 per cent (Rs. 2,22,740.23 per cent) for the year 2005-06. As compared to this, other two sub categories have lower share in total imports. In value terms, this category showed continuous increase for the years 1997-98, 1998-99 and 2001-02.

At constant prices, the share of mineral products imports in total imports was 19.57 per cent (Rs. 9253.80 crs) for the year 1986-87, which increased to 27.60 per cent (Rs. 15,447.03 crs) for the year 1990-91. The share declined to 23.18 per cent (Rs. 26,495.77 crs) for the year 2000-01. The share of this category in total imports further declined to 13.16 per cent (Rs. 48,026.19 crs) for the year 2005-06. The highest share was for the year 1991-92, i.e., 32.59 per cent (Rs. 16,506.84 crs), whereas lowest share was for the year 2005-06, i.e., 13.16 per cent (Rs. 48,026.19 crs). For all the years of study period, the share remained at the level which was higher than or equal to 19 per cent except for the year 2005-06 when it was near to 13 per cent. In value terms (at constant prices), the imports increased continuously except for some of the years (1989-90, 1999-2000 and 2000-01).

Out of three sub categories of mineral products imports, the sub category of mineral oils and products contributed much more than other two sub categories. At constant prices, it had the share of 16.84 per cent (Rs 7966.80 crs) for the year 1986-87, which increased to 25.40 per cent (Rs.13,389.81 crs) for the year 1990-91. The share was 15.59 per cent (Rs. 17823.49 crs) for the year 1995-96, which increased to 20.88 per cent (Rs. 32,374.95 crs) for the year 2000-01. The share of this sub category declined to 12.58 per cent (Rs. 45,921.08 crs) for the year 2005-06.

The category of mineral products imports showed highest share in total imports throughout the study period. This category was major contributor to inflate the bill of aggregate imports of India as our country is highly dependent upon the imports of mineral products especially of mineral fuels, mineral oils and products. The import of petroleum had increased substantially due to heavy demand in our country. The insufficiency of oil production in India necessitated large imports of petroleum, oil and petroleum product, as the expansion of industrial sector is invariably associated with a growing consumption of petroleum products. Also, price rise caused by politics for the profits of oil producing countries and gulf crisis in early nineties were equally responsible factors (Mathur, 2003). Moreover these imports are of essential nature and also helpful in developmental efforts.

Products of Chemical or Allied Industries

With the expansion and diversification of Indian industry, chemicals have emerged as another main item of imports. This category further sub divided into organic chemicals, inorganic chemicals, fertilizers and miscellaneous chemical products. The share of this category in total imports was higher than eight per cent throughout the study period.

At current prices, the share of this category in total imports for the year 1986-87 was 11.41 per cent (Rs. 2294.85 crs), which slightly declined to 10.87 per cent (Rs. 4695.60) for the year 1990-91. The share increased to 13.65 per cent (Rs. 16,754.12 crs) for the year 1995-96, but again declined to 8.47 per cent (Rs. 19,555.56 crs) for the year 2000-01. The share of this category in total imports continued to decline for the year 2005-06, i.e., 8.00 per cent (Rs. 52,853.71 crs). The highest share was for the year 1995-96, i.e., 13.65 per cent (Rs. 16,754.12 crs) and lowest share was for the year 2005-06, i.e., 8.00 per cent (Rs. 52,853.71 crs). The share of this category was more than 10 per cent for the years 1986-87 to 1997-98 (except for the year 1987-88). After the year 1997-98, the share stabilized around 8 per cent for rest of the years of the study period. In value terms, the imports of this category showed an increase except for the years 1987-88, 1996-97 and 1998-99.

At current prices, the sub category of organic chemicals imports of this category accounted for the largest share in total imports. The share of this sub category was higher than three per cent throughout the study period except for the year 1986-87. The share was even higher than five per cent for some of the years. Other important sub categories in this group were inorganic chemicals imports, fertilizers imports and misc. chemical product imports. The share of inorganic chemicals accounted for more than two per cent in total imports throughout the study period (except for the years 1987-88, 2002-03 to 2005-06). The share of fertilizers imports in total imports remained higher than 2 per cent for the years 1986-87 to 1999-2000 (except for the years 1987-88, 1988-89 and 1998-99), but share was less than 1 per cent for the years 2000-01 to 2005-06. The share of misc. chemical products imports in total imports remained less than 1 per cent throughout the study period (except for the year 1998-99).

At constant prices, the share of products of chemical or allied industries imports in total imports was 11.68 per cent (Rs. 5524.43 crs) for the year 1986-87, which declined to 10.72 per cent (Rs. 5651.90 crs) for the year 1990-91. The share further declined to 8.57 per cent (Rs. 9802.89 crs) for the year 1995-96 and to 7.59 per cent (Rs. 11,768.40) for the year 2000-01. The share continued to decline and it was 6.34 per cent (Rs. 23,163.16 crs) for the year 2005-06. The highest share was for the year 1991-92, i.e., 12.52 per cent (Rs. 6342.00 crs), whereas the lowest share was for the year 1989-90, i.e., 5.48 per cent (Rs.2784.47 crs). The share was higher than seven per cent for all the years of study period except for the years 1989-90, 2002-03 and 2005-06 (when it was fluctuating between 5% and 7%). During past eight years of study period, i.e., 1997-98 to 2005-06, the share of this category (at constant prices) fluctuated between six per cent and nine per cent. In value terms, from 1989-90 to 1997-98, the imports of this category showed continuous increase, whereas for rest of the years imports were fluctuating one.

The sub-category of organic chemicals imports contributed more as compared to other sub categories to increase the imports of chemical or allied industries. At constant prices, the share of organic chemical in total imports was higher than two per cent for the years 1986-87 to 1992-93, higher than 4 per cent from 1993-94 to 2000-01. During 2001-02 to 2005-06, the share of organic chemicals was more than 3 per cent in total imports. The highest share of organic chemicals was 9.12 per cent for the year 1999-2000. The share of sub category of inorganic chemicals imports in total imports was more than 2 per cent for the years 1986-87 to 1998-99 (except for the years 1987-88, 1995-96 and 1996-97) and less than two per cent for rest of the years of the study period. The share of fertilizers and misc. chemical products imports in total imports remained higher than 0.50 per cent throughout the study period except for some of the years.

The imports of chemicals remained at the level which was higher than eight per cent (at current prices) and seven per cent (at constant prices) for most of the years of the study period. The higher share of chemicals is due to the reason that organic and inorganic chemicals represent developmental imports (*Report on Currency and Finance*, 1994-95) and the sub category of organic chemical is the major contributor to increase chemical imports.

Plastic and Rubber

This category is comprises of plastic and articles and rubber and articles and its share in total imports mainly fluctuated around two per cent or three per cent for the study period (both at current and constant prices). At current prices, the share of this category was 2.23 per cent (Rs. 448.80 crs) for the year 1986-87, which increased to 3.42 per cent (Rs. 1478.07 crs) for the year 1990-91. The share further increased slightly, i.e., 3.46 per cent (Rs. 4249.09 crs) for the year 1995-96. The share declined to 1.86 per cent (Rs. 4298.36 crs.) for the year 2000-01, which increased to 2.21 per cent (Rs. 14599.58 crs) for the year 2005-06. The highest share was for the year 1989-90, i.e., 3.70 per cent (Rs. 1311.00 crs) and lowest share was for the year 2000-01, i.e., 1.86 per cent (Rs. 4298.36 crs.). The share of this category in total imports was higher than 2 per cent throughout the study period (except for the years 1993-94 and 2000-01). In value terms, the imports of this category increased continuously for the years 1986-87 to 1991-92 and 2001-02 to 2005-06 and were fluctuating one for the years 1992-93 to 2000-01.

The sub-category of plastic and articles had the largest share within this category of imports whereas the sub category of rubber and articles had smaller share in total imports at current prices. The share of sub category of plastic and articles imports was more than two per cent up to the year 1996-97. After the year 1996-97, the share fluctuated between one per cent and two per cent.

At the constant prices, the share of imports of plastic and rubber articles for the year 1986-87 was 3.16 per cent (Rs. 1497.53 crs), which increased slightly to 3.31 per cent (Rs. 1748.16 crs) for the year 1990-91 .The share declined to 2.62 per cent (Rs. 2994.84 crs) for the year 1995-96 and to 1.51 per cent (Rs. 2345.75 crs) for the year 2000-01. The share increased to 2.01 per cent (Rs. 7357.91 crs) for the year 2005-06. The highest share was for the year 1989-90, i.e., 3.49 per cent (Rs. 1775.94 crs), whereas the lowest share was for the year 2000-01, i.e., 1.51 per cent (Rs. 2345.75 crs). The share was higher than 2 per cent for all the years of study period except for the years 1997-98, 2000-01 and 2001-02. In value terms, the imports of this category showed continuous increase for the years 1993-94 to 1996-97 and 2000-01 to 2005-06.

The sub-category of plastic and articles imports had larger share as compared to the imports of rubber and articles. The share of plastic and articles imports in total imports was more than one per cent, whereas share of rubber and articles imports was less than one per cent throughout the study period at constant prices.

Hides and Skins: Leather Products, Furskins and Articles thereof

The share of this category was less than 0.50 per cent at current prices throughout the study period and somewhat higher than 0.50 per cent for some of the years of study period at constant prices. At current prices, the share of this category in total imports was 0.09 per cent (Rs. 18.78 crs) for the year 1986-87, which increased to 0.45 per cent (Rs. 195.13 crs) for the year 1990-91. The share was 0.38 per cent (Rs. 468.00 crs) for the year 1995-96, which slightly increased for the year 2000-01, i.e., 0.39 per cent (Rs. 913.54 crs). The share further declined to 0.22 per cent (Rs 1487.66 crs) for the year 2005-06. The highest share was for the year 1990-91, i.e., 0.45 per cent (Rs. 195.13 crs) whereas lowest share was for the year 1986-87, i.e., 0.09 per cent (Rs. 18.78 crs). Because the share of this category was less than 0.50 per cent in total imports, it can be described as minor category of imports. In value terms, this category showed continuous increase in imports throughout the study period.

At constant prices, the share of hides and skins: leather products, furskins and articles imports in total imports was 0.08 per cent (Rs. 40.89 crs) for the year 1986-87, which increased to 0.46 per cent (Rs. 244.24 crs) for the year 1990-91. The share further increased to 0.75 per cent (Rs. 856.98 crs) for the year 1996-97 and to 1.95 per cent (Rs. 3028.97 crs) for the year 2000-01. The share declined to 0.28 per cent (Rs. 1032.95 crs) for the year 2005-06. The highest share was for the year 2000-01, i.e., 1.95 per cent (Rs. 3028.97 crs), whereas lowest share was for the year 1986-87, i.e., 0.08 per cent (Rs. 40.89 crs). The share of this category in total imports was less than 0.50 per cent for the years 1986-87 to 1993-94 and 2003-04 to 2005-06, for the rest of the years the share fluctuated around 1 per cent. In value terms (at constant prices), the imports of this category increased up to the year 2000-01 (except for the years 1991-92 and 1998-99) and the imports showed declining pattern for the years 2001-02 to 2005-06.

Wood, Cork and Articles thereof, Manufacturing of Plaiting Material: Basketware and Wicker Work

This category witnessed wide fluctuations throughout the study period. At current prices, this category of imports had experienced the share of 0.65 per cent in total imports (Rs. 131.77 crs) for the year 1986-87, which increased to 1.06 per cent (Rs. 459.73 crs) for the year 1990-91. The share declined to 0.68 per cent (Rs. 843.23 crs) for the year 1995-96, which increased to 0.97 per cent (Rs. 2253.14 crs) for the year 2000-01. The share again declined to 0.64 per cent (Rs. 4245.50 crs) for the year 2005-06. The highest share was for the year 1988-89, i.e., 1.29 per cent (Rs. 365.40 crs) and lowest share was for the year 1993-94, i.e., 0.62 per cent (Rs. 454.22 crs). The share of this category was higher than 0.50 per cent for all the years of study period and even more than 1 per cent for the years 1987-88 to 1990-91, 1997-98 and 2001-02. In value terms, the imports of this category were increasing continuously throughout the study period except for the years 1991-92, 1992-93 and 2002-03.

At constant prices, the share of this category in total imports was 0.60 per cent (Rs. 286.95 crs) for the year 1986-87, which increased to 1.09 per cent (Rs. 575.45 crs) for the year 1990-91. The share increased to 1.35 per cent (Rs. 1544.09 crs) for the year 1995-96 and abruptly increased to 4.81 per cent (Rs. 7470.62 crs) for the year 2000-01. Thereafter the imports of this category declined and its share declined to 0.80 per cent (Rs. 2947.85 crs) for the year 2005-06. The highest share was for the year 2000-01, i.e., 4.81 per cent (Rs. 7470.62 crs), whereas lowest share was for the year 1986-87, i.e., 0.60 per cent (Rs. 286.95 crs). For the years 1988-89 to 1990-91 and 1992-93 to 2004-05, the share was higher than 1 per cent, for the rest of the years it was lower than one per cent. In value terms, the imports of this category showed wide fluctuations especially during 2000-01 to 2005-06 period.

Paper and Paper Board and Articles thereof

The imports of various categories of paper, mostly specialty paper are a regular feature of Indian economy, in order to fill the gap between demand and production of paper and paper board (Sarma, 1999). This category of imports is comprises of commodities like pulp of wood or of other material, paper and paper board: articles of paper, of paper pulp and paper board. The share of this category mostly fluctuated between 1 per cent and 3 per cent for most of the years of the study period.

At current prices, this category of imports witnessed the share of 2.64 per cent (Rs. 531.16 crs) for the year 1986-87. The share slightly declined, i.e.; 2.41 per cent (Rs. 1042.64 crs) for the year 1990-91. The share for the year 1995-96 was 2.28 per cent (Rs. 2807.63 crs), which declined to 1.81 per cent (Rs. 4200.07 crs) for the year 2000-01. Further, the share declined to 1.31 per cent (Rs. 8697.12 crs) for the year 2005-06. The highest share was for the year 1987-88, i.e., 2.66 per cent (Rs. 592.74 crs) and the lowest share was for the year 2005-06, i.e., 1.31 per cent (Rs. 8697.12 crs). The share was more than 1.5 per cent for all the years of the study period except last two years (2004-05 and 2005-06). The share was more than 2 per cent for the years 1986-87 to 1990-91 and 1995-96 to 1998-99. In value terms, the imports of this category indicated continuous increase except for the year 1991-92.

The sub-category of pulp of wood or of other material recorded the share which was less than 1 per cent for all the years of study period (except for the years 1986-87, 1987-88 and 1990-91). The share of sub category of paper and paper board imports fluctuated between 0.80 per cent and 1.28 per cent except for the years 2002-03, 2004-05 and 2005-06.

At constant prices, the share of this category was 3.35 per cent (Rs. 1586.49 crs) for the year 1986-87, which declined to 2.47 per cent (Rs. 1301.83 crs) for the year 1990-91. The share further declined to 1.25 per cent (Rs. 1434.07 crs) for the year 1995-96. The share increased to 1.50 per cent (Rs. 2332.2 crs) for the year 2000-01, but again declined to 1.29 per cent (Rs. 4724.89 crs) for the year 2005-06. The highest share was for the year 1986-87, i.e., 3.35 per cent (Rs. 1586.49 crs) and lowest share was for the year 1995-96, i.e., 1.25 per cent (Rs. 1434.07 crs). The share was higher than 2 per cent for the years 1986-87 to 1988-89, 1990-91, 1997-98 and 2003-04. For rest of the years, the share was higher than 1 per cent but less than 2 per cent. In value terms, the imports of this category have been fluctuating throughout the study period.

The sub-category of paper and paper board contributed more as compared to sub category of pulp of wood or of other material. The sub category of paper and paper board had more than 0.70 per cent share for all the years of study period except for the year 2005-06.

Textiles and Textile Articles

This category of imports is sub divided into silk, wool, fine or coarse animal hair, cotton and man-made filaments. The share witnessed by this category was higher than two per cent, except for some of the years of study period. At current prices, the share for this category in total imports was 1.87 per cent (Rs. 373.99 crs) for the year 1986-87, which increased to 2.07 per cent (Rs. 896.08 crs) for the year 1990-91. The share increased to 2.65 per cent (Rs. 3259.55 crs) for the year 1995-96, which declined to 2.31 per cent (Rs. 5347.29 crs) for the year 2000-01. The share declined to 1.79 per cent (Rs 11838.33 crs) for the year 2005-06. The highest share was for the year 1994-95, i.e., 3.29 per cent (Rs. 2963.25 crs) and lowest share was for the year 1991-92, i.e., 1.72 per cent (Rs. 826.33 crs). The share of textiles and textile articles imports in total imports was more than 2 per cent for all the years of study period (except the years 1986-87, 1991-92 and 2005-06). In value terms, the imports of this category recorded continuous increase except for the years 1991-92 and 1996-97.

The sub-category of wool, fine or coarse animal hair had highest share in total imports for the years 1986-87 to 1997-98 (except for the year 1994-95). For the years 1994-95 to 2004-05, the sub category of cotton had the highest share, whereas the man made filaments imports accounted for highest share in total imports within the category of textiles and textiles articles imports.

At constant prices, this category witnessed the share of 1.40 per cent (Rs. 664.16 crs) in total imports for the year 1986-87, which increased to 2.37 per cent (Rs. 1251.50 crs) for the year 1990-91. The share declined slightly to 2.12 per cent (Rs. 2424.17 crs) for the year 1995-96, which increased to 2.53 per cent (Rs. 3927.21 crs) for the year 2000-01. The share increased slightly to 2.58 per cent (Rs. 9416.42 crs) for the year 2005-06. The highest share was 4.17 per cent (Rs. 6794.85 crs) for the year 2001-02, whereas lowest share was for the year 1986-87, i.e., 1.40 per cent (Rs. 664.16 crs). The share was higher than 2 per cent for the study period (except for the years 1986-87, 1991-92, 1996-97 and 1997-98). In value terms, the imports of textile and articles had fluctuated for the years 1986-87 to 1995-96, whereas from 1996-97 to 2005-06 imports of this category increased continuously (except for the years 2000-01 and 2002-03).

The sub-category of wool had highest share as compared to other sub categories for the years 1986-87 to 1997-98 (except for the year 1994-95). For the years 1994-95 and from 1998-99 to 2004-05, the sub category of cotton showed highest share whereas the sub category of man made filaments had the highest share for the year 2005-06.

Footwear, Headgear, Umbrellas: Prepared Feathers and Articles thereof

The share of imports of this category in total imports was lower than 0.50 per cent throughout the study period so it was minor category of imports. The imports of this category recorded the share of 0.08 per cent (Rs. 16.53 crs) for the year 1986-87. The share remained at same level, i.e., 0.08 per cent (Rs. 35.09 crs) for the year 1990-91, which increased to 0.10 per cent (Rs. 130.09 crs) for the year 1995-96. The share of this category in total imports again declined to 0.06 per cent (Rs. 159.82 crs) for the year 2000-01, which increased slightly to 0.07 per cent (Rs. 470.69 crs) for the year 2005-06. The highest share was for the year 1996-97, i.e., 0.32 per cent (Rs. 109.37 crs) and the lowest share was 0.05 per cent (Rs. 152.29 crs) for the year 2002-03. The share of this category was less than 0.10 per cent for all the years of study period (except 1993-94 to 1996-97). In value terms, the imports of this category increased continuously for the years 1986-87 to 1995-96, thereafter the imports increased but with downfall in some of the years (1996-97 and 2001-02).

At constant prices, the share experienced by imports of footwear, headgear, umbrellas, prepared feathers and articles thereof was 0.07 per cent (Rs. 35.99 crs) for the year 1986-87, which increased to 0.09 per cent (Rs. 49.00 crs) for the year 1990-91. The share increased to 0.21 per cent (Rs. 238.21 crs) for the year 1995-96 and to 0.34 per cent (Rs. 529.9 crs) for the year 2000-01. The share of this category declined to 0.09 per cent (Rs. 326.82 crs) for the year 2005-06. The highest share was for the year 2000-01, i.e., 0.34 per cent (Rs. 529.9 crs) and lowest share was 0.05 per cent for the years 1987-88 (Rs. 24.04 crs) and 1988-89 (Rs. 25.90 crs). The share was low and fluctuating one for all the years of study period. In value terms, the imports of this category increased for the study period except for the years 1991-92, 1996-97, 1998-99 and 2001-02 to 2003-04.

Stone, Cement and Similar Material: Ceramic Products, Glass and Glassware

This category consists of articles of stone, plaster, cement, asbestos, mica or similar material, ceramic products and glass and glass ware. The share of this category was higher than 0.50 per cent throughout the study period.

At current prices, the share of this category in total imports recorded as 0.54 per cent (Rs. 110.48 crs) for the year 1986-87, which declined to 0.46 per cent (Rs. 202.06 crs) for the year 1990-91. The share continued to decline, i.e., 0.41 per cent (Rs. 504.89

crs) for the year 1995-96 and 0.36 per cent (Rs. 849.35 crs) for the year 2000-01. The share increased to 0.45 per cent (Rs. 2992.01crs) for the year 2005-06. The highest share was 0.57 per cent (161.43 crs) for the year 1988-89 and lowest share was 0.32 per cent (Rs. 457.86 crs) for the year 1996-97. The share for all the years of study period was more than 0.30 per cent. In value terms, the imports of this category in total imports showed continuous increase for all the years of study period (except for the years 1986-87 and 1996-97).

The sub-category of glass and glassware imports contributed highest share in total imports throughout the study period as compared to other two sub categories within the category of stone, cement and similar material: ceramic products, glass and glassware imports at current prices.

At constant prices, the share of this category in total imports was 1.28 per cent (Rs. 609.71 crs) for the year 1986-87, which declined to 0.75 per cent (Rs. 399.56 crs) for the year 1990-91. The share further declined to 0.42 per cent (Rs. 486.50 crs) for the year 1995-96 and to 0.30 per cent (Rs. 478.26 crs) for the year 2000-01. The share increased to 1.30 per cent (Rs. 4742.44 crs) for the year 2005-06. The highest share for this category in total imports was for the year 2005-06, i.e., 1.30 per cent (Rs. 4742.44 crs) and lowest share was for the year 2000-01, i.e., 0.30 per cent (Rs. 478.26 crs). The share was more than 0.70 per cent for the years 1986-87 to 1991-92, 1999-2000 and 2002-03 to 2005-06. For the rest of the years (1992-93 to 1998-99 and 2000-01 to 2001-02), the share was less than 0.70 per cent. In value terms, this category showed fluctuating imports for the years 1986-87 to 1991-92, whereas the imports increased continuously for the years 1992-93 to 2005-06 (except for the year 2000-01).

The sub-category of glass and glassware contributed highest share in total imports as compared to other sub categories throughout the study period within this category of imports at constant prices.

Pearls, Precious and Semi Precious Stones, Metals and Articles thereof: Imitation, Jewellery and Coins

This is another major category of imports in India. Imports of this category are mainly serving the export oriented industries of pearls, precious and semi precious stones, metals and articles thereof. The share of this category in total imports was higher than seven per cent, almost throughout the study period. The share experienced by this export related category in total imports was 7.73 per cent (Rs. 1555.33 crs) for the year 1986-87. The share showed an increase, i.e., 8.70 per cent (Rs. 3758.94 crs) for the year 1990-91. The share declined slightly for the year 1995-96, i.e., 8.23 per cent (Rs. 10104.17 crs). Further, the share of this category in total imports doubled and increased to 19.20 per cent (Rs. 44347.58 crs) for the year 2000-01, which declined to 13.87 per cent (Rs. 91604.14 crs) for the year 2005-06. The highest share was for the year 1998-99, i.e., 21.17 per cent (Rs. 37769.04 crs) and the lowest share was 7.73 per cent (Rs. 1555.33 crs) for the year 1986-87. The share of this export-oriented category fluctuated between seven per cent and 12 per cent for the years 1986-87 to 1996-97. For rest of the years, the share remained at the level which was more than 17 per cent (except for the years 1997-98 and 2005-06). In value terms, the imports of this export oriented category showed a continuous increase except for some of the years (1990-91, 1994-95, 2000-01 and 2005-06).

At constant prices, the share of this export oriented item in total imports was 7.47 per cent (Rs. 3533.23 crs) for the year 1986-87, which increased to 9.03 per cent (Rs. 4906.59 crs) for the year 1990-91. The share declined to 6.23 per cent (Rs. 7126.15 crs) for the year 1995-96, which abruptly increased to 19.55 per cent (Rs. 30321.05 crs) for the year 2000-01. The share declined to 11.60 per cent (Rs. 42328.97 crs) for the year 2005-06. The highest share of this category in total imports was for the year 1999-2000, i.e., 21.82 per cent (Rs. 34178.03 crs) and lowest share was for the year 1995-96, i.e, 6.23 per cent (Rs. 7126.15 crs).

From 1986-87 to 1996-97, the share fluctuated between 6 per cent and 12 per cent, but the share was higher than 19 per cent for rest of the years (except for the years 1997-98 and 2005-06). In value terms, the imports of this category increased continuously except for the years 1990-91, 1991-92, 1994-95, 2000-01 and 2005-06 at constant prices.

Base metals and Articles of Base Metals

Metal imports are an important raw material for many industries. Imports of this category depend upon the pace of industrial development, infrastructural development and growth in the economy. This category of imports is sub-divided into iron and steel, articles of iron and steel, copper and articles thereof and aluminum and articles thereof. Out of these, the imports of iron and steel highly contributed to increase the imports of this category. The share of this category was higher in mid 80's as compared to the period after 1990-91.

At current prices, the imports of this category experienced the share of 13.50 per cent (Rs. 2714.49 crs) for the year 1986-87. The share declined to 11.20 per cent (Rs. 4841.27 crs) for the year 1990-91 and further to 8.86 per cent (Rs. 10880.62 crs) for the year 1995-96. The share of this category in total imports declined continuously and it was 4.34 per cent (Rs. 10038.25 crs) for the year 2000-01. The share increased to 6.60 per cent (Rs. 43637.98 crs) for the year 2005-06. The highest share was for the year 1986-87, i.e., 13.50 per cent (Rs. 2714.49 crs) and lowest share was for the year 2002-03, i.e., 4.33 per cent (Rs. 12879.58 crs). The share of this category continued to fluctuate between 11 per cent and 13 per cent for the years 1986-87 to 1990-91, also between 6 per cent and 8 per cent for the years 1991-92 to 1998-99. However, the share declined and was around 4 per cent for the years 1999-2000 to 2003-04 but showed increasing trend for the remaining two years. In value terms, the imports showed decline for the years 1987-88, 1991-92, 1997-98, 1998-99 and 2000-01.

The sub-category of iron and steel imports had highest contribution to increase the imports of base metals and articles of base metals. The share of this sub category in total imports was more than five per cent for the years 1986-87 to 1990-91 and fluctuated around four per cent for the years 1991-92 to 1995-96. Thereafter, share fluctuated around two per cent up to the year 2003-04, but was higher than three per cent for last two years of the study period. The share of other sub categories of base metal and articles of base metal imports in total imports mostly fluctuated around one per cent or two per cent throughout the study period.

At constant prices, the share of this category in total imports was 16.50 per cent (Rs. 7804.74 crs.) for the year 1986-87 and it declined to 12.48 per cent (Rs. 6550.92 crs.) for the year 1990-91. The share further declined to 7.46 per cent (Rs. 8531.81 per cent crs) for the year 1995-96 and to 6.60 per cent (Rs. 10246.24 crs.) for the year 2000-01. The share continued to decline and it was 3.98 per cent (Rs. 14545.94 crs.) for the year 2005-06. The highest share was the for year 1988-89, i.e., 16.66 per cent (Rs. 8273.24 crs) and lowest share was 3.48 per cent (Rs. 5449.74 crs.) for the year 1999-2000. The share was higher than 11 per cent for the year 1986-87 to 1990-91 and the share fluctuated between seven per cent and 9 per cent for the years 1991-92 to 1998-99. For the years 2000-01 to 2004-05, the share fluctuated around five per cent or 6 per cent and for years 1999-2000 and 2005-06 it fluctuated between three per cent and four per cent. In value terms, the imports of this category increased for the study period except for the years 1987-88, 1991-92, 1997-98, 1998-99 and 2000-01.

The sub category of iron and steel accounted for largest share in total imports. At constant prices, the share of this sub category was higher than five per cent for the years 1986-87 to 1991-92. Further the share was higher than three per cent for the years 1992-93 to 1995-96 and for the rest of the years, the share fluctuated from one per cent to two per cent.

Machinery and Their Parts, Electrical and Electronic Equipments, Parts thereof

This is a major category of capital goods imports, which plays a significant role in industrial and overall economic development of a country. This category is sub divided into machinery and mechanical apparatus parts, electric machinery and equipment and parts thereof and nuclear reactor, boiler etc.

At current prices, the share of this category in total imports was 19.92 per cent (Rs. 4003.77 crs) for the year 1986-87, which declined to 13.48 per cent (Rs. 5823.23 crs) for the year 1990-91. The share increased to 17.21 per cent (Rs. 21119.57 crs) for the year 1995-96, but share again declined to 13.68 per cent (Rs. 31588.28 crs) for the year 2000-01. The share of this category increased to 17.30 per cent (Rs. 114287.17 crs) for the year 2005-06. The highest share for this category in total imports was for the year 1987-88, i.e., 17.49 per cent (Rs. 3891.04 crs). The lowest share was for the year 1991-92, i.e., 11.48 per cent (Rs. 5496.63 crs). The share showed declining pattern for the years 1986-87 to 1991-92. Thereafter, the share was more than 12 per cent up to the year 2001-02 and even more than 16 per cent for last four years (2002-03 to 2005-06) of the study period. The value of imports of this category experienced a continuous increase for all the years of study period except for the years 1987-88, 1991-92 and 1996-97. The value of machinery and their parts imports was Rs 4003.77 crs for the year 1986-87, which increased to Rs.114287.17 crs for the year 2005-06.

The sub-category of nuclear reactor contributed much to increase the imports of this category. The share of above mentioned sub category in total imports remained around 8 per cent for all the years of study period (except for the years 1991-92, 1992-93 and 1999-2000). The second sub category of electrical machinery equipments imports showed declining trend upto the year 1993-94. The share for this sub category in total imports was more than 4 per cent upto year 1999-2000 and more than 5 per cent for remaining years of study period (except for the year 2004-05).

At constant prices, the imports of this category in total imports witnessed the share of 12.18 per cent (Rs. 5762.47 crs.) for the year 1986-87. The share increased slightly for the year 1990-91, i.e., 12.51 per cent (Rs. 6597.81 crs.), which abruptly increased to 21.31 per cent (Rs. 24367.79 crs.) for the year 1995-96. The share of this category in total imports declined to 15.01 per cent (Rs. 23281.45 crs.) for the year 2000-01, but further increased to 27.57 per cent (Rs. 100596.10 crs.) for the year 2005-06. The highest share was 27.95 per cent (Rs. 13426.76 crs) for the year 1994-95 and lowest share was 11.22 per cent (Rs. 25078.87 crs.) for the year 1998-99.The share of imports of machinery and their parts in total imports fluctuated for the years 1986-87 to 1993-94, whereas share declined continuously for the years 1994-95 to 1998-99. For rest of the years, share of this category increased and was higher than 13 per cent. In value terms, the imports of this category were Rs. 5762.47 crs during 1986-87, which increased to Rs. 25309.63 crs for the year 1993-94 and further to Rs. 100596.10 crs for the year 2005-06.

The share of sub category of nuclear reactors, boilers, machinery etc. imports in total imports increased up to the year 1994-95 except for the years 1990-91 and 1991-92. For the rest of the years, the share showed fluctuating trend. The sub category of electrical equipments imports showed share between 1 per cent and 4 per cent except some of the years (1994-95, 1997-98 and 2002-03).

The share and value of category of machinery imports are bound to increase in a developing economy like India as these imports are essential for progress of any developing economy. Moreover, imports of this category depend upon nature of trade policy and growth of domestic industry and exports sector.

Transport Equipments

This category of imports also falls under capital goods sector. Transport equipment imports comprises of railway/ tramway locomotives, truck etc, road vehicles and parts, aircraft, spacecraft and parts and ship, boat and floating structure. The share of this category in total imports remained at the level which was higher than two per cent throughout the study period (except for some of the years in case of current prices).

At current prices, the imports of this category showed the share of 3.93 per cent (Rs. 789.98 crs) for the year 1986-87. The share slightly declined to 3.86 per cent (Rs. 1670.31 crs) for the year 1990-91 and further to 3.01 per cent (Rs. 3704.59 crs) for the year 1995-96. The share declined to 1.88 per cent (Rs. 4361.26 crs) for the year 2000-01, however it increased to 5.93 per cent (Rs. 39177.05 crs) for the year 2005-06. The highest share of imports of transport equipments in total imports was for the year 2005-06, i.e., 5.93 per cent (Rs. 39177.05 crs) and lowest share was 1.88 per cent (Rs. 3369.21 crs) for the year 1998-99 and (Rs. 4361.26 cr) for the year 2000-01. The share was more than two per cent for all the years of study period except the years 1991-92, 1998-99 and 2000-01. In value terms, the imports of this category fluctuated for the years 1986-87 to 2000-01. Afterwards the category of imports of transport equipments showed continuously increasing values for rest of the years of the study period.

The sub-categories of road vehicles and parts and aircraft, spacecraft and parts had the largest share within this category whereas the sub categories of tramway/railway locomotives, truck etc imports and ship, boat and floating structure had smaller share in total imports. The share of sub category of road vehicles and parts was more than or near to 1 per cent for the years 1986-87 to 1997-98 but for the period 1998-99 onwards the share was between 1 per cent and 0.50 per cent. Similarly, the sub category of aircraft, spacecraft etc. also experienced the share which was more than 0.50 per cent except for some of the years of study period.

At constant prices, the share of transport equipments imports in aggregate imports was 6.72 per cent (Rs. 3177.71 crs.) for the year 1986-87. The share declined to 5.71 per cent (Rs. 3011.19 crs.) for the year 1990-91 and to 2.37 per cent (Rs. 2709.42 crs.) for the year 1995-96. The share slightly increased to 2.48 per cent (Rs. 3853.72 crs) for the year 2000-01 and to 5.27 per cent (Rs. 19231.77 crs) for the year 2005-06. The highest share of this category in total imports was for the year 1986-87, i.e., 6.72 per cent (Rs. 3177.71 crs.), whereas lowest share was for the year 1998-99, i.e., 2.03 per cent (Rs. 2910.51 crs). The share of these imports fluctuated between three per cent and six per cent for the years 1986-87 to 1990-91 and between two per cent and five per cent for the years 1991-92 to 2005-06. In value terms, the imports of transport equipments fluctuated for the years 1986-87 to 1999-2000, but experienced an increase for the years 2000-01 to 2005-06.

The sub-category of road vehicles imports had the highest share in transport equipment imports for the years 1986-87 to 1992-93 and 1996-97 to 1998-99. The sub category of aircraft, spacecraft etc imports accounted for highest share for the years 1993-94 to 1995-96, 2002-03 and 2005-06. The sub category of ship, boat etc imports accounted for highest share for the years 1999-2000 to 2001-02, 2003-04 and 2004-05.

Instruments and Apparatus: Clocks and Watches Parts and Accessories thereof

The major part of share of this category consists of optical measuring, medical and similar instruments and parts thereof. At current prices, the imports of this category showed the share of 2.46 per cent (Rs. 495.84 crs) in total imports for the year 1986-87. The share slightly increased to 2.50 per cent (Rs. 1083.56 crs) for the year 1990-91, which declined to 2.05 per cent (Rs. 2526.06 crs) for the year 1995-96. Further, it declined to 1.96 per cent (Rs. 4533.55 crs) for the year 2000-01 and to 1.83 per cent (Rs. 12,125.33 crs) for year 2005-06. The highest share of imports of this category was for the year 1989-90, i.e., 2.63 per cent (Rs. 934.61 crs) and lowest share was for the year 1996-97, i.e., 1.54 per cent (Rs. 2143.10 crs). The share was higher than 2 per cent for the years 1986-87 to 1992-93. After the year 1992-93, share of this category fluctuated between 1.5 per cent and 2.36 per cent. In value terms, the imports of this category experienced fluctuations for the years 1986-87 to 1997-98, but afterwards imports of instruments and apparatus continuously increased for rest of the years of the study period.

The major sub-category within this category was optical measuring, medical and similar instruments and parts thereof showed higher than two per cent share for the years 1986-87 to 1990-91, 1992-93, 1998-99, 2001-02 and 2002-03. For rest of the years, the share of this sub category in total imports was less than 2 per cent but higher than 1 per cent.

At constant prices, the share of instruments and apparatus: clocks, watches etc. imports in total imports was 4.66 per cent (Rs. 2203.73 crs) for the year 1986-87. The share declined to 3.07 per cent (Rs. 1619.67 crs) for the year 1990-91 and further to 2.72 per cent (Rs. 3111.29 crs) for the year 1995-96. The share abruptly increased to 11.95 per cent (Rs. 18534.54 crs) for the year 2000-01, but again declined to 3.48 per cent (Rs. 12,727.33 crs) for the year 2005-06. The highest share of this category was 14.86 per cent (Rs. 24,179.90 crs) for the year 2001-02, whereas lowest share was 1.96 per cent (Rs. 2232.62 crs) for the year 2005-06. The share was higher than one per cent, but less than five per cent for the years 1986-87 to 1996-97 and 2005-06. The share was higher than six per cent for the rest of the years (1997-98 to 2004-05). In value terms, the imports of this category had fluctuated for the years 1986-87 to 2001-02 and declined for rest of the years of study period (except for the year 2003-04).

The sub-category of optical measuring, medical instruments and similar parts imports showed higher than three per cent share for the period 1994-95 onward, whereas share was less than three per cent for the years 1986-87 to 1993-94.

Arms and Ammunition: Parts and Accessories thereof

At current prices, this category had a very small share in total imports so it can be considered as minor category of imports. The share of this category in total imports was 0.005 per cent (Rs. 1.09 crs) for the year 1986-87. The share further declined to 0.001 per cent (Rs. 0.28 crs) for the year 1990-91, which remained at same level, i.e., 0.001 per cent (Rs. 1.67 crs) for the year 1995-96. The share was again at the same level, i.e., 0.001 per cent (Rs. 1.96 crs) for the year 2000-01 and 0.001 per cent (Rs. 4.88 crs) for the year 2005-06. In value terms, the imports of this category fluctuated for the years 1986-87 to 1998-99, but experienced an increase for the rest of the years of study period.

At constant prices, the share of imports of arms, ammunition: parts and accessories thereof was 0.005 per cent (Rs. 2.37 crs) for the year 1986-87, which declined to 0.001 per cent (Rs. 0.35 crs) for the year 1990-91. The share was 0.003 per cent (Rs. 3.05 crs) for the year 1995-96 and slightly increased to 0.004 per cent (Rs. 6.49 crs) for the year 2000-01. The share was 0.001 per cent (Rs. 3.38 crs) for the year 2005-06. The highest share was 0.010 per cent (Rs. 16.08 crs) for the year 1999-2000 and the share for the year 1988-89 was almost zero. This category had negligible, low and highly fluctuated share in total imports.

Miscellaneous Manufactured Articles

At current prices, this category had less than 0.50 per cent share in the total imports throughout the study period (except for some of the years at constant prices). At current prices, the share of this category in total imports was 0.10 per cent (Rs. 20.91 crs) for the year 1986-87. The share increased to 0.12 per cent (Rs. 54.92 crs) for the year 1990-91. The share further increased to 0.20 per cent (Rs. 251.16 crs) for the year 1995-96 and to 0.27 per cent (Rs. 631.74 crs) for the year 2000-01. The share of this category in total imports increased to 0.34 per cent (Rs. 2259.63 crs) for the year 2005-06. The highest share was for the year 2000-01, i.e., 0.27 per cent (Rs. 631.74 crs) and lowest share was for the year 1986-87, i.e., 0.10 per cent (Rs. 20.91 crs). The share of this category fluctuated between 0.10 per cent and 0.14 per cent for the years 1986-87 to 1993-94, the share was equal to or more than 0.20 per cent for the rest of the years of study period. Although, the value of imports of miscellaneous articles had shown continuous increase throughout the study period, but at the same time it was at very low level.

At constant prices, the share of miscsllaneous manufactured articles imports was 0.09 per cent (Rs. 45.53 crs) for the year 1986-87. The share increased to 0.13 per cent (Rs. 68.74 crs) for the year 1990-91 and further increased to 0.40 per cent (Rs. 459.91

crs) for the year 1995-96. The share increased to 1.35 per cent (Rs. 156.53 crs) for the year 2000-01 and declined to 0.43 per cent (Rs. 1568.53 crs) for the year 2005-06. The highest share was for the year 2000-01, i.e., 1.35 per cent (Rs. 156.53 crs) and lowest share was 0.09 per cent for the years 1986-87 (Rs. 45.53 crs) and 1987-88 (Rs. 43.38 crs). The share increased continuously for the years 1986-87 to 2000-01 except for the years 1991-92, 1993-94 and 1998-99. Thereafter, the share of this category in total imports declined for the years 2001-02 to 2005-06. In value terms, the imports of this category increased continuously for the years 1986-87 to 2000-01 (except for the years 1987-88, 1991-92 and 1998-99), thereafter imports showed fluctuating pattern.

Work of Art, Collectors Pieces and Antiques

The category of imports of work of art collector pieces and antiques experienced very small share in total imports and described as minor category of imports. At current prices, the share was 0.001 per cent (Rs. 0.11 crs) for the year 1986-87, which was again at same level with different value, i.e, 0.001 per cent (Rs. 0.20 crs) for the year 1990-91. The share was 0.001 per cent (Rs. 0.57 crs) for the year 1995-96, which was again 0.001 per cent (1.94 crs) for the year 2000-01. The share was 0.01 per cent (Rs. 65.55 crs) for the year 2005-06. In value terms, this category showed fluctuating and also very low valued imports throughout the study period.

The share of this category in total imports was almost negligible for the years 1986-87 to 1993-94 at constant prices because this category was minor one. For the year 1995-96 the share was 0.001 per cent (Rs. 1.04 crs), which increased to 0.004 per cent (Rs. 6.43 crs) for the year 2000-01. The share further increased to 0.012 per cent (Rs. 45.5 crs) for the year 2005-06, which was also highest share of this category.

Project Goods: Some Special Uses

The project goods imports fall in the category of capital goods imports. The share of this category in total imports was at higher level for the years 1986-87 to 1999-2000, but afterwards it declined. At current prices, the share of this category in total imports was 7.03 per cent (Rs. 1414.45 crs) for the year 1986-87, which declined to 5.90 per cent (Rs. 2551.12 crs) for the year 1990-91. The share increased to 6.51 per cent (Rs. 7997.83 crs) for the year 1995-96, but it abruptly declined to 1.50 per cent (Rs. 3470.47 crs) for the year 2000-01. The share of this category further declined to 0.60 per cent (Rs. 4006.28 crs) for the year 2005-06. The highest share was 7.75 per cent (Rs. 1725.68 crs) for the year 1987-88 and lowest share was for the year 2003-04, i.e., 0.51 per cent (Rs. 1848.07 crs). The share of this category in total imports fluctuated between 5 per cent and 7 per cent for the years 1986-87 to 1996-97, after this the share showed declining trend. In value terms, the imports showed almost continuous increase for the years 1986-87 to 1995-96, afterwards the imports showed decline, but for last year of the study period the imports increased again.

At constant prices, this category recorded the share as 6.51 per cent (Rs. 3080.24 crs) for the year 1986-87, which slightly declined to 6.05 per cent (Rs. 3193.29 crs) for the year 1990-91. The share doubled for the year 1995-96, i.e., 12.18 per cent (Rs. 14,645.75 crs), but declined to 7.42 per cent (Rs. 11,506.85 crs) for the year 2000-01. The share abruptly declined to 0.76 per cent (Rs. 2781.75 crs) for the year 2005-06. The highest share was for the year 1998-99, i.e., 19.15 per cent (Rs. 27,382.56 crs) and lowest share was for the year 2005-06, i.e., 0.76 per cent (Rs. 2781.75 crs). The share of this category in total imports fluctuated between 4 per cent and 7 per cent for the years 1986-87 to 1993-94. For the year 1994-95, the share was around 10 per cent but the share remained at the level which was higher than 12 per cent for the years 1995-96 to 1998-99. The share started to decline from the year 1999-2000 and reached at its lowest level in year 2005-06. In value terms, the imports of project goods declined for the years 1986-87 to 1989-90, whereas the imports increased continuously for the years 1991-92 to 1999-2000. The years 2000-01 to 2003-04 experienced continuous decline, whereas the imports of project goods increased again for last two years of the study period.

Miscellaneous Goods

Imports of miscellaneous goods had a share less than 0.50 per cent at current prices throughout the study period. However, at constant prices the share was higher than 0.50 per cent for some of the years.

At current prices, the share of this category in total imports was 0.13 per cent (Rs 27.72 crs) for the year 1986-87. The share increased to 0.28 per cent (Rs. 121.59 crs) for the year 1990-91 and to 0.45 per cent (Rs. 562.41 crs) for the year 1995-96. The share of this category in total imports declined to 0.30 per cent (Rs. 695.66 crs) for the year 2000-01, but increased to 0.33 per cent (Rs. 2225.33 crs) for the year 2005-06. The highest share was for the year 1995-96, i.e., 0.45 per cent (Rs. 562.41 crs) and lowest share was for the year 1989-90, i.e., 0.10 per cent (Rs. 35.97 crs). The share of this category in total imports was less than 0.30 per cent for all years of study period except for the years 1991-92, 1995-96 and 2005-06. In value terms, the imports of this category showed fluctuating trend.

At constant prices, the share of miscellaneous imports in total imports was 0.12 per cent (Rs. 60.36 crs) for the year 1986-87. The share was 0.28 per cent (Rs. 152.19 crs) for the year 1990-91, which increased to 0.90 per cent (Rs 1029.86 crs) for the year 1995-96. The share of this category in total imports further increased to 1.48 per cent (Rs. 2306.56 crs) for the year 2000-01, but declined to 0.42 per cent (Rs 1545.45 crs) for the year 2005-06. The highest share was for the year 2000-01, i.e., 1.48 per cent (Rs. 2306.56 crs) and lowest share was for the year 1989-90, i.e., 0.10 per cent (Rs 52.53 crs). In value terms, the imports of this category increased continuously for the years 1986-87 to 1995-96 (except for the years 1992-93 and 1994-95), thereafter imports showed fluctuated pattern.

On the whole, there were some categories which had very high share in total imports like mineral products, machinery and their parts, pearls, precious and semi-precious stones, chemicals and allied industries and base metals and articles of base metals. Whereas some of the categories had experienced relatively lower share in total imports like live animals: animal products, arms, ammunition: parts and accessories and work of art, collectors and antiques.

The imports whose share in total imports was very low in 1986-87 and continued to be so through out the study period, can be described as low and constant imports (with share less than 0.5%). The imports, whose share in total imports, generally increased and have higher share in total imports during the study period, may be described as leading imports. The imports, whose share in total imports, generally declined during study period may be described as lagging imports.

The analysis of structure of Indian imports showed that the group of low and constant imports includes live animals: animal products, hides and skins: leather products, furskins and articles thereof, footwear, headgear, umbrellas: prepared feathers and articles thereof, stone, cement and similar materials, ceramic products, glass and glassware, arms and ammunition: parts and accessories thereof, miscellaneous manufactured articles, work of art, collectors and antiques and miscellaneous goods. The category of paper and paper board and articles thereof was under the group of constant imports.

The group of leading imports includes mineral products, pearls, precious and semi precious stones, metals, jewellery and coins, machinery and their parts: electrical and electronic equipment parts thereof, chemicals or allied industries, transport equipment, base metals and articles of base metals and animal or vegetable oils and fats.

The group of lagging imports consists of vegetable products, prepared food stuffs, beverages and tobacco, wood, cork and articles thereof, textiles and textile articles, instruments and apparatus and project goods.

During post-2000-01 period, the share of imports of mineral products in total imports has been increasing and remained higher than 30 per cent. Similarly, the share of machinery and their parts and pearls, precious and semi precious stones remained more than 12 per cent. The share of chemicals and allied industries imports has been stabilized around eight per cent and of base metals and articles of base metal imports around four per cent. Similarly, the share of categories of transport equipments and animals or vegetables fats and oils fluctuated between one per cent and five per cent. The categories of vegetable products, plastic and rubber, instruments and apparatus and textiles and textile articles had the share which fluctuated between one per cent and three per cent. The category of paper and paper board and articles thereof had the share which fluctuated between one per cent and two per cent. The categories of wood, cork and articles thereof (except year 2001-02) and project goods (except years 2000-01 and 2001-02) had the share between 0.5 per cent and one per cent. The categories for which the share was between 0.1 per cent and 0.5 per cent are prepared food stuffs, beverages and tobacco (except the year 2004-05), hides and skins: leather, für skins and articles thereof, stones, cement and similar material, miscellaneous manufactured articles and miscellaneous goods. The categories of live animals: animal products, footwear, headgear, umbrellas, arms and ammunition and work of art, collectors and antiques had showed the share which was lesser than 0.1 per cent during last six years of study period.

The analysis of structure of India's imports shows that the changes in imports structure reflect the changes in trade policy regimes as well as those in structure of India's economy and its growth. There are certain categories in case of which India has import dependence like petroleum imports and hence their share is high. The share of mineral products imports has increased also due to rising international price of petroleum products during the study period. The capital goods imports are high because of India's import dependence in this category and also due to liberalization and fast growth of the economy. Imports of industrial raw materials and intermediate goods like base metals and articles of base metals, chemical and allied industries products imports etc., are high due to fast growth of related industries and rising demand. Thus, India's imports primarily consist of essential imports and developmental imports. As far as agricultural imports are concerned they are very low throughout the study period as India has near self sufficiency in agricultural sector. However, import dependence is high in case of edible oils and fertilizers. Apart from the above mentioned categories of imports, another major category is that of imports of pearls, precious and semi precious stones, metals and articles. These imports are primarily for export oriented pearls and jewellery industry, in which India specializes. Hence, the present structure of Indian imports helps Indian economy in strengthening its base through betterment of infrastructure, industry and export sectors.

Table 5.1 : India's Foreign Trade

Years	Imports (Rs. in crs)	Exports (Rs. in crs)	Trade Balance	Foreign Trade/ GDP	Imports/ GDP	Exports/ GDP	Imports % Change	Exports % Change	Import/ Export % Ratio
1	2	3	4	5	6	7	8	9	10
1986-87	20096	12452	-7644	11.47	6.38	3.96	2.23	14.29	161.38
1987-88	22244	15674	-6570	11.79	6.22	4.38	10.69	25.88	141.91
1988-89	28235	20231	-8004	12.62	6.65	4.77	26.93	29.07	139.56
1989-90	35328	27658	-7670	14.24	7.24	5.67	25.12	36.71	127.73
1990-91	42095	32558	-9537	14.49	7.39	5.72	19.16	17.72	129.29
1991-92	47851	44042	-3809	15.46	7.31	6.73	13.65	35.27	108.64
1992-93	63375	53688	-9687	17.17	7.42	7.13	32.47	21.90	118.04
1993-94	73177	69749	-3428	18.04	8.45	8.06	15.47	29.91	104.91
1994-95	89971	82673	-7298	18.65	8.86	8.14	22.95	18.53	108.82
1995-96	122678	106352	-16326	21.14	10.29	8.92	36.35	28.64	115.35
1996-97	138920	118817	-20103	20.44	10.08	8.62	13.24	11.72	116.91
1997-98	154176	130101	-24075	20.27	10.10	8.52	10.98	9.50	118.50
1998-99	178332	139752	-38580	19.68	10.18	7.98	15.67	7.42	127.60

...(*Contd.*)

Table 5.1 (*Contd.*)

1	2	3	4	5	6	7	8	9	10
1999-2000	215529	159095	-56434	20.96	11.04	8.15	20.86	13.84	135.47
2000-01	228307	201356	-26951	22.31	10.86	9.58	5.93	26.56	113.38
2001-02	245200	209018	-36182	21.63	10.75	9.16	7.40	3.80	117.31
2002-03	297206	255137	-42069	24.38	12.09	10.38	21.21	22.06	116.48
2003-04	359108	293367	-65741	25.59	12.99	10.61	20.83	14.98	122.40
2004-05	501064	375340	-125724	30.68	16.03	12.00	39.53	27.94	133.49
2005-06	660408	456418	-203990	34.35	18.51	12.79	31.80	21.60	144.69

Source: (*i*) CMIE Reports (Various Issues).
(*ii*) Economic Survey (Various Issues).

Table 5.2 : Structure of India's Imports at Current Prices 1986-87—2005-06 (Rupees in Crores)

Sl. No.	Categories	1986-87	1987-88	1988-89	1989-90	1990-91	1991-92	1992-93	1993-94	1994-95	1995-96
1	2	3	4	5	6	7	8	9	10	11	12
1.	Live animals : animal products	32.42	148.50	116.38	62.89	9.22	35.79	58.85	35.45	57.04	117.05
2	Vegetable products	478.68	471.88	1322.42	817.81	929.59	773.43	1818.72	1645.70	1810.82	2062.88
	(*a*) Edible vegetable and certain roots and tubers	233.73	283.54	423.03	253.21	541.63	299.09	342.06	595.99	624.92	709.83
	(*b*) Edible fruits and nuts: peel of citrus fruits or melons	131.30	127.95	125.29	172.31	240.09	366.73	565.25	700.57	1004.73	1091.21
	(*c*) Cereals	46.02	11.27	687.17	327.82	61.80	11.16	783.57	181.02	9.27	10.67
	(*d*) Coffee, tea, mate and spices	33.23	11.99	45.33	12.83	20.40	27.76	43.44	57.49	41.98	67.01
	(*e*) Oil seeds and oleaginous fruits: misc. grams seeds & fruits: industries or med	11.51	15.70	15.60	11.82	16.49	31.73	33.46	32.69	42.78	68.75
	(*f*) Lac: gums, resins and other veg. sabs and extracts	18.03	19.50	23.60	27.55	48.18	34.76	49.11	72.15	71.56	83.11
3.	Animal or vegetable fats and oils and their cleavage products: animal or vegetable waxes	670.88	1016.48	781.70	251.37	364.26	342.07	286.99	345.99	876.51	2550.23
4.	Prepared foodstuffs, beverages and tobacco	283.15	285.59	106.45	214.09	172.90	223.18	308.82	361.17	2783.44	658.14
5.	Mineral products	3509.97	4749.93	5475.82	7765.64	12807.21	15443.80	20036.13	20953.70	23203.83	31124.59
	(*a*) Salt, sulphur, earths and stone, plastering materials lime and cement	416.97	402.44	577.66	726.45	817.26	982.65	1059.31	863.67	1237.00	1451.28

...(*Contd.*)

Table 5.2 (*Contd.*)

1	2	3	4	5	6	7	8	9	10	11	12
	(*b*) Ores, slag and ash	71.19	66.88	89.71	134.16	201.59	145.01	271.45	248.87	557.14	636.05
	(*c*) Mineral fuels, min. oil and products: bituminous sub-stances: min waxes	3021.81	4280.61	4808.44	6905.03	11788.39	14316.14	18705.37	19841.16	21409.69	29037.26
6.	Products of the chemical or allied industries	2294.85	1848.35	3099.08	4254.96	4695.60	6416.84	8103.83	8411.04	11783.31	16754.12
	(*a*) Inorganic Chemicals	594.66	408.85	813.47	797.21	897.93	2046.37	2279.01	1541.78	2394.47	2912.13
	(*b*) Organic Chemicals	557.73	719.91	1182.68	1448.21	1589.76	1604.05	2420.18	3333.78	4973.08	6658.11
	(*c*) Fertilizers	586.49	187.95	492.37	1226.04	1141.33	1591.16	2023.17	1981.59	2409.51	4621.16
	(*d*) Misc. Chemical Products	149.37	191.50	184.88	213.25	284.31	335.90	481.52	505.16	612.21	797.94
7.	Plastic and rubber	619.38	752.52	1067.68	1311.00	1478.07	1754.57	1684.33	1970.64	2696.28	4249.09
	(*a*) Plastic and articles thereof	448.80	582.62	842.81	1051.41	1150.60	1451.78	1277.91	1445.90	2118.18	3175.69
	(*b*) Rubber and articles thereof	170.58	169.90	224.87	259.59	327.47	302.79	406.42	524.74	578.10	1073.40
	8. Hides and skins: leather products, furskins and article thereof	18.78	25.22	50.64	105.19	195.13	192.11	246.87	363.52	396.91	468.00
9.	Wood, cork and article thereof, manuf. of plaiting material: basketware wicker work	131.77	240.53	365.40	401.01	459.73	418.77	574.71	454.22	709.37	843.23
	(*a*) Wood and articles of wood : wood charcoal	129.98	239.11	360.59	394.82	454.85	415.57	570.14	450.03	703.45	835.94
10.	Paper and paper board and article thereof	531.16	592.74	694.59	759.42	1042.64	886.16	1134.01	1401.96	1621.36	2807.63
	(*a*) Pulp of wood or of other material : waste and scrap of paper and paperboard	243.51	238.54	259.64	303.88	457.98	298.69	409.02	497.33	635.35	920.83

	(*b*) Paper and paper board: articles of paper pulp, of paper and paper board	217.68	270.01	303.41	357.81	456.04	487.89	513.23	695.96	773.05	1582.48
11.	Textile and Textile articles	373.99	452.05	690.13	776.15	896.08	826.33	1397.97	1698.70	2963.25	3259.55
	(*a*) Silk	47.59	58.45	71.84	108.74	122.78	176.11	259.70	305.15	295.23	369.69
	(*b*) Wool, fine or coarse animal hair	96.67	168.61	206.35	236.62	239.37	236.85	348.25	417.63	435.14	605.27
	(*c*) Cotton	20.10	26.66	128.44	53.28	57.19	41.80	265.70	78.36	570.02	602.54
	(*d*) Man-made filaments	71.38	86.98	129.83	163.73	225.54	121.23	153.25	311.98	449.33	407.51
12.	Footwear, headgear, umbrellas: prepared feather and articles thereof	16.53	13.92	16.75	23.11	35.09	40.99	53.29	81.41	97.05	130.09
13.	Stone, cement and similar material: ceramic products, glass and glassware	110.48	101.44	161.43	168.35	202.06	218.71	261.85	279.62	421.23	504.89
	(*a*) Articles of stone, plaster, cement, asbestos, mica or similar materials	14.37	11.80	16.28	23.68	32.98	37.17	54.25	54.51	72.20	96.18
	(*b*) Ceramic products	38.62	23.82	28.26	40.87	60.46	73.43	68.96	80.78	115.77	136.36
	(*c*) Glass and glassware	57.49	65.82	116.90	103.79	108.62	108.12	138.64	144.33	233.26	272.35
14.	Pearls, precious or semi-precious stones, metals and articles thereof: imitation jewellery and coins	1555.33	2037.67	3204.98	4288.93	3758.94	4865.30	7756.03	9110.00	7435.83	10104.17
15.	Base metals and articles of base metals	2714.49	2570.97	3620.37	4768.63	4841.27	4148.73	5452.48	5668.27	8352.49	10880.62

...(*Contd.*)

Table 5.2 (*Contd.*)

1	2	3	4	5	6	7	8	9	10	11	12
	(*a*) Iron and steel	1408.29	1326.15	2050.35	2449.22	2591.09	2097.94	3108.50	2440.01	4370.88	5453.55
	(*b*) Articles of iron and steel	628.81	430.14	520.97	655.20	653.73	679.66	687.99	1047.79	928.87	1197.37
	(*c*) Copper and articles thereof	205.27	321.68	480.78	740.55	824.13	729.00	1001.06	1228.83	1482.46	2083.61
	(*d*) Aluminium and articles thereof	201.87	180.07	82.67	256.58	128.65	107.52	87.50	251.55	615.66	864.08
16.	Machinery and their parts, electrical and electronic equipments, parts thereof	4003.77	389.04	4333.92	5324.37	5823.23	5496.63	7473.43	9498.48	13426.76	21119.57
	(*a*) Nuclear reactors, boilers, machinery and mechanical appliances, parts thereof	2758.64	2667.54	2656.25	3247.07	3985.98	3794.46	5061.01	6748.50	9316.76	14134.15
	(*b*) Elec. mach. and equip and parts thereof: sound and TV recorder and reproducers and parts thereof	1245.13	1223.49	1677.67	2077.30	1837.25	1702.17	2412.42	2749.98	4110.00	6985.42
17.	Transport equipments	789.98	760.17	754.93	1534.81	1670.31	917.09	1339.50	3986.44	3498.64	3704.59
	(*a*) Railway/tramway locomotives truck etc., equipment and parts thereof	42.55	78.97	99.96	112.23	139.36	140.14	124.36	98.30	51.75	167.87
	(*b*) Road vehicles and parts	408.72	260.78	350.75	381.79	521.83	482.06	573.09	700.21	920.51	1557.79
	(*c*) Aircraft, spacecraft and parts	165.02	279.69	176.40	980.62	525.80	159.14	357.33	2933.37	2300.28	1631.65
	(*d*) Ship, boat and floating structure	173.68	140.73	127.81	60.17	483.33	135.75	283.72	254.56	226.10	347.28
18.	Instrument and appratus: clocks and watches: parts and accessories thereof	495.84	504.10	694.55	934.61	1083.56	971.71	1451.65	1442.05	1694.59	2526.06

	(*a*) Optical measuring, medical and similar instruments and parts thereof	445.17	463.61	655.31	868.42	1030.65	926.87	1404.89	1389.47	1639.99	2429.47
19.	Arms and Ammunitions: parts & Accessories thereof	1.09	0.66	0.13	1.58	0.28	0.40	0.96	0.30	0.34	1.67
20.	Misc. manufactured articles	20.91	25.11	40.36	44.04	54.92	63.18	78.63	97.42	158.57	251.16
21.	Work of art, collectors pieces and antiques	0.11	0.01	0.03	0.43	0.20	0.28	0.12	0.18	0.43	0.57
22.	Project goods: some special uses	1414.45	1725.68	1574.94	1579.64	2551.12	3626.41	3702.79	5090.86	5820.18	7997.83
23.	Misc. goods	27.72	29.16	62.52	35.97	121.59	188.33	152.54	203.89	162.42	562.41
	Total Imports	**20095.76**	**22243.74**	**28235.22**	**35415.90**	**43192.85**	**47850.84**	**63374.52**	**73101.01**	**89970.66**	**122678.14**

Table 5.2 (*Contd.*)

Sl.No.	Categories	1996-97	1997-98	1998-99	1999-00	2000-01	2001-02	2002-03	2003-04	2004-05	2005-06
1	2	13	14	15	16	17	18	19	20	21	22
1.	Live animals : animal products	46.28	101.37	147.90	272.39	146.40	134.81	195.03	238.55	185.67	204.99
2.	Vegetable products	2768.11	3949.01	4224.00	3718.59	2871.32	5378.22	5882.19	5736.33	6111.52	7815.47
	(*a*) Edible vegetable and certain roots and tubers	941.97	1286.38	812.84	428.46	518.27	3425.31	3049.99	2622.17	2018.73	2823.04
	(*b*) Edible fruits and nuts: peel of citrus fruits or melons	1143.63	1342.30	1639.43	1789.51	1763.48	1189.49	1883.96	2174.93	2911.65	3484.68
	(*c*) Cereals	404.27	989.38	1171.45	919.18	36.20	4.48	1.76	2.39	6.67	30.46
	(*d*) Coffee, tea, mate and spices	87.44	138.05	323.02	234.48	259.98	456.51	587.84	521.22	647.78	845.51
	(*e*) Oil seeds and oleaginous fruits: misc. grams seeds & fruits: industries or med	44.96	51.45	90.75	120.47	119.04	115.97	184.73	212.94	256.71	320.51
	(*f*) Lac: gums, resins and other veg. sabs and extracts	101.73	112.09	110.46	126.44	113.19	138.53	135.78	157.37	210.30	241.31
3.	Animal or vegetable fats and oils and their cleavage products: animal or vegetable waxes	3069.08	2912.62	8036.54	8469.27	6467.15	7079.98	9052.36	11868.59	11372.75	10151.70
4.	Prepared foodstuffs, beverages and tobacco	499.01	990.19	1682.16	1632.74	659.35	839.61	933.8	982.41	2942.75	2707.69
5.	Mineral products	42515.10	39363.99	36346.18	65423.69	83480.64	79141.64	99476.46	108488.25	163913.10	232951.08
	(*a*) Salt, sulphur, earths and stone, plastering materials lime and cement	1226.27	1424.23	1640.17	1997.35	2008.00	1757.51	2024.69	1849.78	2905.41	3372.98
	(*b*) Ores, slag and ash	589.60	523.17	867.81	1243.10	1318.72	2195.67	2206.91	2327.39	4562.23	6837.87
	(*c*) Mineral fuels, min. oil and products: bituminous substances: min waxes	40699.23	37416.59	33838.19	62183.25	80153.92	75218.46	95244.86	104311.08	156445.46	222740.23

6.	Products of the chemical or allied industries	15673.55	18838.12	15024.48	17347.21	19555.56	23198.57	25312.62	31179.57	41110.62	52853.71
	(*a*) Inorganic Chemicals	3251.86	4488.01	5415.89	5787.48	4962.24	5729.85	5579.41	5916.25	8130.10	10445.86
	(*b*) Organic Chemicals	7007.41	7394.58	6840.44	7564.00	7307.95	8795.15	10694.87	14363.01	18784.84	22775.24
	(*c*) Fertilizers	2434.38	3138.07	3414.59	4677.43	2032.46	2173.12	1736.06	2313.94	4320.68	7423.84
	(*d*) Misc. Chemical Products	1216.37	1508.33	2051.82	2066.95	1797.74	2442.44	2572.25	3362.05	4045.33	5024.69
7.	Plastic and rubber	3930.60	3822.67	4247.63	4595.24	4298.36	5218.03	6050.36	7932.86	10536.73	14599.58
	(*a*) Plastic and articles thereof	2963.11	2766.88	3077.83	3423.36	3003.37	3726.04	4387.40	5685.27	7491.70	11318.34
	(*b*) Rubber and articles thereof	967.49	1055.79	1169.79	1171.88	1294.99	1491.99	1662.96	2247.58	3045.03	3281.24
8.	Hides and skins: leather products, furskins and article thereof	507.75	563.14	644.58	680.33	913.54	1080.46	1031.86	1123.84	1340.44	1487.66
9.	Wood, cork and article thereof, manuf. of plaiting material: basketware wicker work	966.68	1579.88	1618.05	2003.04	2253.14	2638.79	2004.72	3335.65	4088.54	4245.50
	(*a*) Wood and articles of wood : wood charcoal	959.73	1571.72	1609.54	1994.33	2243.38	2630.78	1994.79	3325.38	4077.11	4230.53
10.	Paper and paper board and article thereof	2895.30	3448.22	3625.55	3630.22	4200.07	4576.66	4791.55	6197.45	7045.86	8697.12
	(*a*) Pulp of wood or of other material : waste and scrap of paper and paperboard	822.70	1055.29	991.79	1105.64	1289.59	1405.24	1661.76	1880.04	2199.46	2537.15
	(*b*) Paper and paper board: articles of paper pulp, of paper and paper board	1767.91	1836.18	1921.50	1901.35	2029.26	2084.27	2126.24	2961.85	3188.16	4056.51
11.	Textile and Textile articles	2779.76	3118.12	3581.59	4884.21	5347.29	7305.83	7942.71	9266.62	10041.48	11838.33
	(*a*) Silk	297.17	283.51	329.68	479.78	567.95	806.54	950.42	1173.37	1449.29	1762.35
	(*b*) Wool, fine or coarse animal hair	717.54	708.18	554.37	531.72	503.44	682.28	955.35	1102.42	1086.24	1175.44
	(*c*) Cotton	128.42	249.87	628.54	1361.40	1325.59	2285.94	1662.51	2222.91	2015.28	1939.57
	(*d*) Man-made filaments	316.69	326.39	498.03	825.67	867.00	1219.48	1614.79	1547.24	1784.33	2023.30

...(*Contd.*)

Table 5.2 (*Contd.*)

1	2	13	14	15	16	17	18	19	20	21	22
12.	Footwear, headgear, umbrellas: prepared feather and articles thereof	109.37	117.69	136.32	150.84	159.82	142.28	152.29	197.03	291.52	470.69
13.	Stone, cement and similar material: ceramic products, glass and glassware	457.86	561.58	711.28	750.84	849.35	1124.96	1185.02	1584.23	2238.70	2992.01
	(*a*) Articles of stone, plaster, cement, asbestos, mica or similar materials	85.06	101.76	130.29	120.94	160.08	190.10	247.26	351.80	481.05	608.40
	(*b*) Ceramic products	122.36	189.25	206.10	193.42	210.55	287.75	358.63	490.01	783.01	1076.63
	(*c*) Glass and glassware	250.44	270.57	374.87	436.48	478.72	647.11	579.13	742.42	974.65	1306.97
14.	Pearls, precious or semi-precious stones, metals and articles thereof: imitation jewellery and coins	14089.63	24506.17	37769.04	44380.18	44347.58	44599.22	50695.72	65044.51	93387.35	91604.14
15.	Base metals and articles of base metals	12214.79	12097.87	10707.99	10725.64	10038.25	12183.89	12879.58	17940.3	28334.31	43637.98
	(*a*) Iron and steel	5333.13	5274.52	4441.84	4800.01	4369.61	5264.29	5365.42	8155.31	15077.42	24113.34
	(*b*) Articles of iron and steel	1520.00	1826.39	1870.04	1434.79	1398.40	1702.87	2121.99	2951.19	3983.79	5789.12
	(*c*) Copper and articles thereof	2643.21	2376.76	1535.36	1386.82	1057.61	1235.93	1043.08	1513.99	2408.18	3922.49
	(*d*) Aluminium and articles thereof	1169.44	785.71	997.78	923.82	1050.61	1451.35	1486.79	1721.54	2162.91	3676.50
16.	Machinery and their parts, electrical and electronic equipments, parts thereof	20790.23	24068.53	25078.87	26728.78	31588.28	35439.89	49352.43	62023.14	83460.28	114287.17
	(*a*) Nuclear reactors, boilers, machinery and mechanical appliances, parts thereof	15129.98	16664.36	16763.03	16805.86	19355.69	20265.19	24829.37	31857.46	43366.97	61606.78
	(*b*) Elec. mach. and equip and parts thereof: sound and TV recorder and reproducers and parts thereof	5660.25	7404.17	8315.84	9922.92	12232.58	15174.70	24523.06	30165.67	40193.31	52680.40

17.	Transport equipments	5275.46	3913.40	3369.21	4944.04	4361.26	5491.71	9188.45	14840.29	19459.48	39177.05
	(*a*) Railway/tramway locomotives truck etc., equipment and parts thereof	478.31	101.61	401.26	153.19	175.97	80.48	134.73	511.00	556.41	604.08
	(*b*) Road vehicles and parts	2056.96	1555.85	1253.63	1910.40	1475.42	1455.39	1646.57	2594.51	3794.41	4523.34
	(*c*) Aircraft, spacecraft and parts	1783.90	1325.89	792.64	406.03	1178.35	1231.21	4712.30	5371.49	7153.92	22045.59
	(*d*) Ship, boat and floating structure	956.28	930.04	921.68	2474.42	1531.52	2724.63	2694.85	6363.29	7954.74	12004.04
18.	Instrument and appratus: clocks and watches: parts and accessories thereof	2143.10	3114.25	3982.46	4242.32	4533.55	5788.67	6713.22	7354.93	9321.85	12125.33
	(*a*) Optical measuring, medical and similar instruments and parts thereof	2015.16	3014.53	3851.60	4048.22	4376.75	5643.85	6548.93	7143.03	9053.55	11759.35
19.	Arms and Ammunitions: parts & Accessories thereof	1.77	3.79	3.35	5.42	1.96	4.82	12.67	14.99	13.01	4.88
20.	Misc. manufactured articles	248.80	336.72	387.61	520.88	631.74	703.69	908.99	1160.39	1539.72	2259.63
21.	Work of art, collectors pieces and antiques	1.41	1.18	0.71	0.56	1.94	2.50	5.90	6.20	4.76	65.55
22.	Project goods: some special uses	7520.11	6464.52	11309.00	4273.73	3470.47	2713.55	2626.34	1848.07	2711.22	4006.28
23.	Misc. goods	415.75	303.20	281.44	360.75	695.66	411.84	811.53	743.34	1512.82	2225.33
	Total Imports	**138919.66**	**154176.28**	**178331.86**	**215528.44**	**230872.76**	**245199.72**	**297205.86**	**359104.64**	**501064.56**	**660408.88**

Source: DGFTI, Ministry of Commerce, Government of India (Various Issues).

Table 5.3 : Structure of India's Imports at Current Prices (1986-87 to 2005-06 (Percentage Share)

Sl.No.	Categories	1986-87	1987-88	1988-89	1989-90	1990-91	1991-92	1992-93	1993-94	1994-95	1995-96
1	2	3	4	5	6	7	8	9	10	11	12
1.	Live animals : animal products	0.16	0.66	0.41	0.17	0.02	0.07	0.09	0.04	0.06	0.09
2.	Vegetable products	2.38	2.12	4.68	2.30	2.15	1.61	2.86	2.25	2.01	1.68
	(*a*) Edible vegetable and certain roots and tubers	1.16	1.27	1.49	0.71	1.25	0.62	0.53	0.81	0.69	0.57
	(*b*) Edible fruits and nuts: peel of citrus fruits or melons	0.65	0.57	0.44	0.48	0.55	0.76	0.89	0.95	1.11	0.88
	(*c*) Cereals	0.22	0.05	2.43	0.92	0.14	0.02	1.23	0.24	0.01	0.01
	(*d*) Coffee, tea, mate and spices	0.16	0.05	0.16	0.03	0.04	0.05	0.06	0.07	0.04	0.05
	(*e*) Oil seeds and oleaginous fruits: misc. grams seeds & fruits: industries or med	0.05	0.07	0.05	0.03	0.03	0.06	0.05	0.04	0.04	0.05
	(*f*) Lac: gums, resins and other veg. sabs and extracts	0.08	0.08	0.08	0.07	0.11	0.07	0.07	0.09	0.07	0.06
3.	Animal or vegetable fats and oils and their cleavage products: animal or vegetable waxes	3.33	4.56	2.76	0.70	0.84	0.71	0.45	0.47	0.97	2.07
4.	Prepared foodstuffs, beverages and tobacco	1.40	1.28	0.37	0.60	0.40	0.46	0.48	0.49	3.09	0.53
5.	Mineral products	17.46	21.35	19.39	21.92	29.65	32.27	31.61	28.66	25.79	25.37
	(*a*) Salt, sulphur, earths and stone, plastering materials lime and cement	2.07	1.80	2.04	2.05	1.89	2.05	1.67	1.18	1.37	1.18
	(*b*) Ores, slag and ash	0.35	0.30	0.31	0.37	0.46	0.30	0.42	0.34	0.61	0.51
	(*c*) Mineral fuels, min. oil and products: bituminous substances: min waxes	15.03	19.24	17.02	19.49	27.29	29.91	29.51	27.14	23.79	23.66

6.	Products of the chemical or allied industries	11.41	8.30	10.97	12.01	10.87	13.41	12.78	11.50	13.09	13.65
	(*a*) Inorganic Chemicals	2.95	1.83	2.88	2.25	2.07	4.27	3.59	2.10	2.66	2.37
	(*b*) Organic Chemicals	2.77	3.23	4.18	4.08	3.66	3.35	3.81	4.56	5.52	5.42
	(*c*) Fertilizers	2.91	0.84	1.74	3.46	2.64	3.32	3.19	2.71	2.67	3.76
	(*d*) Misc. Chemical Products	0.74	0.01	0.65	0.60	0.65	0.70	0.75	0.69	0.68	0.65
7.	Plastic and rubber	3.08	3.38	3.78	3.70	3.42	3.66	2.65	2.69	2.99	3.46
	(*a*) Plastic and articles thereof	2.23	2.61	2.98	2.96	2.66	3.03	2.01	1.97	2.35	2.58
	(*b*) Rubber and articles thereof	0.84	0.76	0.79	0.73	0.75	0.63	0.64	0.71	0.64	0.87
8.	Hides and skins: leather products, furskins and article thereof	0.09	0.11	0.17	0.29	0.45	0.40	0.38	0.49	0.44	0.38
9.	Wood, cork and article thereof, manuf. of plaiting material: basketware wicker work	0.65	1.08	1.29	1.13	1.06	0.87	0.90	0.62	0.78	0.68
	(*a*) Wood and articles of wood : wood charcoal	0.64	1.07	1.27	1.11	1.05	0.86	0.89	0.61	0.78	0.68
10.	Paper and paper board and article thereof	2.64	2.66	2.46	2.14	2.41	1.85	1.78	1.91	1.80	2.28
	(*a*) Pulp of wood or of other material : waste and scrap of paper and paperboard	1.21	1.07	0.91	0.85	1.06	0.62	0.64	0.68	0.70	0.75
	(*b*) Paper and paper board: articles of paper pulp of paper and paper board	1.08	1.21	1.07	1.01	1.05	1.01	0.80	0.95	0.85	1.28
11.	Textile and Textile articles	1.87	2.03	2.44	2.19	2.07	1.72	2.20	2.32	3.29	2.65
	(*a*) Silk	0.23	0.26	0.32	0.30	0.28	0.36	0.40	0.41	0.32	0.30
	(*b*) Wool, fine or coarse animal hair	0.48	0.75	0.73	0.66	0.55	0.49	0.54	0.57	0.48	0.49
	(*c*) Cotton	0.10	0.11	0.45	0.15	0.13	0.08	0.41	0.10	0.63	0.49
	(*d*) Man-made filaments	0.35	0.39	0.45	0.46	0.52	0.25	0.24	0.42	0.49	0.33

...(*Contd.*)

Table 5.3 (*Contd.*)

1	2	3	4	5	6	7	8	9	10	11	12
12.	Foot wear, headgear, umbrellas: prepared feather and articles thereof	0.08	0.06	0.05	0.06	0.08	0.08	0.08	0.11	0.10	0.10
13.	Stone, cement and similar material: ceramic products, glass and glassware	0.54	0.45	0.57	0.47	0.46	0.45	0.41	0.38	0.46	0.41
	(*a*) Articles of stone, plaster, cement, asbestos, mica or similar materials	0.07	0.05	0.05	0.06	0.07	0.07	0.08	0.07	0.08	0.07
	(*b*) Ceramic products	0.19	0.10	0.10	0.11	0.13	0.15	0.10	0.11	0.12	0.11
	(*c*) Glass and glassware	0.28	0.29	0.41	0.29	0.25	0.22	0.21	0.19	0.25	0.22
14.	Pearls, precious or semi-precious stones, metals and articles thereof: imitation jewellery and coins	7.73	9.16	11.35	12.11	8.70	10.16	12.23	12.46	8.26	8.23
15.	Base metals and articles of base metals	13.50	11.55	12.82	13.46	11.20	8.67	8.60	7.75	9.28	8.86
	(*a*) Iron and steel	7.00	5.96	7.26	6.91	5.99	4.38	4.90	3.33	4.85	4.44
	(*b*) Articles of iron and steel	3.12	1.93	1.84	1.85	1.51	1.42	1.08	1.43	1.03	0.97
	(*c*) Copper and articles thereof	1.02	1.44	1.70	2.09	1.90	1.52	1.57	1.68	1.64	1.69
	(*d*) Aluminium and articles thereof	1.00	0.80	0.29	0.72	0.29	0.22	0.13	0.34	0.68	0.70
16.	Machinery and their parts, electrical and electronic equipments, parts thereof	19.92	17.49	15.34	15.03	13.48	11.48	11.79	12.99	14.92	17.21
	(*a*) Nuclear reactors, boilers, machinery and mechanical appliances, parts thereof	13.72	11.99	9.40	9.16	9.22	7.92	7.98	9.23	10.35	11.52
	(*b*) Elec. mach. and equip and parts thereof: sound and TV recorder and reproducers and parts thereof	6.19	5.50	5.94	5.86	4.25	3.55	3.80	3.76	4.56	5.69
17.	Transport equipments	3.93	3.41	2.67	4.33	3.86	1.91	2.11	5.45	3.88	3.01

	(*a*) Railway/tramway locomotives truck etc., equipment and parts thereof	0.21	0.35	0.35	0.31	0.32	0.29	0.19	0.13	0.05	0.13
	(*b*) Road vehicles and parts	2.03	1.17	1.24	1.07	1.20	1.00	0.90	0.95	1.02	1.26
	(*c*) Aircraft, spacecraft and parts	0.82	1.25	0.62	2.76	1.21	0.33	0.56	4.01	2.55	1.33
	(*d*) Ship, boat and floating structure	0.86	0.63	0.45	0.16	1.11	0.28	0.44	0.34	0.25	0.28
18.	Instrument and appratus: clocks and watches: parts and accessories thereof	2.46	2.26	2.45	2.63	2.50	2.03	2.29	1.97	1.88	2.05
	(*a*) Optical measuring, medical and similar instruments and parts thereof	2.21	2.08	2.32	2.45	2.38	1.93	2.21	1.90	1.82	1.98
19.	Arms and Ammunitions: parts & Accessories thereof	0.005	0.003	0.000	0.000	0.001	0.001	0.001	0.000	0.000	0.001
20.	Misc. manufactured articles	0.10	0.11	0.14	0.12	0.12	0.13	0.12	0.13	0.17	0.20
21.	Work of art, collectors pieces and antiques	0.005	0.000	0.000	0.001	0.001	0.001	0.000	0.000	0.006	0.006
22.	Project goods: some special uses	7.03	7.75	5.57	4.46	5.90	7.57	5.84	6.96	6.46	6.51
23.	Misc. goods	0.13	0.13	0.22	0.10	0.28	0.39	0.24	0.27	0.18	0.45

...(*Contd.*)

Table 5.3 (*Contd.*)

Sl.No.	Categories	1996-97	1997-98	1998-99	1999-00	2000-01	2001-02	2002-03	2003-04	2004-05	2005-06
1	2	13	14	15	16	17	18	19	20	21	22
1.	Live animals : animal products	0.03	0.06	0.08	0.12	0.06	0.05	0.06	0.06	0.03	0.03
2.	Vegetable products	1.99	2.56	2.36	1.72	1.24	2.19	1.97	1.59	1.21	1.18
	(*a*) Edible vegetable and certain roots and tubers	0.67	0.83	0.45	0.19	0.22	1.39	1.02	0.73	0.40	0.42
	(*b*) Edible fruits and nuts: peel of citrus fruits or melons	0.82	0.87	0.91	0.83	0.76	0.48	0.63	0.60	0.58	0.52
	(*c*) Cereals	0.29	0.64	0.65	0.42	0.01	0.00	0.00	0.00	0.001	0.004
	(*d*) Coffee, tea, mate and spices	0.06	0.08	0.18	0.10	0.11	0.18	0.19	0.14	0.12	0.12
	(*e*) Oil seeds and oleaginous fruits: misc. grams seeds & fruits: industries or med	0.03	0.03	0.05	0.05	0.05	0.04	0.06	0.05	0.05	0.04
	(*f*) Lac: gums, resins and other veg. sabs and extracts	0.07	0.07	0.06	0.05	0.04	0.05	0.04	0.04	0.04	0.03
3.	Animal or vegetable fats and oils and their cleavage products: animal or vegetable waxes	2.20	1.88	4.50	3.92	2.80	2.88	3.04	3.30	2.26	1.53
4.	Prepared foodstuffs, beverages and tobacco	0.35	0.64	0.94	0.75	0.28	0.34	0.31	0.27	0.58	0.41
5.	Mineral products	30.60	25.53	20.38	30.35	36.15	32.27	33.47	30.21	32.71	35.27
	(*a*) Salt, sulphur, earths and stone, plastering materials lime and cement	0.88	0.92	0.91	0.92	0.86	0.70	0.68	0.51	0.57	0.51
	(*b*) Ores, slag and ash	0.42	0.33	0.48	0.57	0.57	0.89	0.74	0.64	0.91	1.03
	(*c*) Mineral fuels, min. oil and products: bituminous substances: min waxes	29.29	24.26	18.97	28.85	34.71	30.67	32.04	29.04	31.22	33.72

6.	Products of the chemical or allied industries	11.28	12.21	8.42	8.04	8.47	9.46	8.51	8.68	8.20	8.00
	(*a*) Inorganic Chemicals	2.34	2.91	3.03	2.68	2.14	2.33	1.87	1.64	1.62	1.58
	(*b*) Organic Chemicals	5.04	4.79	3.83	3.50	3.16	3.58	3.59	3.99	3.74	3.44
	(*c*) Fertilizers	1.75	2.03	1.91	2.17	0.88	0.88	0.58	0.64	0.86	1.12
	(*d*) Misc. Chemical Products	0.87	0.97	1.15	0.95	0.77	0.99	0.86	0.93	0.80	0.76
7.	Plastic and rubber	2.82	2.47	2.38	2.13	1.86	2.12	2.03	2.20	2.10	2.21
	(*a*) Plastic and articles thereof	2.13	1.79	1.72	1.58	1.30	1.51	1.47	1.58	1.49	1.71
	(*b*) Rubber and articles thereof	0.69	0.68	0.65	0.54	0.56	0.60	0.55	0.62	0.60	0.49
8.	Hides and skins: leather products, furskins and article thereof	0.36	0.36	0.36	0.31	0.39	0.44	0.34	0.31	0.26	0.22
9.	Wood, cork and article thereof, manuf. of plaiting material: basketware wicker work	0.69	1.02	0.90	0.92	0.97	1.07	0.67	0.92	0.81	0.64
	(*a*) Wood and articles of wood : wood charcoal	0.69	1.01	0.90	0.92	0.97	1.07	0.67	0.92	0.81	0.64
10.	Paper and paper board and article thereof	2.08	2.23	2.03	1.68	1.81	1.86	1.61	1.72	1.40	1.31
	(*a*) Pulp of wood or of other material : waste and scrap of paper and paperboard	0.59	0.68	0.55	0.51	0.55	0.57	0.55	0.52	0.43	0.38
	(*b*) Paper and paper board: articles of paper pulp, of paper and paper board	1.27	1.19	1.07	0.88	0.87	0.85	0.71	0.82	0.63	0.61
11.	Textile and Textile articles	2.00	2.02	2.00	2.26	2.31	2.97	2.67	2.58	2.00	1.79
	(*a*) Silk	0.21	0.18	0.18	0.22	0.24	0.32	0.31	0.32	0.28	0.26
	(*b*) Wool, fine or coarse animal hair	0.51	0.45	0.31	0.24	0.21	0.27	0.32	0.30	0.21	0.17
	(*c*) Cotton	0.09	0.16	0.35	0.63	0.57	0.93	0.55	0.61	0.40	0.29
	(*d*) Man-made filaments	0.22	0.21	0.27	0.38	0.37	0.49	0.54	0.43	0.35	0.30

...(*Contd.*)

Table 5.3 (*Contd.*)

1	2	13	14	15	16	17	18	19	20	21	22
12.	Footwear, headgear, umbrellas: prepared feather and articles thereof	0.32	0.07	0.07	0.06	0.06	0.05	0.05	0.05	0.05	0.07
13.	Stone, cement and similar material: ceramic products, glass and glassware	0.32	0.36	0.39	0.34	0.36	0.45	0.39	0.44	0.44	0.45
	(*a*) Articles of stone, plaster, cement, asbestos, mica or similar materials	0.06	0.06	0.07	0.05	0.06	0.07	0.08	0.09	0.09	0.09
	(*b*) Ceramic products	0.08	0.12	0.11	0.08	0.09	0.11	0.12	0.13	0.15	0.16
	(*c*) Glass and glassware	0.18	0.17	0.21	0.20	0.20	0.26	0.19	0.20	0.19	0.19
14.	Pearls, precious or semi-precious stones, metals and articles thereof: imitation jewellery and coins	10.14	15.89	21.17	20.59	19.20	18.18	17.05	18.11	18.63	13.87
15.	Base metals and articles of base metals	8.79	7.84	6.00	4.97	4.34	4.96	4.33	4.99	5.65	6.60
	a. Iron and steel	3.83	3.42	2.49	2.22	1.89	2.14	1.80	2.27	3.00	3.65
	b. Articles of iron and steel	1.09	1.18	1.04	0.66	0.60	0.69	0.71	0.82	0.79	0.87
	c. Copper and articles thereof	1.90	1.54	0.86	0.64	0.45	0.50	0.35	0.42	0.48	0.59
	d. Aluminium and articles thereof	0.84	0.50	0.55	0.42	0.45	0.59	0.50	0.47	0.43	0.55
16.	Machinery and their parts, electrical and electronic equipments, parts thereof	14.96	15.61	14.06	12.40	13.68	14.45	16.60	17.27	16.65	17.30
	(*a*) Nuclear reactors, boilers, machinery and mechanical appliances, parts thereof	10.89	10.80	9.30	7.79	8.38	8.26	8.35	8.87	8.65	9.32
	(*b*) Elec. mach. and equip and parts thereof: sound and TV recorder and reproducers and parts thereof	4.07	4.80	4.66	4.60	5.29	6.18	8.25	8.40	8.02	7.97

Table 5.4 : Structure of India's Imports at Constant Prices (1986-87 to 2005-06) (Rupees in Crores)

Sl.No.	Categories	1986-87	1987-88	1988-89	1989-90	1990-91	1991-92	1992-93	1993-94	1994-95	1995-96
1	2	3	4	5	6	7	8	9	10	11	12
1.	Live animals : animal products	91.63	698.49	297.49	140.88	14.05	82.27	64.16	35.45	133.11	215.87
2	Vegetable products	1517.21	1323.64	3276.56	1856.54	1751.62	943.66	1797.86	1645.70	1612.62	1603.10
	(*a*) Edible vegetable and certain roots and tubers	740.82	795.34	1048.14	574.82	1020.59	364.92	338.13	595.99	556.52	551.52
	(*b*) Edible fruits and nuts: peel of citrus fruits or melons	416.16	358.90	310.43	391.16	452.4	447.44	558.76	700.57	894.76	848.00
	(*c*) Cereals	63.52	15.00	1531.12	482.15	88.57	10.77	773.28	181.02	5.85	4.45
	(*d*) Coffee, tea, mate and spices	25.34	8.56	39.78	15.60	19.32	28.71	45.99	57.49	62.97	86.16
	(*e*) Oil seeds and oleaginous fruits: misc. grams seeds & fruits: industries or med	23.14	49.43	67.24	-	-	36.10	-	32.69	28.46	-
	(*f*) Lac: gums, resins and other veg. sabs and extracts	36.26	61.39	101.72	-	-	39.54	-	72.15	47.62	-
3.	Animal or vegetable fats and oils and their cleavage products: animal or vegetable waxes	2382.38	2976.51	1694.92	571.16	855.07	456.15	258.75	345.99	707.24	1741.12
4.	Prepared foodstuffs, beverages and tobacco	1470.14	911.55	267.32	527.18	323.23	360.72	352.45	361.17	3151.53	702.31
5.	Mineral products	9253.80	10281.23	12344.04	9819.97	14547.03	16506.84	19765.34	20953.7	22582.42	26495.77
	(*a*) Salt, sulphur, earths and stone, plastering materials lime and cement	966.55	766.55	830.44	861.94	863.54	846.74	627.21	863.67	750.24	1446.50
	(*b*) Ores, slag and ash	165.02	127.39	128.96	159.18	213.00	124.95	160.72	248.87	337.90	633.95
	(*c*) Mineral fuels, min. oil and products: bituminous substances: min waxes	7966.80	9265.38	10839.58	8731.70	13389.81	15301.56	18452.56	19841.16	20836.68	17823.49

...(*Contd.*)

Table 5.4 (*Contd.*)

1	2	3	4	5	6	7	8	9	10	11	12
6.	Products of the chemical or allied industries	5524.43	3775.22	4642.12	2784.47	5651.90	6342.00	7401.43	8411.04	9781.11	9802.89
	(*a*) Inorganic Chemicals	1225.09	903.53	1402.05	1234.26	1255.31	2069.13	2153.46	1541.78	1935.39	1480.41
	(*b*) Organic Chemicals	1323.2	1135.68	1198.37	1472.35	1401.57	1583.46	1780.32	3333.78	4411.10	5643.90
	(*c*) Fertilizers	1539.34	437.39	734.66	453.63	1375.59	1332.07	1599.59	1981.59	1841.99	2709.72
	(*d*) Misc. Chemical Products	359.58	391.13	276.93	139.55	342.21	331.98	439.78	505.16	508.18	466.87
7.	Plastic and rubber	1497.53	1423.34	1282.65	1775.94	1748.16	1696.87	1532.04	1970.64	2373.27	2994.84
	(*a*) Plastic and articles thereof	1085.10	1101.98	1012.50	1484.28	1360.85	1404.04	1162.37	1445.90	1864.43	2238.29
	(*b*) Rubber and articles thereof	412.42	321.35	270.14	351.65	387.3	292.83	369.67	524.74	508.84	756.55
8.	Hides and skins: leather products, furskins and article thereof	40.89	43.57	78.30	153.62	244.24	168.32	311.15	363.52	607.80	856.98
9.	Wood, cork and article thereof, manuf. of plaiting material: basketware wicker work	286.95	415.56	565.02	585.67	575.45	366.92	724.36	454.22	1165.57	1544.09
	(*a*) Wood and articles of wood : wood charcoal	283.05	413.11	557.58	576.63	569.34	364.11	718.60	450.03	1155.84	1530.74
10.	Paper and paper board and article thereof	1586.49	1188.33	1098.51	1013.37	1301.83	871.94	1136.73	1401.96	1463.71	1434.07
	(*a*) Pulp of wood or of other material : waste and scrap of paper and paperboard	615.39	488.71	346.51	357.67	590.40	332.98	363.05	497.33	474.03	416.47
	(*b*) Paper and paper board: articles of paper pulp, of paper and paper board	650.17	541.31	479.85	477.46	569.40	480.06	514.46	695.96	697.88	808.29
11.	Textile and Textile articles	664.16	945.51	1137.51	1095.17	1251.5	895.94	1182.71	1698.7	2914.00	2424.17
	(*a*) Silk	84.51	122.25	118.41	153.43	171.48	190.94	219.71	305.15	290.32	274.94
	(*b*) Wool, fine or coarse animal hair	171.67	352.66	340.11	333.87	334.31	256.8	294.62	417.63	427.90	450.14

	(c) Cotton	35.69	55.76	211.7	75.17	79.87	45.32	224.78	78.36	560.54	448.11
	(d) Man-made filaments	126.76	181.92	213.99	231.02	31.50	131.44	129.65	311.98	441.86	303.07
12.	Footwear, headgear, umbrellas: prepared feather and articles thereof	35.99	24.04	25.90	33.75	49.00	35.91	67.16	81.41	159.46	238.21
13.	Stone, cement and similar material: ceramic products, glass and glassware	609.71	410.52	535.60	405.56	399.56	405.99	253.90	279.62	415.78	486.50
	(a) Articles of stone, plaster, cement, asbestos, mica or similar materials	79.30	47.75	54.01	57.04	65.21	68.99	52.60	54.51	71.26	92.67
	(b) Ceramic products	213.13	96.39	93.76	98.45	119.55	136.30	66.86	80.78	114.27	131.39
	(c) Glass and glassware	317.27	266.39	387.85	250.03	214.79	200.70	134.43	144.33	230.24	262.43
14.	Pearls, precious or semi-precious stones, metals and articles thereof: imitation jewellery and coins	3533.23	4404.82	5651.52	5709.43	4906.59	4829.56	5460.83	9110.00	6253.85	7126.15
15.	Base metals and articles of base metals	7804.74	5187.59	8273.24	8267.38	6550.22	4771.39	5824.05	5668.27	6686.27	8531.81
	(a) Iron and steel	5018.85	3605.59	3477.52	3450.09	3625.93	2600.96	2684.36	2440.01	4164.72	4007.60
	(b) Articles of iron and steel	2240.94	1169.17	883.59	922.94	914.81	842.62	594.11	1047.79	885.05	879.9
	(c) Copper and articles thereof	709.29	988.87	1089.95	1145.12	1047.97	775.44	870.71	1228.83	1307.62	1447.85
	(d) Aluminium and articles thereof	529.28	350.74	104.36	285.94	147.39	120.16	69.49	251.54	430.44	504.89
16.	Machinery and their parts, electrical and electronic equipments, parts thereof	5762.47	552.45	5956.45	7931.43	6597.81	6035.60	8795.37	9498.48	25309.63	23552.54
	(a) Nuclear reactors, boilers, machinery and mechanical appliances, parts thereof	-	-	1603.62	1837.82	1794.83	2454.37	2967.46	6748.50	18749.76	6031.21
	(b) Elec. mach. and equip and parts thereof: sound and TV recorder and reproducers and parts thereof	498.07	585.48	1158.05	1543.19	1291.11	1459.08	2476.05	2749.98	7456.45	4223.86

...(*Contd.*)

Table 5.4 (*Contd.*)

1.	2	3	4	5	6	7	8	9	10	11	12
17.	Transport equipments	3177.71	1797.09	1507.14	2766.91	3011.19	1454.08	1739.83	3986.44	2622.86	2709.42
	(*a*) Railway/tramway locomotives truck etc., equipment and parts thereof	171.15	186.69	199.56	202.32	251.23	222.19	161.52	98.30	38.79	122.77
	(*b*) Road vehicles and parts	1644.08	616.50	700.23	688.28	940.74	764.32	745.66	700.21	690.08	1139.31
	(*c*) Aircraft, spacecraft and parts	663.79	661.20	352.16	1767.83	947.89	252.32	464.12	2933.37	1724.47	1193.33
	(*d*) Ship, boat and floating structure	698.63	332.69	255.16	108.47	871.33	215.23	368.51	254.56	169.50	253.98
18.	Instrument and appratus: clocks and watches: parts and accessories thereof	2203.73	1424.81	1275.10	1541.49	1619.67	1107.23	1547.10	1442.05	1655.51	3111.29
	(*a*) Optical measuring, medical and similar instruments and parts thereof	920.15	803.48	1032.96	1353.73	1529.6	793.28	2085.02	1389.47	2895.97	4876.49
19.	Arms and Ammunitions: parts & Accessories thereof	2.37	1.14	0.20	2.30	0.35	0.35	1.20	0.30	0.55	3.05
20.	Misc. manufactured articles	45.53	43.38	62.40	64.32	68.74	55.34	99.10	97.42	260.54	459.91
21.	Work of art, collectors pieces and antiques	0.23	0.01	0.04	0.62	0.25	0.24	0.15	0.18	0.70	1.04
22.	Project goods: some special uses	3080.24	2981.47	2435.34	2307.05	3193.29	3177.43	4666.99	5090.86	9563.22	14645.35
23.	Misc. goods	60.36	50.38	96.67	52.53	152.19	165.01	192.26	203.89	266.87	1029.86
	Total Imports	**47284.14**	**45469.62**	**49639.97**	**50797.33**	**52706.34**	**50641.16**	**62610.66**	**73101.01**	**90531.95**	**114299.95**

Sl.No.	Categories	1996-97	1997-98	1998-99	1999-00	2000-01	2001-02	2002-03	2003-04	2004-05	2005-06
1	2	13	14	15	16	17	18	19	20	21	22
1.	Live animals : animal products	38.78	215.36	162.40	277.8	128.28	115.18	165.49	233.25	178.15	122.36
2	Vegetable products	2943.23	3078.66	3748.00	3733.89	2633.99	5537.13	5335.80	4777.09	4008.86	4036.08
	(a) Edible vegetable and certain roots and tubers	1001.56	1002.86	721.24	430.32	475.43	3526.52	2766.68	2183.68	1324.19	1457.88
	(b) Edible fruits and nuts: peel of citrus fruits or melons	1215.98	1046.46	1454.68	1796.87	1617.72	1224.63	1708.96	1811.23	1909.90	1799.56
	(c) Cereals	312.58	757.21	921.6	801.65	21.43	1.90	0.57	0.92	2.50	8.76
	(d) Coffee, tea, mate and spices	99.62	128.09	338.06	92.96	103.07	91.09	194.5	291.37	204.56	279.76
	(e) Oil seeds and oleaginous fruits: misc. grams seeds & fruits: industries or med		43.21		129.41		158.42		186.65	244.55	364.87
	(f) Lac: gums, resins and other veg. sabs and extracts		94.14		135.82		189.24		137.94	200.34	274.71
3.	Animal or vegetable fats and oils and their cleavage products: animal or vegetable waxes	2173.79	1946.41	4061.31	3441.11	6654.81	3751.38	3595.63	7912.92	7161.68	7136.52
4.	Prepared foodstuffs, beverages and tobacco	442.11	692.39	1503.67	1596.18	656.13	861.13	1080.53	898.98	2409.12	2247.97
5.	Mineral products	28497.28	31711.9	36018.41	35799.55	33718.65	37098.22	38567.23	42061.12	47158.38	48026.19
	(a) Salt, sulphur, earths and stone, plastering materials lime and cement	742.24	805.01	1000.89	1231.41	1331.3	1284.91	1572.45	1523.70	2039.31	2145.79
	(b) Ores, slag and ash	356.87	295.70	529.57	766.39	874.30	1605.25	1713.97	1917.12	3202.23	4350.06
	(c) Mineral fuels, min. oil and products: bituminous substances: min waxes	27280.13	30143.06	33533.05	34026.40	32374.95	35259.20	36926.63	40441.12	45009.91	45921.08

...(*Contd.*)

Table 5.4 (*Contd.*)

1	2	13	14	15	16	17	18	19	20	21	22
6.	Products of the chemical or allied industries	10119.14	13116.64	10167.47	11669.05	11768.40	12448.92	12134.52	20169.20	19763.77	23163.16
	(*a*) Inorganic Chemicals	1546.95	2794.87	3072.49	3037.88	2008.35	2702.24	2779.69	3191.07	3390.64	3623.00
	(*b*) Organic Chemicals	6478.74	6083.07	11376.08	14287.87	11126.59	5787.80	6221.92	10642.41	10907.49	13325.86
	(*c*) Fertilizers	1474.22	2111.18	1911.43	2699.97	1050.31	1107.54	837.50	1149.21	1457.32	2679.89
	(*d*) Misc. Chemical Products	785.31	1050.22	1388.52	1390.38	1081.86	1310.67	1233.1	2174.81	1944.77	2202.07
7.	Plastic and rubber	3108.91	2483.54	3614.08	3363.02	2345.75	3235.98	3917.35	5118.96	5514.01	7357.91
	(*a*) Plastic and articles thereof	2343.67	1797.60	2618.76	2505.38	1639.03	2310.72	2840.66	3668.62	3920.50	5704.23
	(*b*) Rubber and articles thereof	765.23	685.93	995.31	857.64	706.71	925.26	1076.69	1450.33	1593.50	1653.68
8.	Hides and skins: leather products, furskins and article thereof	1099.26	1631.81	1560.72	2019.38	3028.97	2173.08	1282.92	1063.23	1021.36	1032.95
9.	Wood, cork and article thereof, manuf. of plaiting material: basketware wicker work	2092.83	4578.03	3917.79	5945.50	7470.62	5307.30	2492.50	3155.77	3115.31	2947.85
	(*a*) Wood and articles of wood : wood charcoal	2077.78	4554.39	3897.19	5919.64	7438.26	5291.19	2480.15	3146.05	3106.60	2937.46
10.	Paper and paper board and article thereof	1934.84	2629.41	2345.72	2472.39	2332.20	2595.36	3305.42	4432.76	4184.49	4724.89
	(*a*) Pulp of wood or of other material : waste and scrap of paper and paperboard	580.67	742.06	682.20	668.34	624.22	828.31	961.55	1078.00	1157.79	1322.67
	(*b*) Paper and paper board: articles of paper pulp, of paper and paper board	1181.44	1400.16	1243.2	1294.93	1126.8	1181.96	1466.77	2118.48	1893.43	2203.78
11.	Textile and Textile articles	2109.23	2281.82	3369.00	4849.29	3927.21	6794.85	6775.32	7681.85	8341.48	9416.42
	(*a*) Silk	225.48	207.47	310.11	476.35	417.11	750.13	810.73	972.70	1203.92	1401.80
	(*b*) Wool, fine or coarse animal hair	544.45	518.24	521.46	527.91	369.74	634.56	814.93	913.88	902.34	934.96

...(*Contd.*)

	(*c*) Cotton	97.44	182.85	591.23	1351.66	973.55	2126.06	1418.16	1842.75	1674.09	1542.76
	(*d*) Man-made filaments	240.29	238.85	468.46	819.76	636.75	1134.18	1400.48	1282.63	1482.24	1609.37
12.	Footwear, headgear, umbrellas: prepared feather and articles thereof	236.78	341.03	330.07	447.72	529.9	286.16	189.34	186.4	222.12	326.82
13.	Stone, cement and similar material: ceramic products, glass and glassware	652.4	794.65	820.84	1915.4	478.26	1002.72	1319.91	1958.74	2613.47	4742.44
	(*a*) Articles of stone, plaster, cement, asbestos, mica or similar materials	121.2	143.99	150.36	308.52	90.14	169.44	275.4	434.96	561.58	964.33
	(*b*) Ceramic products	174.35	267.79	237.85	493.41	118.55	256.48	399.45	605.84	914.09	1706.49
	(*c*) Glass and glassware	356.85	382.86	432.62	1113.46	269.56	576.79	645.05	917.92	1137.81	2071.59
14.	Pearls, precious or semi-precious stones, metals and articles thereof: imitation jewellery and coins	10647.34	17592.36	27506.4	34178.03	30321.05	32014.37	36987.97	46610.18	49724.37	42328.97
15.	Base metals and articles of base metals	11268.25	9213.91	10039.36	5449.74	10246.24	10105.24	10406.9	11092.74	16710.49	14545.99
	(*a*) Iron and steel	3267.84	3733.64	2840.77	2975.45	2276.07	2772.86	2966.12	1443.26	6631.8	10454.06
	(*b*) Articles of iron and steel	931.37	1292.83	1195.98	889.4	728.4	896.48	1173.08	1443.26	1752.27	2509.8
	(*c*) Copper and articles thereof	2056.33	1766.71	1388.58	1354.44	1043.11	1314.67	1177.02	1044.77	1462.42	1906.15
	(*d*) Aluminium and articles thereof	772.72	485.45	621.16	494.57	513.99	742.03	768.8	884.56	1000.74	1584.56
16.	Machinery and their parts, electrical and electronic equipments, parts thereof	19594.93	17498.02	16042.26	20628.83	23281.45	27754.63	36500.57	41415.02	45701.6	100596.1
	(*a*) Nuclear reactors, boilers, machinery and mechanical appliances, parts thereof	5224.93	4885.47	5553.61	6553.52	6360.93	4262.22	18913.29	13014.73	9790.7	14811.1

...(*Contd.*)

Table 5.4 (*Contd.*)

1	2	13	14	15	16	17	18	19	20	21	22
	(*b*) Elec. mach. and equip and parts thereof: sound and TV recorder and reproducers and parts thereof	4505.13	5500.46	3907.45	4961.71	5713.48	6132.92	9152.44	5809.69	7125.21	11477.96
17.	Transport equipments	3572.22	2690.54	2910.51	4050.16	3853.72	4315	6423.69	9851.49	11539.06	19231.77
	(*a*) Railway/tramway locomotives truck etc., equipment and parts thereof	323.88	69.85	346.63	125.49	155.49	63.23	94.19	339.21	329.93	296.53
	(*b*) Road vehicles and parts	1392.84	1069.68	1082.95	1565.00	1303.72	1143.54	1151.12	1722.32	2250	2220.48
	(*c*) Aircraft, spacecraft and parts	1207.94	911.57	684.72	332.62	1041.22	967.4	3294.39	3665.77	4242.12	10822.04
	(*d*) Ship, boat and floating structure	647.53	639.42	796.19	2027.05	1353.29	2140.82	1883.98	4224.17	4716.99	5892.71
18.	Instrument and appratus: clocks and watches: parts and accessories thereof	2232.62	12680.17	11744.2	21393.44	18534.54	24179.9	18297.13	19138.51	15802.42	12727.33
	(*a*) Optical measuring, medical and similar instruments and parts thereof	5406.92	10384.18	12497.07	14483.79	17451.15	12304.01	8460.05	6470.72	7540.22	9678.47
19.	Arms and Ammunitions: parts & Accessories thereof	3.83	10.98	8.11	16.08	6.49	9.69	15.75	14.18	9.91	3.38
20.	Misc. manufactured articles	538.64	975.71	938.52	1546.09	2094.62	1415.3	1204.76	1097.81	1173.2	1568.53
21.	Work of art, collectors pieces and antiques	3.05	3.41	1.71	1.66	6.43	5.02	7.33	5.86	3.62	45.51
22.	Project goods: some special uses	16280.81	18732.3	27382.56	12685.45	11506.85	5457.66	3265.37	1748.41	2065.84	2781.75
23.	Misc. goods	900.08	878.58	681.45	1070.79	2306.56	828.31	1008.98	703.25	1152.71	1545.45
	Total Imports	**113570.68**	**124798.67**	**142928.47**	**156622.65**	**155031.39**	**162642.42**	**177999.55**	**215473.2**	**239194.46**	**364806.32**

Source: (i) DGFTI, Ministry of Commerce, Government of India (Various Issues).
(ii) www.rbi.org.in

Table 5.5 : Structure of India's Imports at Constant Prices (1986-87 to 2005-06) (Percentage Share)

Sl.No.	Categories	1986-87	1987-88	1988-89	1989-90	1990-91	1991-92	1992-93	1993-94	1994-95	1995-96
1	2	3	4	5	6	7	8	9	10	11	12
1.	Live animals : animal products	0.19	1.53	0.59	0.27	0.02	0.16	0.10	0.04	0.14	0.18
2	Vegetable products	3.20	2.91	6.60	3.65	3.32	1.86	2.87	2.25	1.78	1.40
	(*a*) Edible vegetable and certain roots and tubers	1.56	1.74	2.11	1.13	1.93	0.72	0.54	0.81	0.61	0.48
	(*b*) Edible fruits and nuts: peel of citrus fruits or melons	0.88	0.78	0.62	0.77	0.85	0.88	0.89	0.95	0.98	0.74
	(*c*) Cereals	0.13	0.03	3.08	0.94	0.16	0.02	1.23	0.24	0.00	0.00
	(*d*) Coffee, tea, mate and spices	0.05	0.01	0.08	0.03	0.03	0.05	0.07	0.07	0.07	0.07
	(*e*) Oil seeds and oleaginous fruits: misc. grams seeds & fruits: industries or med	0.04	0.109	0.13			0.07		0.04	0.03	
	(*f*) Lac: gums, resins and other veg. sabs and extracts	0.07	0.13	0.20	0.02		0.07		0.09	0.05	
3.	Animal or vegetable fats and oils and their cleavage products: animal or vegetable waxes	5.03	6.54	3.4	1.12	1.62	0.90	0.41	0.47	0.78	1.52
4.	Prepared foodstuffs, beverages and tobacco	3.10	2.00	0.5	1.04	0.613	0.71	0.56	0.49	3.48	0.61
5.	Mineral products	19.57	22.61	24.86	19.33	27.60	32.59	31.56	28.66	24.94	23.18
	(*a*) Salt, sulphur, earths and stone, plastering materials lime and cement	2.04	1.68	1.67	1.70	1.63	1.67	1.00	1.18	0.82	1.26
	(*b*) Ores, slag and ash	0.34	0.28	0.26	0.31	0.40	0.24	0.25	0.34	0.37	0.55
	(*c*) Mineral fuels, min. oil and products: bituminous substances: min waxes	16.84	20.37	21.83	17.18	25.40	30.21	29.47	27.14	23.01	15.59

...(*Contd.*)

Table 5.5 (*Contd.*)

1	2	3	4	5	6	7	8	9	10	11	12
6.	Products of the chemical or allied industries	11.68	8.30	9.35	5.48	10.72	12.52	11.82	11.50	10.80	8.57
	(*a*) Inorganic Chemicals	2.59	1.98	2.82	2.43	2.38	4.08	3.43	2.10	2.13	1.29
	(*b*) Organic Chemicals	2.79	2.49	2.41	2.89	2.65	3.12	2.84	4.56	4.87	4.93
	(*c*) Fertilizers	3.25	0.96	1.48	0.89	2.61	2.63	2.55	2.71	2.03	2.37
	(*d*) Misc. Chemical Products	0.76	0.86	0.55	0.27	0.64	0.65	0.70	0.69	0.56	0.40
7.	Plastic and rubber	3.16	3.13	2.58	3.49	3.31	3.35	2.44	2.69	2.62	2.62
	(*a*) Plastic and articles thereof	2.29	2.42	2.04	2.92	2.58	2.77	1.85	1.97	2.05	1.95
	(*b*) Rubber and articles thereof	0.87	0.70	0.54	0.69	0.73	0.57	0.59	0.71	0.56	0.66
8.	Hides and skins: leather products, furskins and article thereof	0.08	0.09	0.15	0.30	0.46	0.33	0.49	0.49	0.67	0.75
9.	Wood, cork and article thereof, manuf. of plaiting material: basketware wicker work	0.60	0.91	1.13	1.15	1.09	0.72	1.15	0.62	1.28	1.35
	(*a*) Wood and articles of wood : wood charcoal	0.59	0.90	1.12	1.13	1.08	0.71	1.14	0.61	1.27	1.33
10.	Paper and paper board and article thereof	3.35	2.61	2.21	1.99	2.47	1.72	1.81	1.91	1.61	1.25
	(*a*) Pulp of wood or of other material : waste and scrap of paper and paperboard	1.30	1.07	0.69	0.70	1.12	0.65	0.58	0.68	0.52	0.36
	(*b*) Paper and paper board: articles of paper pulp, of paper and paper board	1.37	1.19	0.96	0.94	1.08	0.94	0.82	0.95	0.77	0.70
11.	Textile and Textile articles	1.40	2.07	2.29	2.15	2.37	1.76	1.88	2.32	3.21	2.12
	(*a*) Silk	0.17	0.26	0.23	0.30	0.32	0.37	0.35	0.41	0.32	0.24
	(*b*) Wool, fine or coarse animal hair	0.36	0.77	0.68	0.65	0.63	0.50	0.47	0.57	0.47	0.39
	(*c*) Cotton	0.07	0.12	0.42	0.14	0.15	0.08	0.35	0.10	0.61	0.39
	(*d*) Man-made filaments	0.26	0.40	0.43	0.45	0.59	0.26	0.20	0.42	0.48	0.26

12.	Footwear, headgear, umbrellas: prepared feather and articles thereof	0.07	0.05	0.05	0.06	0.09	0.07	0.10	0.11	0.17	0.20
13.	Stone, cement and similar material: ceramic products, glass and glassware	1.28	0.90	1.07	0.79	0.75	0.80	0.40	0.38	0.45	0.42
	(*a*) Articles of stone, plaster, cement, asbestos, mica or similar materials	0.16	0.10	0.10	0.11	0.12	0.13	0.08	0.07	0.07	0.08
	(*b*) Ceramic products	0.45	0.21	0.18	0.19	0.22	0.26	0.10	0.11	0.12	0.11
	(*c*) Glass and glassware	0.67	0.58	0.78	0.49	0.40	0.39	0.21	0.19	0.25	0.23
14.	Pearls, precious or semi-precious stones, metals and articles thereof: imitation jewellery and coins	7.47	9.68	11.38	11.24	9.30	9.53	8.72	12.46	6.90	6.23
15.	Base metals and articles of base metals	16.50	11.40	16.66	16.275	12.42	9.42	9.30	7.75	7.38	7.46
	(*a*) Iron and steel	10.61	7.93	7.00	6.79	6.87	5.13	4.28	3.33	4.60	3.50
	(*b*) Articles of iron and steel	4.73	2.57	1.78	1.81	1.73	1.66	0.94	1.43	0.97	0.77
	(*c*) Copper and articles thereof	1.50	2.17	2.19	2.25	1.98	0.00	1.39	1.68	1.44	1.26
	(*d*) Aluminium and articles thereof	1.11	0.77	0.21	0.56	0.28	0.23	0.11	0.34	0.47	0.44
16.	Machinery and their parts, electrical and electronic equipments, parts thereof	12.18	12.14	11.99	15.61	12.51	11.91	14.04	12.99	27.95	20.60
	(*a*) Nuclear reactors, boilers, machinery and mechanical appliances, parts thereof	1.28		3.23	3.61	3.40	2.95	4.74	9.23	20.71	5.27
	(*b*) Elec. mach. and equip and parts thereof: sound and TV recorder and reproducers and parts thereof	1.05	1.28	2.33	3.03	2.45	2.88	3.95	3.76	8.23	3.69

...(*Contd.*)

Table 5.5 (*Contd.*)

1	2	3	4	5	6	7	8	9	10	11	12
17.	Transport equipments	6.72	3.95	3.03	5.44	5.71	2.87	2.77	5.45	2.89	2.37
	(*a*) Railway/tramway locomotives truck etc., equipment and parts thereof	0.36	0.41	0.40	0.39	0.47	0.43	0.25	0.13	0.04	0.10
	(*b*) Road vehicles and parts	3.47	1.35	1.41	1.35	1.78	1.50	1.19	0.95	0.76	0.99
	(*c*) Aircraft, spacecraft and parts	1.40	1.45	0.70	3.48	1.79	0.49	0.74	4.01	1.90	1.04
	(*d*) Ship, boat and floating structure	1.47	0.73	0.51	0.21	1.65	0.42	0.58	0.34	0.18	0.22
18.	Instrument and appratus: clocks and watches: parts and accessories thereof	4.66	3.13	2.56	3.03	3.07	2.18	2.47	1.97	1.82	2.72
	(*a*) Optical measuring, medical and similar instruments and parts thereof	1.94	1.7	2.08	2.66	2.90	1.56	3.33	1.90	3.19	4.26
19.	Arms and Ammunitions: parts & Accessories thereof	0.00	0.00	0.00	0.00	0.00	0.00	0.00	0.00	0.00	0.00
20.	Misc. manufactured articles	0.09	0.09	0.12	0.12	0.13	0.10	0.15	0.1	0.28	0.40
21.	Work of art, collectors pieces and antiques	0.00	0.00	0.00	0.00	0.00	0.00	0.00	0.00	0.00	0.00
22.	Project goods: some special uses	6.51	6.55	4.90	4.54	6.05	6.27	7.45	6.96	10.56	12.81
23.	Misc. goods	0.12	0.11	0.19	0.10	0.28	0.32	0.30	0.27	0.29	0.90

Sl.No.	Categories	1996-97	1997-98	1998-99	1999-00	2000-01	2001-02	2002-03	2003-04	2004-05	2005-06
1	2	13	14	15	16	17	18	19	20	21	22
1.	Live animals : animal products	0.03	0.17	0.11	0.17	0.08	0.07	0.09	0.10	0.07	0.03
2	Vegetable products	2.59	2.46	2.62	2.38	1.69	3.40	2.99	2.21	1.67	1.10
	(*a*) Edible vegetable and certain roots and tubers	0.88	0.80	0.57	0.27	0.30	2.16	1.55	1.01	0.55	0.40
	(*b*) Edible fruits and nuts: peel of citrus fruits or melons	1.07	0.83	1.01	1.14	1.04	0.75	0.96	0.84	0.79	0.49
	(*c*) Cereals	0.27	0.60	0.64	0.51	0.01	0.00	0.00	0.00	0.00	0.00
	(*d*) Coffee, tea, mate and spices	0.08	0.10	0.23	0.05	0.06	0.05	0.10	0.13	0.08	0.07
	(*e*) Oil seecs and oleaginous fruits: misc. grams seeds & fruits: industries or med		0.03		0.08		0.09		0.08	0.10	0.10
	(*f*) Lac: gums, resins and other veg. sabs and extracts		0.07		0.08		0.11		0.06	0.08	0.07
3.	Animal or vegetable fats and oils and their cleavage products: animal or vegetable waxes	1.91	1.56	2.84	2.19	4.29	2.30	2.02	3.67	2.99	1.95
4.	Prepared foodstuffs, beverages and tobacco	0.38	0.55	1.05	1.01	0.42	0.52	0.60	0.41	1.00	0.61
5.	Mineral products	25.09	25.41	25.20	22.85	21.75	22.81	21.66	19.52	19.71	13.16
	(*a*) Salt, sulphur, earths and stone, plastering materials lime and cement	0.65	0.64	0.70	0.78	0.85	0.79	0.88	0.70	0.85	0.58
	(*b*) Ores, slag and ash	0.31	0.23	0.37	0.48	0.56	0.98	0.96	0.89	1.33	1.19
	(*c*) Mineral fuels, min. oil and products: bituminous substances: min waxes	24.02	24.15	23.46	21.72	20.883	21.67	20.74	18.76	18.81	12.58

...(*Contd.*)

Table 5.5 (*Contd.*)

1	2	13	14	15	16	17	18	19	20	21	22
6.	Products of the chemical or allied industries	8.91	10.51	7.11	7.45	7.59	7.65	6.81	9.36	8.26	6.34
	(*a*) Inorganic Chemicals	1.36	2.24	2.15	1.94	1.29	1.66	1.56	1.48	1.41	0.99
	(*b*) Organic Chemicals	5.70	4.87	7.95	9.12	7.17	3.55	3.49	4.93	4.56	3.65
	(*c*) Fertilizers	1.29	1.69	1.33	1.72	0.67	0.68	0.47	0.53	0.60	0.73
	(*d*) Misc. Chemical Products	0.69	0.84	0.97	0.88	0.69	0.80	0.69	1.00	0.81	0.60
7.	Plastic and rubber	2.73	1.99	2.52	2.14	1.51	1.99	2.20	2.37	2.30	2.01
	(*a*) Plastic and articles thereof	2.06	1.44	1.83	1.60	1.05	1.42	1.59	1.70	1.63	1.5
	(*b*) Rubber and articles thereof	0.67	0.55	0.69	0.54	0.45	0.56	0.60	0.67	0.66	0.45
8.	Hides and skins: leather products, furskins and article thereof	0.96	1.30	1.09	1.28	1.95	1.33	0.72	0.49	0.42	0.28
9.	Wood, cork and article thereof, manuf. of plaiting material: basketware wicker work	1.84	3.66	2.74	3.79	4.81	3.2	1.40	1.46	1.30	0.80
	(*a*) Wood and articles of wood : wood charcoal	1.83	3.64	2.72	3.78	4.79	3.25	1.39	1.46	1.29	0.80
10.	Paper and paper board and article thereof	1.70	2.10	1.64	1.57	1.50	1.59	1.85	2.05	1.74	1.29
	(*a*) Pulp of wood or of other material : waste and scrap of paper and paperboard	0.51	0.59	0.47	0.42	0.40	0.50	0.54	0.50	0.48	0.36
	(*b*) Paper and paper board: articles of paper pulp, of paper and paper board	1.04	1.12	0.87	0.82	0.72	0.72	0.82	0.98	0.79	0.60
11.	Textile and Textile articles	1.85	1.82	2.35	3.09	2.53	4.17	3.8	3.56	3.48	2.58
	(*a*) Silk	0.19	0.16	0.21	0.30	0.26	0.46	0.49	0.45	0.50	0.38
	(*b*) Wool, fine or coarse animal hair	0.47	0.41	0.36	0.33	0.23	0.39	0.45	0.42	0.37	0.25
	(*c*) Cotton	0.08	0.14	0.41	0.86	0.62	1.30	0.79	0.85	0.70	0.42

	(*d*) Man-made filaments	0.21	0.19	0.32	0.52	0.41	0.69	0.78	0.59	0.62	0.44
12.	Footwear, headgear, umbrellas: prepared feather and articles thereof	0.20	0.27	0.23	0.28	0.34	0.17	0.10	0.08	0.09	0.09
13.	Stone, cement and similar material: ceramic products, glass and glassware	0.57	0.63	0.57	1.22	0.30	0.61	0.74	0.90	1.09	1.30
	(*a*) Articles of stone, plaster, cement, asbestos, mica or similar materials	0.10	0.11	0.10	0.19	0.05	0.10	0.15	0.20	0.23	0.26
	(*b*) Ceramic products	0.15	0.21	0.16	0.31	0.07	0.15	0.22	0.28	0.38	0.46
	(*c*) Glass and glassware	0.31	0.30	0.30	0.71	0.17	0.35	0.36	0.42	0.47	0.56
14.	Pearls, precious or semi-precious stones, metals and articles thereof: imitation jewellery and coins	9.37	14.09	19.24	21.82	19.55	19.68	20.78	21.63	20.78	11.60
15.	Base metals and articles of base metals	9.92	7.38	7.02	3.48	6.60	6.21	5.84	5.14	6.98	3.98
	(*a*) Iron and steel	2.87	2.99	1.98	1.90	1.46	1.70	1.66	0.67	2.77	2.86
	(*b*) Articles of iron and steel	0.82	1.03	0.83	0.56	0.47	0.55	0.65	0.67	0.73	0.68
	(*c*) Copper and articles thereof	1.81	1.41	0.97	0.86	0.67	0.80	0.66	0.48	0.61	0.52
	(*d*) Aluminium and articles thereof	0.68	0.38	0.43	0.31	0.33	0.45	0.43	0.41	0.41	0.43
16.	Machinery and their parts, electrical and electronic equipments, parts thereof	17.25	14.02	11.22	13.17	15.01	17.06	20.50	19.22	19.10	27.57
	(*a*) Nuclear reactors, boilers, machinery and mechanical appliances, parts thereof	4.60	3.91	3.88	4.18	4.10	2.62	10.62	6.04	4.09	4.06
	(*b*) Elec. mach. and equip and parts thereof: sound and TV recorder and reproducers and parts thereof	3.96	4.40	2.73	3.16	3.68	3.77	5.14	2.69	2.97	3.14

...(*Contd.*)

Table 5.5 (*Contd.*)

1	2	13	14	15	16	17	18	19	20	21	22
17.	Transport equipments	3.14	2.15	2.03	2.58	2.48	2.65	3.60	4.57	4.82	5.27
	(*a*) Railway/tramway locomotives truck etc., equipment and parts thereof	0.28	0.05	0.24	0.08	0.10	0.03	0.05	0.15	0.13	0.08
	(*b*) Road vehicles and parts	1.22	0.85	0.75	0.99	0.84	0.70	0.64	0.79	0.9	0.60
	(*c*) Aircraft, spacecraft and parts	1.06	0.73	0.47	0.21	0.67	0.59	1.85	1.70	1.77	2.96
	(*d*) Ship, boat and floating structure	0.57	0.51	0.55	1.29	0.87	1.31	1.05	1.96	1.97	1.61
18.	Instrument and appratus: clocks and watches: parts and accessories thereof	1.96	10.16	8.21	13.65	11.95	14.86	10.27	8.88	6.60	3.48
	(*a*) Optical measuring, medical and similar instruments and parts thereof	4.76	8.32	8.74	9.24	11.25	7.56	4.75	3.0	3.15	2.65
19.	Arms and Ammunitions: parts & Accessories thereof	0.00	0.00	0.00	0.01	0.00	0.00	0.00	0.00	0.00	0.00
20.	Misc. manufactured articles	0.47	0.78	0.65	0.98	1.35	0.87	0.67	0.50	0.4	0.43
21.	Work of art, collectors pieces and antiques	0.00	0.00	0.00	0.00	0.00	0.00	0.00	0.00	0.00	0.01
22.	Project goods: some special uses	14.33	15.01	19.15	8.09	7.42	3.35	1.83	0.81	0.86	0.76
23.	Misc. goods	0.79	0.70	0.47	0.68	1.48	0.50	0.56	0.32	0.48	0.42

Source: Author's Calculations.

CHAPTER

6

Determinants of India's Imports

For any developing country, high import is one of the prerequisites, during the initial stages of economic development. The demand for imports depends upon a large number of macro variables including size, composition and growth rate of population, level and growth rate of GNP, relative prices, rate of capital formation, size and growth of export earnings. Besides, many other factors can influence imports at aggregate and disaggregate level like tastes and preferences of consumers, natural calamities, availability or non availability of substitutes to important import items, level of domestic production etc. (Kutty, 2001 and Mathur, 2003).

The present chapter is devoted to the estimation of import demand functions for India's total imports and for some of its major categories. The determinants taken at aggregate level for total imports are Relative Prices (RP), which is the ratio of unit value indices of imports to whole sale price indices, Gross Domestic Product at Factor cost (GDPFC) as income measure, Foreign Exchange Reserves (FR) as measure of capacity to import and a Dummy (Dum) variable is included to capture the impact of liberalisation policies. The value of dummy variable is '0' for 1986-

87 to 1990-91 and '1' for 1991-92 to 2003-04. In addition to these, the Domestic Production (DP) variable is also considered in case of all major categories of imports except for mineral products imports and pearls, precious and semi precious stones imports. Both of these categories are import dependent i.e., mineral products imports for domestic needs due to less domestic production and pearls, precious and Semi precious stones imports for exports need as it is a export related item. The domestic production variable helps us to determine whether the imports of particular category are acting as substitute or supplement for domestic production of some category. The variable of Gross Domestic Capital Formation (GDCF) is considered as a determinant in case of machinery and their parts imports. The Exports in previous year (Exp_{t-1}) variable is also taken as one of the determinant in case of imports of pearls, precious and semi-precious stones.

In literature we find many studies measuring regression equations, using both linear as well as log linear forms. Our study uses both the forms to measure the impact of independent variables on the dependent variables. Further each form has two models or regression equations, one is without dummy variable and other is with dummy variable. On the whole, the linear and double log forms have been estimated with and without dummy variable for total imports (TI) and for the sub categories of Agricultural Imports (AI), Chemical or Allied Industries Imports (CI), Base Metals and Articles of metals (BI), Machinery and their parts imports (MhI), Textiles and Textile articles imports (TxI), Mineral products imports (MnI) and Pearls, precious and Semi Precious Stones imports (PI). Imports at aggregate level, categories of imports and all the variables have been taken at a constant price except in case of pearls, precious and semi precious stones imports. Following are the results in both the forms, for total imports and various categories of imports.

Total Imports (TI)

Total imports have been assumed to be dependent upon income (GDPFC), relative prices (RP), foreign reserves (FR) and dummy variable (Dum) for studying the impact of liberalization.

Linear Form

Model 1

$$TI = 9441.876 + 0.177\,(GDPFC) - 73631.840\,(RP) + 0.032\,(FR)$$

(0.637) (15.676)* (–5.383)* (1.341)

$R^2 = 0.992$ $\bar{R}^2 = 0.991$

F ratio = 627.646 D-W = 1.847

Model 2

$$TI = 8863.380 + 0.178\,(GDPFC) - 73454.10\,(RP) + 0.03\,(FR) - 337.28\,(Dum)$$

(0.515) (10.96)* (–5.104)* (1.095) (–0.070)

$R^2 = 0.992$ $\bar{R}^2 = 0.990$

F ratio = 437.299 D-W = 1.842

Total imports are positively related with respect to income. The income variable has been found to be significant at one per cent level. Total imports are negatively related with respect to relative prices and this variable has also been found to be significant at one per cent level. The sign of foreign reserves variable is appropriate but it has been found to be non significant one. The sign of dummy variable (representing liberalisation policies) is negative and it has been found be nonsignificant. Results of import demand function with dummy variable in linear form gives similar results. Both income and price variable are highly significant. The values of R^2 and $\bar{R}^2$ are 0.99 and 0.99, respectively, in both models 1 and 2 (i.e., with and without dummy variable). The F-ratio is significant in both the models and value of D-W statistics is near about 1.8 in both the models.

Double Log Form

Model 3

$$\text{Log}\,TI = -5.067 + 1.673\,\text{Log}\,(GDPFC) - 0.939\,\text{Log}\,(RP) + 0.014\,\log\,(FR)$$

(-6.004)* (10.003)* (-6.132)* (0.428)

$R^2 = 0.993$ $\bar{R}^2 = 0.992$

F ratio = 712.840 D-W = 1.833

Model 4

$$\text{Log TI} = -6.074 + 1.898\,\text{Log (GDPFC)} - 1.185\,\text{Log (RP)} - 0.055\,\text{Log (FR)}$$
$$(-5.823)^{*} \quad (8.718)^{*} \qquad\qquad (-5.445)^{*} \qquad\qquad (-0.988)$$
$$+\,0.014\,\text{Log (Dum)}$$
$$(1.526)$$
$$R^2 = 0.994 \qquad\qquad \bar{R}^2 = 0.992$$
$$\text{F ratio} = 584.250 \qquad\qquad \text{D-W} = 2.373$$

In case of double log form, both models (with and without dummy variable), total imports have been found to be both price elastic as well as income elastic. The income variable is positively related with total imports and also found to be significant at one per cent level. The coefficient of income implies that demand for imports increases more than proportionally to the increase in GDPFC. The price variable is negatively related with respect to total imports and also significant at one per cent level. The sign of foreign reserves is positive in case of without dummy variable model, while sign is negative in case of with dummy variable model. The sign of dummy variable is positive, i.e., with the coming up of liberalisation policies total imports show an increase. But dummy variable has been found to be non significant. The values of R^2 and $\bar{R}^2$ are at very high level. The value of D-W statistics is near to 2 in model 3, whereas higher than 2 in case model 4.

On the whole the dummy variable which is introduced to capture the impact of liberalisation policies, has been found to be non significant in both the forms. However, it doesn't mean that there was no impact of liberalisation on imports. The liberalisation affected imports through its positive impact on GDP growth. The import elasticity coefficient with respect to income is more than one in both the models, where as with respect to prices coefficient is less than one in without dummy variable model and is more than one when dummy variable is added to the model. In case of all the models R^2 and $\bar{R}^2$ are very high and F-ratio is significant. The value of D-W statistic is appropriate in models 1, 2 and 3, but in case of model 4 it is higher than 2.

Agricultural Imports (AI)

Agricultural imports have been assumed to be dependent pon gross domestic product at factor cost (GDPFC), relative price (RP), domestic production (DP) and foreign reserves (FR).

Linear Form

Model 1

$$AI = 2863.185 + 0.015\,(GDPFC) - 9771.36\,(RP) - 0.015\,(DP) - 0.001\,(FR)$$

(0.801) (1.962)*** (-3.998)* (-0.686) (-0.096)

$R^2 = 0.891$ $\bar{R}^2 = 0.858$

F- ratio = 26.817 D-W = 1.840

Model 2

$$AI = 6180.533 + 0.012\,(GDPFC) - 11756.64\,(RP) - 0.017\,(DP)$$

(1.251) (1.429) (-3.690)* (-0.808)

$$+ 0.002\,(FR) + 1923.604\,(Dum)$$

(0.193) (0.974)

$R^2 = 0.899$ $\bar{R}^2 = 0.858$

F-ratio = 21.559 D-W = 1.834

In case of linear form, the agricultural imports are positively related with respect to income. The income variable has been found to be significant at 10 per cent level in model 1 (i.e., without dummy variable), while it is found to be non-significant in case of model 2 (i.e., with dummy variable). The sign of relative prices is negative and it has been found to be significant at one per cent level. In both the models the sign of domestic production is appropriate, whereas domestic production variable has been found to be non-significant in both the models. The variable of foreign reserves has been found to be negative in case of model 1 (i.e., without dummy variable) and positive in case of model 2 (i.e., with dummy variable). But in both the models (1 and 2) the foreign reserves variable has been found to be non significant. The dummy variable has been found to be positively related with respect to agricultural imports, but it is nonsignificant. The values of R^2 and $\bar{R}^2$ are almost same and are at appropriate level. The values of D-W statistics are near to 1.8 in both the models.

Double Log Form

Model 3

$$\text{Log AI} = -1.376 + 1.313\ \text{Log (GDPFC)} - 1.832\ \text{Log (RP)} - 0.793\ \text{Log (DP)}$$
$$(-0.412)\quad (1.528)\qquad (-6.438)^{*}\qquad (-2.455)^{**}$$

$$+ 0.263\ \text{Log (FR)}$$
$$(1.967)^{***}$$

$R^2 = 0.955$ $\qquad$ $\bar{R}^2 = 0.942$

F-ratio = 70.209 $\qquad$ D-W = 1.293

Model 4

$$\text{Log AI} = -0.953 + 1.035\ \text{Log (GDPFC)} - 1.760\ \text{Log (RP)} - 0.628\ \text{Log (DP)}$$
$$(-0.279)\quad (1.109)\qquad (-5.842)^{*}\qquad (-1.640)$$

$$+0.337\ \text{Log (FR)} - 0.030\ \text{Log (Dum)}$$
$$(2.072)^{***}\qquad (-0.822)$$

$R^2 = 0.958$ $\qquad$ $\bar{R}^2 = 0.940$

F-ratio = 54.998 $\qquad$ D-W = 1.428

In case of double log form, the agricultural imports have been found to be income elastic but income variable is non significant in both the models 3 and 4. Agricultural imports have been found to be elastic with respect to relative prices and also significant at one per cent level, in both the models 3 and 4 (i.e., with and without dummy variable). The domestic production variable is negatively related with agricultural imports and it has been found to be significant at five per cent level only in case of model 3 (i.e., without dummy variable). The foreign reserves are positively related with respect to agricultural imports and significant at 10 per cent level, in both the models (3 and 4). The sign of dummy variable is negative, i.e., liberalisation has no positive impact on Agricultural imports. The values of R^2 and $\bar{R}^2$ are almost same in both the models and are at appropriate level. The values of D-W statistics are 1.29 and 1.42 in model 3 and model 4 respectively.

Thus, agricultural imports are found to be significant with respect to relative prices in all the four models, where as with respect to income variable imports are significant in case of model

1 only. This is due to the fact that agricultural imports as a category has very small share in total imports. As a result of which GDP growth does not have any significant impact on agricultural imports. The import elasticity coefficient for agricultural imports with respect to both income and price is more than one, but coefficient of relative prices is greater than coefficient of income. The agricultural imports are less elastic with respect to domestic production and foreign reserves (as coefficients of both are less than one). The dummy variable has been found to be non significant in all the models, showing lesser impact of liberalisation policies on these imports. In case of double log form values of R^2 and $\bar{R}^2$ are better as compare to linear form. The F- ratio is significant in all the cases. The value of D-W statistic is better in case of linear models.

Products of Chemical or Allied Industries Imports (CI)

Chemical and allied industries imports include inorganic chemicals, organic chemicals, fertilizers and miscellaneous chemical products. These imports have been assumed to be dependent on income (GDPFC), relative prices (RP), domestic production (DP), foreign reserves (FR) and dummy (Dum) variable for capturing the impact of liberalisation policies.

Linear Form

Model 1

CI = 5468.756 – 0.007 (GDPFC) – 1980.676 (RP) + 0.164 (DP) + 0.011(FR)
(1.969)*** (-0.985) (-1.923)*** (2.729)** (1.691)

R^2 = 0.920 $\bar{R}^2$ = 0.896

F-ratio = 37.673 D-W = 1.233

Model 2

CI = 7534.468 – 0.011(GDPFC) – 1666.109 (RP) + 0.151(DP)
(2.838)** (-1.686) (-1.797)*** (2.806)**

+ 0.018 (FR) + 2191.197 (Dum)
(2.683)** (2.114)**

R^2 = 0.942 $\bar{R}^2$ = 0.918

F-ratio = 39.070 D-W = 1.933

In case of linear form, the income variable has been found to be negatively related with respect to chemical imports (which is an inappropriate sign) and also income variable is non-significant in both the models (1 and 2). The relative prices are negatively related with respect to imports of this category and found to be significant at 10 per cent level in both the models. The sign of domestic production variable is positive and it has been found to be significant at five per cent level in both the models. The sign of foreign reserves is positive in both the models, but found to be significant at five per cent level only in case of model 2 (i.e., with dummy variable). The positive sign of dummy variable shows that with the coming up of liberalisation measures, the imports of chemical products also show higher growth. The dummy variable has been found to be significant at five per cent level. The positive sign of domestic production confirms about an increase in raw material imports of this category. The values of R^2 and $\bar{R}^2$ are found to be appropriate in case of model 1 and model 2, whereas the value of D-W statistic is better in case of model 2 (i.e., with dummy variable). The F- ratio has been found to be significant in both models.

Double Log Form

Model 3

$$\underset{}{\text{Log CI}} = \underset{(0.818)}{2.603} \underset{(-0.850)}{-0.759 \text{ Log (GDPFC)}} \underset{(-2.578)^{**}}{- 0.488 \text{ Log (RP)}}$$

$$\underset{(1.997)^{***}}{+1.058 \text{ Log (DP)}} \underset{(1.513)}{+ 0.163 \text{ Log (FR)}}$$

R^2 = 0.918 $\bar{R}^2$ = 0.893

F-ratio = 36.790 D-W = 1.767

Model 4

$$\text{Log CI} = \underset{(-0.572)}{-2.072} \underset{(0.727)}{+0.793 \text{ Log (GDPFC)}} \underset{(-3.496)^{*}}{- 0.652 \text{ Log (RP)}} \underset{(0.552)}{+0.325 \text{ Log (DP)}}$$

$$\underset{(-0.340)}{- 0.047 \text{ Log (FR)}} \underset{(2.081)^{***}}{+ 0.057 \text{ Log (Dum)}}$$

R^2 = 0.940 $\bar{R}^2$ = 0.915

F-ratio = 37.765 D-W = 1.905

In case of double log form, the sign of income variable is negative in case of without dummy variable model 3 and positive in case of model 4 (i.e., with dummy variable). The sign of relative price has been found to be negative in both the models. The relative prices are significant at five per cent level in model 3 (i.e., without dummy variable), whereas it is significant at one per cent level in case of model with dummy variable. The chemical imports have been found to be positively related with respect to domestic production but are significant only in case of model 3 (i.e., without dummy variable). The sign of foreign reserves is positive in case of model 3 and sign is negative in case of model 4. The foreign reserves have been found to be non-significant in both the models. The sign of dummy variable is positive and variable has been found to be significant at 10 per cent level. This shows that the liberalisation has positive impact on the imports of this category. The values of R^2, $\bar{R}^2$ and D-W are appropriate in case of both the models.

The category of chemical and allied industries is basically import dependent in nature, as imports of this category consist of intermediates or raw material required by domestic industry, the same idea is also given by positive sign of domestic production in all the models. These imports supplement and support the domestic production and are not of substitute nature. This is so because chemical imports are of essential nature. The relative price variable has been found to be significant in all the models with appropriate sign. The income variable has been found to be non significant with inappropriate sign in all the models except model 4. The foreign reserves variable is found to be significant only in model 2.The dummy variable has been found to be significant at five per cent level in model 2 and at 10 per cent in model 4. The positive sign of dummy variable confirms that import of this category show an increase with coming up of liberalisation measures. The values of R^2 and $\bar{R}^2$ are appropriate and almost at same level in models 1 and 3, similar is the case fors models 2 and 4. The F-ratio has been found to be significant in all the models. The value of D-W statistic is nearer to 2 in models 2, 3 and 4, but in model 1, it is somewhat on lower side.

Base Metals and Articles of Base Metals Imports (BI)

The category of base metals and articles of base metal imports include iron and steel, articles of iron and steel, copper and articles and aluminium and articles. The imports of this category are assumed to be dependent upon, income (GDPFC), relative prices (RP), domestic production (DP), foreign reserves (FR) and dummy (Dum) variable.

Linear Form

Model 1

$$BI = \underset{(4.348)^{*}}{8051.736} + \underset{(0.607)}{0.002}(GDPFC) - \underset{(-5.090)^{*}}{8577.732}(RP) + \underset{(1.717)^{***}}{0.093}(DP) - \underset{(-1.339)}{0.007}(FR)$$

$R^2 = 0.815$ $\bar{R}^2 = 0.758$

F-ratio = 14.383 D-W = 1.933

Model 2

$$BI = \underset{(3.886)^{**}}{6999.272} + \underset{(0.781)}{0.003}(GDPFC) - \underset{(-4.540)^{*}}{8197.329}(RP) + \underset{(1.784)^{***}}{0.101}(DP)$$

$$- \underset{(-1.483)}{0.009}(FR) - \underset{(-0.692)}{717.301}(Dum)$$

$R^2 = 0.822$ $\bar{R}^2 = 0.748$

F-ratio=11.141 D-W=2.000

In case of linear form, the base metal and articles of base metals imports have been found to be positively related with respect to income variable but variable is found to be non significant. The sign of price variable is appropriate one and found be significant at one per cent level in both the models. The domestic production is positively related with respect to Base Metal alloys imports and found to be significant at 10 per cent level in both the models. The foreign reserves have been found to be negatively related with respect to the imports of this category and also found to be non-significant in case of both the models. The sign of dummy variable has been found to be negative and also found to be non significant. The values of R^2 and $\bar{R}^2$ are 0.815 and 0.758 respectively in model 1 (i.e., without dummy variable). The values of R^2 and $\bar{R}^2$ are 0.822 and 0.748 respectively, in case of model 2 (i.e., with dummy variable). The values of D-W statistics are almost 2 in both the models. The F-ratio has been found to be significant in both the models.

Double Log Form

Model 3

$$\text{Log BI} = \underset{(0.029)}{0.064} - \underset{(-0.248)}{0.180}\ \text{Log (GDPFC)} - \underset{(-4.815)^*}{1.138}\ \text{Log (RP)}$$

$$+\underset{(1.684)}{1.035}\ \text{Log (DP)} - \underset{(-0.325)}{0.027}\ \text{Log (FR)}$$

$R^2 = 0.781$ $\quad$ $= 0.713$

F-ratio = 11.602 $\quad$ D-W = 1.732

Model 4

$$\text{Log BI} = \underset{(0.165)}{0.383} - \underset{(-0.405)}{0.311}\ \text{Log (GDPFC)} - \underset{(-3.936)^*}{1.059}\ \text{Log (RP)} + \underset{(1.719)}{1.089}\ \text{Log (DP)}$$

$$+\underset{(0.118)}{0.012}\ \text{Log (FR)} - \underset{(-0.662)}{0.017}\ \text{Log (Dum)}$$

$R^2 = 0.788$ $\quad$ $\bar{R}^2 = 0.700$

F ratio = 8.965 $\quad$ D-W = 1.763

In case of double log form, the sign of income variable has been found to be inappropriate one (i.e., negative) and also found to be non-significant in both the models. The base metals and articles of base metals imports have been found to be elastic with respect to relative prices variable which is significant at one per cent level in both the models. The sign of domestic production is negative but found to be non significant in both the models. The sign of foreign reserves is negative in case of first model, while it is positive in case of second model. In both the models the foreign reserves variable is non-significant. The dummy variable is negative and-non significant. The values of R^2 and $\bar{R}^2$ are almost same in the case of both the models. The F-ratio is significant in both the models. The value of D-W statistics is around 1.75 in both the models.

On the whole, the sign of income variable is positive in case of model 1 and model 2, but it is negative in case of model 3 and model 4. In all the models, income variable is found to be non-significant. The price variable has been found to be significant at 1 per cent level in case of all the models, i.e., Prices play an important role in determining the imports of this category. The domestic production variable has positive sign in all the models, but found to be significant only in case of linear form (model 1 and model 2). The positive sign of domestic production gives an idea about increased raw material imports of this category, which confirms about complementary role of imports and indicates that home industries of base metals are import dependent. The dummy variable has negative sign in all the models showing that liberalisation policies have not lead to increased imports of this category. The foreign reserves variable is positive in case of model 4 only and non significant in all the models. The values of R^2 and $\bar{R}^2$ have been found to be better in models 1 and 2 (i.e., linear form) as compared to models 3 and 4 (i.e., double log form). The F-ratio is significant in all the models. The value of D-W statistic is relatively better in the models 1 and 2.

Machinery and their Parts Imports (MhI)

Imports of this category include nuclear reactor, boiler, machine and mechanical apparatus, electrical and electronic equipment. These imports have been assumed to be dependent upon income (GDPFC), relative prices (RP), domestic production (DP), foreign reserves (FR), gross domestic capital formation (GDCF) and dummy (Dum) variable for measuring the impact of liberalisation policies.

Linear Form

Model 1

$$MhI = 204.615 - 0.011\,(GDPFC) - 181.257\,(RP) + 0.201(DP)$$
$$(2.962)^{**} \quad (-0.780) \quad (-5.256)^{*} \quad (1.127)$$

$$+0.046\,(FR) + 0.032\,(GDCF)$$
$$(3.331)^{**} \quad (0.558)$$

$R^2 = 0.960$ $\bar{R}^2 = 0.950$

F ratio = 66.790 D-W = 1.610

Model-2

$$MhI = 211.426 - 0.002\,(GDPFC) - 20836.770\,(RP) + 0.275(DP)$$
$$(3.034)^{*} \quad (-0.140) \quad (-4.657)^{*} \quad (1.409)$$

$$+0.043\,(FR) + 0.001\,(GDCF) - 2699.213\,(Dum)$$
$$(2.960)^{*} \quad (0.018) \quad (-0.956)$$

$R^2 = 0.967$ $\bar{R}^2 = 0.950$

F- ratio = 55.421 D-W = 1.772

In case of linear form, machinery imports have been found to be negatively related with respect to income variable (non-significant) in both the models. These imports are negatively related to relative price variable, which is highly significant at one per cent level of significance. The domestic production has positive sign and found to be non-significant in both the models. The sign of foreign reserves is positive and found to be significant in both the models (at 5 per cent level in model 1 and at one per cent level in model 2). The gross domestic capital formation has been found to be positively related with respect to machinery imports, but non-significant in both the models. The sign of dummy variable is negative, i.e., liberalisation policies have no impact on this category of imports. The dummy variable has also been found to be non significant. The values of R^2 and $\bar{R}^2$ are 0.96 and 0.95 respectively, in the models 1 and 2. The F-ratio is found to be significant at one per cent level. The values of D-W statistics are 1.61 and 1.77 in models 1 and 2 respectively.

Double Log Form

Model 3

$$\text{Log MhI} = -20.217 + 5.564 \text{ Log (GDPFC)} - 1.602 \text{ Log (RP)}$$
$$(-1.774)^{***} \quad (1.350) \quad (-2.377)^{*}$$
$$- 0.224 \text{ Log (DP)} - 0.237 \text{ Log (FR)} - 1.223 \text{ Log (GDCF)}$$
$$(-0.099) \quad (-0.690) \quad (-0.370)$$
$$R^2 = 0.794 \qquad \bar{R}^2 = 0.708$$
$$\text{F ratio} = 9.268 \qquad \text{D-W} = 2.748$$

Model 4

$$\text{Log MhI} = -20.297 + 5.639 \text{ Log (GDPFC)} - 1.634 \text{ Log (RP)} - 0.137 \text{ Log (DP)}$$
$$(-1.696) \quad (1.260) \quad (-1.847)^{***} \quad (-0.050)$$
$$- 0.228 \text{ Log (FR)} - 1.376 \text{ Log (GDCF)} - 0.006 \text{ Log (Dum)}$$
$$(-0.589) \quad (-0.323) \quad (-0.061)$$
$$R^2 = 0.794 \qquad \bar{R}^2 = 0.682$$
$$\text{F-ratio} = 7.086 \qquad \text{D-W} = 2.758$$

In case of double log form, the imports of this category have been found to be highly elastic with respect to price and income. Only relative prices variable has been found to be significant (at one per cent level in model 3 and at 10 per cent level in model 4). The imports of machinery and their parts are positively related with respect to income, but the variable has been found to be non significant, in both the models 3 and 4. The sign of domestic production is negative but found to be non significant. The sign of foreign reserves is inappropriate one (i.e. negative) and this variable found to be non-significant. The gross domestic capital formation has also been found to be negatively related with respect to imports of this category in both the models. Moreover, the sign of dummy variable is also negative and found to be non-significant. Thus imports of this category are relatively more affected by prices than any other variables. The values of R^2 and $\bar{R}^2$ are 0.79 and 0.71 respectively in case of model 3 and are 0.79 and 0.68 respectively in case of model 4. The values of F-ratio have been found to be significant at 1 per cent level.

The income variable has negative sign in models 1 and 2 of linear form, whereas it has positive sign in case of double log form (model 3 and model 4). But income variable has been found to be non significant in both the forms. This might be due to import dependence of India in case of this category. The relative price variable has been found to be significant in all the models, with appropriate sign. The imports of machinery and their parts are both price as well as income elastic (coefficients being greater than one) in both the models 3 and 4. But only relative price is found to be significant. The gross capital formation variable has a coefficient which is more than one but with inappropriate sign in model 3 and 4 and also found to be non significant in all the models. The models 2 and 4 also confirm about non significant dummy variable with negative sign. The imports of machinery and their parts are of essential type; moreover the home industry of this category is also import dependent. Imports of this category are not of substitute nature, but help home industry to enhance its production. The non significance of variables including income, policy and gross domestic capital formation also confirms about this fact. Only the price variable affects these imports, i.e. even with low income, low capital formation and restriction, these imports would have increased. In case of machinery and their parts imports linear form is better fit. The values of R^2 and $\bar{R}^2$ have been found to be better in linear form, the D-W statistic is also relatively better in case of models 1 and 2. The F-ratio has been found to be significant in all the models.

Textiles and Textile Article Imports (T_xI)

The textiles and textiles articles imports include silk, wool, cotton, man made filaments etc. Imports of this category depend upon income (GDPFC), relative prices (RP), domestic production (DP), foreign reserves (FR) and policy (Dum) variables.

Linear Form

Model -1

$$TxI = -176.938 + 0.008\,(GDPFC) - 2786.459\,(RP) - 0.042\,(DP) + 0.005\,(FR)$$

(-0.116) (2.775)** (-3.000)* (-1.603) (2.027)***

$R^2 = 0.972$ $\bar{R}^2 = 0.963$

F-ratio = 113.528 D-W = 2.340

Model-2

$$TxI = -145.451 + 0.008\,(GDPFC) - 2800.091(RP) - 0.042(DP)$$
$$(-0.078) \quad (2.459)^{**} \quad (-2.654)^{**} \quad (-1.525)$$
$$+ 0.005\,(FR) + 13.230\,(Dum)$$
$$(1.801)^{***} \quad (0.032)$$
$$R^2 = 0.972 \qquad \bar{R}^2 = 0.960$$
$$\text{F-ratio} = 83.844 \qquad \text{D-W} = 2.342$$

In case of linear form, the imports of textiles and textiles articles are found to be positively related with respect to income variable. The income variable has also been found to be significant at five per cent level in both the models (1 and 2). The sign of relative prices is negative in both the models and the variable has been found to be significant at one per cent level in case of model 1 and at five per cent level in case of model 2. The domestic production is negatively related with respect to textiles imports, but found to be non significant in both the models. The sign of foreign reserves variable has been found to be positive and significant at 10 per cent level in both the models. The sign of dummy variable has been found to be positive but also non significant. The values of R^2 and $\bar{R}^2$ are 0.97 and 0.96 respectively, in both the models. The F-ratio has also been found to be significant. But the values of D-W statistics show the presence of autocorrelation in the models.

Double Log Form

Model -3

$$\text{Log}\,T_xI = -9.720 + 2.500\,\text{Log}\,(GDPFC) - 1.314\,\text{Log}\,(RP)$$
$$(-4.762)^{*} \quad (4.118)^{*} \quad (-4.647)^{*}$$
$$-0.486\,\text{Log}\,(DP) + 0.109\,\text{Log}\,(FR)$$
$$(-1.152) \quad - \quad (1.525)$$
$$R^2 = 0.979 \qquad \bar{R}^2 = 0.973$$
$$\text{F-ratio} = 157.883 \qquad \text{D-W} = 2.384$$

Model -4

$$\text{Log}\,T_xI = -9.365 + 2.350\,\text{Log}\,(GDPFC) - 1.217\,\text{Log}\,(RP) - 0.412\,\text{Log}\,(DP)$$
$$(-4.394)^{*} \quad (3.614)^{*} \quad (-3.848)^{*} \quad (-0.933)$$
$$+ 0.145\,\text{Log}\,(FR) - 0.015\,\text{Log}\,(Dum)$$
$$(1.655) \quad (-0.736)$$
$$R^2 = 0.980 \qquad \bar{R}^2 = 0.972$$
$$\text{F-ratio} = 122.158 \qquad \text{D-W} = 2.220$$

In case of double log form, the textiles imports have been found to be price elastic as well as income elastic in both the models. The income and price variables have also been found to be significant at one per cent level in both the models. The domestic production variable has been found to be negatively related with respect to imports of this category, but is non-significant in both the models. The sign of foreign reserves is positive, but found to be non-significant in both the models. The dummy variable has been found to be negatively related with respect to textiles imports. The values of R^2 and $\bar{R}^2$ are 0.98 and 0.97 in both the models. The values of D-W statistics are more than 2. The F-ratio has been found to be significant in both the models.

Thus, in case of textiles and textiles articles imports, price and income variables have been found to be significant in all the models. These imports are also found to be highly price as well as income elastic. However, the import elasticity coefficient with respect to income is higher than relative prices. The dummy variable shows positive impact of liberalisation polices in model 2, whereas negative impact in model 4, but found to be non-significant in both the models. The foreign reserves variable has been found to be significant in case of linear form only. The variable of domestic production has been found to be non significant in all the models. In case of Textiles and Textiles articles imports the values of R^2 and $\bar{R}^2$ have been found to be at appropriate level in all the models. The F ratio is also found to be significant in all the models.

Mineral Products Imports (MnI)

The mineral products imports include salt, sulphur, earths and stones, plastering materials, ores, slag and ash and mineral fuels, mineral oils and products. This category has highest share in aggregate imports and the sub category of mineral fuels, mineral oils and products is major contributor to the imports of this category. The mineral products imports have been assumed to be dependent upon income (GDPFC), relative prices (RP), foreign reserves (FR) and dummy (Dum) variable.

Linear Form

Model-1

$$MnI = -15874.640 + 0.054\,(GDPFC) - 5633.033\,(RP) - 0.034\,(FR)$$
$$(-5.289)^{*} \quad (13.030)^{*} \quad (-2.389)^{**} \quad (-3.957)^{*}$$

$R^2 = 0.979$ $\bar{R}^2 = 0.974$

F-ratio $= 221.443$ D-W $= 1.011$

Model-2

$$MnI = -10856.760 + 0.045(GDPFC) - 6246.33(RP) - 0.023(FR)$$
$$(-4.015)^{*} \quad (10.946)^{*} \quad (-3.492)^{*} \quad (-3.171)^{*}$$
$$+3811.259(Dum)$$
$$(3.401)^{*}$$

$R^2 = 0.989$ $\bar{R}^2 = 0.985$

F-ratio $= 294.333$ D-W $= 1.942$

For mineral products imports, in case of linear form, the income variable has positive sign and significant at 1 per cent level, in both the models (1 and 2). The price variable has been found to be negatively related with respect to imports of this category. The relative prices variable is significant at five per cent levels in case of model 1(i.e. without dummy variable) and at one per cent level in case of model 2 (i.e. without dummy variable). The sign of foreign reserves have been found to be negative and also significant at one per cent level in both the models. The sign of dummy variable is positive and also found to be significant at one per cent level, i.e., with increase in liberalization measures, the mineral products imports also show an increase. The values of R^2 and $\bar{R}^2$ are at appropriate level. The value of D-W is near to 1 in first model, but it is near to 2 in second model. The F-ratio has been found to be significant in both the models.

Double Log Form

Model-3

$$Log\,MnI = -1.590 + 0.882\,Log\,(GDPFC) + 0.105\,Log\,(RP) + 0.148\,Log\,(FR)$$
$$(-0.727) \quad (2.050)^{***} \quad (0.607) \quad (1.792)^{***}$$

$R^2 = 0.946$ $\bar{R}^2 = 0.935$

F-ratio $= 82.749$ D-W $= 1.508$

Model-4

$$\text{Log MnI} = -5.489 + 1.766\,\text{Log (GDPFC)} - 0.326\,\text{Log (RP)} - 0.130\,\text{Log (FR)}$$
$$\quad (-3.426)^{*} \quad (5.374)^{*} \quad (-2.295)^{**} \quad (-1.653)$$
$$+ 0.070\,\text{Log (Dum)}$$
$$(4.745)^{*}$$

$R^2 = 0.980$ $\bar{R}^2 = 0.974$

F-ratio = 162.437 D-W = 2.413

In case of double log form, the mineral products imports have been found to income elastic in case of model 4 (significant at one per cent level). The income variable is significant at 10 per cent level in model 3. The relative price variable has been found to be significant at five per cent level only in case of without dummy variable model (i.e. model 3). The sign of relative prices is inappropriate one (i.e., positive) and also this variable has been found to be non significant in case of without dummy variable model (i.e. model 3). The foreign reserves variable has been found to be significant at 10 per cent level with positive sign in model 3, but it is negative and also non significant in case of model 4. The dummy variable has been found to be positively related with mineral products imports, the variable is also significant at one per cent level. So with the coming up of liberalisation policies the imports of this category also show an increase. The values of R^2 and $\bar{R}^2$ are at appropriate level in both the models. The value of D-W statistics is 1.50 in case of model 3, whereas it is 2.41 in case of model 4.

In case of mineral products imports, income variable has been found to be significant in all the models. The relative price variable has been found to significant in all the models except model 3. The dummy variable has been found to be significant in both the forms (i.e. in models 2 and 4), i.e., with the advent of liberalisation polices, the mineral products imports have also increase as this category of imports includes essential imports. The import elasticity coefficient with respect to income is more than one, whereas as with respect to relative prices it is less than one in model 4. These imports are income sensitive and not price sensitive. The model 2 is better fit as all variables have been found to be significant with appropriate R^2, $\bar{R}^2$ and D-W.

Pearls, Precious and Semi-precious Stones Imports (PI)

The pearls, precious and semi-precious stones imports have been assumed to be dependent upon income (GDPFC), foreign reserves (FR), and exports in previous year (ExP_{t-1}) and dummy (Dum) variable for measuring the impact of liberalisation policies.

Linear Form

Model-1

$$PI = -8525.395 + 0.025\,(GDPFC) + 0.043\,(FR) - 0.266\,(ExP_{t-1})$$

(-2.289)*** (2.155)*** (1.436) (-0.348)

$R^2 = 0.953$ $\bar{R}^2 = 0.943$

F-ratio = 94.980 D-W = 0.623

Model-2

$$PI = -9967.501 + 0.038(GDPFC) + 0.022(FR) - 0.585(EXP_{t-1}) - 8237.637(Dum)$$

(-2.987)* (3.232)* (0.777) (-0.848) (-2.251)**

$R^2 = 0.966$ $\bar{R}^2 = 0.955$

F-ratio = 93.180 D-W = 1.022

In the case of linear form, these imports have been found to be positively related with respect to income. The income variable has been found to be significant at 10 per cent level in model 1 (i.e., without dummy variable) and at one per cent level in model 2 (i.e., with dummy variable). The sign of foreign reserves is positive but this variable has been found to be non significant in both of the models (1 and 2). The variable which show exports in previous year has been found to be negative and also non significant in both of the models. The dummy variable is negative, but significant at 5 per cent level. The values of R^2 and $\bar{R}^2$ have been found to be appropriate in both of the models. The value of D-W statistics is less than 1 in case of model without dummy variable whereas it is slightly higher than 1 in case of with dummy variable model. The values of F-ratio have been found to be significant at 1 per cent level in both of the models.

Double Log Form

Model-3

$$\text{Log PI} = \underset{(-4.640)^{**}}{-12.022} + \underset{(4.529)^{*}}{3.554}\,\text{Log(GDPFC)} - \underset{(-1.310)}{0.166}\,\text{Log(FR)} - \underset{(-2.377)^{**}}{1.078}\,\text{Log}(\text{ExP}_{t-1})$$

$R^2 = 0.978$ $\bar{R}^2 = 0.974$

F-ratio = 214.312 D-W = 1.467

Model-4

$$\text{Log PI} = \underset{(-4.759)^{*}}{-11.975} + \underset{(4.495)^{*}}{3.450}\,\text{Log(GDPFC)} - \underset{(-0.849)}{0.110}\,\text{Log(FR)} - \underset{(-2.238)^{**}}{1.008}\,\text{Log}(\text{ExP}_{t-1})$$

$$-\underset{(-1.255)}{0.032}\,(\text{Dum})$$

$R^2 = 0.980$ $\bar{R}^2 = 0.975$

F-ratio = 167.185 D-W = 1.583

In case of double log form, the imports of pearls, precious and semi precious stones have been found to be income elastic. The income variable has been found to be significant at 1 per cent level in both the models (i.e., 3 and 4). The foreign reserves variable has negative sign and also found to be non significant in both the models. Imports of this category have been found to be negatively related with respect to export in previous year variable and it has been found to be significant in model 4. The dummy variable has negative sign and also found to be non significant in both the models. The values of R^2 and $\bar{R}^2$ are quite good. The values of D-W statistics are around 1.5 in both the models. The F-ratio has been found to be significant at 1 per cent level in both the models.

In case of pearls, precious and semi-precious stones imports, the income variable has been found to be significant in all the models whereas foreign reserves variable has been found to be non significant in all the estimated models. The variable showing exports in previous year has been found to be significant in double log form, but with an inappropriate sign. The dummy variable showing the impact of liberalisation policies, has negative sign in models 2 and 4 and significant in case of model 4 only. These imports are highly income elastic in nature that might be because of being export related item, as higher income leads to increased imports, which in turn increases exports. The values of R^2 and $\bar{R}^2$ are at appropriate level in all the models. The F ratio is also found to be significant in all the models.

Conclusion

The total imports (TI) have been found to be income elastic as well as and price elastic. The coefficients of price and income variables have also been found to be highly significant in all the models. The foreign reserves variable has been found to be non significant. The dummy variable is negative in case of linear form whereas it is positive in case of double log form. In both the forms the dummy variable (for capturing effect of liberalisation policies) has been found to be non significant but has positive sign. Dummy variable is not statistically significant in the aggregate import demand function. The values of R^2 and $\bar{R}^2$ are quite good in all the models for both the forms (linear and double log).

The agricultural imports (AI) have been found to be price elastic and also income elastic. The price variable is found to be highly significant in all the models and income variable has been found to be nonsignificant in all models except in model 1. The domestic production variable has been found to be significant in case of model 3 only. The foreign reserves variable has been found to be significant in case of double log form. The dummy variable is positive in linear form, while negative in double log form, but non-significant in both the forms. The addition of dummy variable reduces the significant variables in both the forms. The values of R^2 and $\bar{R}^2$ are better in case of double log form, whereas the values of D-W statistics are better in case of linear form.

In case of products of chemical or allied industries imports (CI), relative price variable has been found to be significant in all the models, whereas the income variable has been found to be non significant in all the models. Imports of this category have been found to be significant with respect to domestic production in case of all models except model 4. The positive sign of domestic production confirms about increased raw material imports of this category. Thus these imports support and supplement home industry and are not of substitute nature. The foreign reserves variable has been found to be non significant except in model 2. The dummy variable is significant in both the forms, which confirms about increased imports of chemicals with the coming up of liberalisation measures. The values of R^2 and $\bar{R}^2$ are at appropriate level. The values of D-W statistics are found to be better when dummy variable is added in both the forms (i.e., model 2 and model 4).

In case of base metals and articles of base metals imports (BI) the income variable is found to be non-significant in all the models. The sign of income variable is positive in case of linear form, whereas it is negative in case of double log form. The price variable has been found to be highly significant in all the models. The imports of this category have been found to be price elastic, as prices play an important role in deciding about import quantity of this category. The domestic production variable has been found to be significant in case of linear form only. The positive sign of domestic production confirms about complimentarity of imports with domestic production. The foreign reserves variable has been found to be non significant in all the models and has appropriate sign only in double log form of model with dummy variable. The negative sign of dummy variables shows that liberalisation policies have very less impact on this category of imports. The values of R^2 and $\bar{R}^2$ have been found to be better in case of linear form. The values of D-W statistics are relatively linear form. The F-ratio has been found to be significant in all the models.

In case of machinery and their parts imports (M_hI), the income variable has been found to be non significant in all the models whereas the price variable has been found to be significant in all the models. These imports are highly income elastic as well as price elastic (coefficients being greater one). The domestic production variable has been found to be non significant in all the cases. The foreign reserves have been found to be significant in case of linear form only. The gross domestic capital formation has also been found to be non significant with positive sign in case of linear form and negative sign in case of double log form. The dummy variable is also non-significant in both the forms (with negative sign). In case of these imports, price variable is most important one, as all other variables i.e., policy, capital formation and income variable, have been found to be non-significant. Only foreign reserves variable has been found to be significant (only in case of linear form). The values of R^2, $\bar{R}^2$ and D-W have been found to be better in case of linear form. The F-ratio has been found to be significant in all the cases.

In case of textiles and textiles articles imports (TxI), the income and price variables have been found to be significant in both the forms. The imports of this category have been found to be price elastic and also highly income elastic. These imports are more elastic with respect to income as compared to prices. The foreign reserves variable has been found to be significant in case of linear form only. The sign of domestic production is negative and variable is also non-significant in both the forms (in case of all the models).The sign of dummy variable is positive in case of linear form, while sign is negative in case of double log form. The dummy variable is also non significant in both the forms, showing less impact of liberalisation policies on imports of textiles and textiles articles imports. The values of R^2 and $\bar{R}^2$ have been found to at appropriate level.

In case of mineral products imports (MnI), income variable has been found to be significant in both the forms (i.e., in case of all the models). The price variable has been found to be significant in all the cases except in case of without dummy variable model (i.e., model 3) of double log form. The mineral imports are price inelastic but income elastic in case of model 4 of double log form. The foreign reserve variable has been found to be significant except in model 4 of double log form. The dummy variable has positive sign and is highly significant in both the forms. Thus, irrespective of changes in prices, the imports of minerals are more responsive to income. The values of R^2 and $\bar{R}^2$ have been found to at appropriate level. The value of D-W statistics has been found to be better in case of linear form. The F-ratio has been found to be significant in all the cases.

In case of pearls, precious and semi precious stones imports (PI), the income variable has been found to be significant in both the forms (in case of both the models). The foreign reserves variable has been found to be non-significant in all the models. The export in the previous year variable has been found to be non-significant in case of linear form, while found to be significant in case of double log form. This variable has negative sign in all the models. The dummy variable has negative sign in both the forms, but found to be significant in case linear form. The imports of this category are found to be highly elastic with respect to income. The values of R^2 and $\bar{R}^2$ have been found to at appropriate level. The value of D-W statistics has been found to be better in case of double log form.

CHAPTER

Imports – Growth Causality in India

One of the principle components of economic reforms in India is import liberalization. Import policy reforms, as a part of broader economic reforms initiated in 1991, aimed at promoting rapid economic growth through growth of industrial and export sectors. The positive relationship between liberalization and growth is empirically well-established (Frankel and Romer, 1999). However, the empirical studies generally concentrate on export promotion as the ultimate objective of liberalization with lesser emphasis on the role of import sector in promoting economic growth and hence exports. Further, the large demand for imports in developing countries is not satisfied fully due to limited export growth. The economic development is affected by openness as measured by exports and imports (Afxentiou and Serletis, 2000), and as India is now passing through the phase of rapid growth, imports are crucial for attaining developmental goals.

Imports play an important role in the growth process. Imports are the source of raw materials not available domestically, as well as of technology and capital goods for raising productive capacity of the economy. Imports also help in generating economic efficiency as well as price stability (Shirazi and Manap, 2004). Aggregate imports of a country depend upon a large number of factors such as size, structure and growth rate of gross domestic product, relative prices of imports, foreign exchange reserves etc. At disaggregate level, the various categories of imports also depend upon their domestic production.

Causality

One way of looking at relationship between imports and growth is to investigate the causal relation between two. The causal behaviour between given pair of variables can be put into one of the following four categories.

1. ***Unidirectional causality :*** When X causes Y (X →Y) or when X is caused by Y (X←Y) after some lag. In other words, it indicates if the estimated coefficients on lagged X are statistically different from zero as a group and set of estimated coefficients on lagged Y is not statistically different from zero and *vice versa.*
2. ***Feedback or bilateral causality :*** When both the variables X and Y, are cause of one another with some lag (X ↔ Y) or when the sets of X and Y coefficients are statistically different from zero in both regressions.
3. ***Instantaneous Causality :*** When both the variables X and Y are simultaneously the cause of one another without any lag.
4. ***No Causality :*** When one of the variables, say X, does not or is affected by the other, say Y, (With or without any lag), i.e., there is no indication of causality.

Most of the studies conducted on causal relationships are based on aggregates (like imports and GNP, exports and GNP etc). India being a large country, the major categories of imports such Mineral imports, Machinery and their parts imports, pearls and semi-precious stones imports, Chemical and allied imports, Base metal and articles imports, Textile imports and agricultural imports are very large in themselves and hence can have causal relation with gross domestic product at factor cost (GDPFC) as well as their domestic production (DP). In case of imports of capital goods (as measured broadly by Machinery and Machine tool imports), gross domestic capital formation (GDCF) of our country can also be an important factor. Here it is important to mention that domestic production is the production of considered import categories with in our country (as reported in Annual Survey of Industries, Factory Sector).

We have studied the causal relationship in the following cases:

1. Total imports (TI) and Gross Domestic Product at Factor Cost (GDPFC).
2. Agricultural imports (AI) and GDPFC.
3. Products of Chemicals or Allied Industries Imports (CI) and GDPFC.
4. Products of Chemicals or Allied Industires Imports (CI) and Domestic Production (DP).
5. Base Metals and Articles of Base Metals Imports (BI) and GDPFC.
6. Base Metals and Articles of Base Metals Imports (BI) and Domestic Production (DP).
7. Machinery and Their Parts Imports (MhI) and GDPFC.
8. Machinery and Their Parts Imports (MhI) and Domestic Production (DP).
9. Machinery and Their Parts imports (MhI) and Gross Domestic Capital Formation (GDCF).
10. Textiles and Textiles Articles imports (TxI) and GDPFC.
11. Textiles and Textiles Articles imports (TxI) and Domestic Production (DP).
12. Mineral Products Imports (MnI) and GDPFC.

13. Pearls, Precious and Semi Precious Stones Imports (PI) and GDPFC.

To study the causal relationship, the well-known Granger causality test has been applied. This test procedure assumes that the information relevant to the prediction of respective variables is contained solely in the time series data on the variables. More generally, since the future cannot predict the past, if variable X (Granger) causes Y, then changes in X should precede changes in Y (Gujrati, 2004; Granger, 1969; Greene, 2003).

Granger test of causality presupposes the stationarity in the data. Data used in our study, have been investigated and found to be stationary. The Unit Root test is used for checking stationarity of the data and results of unit root test are shown in Table 7.9. This test has been performed as follows :

(1) The following regression has been estimated :

$\Delta Y_{t-} = A_1 + A_2 t + A_3 Y_{t-1} + U_t$

Δ is first difference operator, t is trend variable and Y_{t-1} is the one period lagged value of Y

(2) The null hypothesis (H_o) is that A_3 is zero, which is a coefficient of Y_{t-1} or time series is non-stationary. This is a Unit Root hypothesis.

(3) In order to calculate the values for Dickey-Fuller (DF) test, there are two approaches as follows :

$DF_{\tau =} \hat{A}_3 - 1/S.E.(\hat{A}_3)$

or

$DF_{\gamma} = T(\hat{A}_3 - 1)$

where $\hat{A}_3$ is estimated coefficient of Y_{t-1}, T is time period of present study, S.E.($\hat{A}_3$) is standard error of $\hat{A}_3$.

(4) The computed values of DF_{τ} and DF_{γ} have been compared with their critical values. If the computed values are greater than the critical values then we reject the null hypothesis (H_o) and conclude that time series is stationary (Gujrati, 2004 and Greene, 2003).

In present study, we have applied Unit Root test and estimated the coefficient of Y_{t-1}. After comparing the absolute calculated values of DF_τ and DF_γ with their absolute critical values, we get significant values at one per cent level of significance in all the considered cases. The 1 per cent critical value of DF_τ for 25 observations (we have thirty, so this is close enough) is -4.38 per cent and -3.75 per cent for with trend and without trend cases respectively. Similarly 1 per cent critical values of DF_γ for twenty five observations are -22.5 per cent and -17.2 per cent with and without trend respectively. The results of Unit Root test (computed value DF_τ and DF_γ) are given in Table 7.9. As all calculated values are greater than critical values so we rejected the null hypothesis and concluded that considered time series are stationary.

In Granger causality test $\bar{R}^2$ is used for finding out appropriate number of lags, i.e. we will consider a particular lag if $\bar{R}^2$, improves by adding it in regression equation. In most of the cases $\bar{R}^2$ is almost same in double lag and in single lag, only in few cases it slightly improved and hence we have presented the results for both single lag and double lag. After this, value of F statistics is calculated for all possible directions of causality, which helps us to decide about the type of causation existing in the given variables. Results of Granger causality test are shown in Tables 7.1 to 7.8, for the total imports and for different categories of imports (both for single lag and double lag). As we have already confirmed stationarity in our data. Further steps involved in implementing Granger causality test are as follows:

For example to study whether Y causes X or X causes Y, we have to consider following equations:

$$\text{(A) } Y_t = \sum_{i=1}^{n} \alpha_i y_{t-i} + u_{1t}$$

$$\text{(A}_1\text{) } Y_t = \sum_{i=1}^{n} \alpha_i y_{t-i} + \sum_{j=1}^{n} \beta_j x_{t-j} + u_{2t}$$

$$(D)\ X_t = \sum_{i=1}^{n} \lambda_i x_{t-i} + u_{3t}$$

$$(B_1)\ X_t = \sum_{i=1}^{n} \lambda_i y_{t-i} + \sum_{j=1}^{n} \delta_j x_{t-j} + u_{4t}$$

Equations (A) and (A_1) help us to find out whether X causes Y or not. Similarly equations (B) and (B_1) give the results whether Y causes X or not. Following are the steps involved in this process.

5. Firstly, regress current values of Y on all lagged Y terms and by not including the lagged X variables in this regression. This is a restricted regression, from which we obtain restricted residual sum of squares (RSS_r).
6. Now run regression A_1, where current values of Y regressed on all lagged values of Y terms and also on all lagged values of X terms. This is unrestricted regression, which provides us with unrestricted residual sum of squares (RSS_{ur}).
7. Set the null hypothesis, Ho: $\Sigma\beta j = 0$, i.e., lagged X terms do not belong to the regression.
8. To test this hypothesis we apply the F-test i.e.

   $$(C)\ F = \frac{RSS_r - RSS_{ur}/m}{RSS_{ur}/(n-k)}$$

   Which follows F-test with 'm' and 'n.k' d.f. where m is number of lagged X terms and k is number of parameters estimated in unrestricted regression.
9. If computed F value is greater than the tabulated or critical F value at chosen level of significance, we reject the null hypothesis, in which case lagged X terms belong to the regression. or X causes Y. Step 1 to 5 can be repeated to test the models (B) and (B_1), i.e., whether Y causes X (Gujrati, 2004; Nandi and Kumar, 2005).

Total Imports and Gross Domestic Product at Factor Cost

Table 7.1 gives the results in case of Total imports (TI), it indicates that GDPFC (gross domestic product at factor cost) causes Total imports (GDPFC → TI), in both the cases of single lag and double lag. But there is no reverse causation (TI → GDPFC) experienced in both the cases of single lag and double lag. Thus, there is unidirectional causality between the Total imports (TI) and GDP of India. It means changes in income causes changes in total imports of India. In case of GDPFC → TI, calculated value of F-statistics is found to be significant at 10 per cent level in case of single lag and at 1 per cent level in case of double lag. The values of $\bar{R}^2$ are better in case of double lag for GDPFC → TI.

Agricultural Imports and Gross Domestic Product at Factor Cost

In Table 7.2, results of Agricultural imports show that GDP causes Agricultural imports i.e., (GDPFC → AI), but there is no reverse causation (AI → GDPFC) present in both the cases of single and double lag. So there is unidirectional causality from GDP to Agricultural imports. The calculated value of F-statistics is significant at one per cent level in case of both single lag as well as double lag. The values of $\bar{R}^2$ are between 0.85 and 0.90 in all the cases. The value of $\bar{R}^2$ is better in case of double lag for unrestricted regression for GDPFC → AI.

Products of Chemicals or Allied Industries Imports and Domestic Production

Table 7.3 gives the results of Chemical or Allied Industries imports and it show that domestic production causes Chemical imports i.e. (DP → CI), both in single lag and double lag case. The reverse causation (CI→DP) i.e. Chemical import to domestic production is present in case of double lag, but not in case of single lag. So with the increase or decrease in domestic production of chemicals,

Table 7.1 : Total Imports - Causality Analysis

	Single lag					Double lag				
	F_{cal}	F_{tab} (1,27)	Decision	$\bar{R}^2_r$	$\bar{R}^2_{ur}$	F_{cal}	F_{tab} (2,25)	Decision	$\bar{R}^2_r$	$\bar{R}^2_{ur}$
TI → GDPFC	3.04***	2.90(10%)	Rejected	0.979	0.980	8.03*	5.57(1%)	Rejected	0.978	0.986
GDPFC → TI	2.01	2.90(10%)	Not Rejected	0.998	0.998	2.02	2.53(10%)	Not Rejected	0.998	0.998

Source: Author's Calculations.

Table 7.2 : Agricultural Imports - Causality Analysis

	Single lag					Double lag				
	F_{cal}	F_{tab} (1,27)	Decision	$\bar{R}^2_r$	$\bar{R}^2_{ur}$	F_{cal}	F_{tab} (2,25)	Decision	$\bar{R}^2_r$	$\bar{R}^2_{ur}$
GDPFC → AI	8.45*	7.68(1%)	Rejected	0.863	0.891	7.86*	5.57(1%)	Rejected	0.858	0.906
AI → GDPFC	2.23	2.90(10%)	Not Rejected	0.806	0.998	0.98	2.53(10%)	Not Rejected	0.998	0.998

Source: Author's Calculations.

Table 7.3 : Products of Chemical or Allied Industries Imports - Causality Analysis

	Single lag					Double lag				
	F_{cal}	F_{tab} (1,27)	Decision	$\bar{R}^2_r$	$\bar{R}^2_{ur}$	F_{cal}	F_{tab} (2,25)	Decision	$\bar{R}^2_r$	$\bar{R}^2_{ur}$
DP→CI	5.65**	4.21(5%)	Rejected	0.644	0.695	4.31**	3.39(5%)	Rejected	0.636	0.709
CI→DP	2.03	2.90(10%)	Not Rejected	0.954	0.956	4.01**	3.39(5%)	Rejected	0.966	0.965
GDPFC→CI	3.65***	2.90(10%)	Rejected	0.644	0.675	1.66	2.53(10%)	Not Rejected	0.636	0.654
CI→GDPFC	0.18	2.90(10%)	Not Rejected	0.998	0.998	0.41	2.53(10%)	Not Rejected	0.998	0.998

Source: Author's Calculations.

the imports of this category also increase or decrease. This indicates toward enhanced industrial activity in chemicals industry. Similarly, with the changes in imports of Chemicals,'the domestic production of chemicals also changes. Thus, causal relation present here is bidirectional in nature. The calculated value of F-statistics is found to be significant at 5 per cent level in both the lags for DP → CI. The calculated value of F-statistics for CI→DP is also significant at 5 per cent level, but in case of double lag only. The value of ^{2} are better in case of double lag form.

Products of Chemicals or Allied Industries Imports and Gross Domestic Product at Factor Cost

Similarly in case of income, changes in Chemical imports are not causing changes in GDP in case of both the lags, while GDP causes Chemical imports (GDPFC → CI) in case of single lag only. So, with the change in income, the imports of Chemicals and Allied Industries also show a change. Thus here we have unidirectional causality. The calculated value of F-statistic for GDPFC → CI (in case of single lag) is significant at 10 per cent level. The values of $\bar{R}^2$ are better in case of single lag. The F statistic is also found to be significant in case of single lag only.

Base Metals and Articles of Base Metal Imports and Domestic Production

The results of Base Metals and Articles of Base Metal imports (BI) are there in Table 7.4 which indicate that there is no causation between base metal imports to domestic production (BI→DP) in both the cases of single and double lag. The domestic production causes Base Metal imports in case of single lag but not in case of double lag. It means domestic production of base metal is having causal relationship with its imports (DP → BI). So with the growth in domestic production of Base Metals, there is higher demand for raw materials and intermediates. The calculated value of F-statistic is significant at 5 per cent level for DP → BI (single lag).

Table 7.4 : Base Metals and Article of Base Metals Imports - Causality Analysis

	Single lag					Double lag				
	F_{cal}	F_{tab} (1,27)	Decision	$\bar{R}^2_r$	$\bar{R}^2_{ur}$	F_{cal}	F_{tab} (2,25)	Decision	$\bar{R}^2_r$	$\bar{R}^2_{ur}$
DP→BI	4.55**	4.21(5%)	Rejected	0.851	0.868	1.06	2.53(10%)	Not Rejected	0.870	0.871
BI→DP	0.95	2.90(10%)	Not Rejected	0.965	0.965	1.25	2.53(10%)	Not Rejected	0.964	0.965
GDPFC→BI	14.56*	7.68(1%)	Rejected	0.851	0.900	4.94**	3.39(5%)	Rejected	0.870	0.900
BI→GDPFC	0.11	2.90(10%)	Not Rejected	0.998	0.998	2.79***	2.53(10%)	Rejected	0.998	0.998

Source: Author's Calculations.

Base Metals and Articles of Base Metal Imports and Gross Domestic Product at Factor Cost

The results of Table 7.4 show the presence of causation from GDP to Base Metals and Articles imports (GDPFC → BI), the reverse causation (BI → GDPFC) is also present in case of double lag, but not in case of single lag. Thus, the results show strong causation for GDPFC → BI, i.e. with the growth in income, the requirement for the imports of this category also increases. For GDPFC→BI, the calculated value of F statistics is significant at one per cent level in case of single lag and at 5 per cent level in case of double lag. The calculated value of F-statistics is found to be significant at 10 per cent level for BI → GDPFC in case of double lag only. The values of $\bar{R}^2$ are almost same in both the lags except $\bar{R}^2$ for restricted regression, which is better in double lag as compared to single lag.

Machinery and Their Parts Imports and Domestic Production

In Table 7.5, results of Machinery and Their Parts imports (M_hI) indicate that these imports cause domestic production ($M_hI \rightarrow DP$) in both the cases of single lag as well as double lag. The reverse causation ($DP \rightarrow M_hI$) is present in case of double lag, but not in case of single lag. Thus in case of double lag we have bidirectional causality, whereas in case of single lag there is presence of unidirectional causality. The domestic production of this category is strongly import oriented and also need based. The calculated values of F-statistic are significant at 10 per cent level for $DP \rightarrow M_hI$ in case of double lag only. For $M_hI \rightarrow DP$ the calculated values of F-statistics are significant at one per cent level in case of single lag and at 5 per cent level in case of double lag. For unrestricted regression $\bar{R}^2$ is better in case of single lag for $M_hI \rightarrow DP$ and is better in case of double lag for $DP \rightarrow M_hI$. For restricted regression $\bar{R}^2$ is better for $DP \rightarrow M_hI$ in case of single lag, whereas the value of $\bar{R}^2$ is almost same in both the lags for $M_hI \rightarrow DP$.

Machinery and Their Parts Imports and Gross Domestic Product at Factor Cost

The results of Table 7.5 also show the causality for GDPFC → M^hI in both the cases of single lag as well as double lag, but reverse causation (M_hI → GDPFC) is absent in both the cases. As development takes place, the income of country also increases, which in turn creates greater requirements of capital goods within the country that is why GDP causes Machinery and their Parts imports. The calculated value of F-statistic is significant at five per cent level in case of single lag and at one per cent level in case of double lag for GDPFC → M_hI. The value of $\bar{R}^2$ is better in case of single iag for GDPFC → M_hI for restricted regression and better in case of double lag for unrestricted regression.

Machinery and Their Parts Imports and Gross Domestic Capital Formation

The results further indicate that gross domestic capital formation (GDCF) causes machinery imports (GDCF → M_hI) in both the cases of single lag and in case of double lag, but there is no reverse causation (M_hI → GDCF) present in both the cases. So the capital formation also cause the changes in capital goods imports, i.e., higher the capital formation higher will be the imports. The calculated values of F-statistics are significant at 5 per cent level in both the lags for GDCF → M_hI. In case of GDCF → M_hI, the value of $\bar{R}^2$ is better in case of restricted regression both in single and double lags. For M_hI → GDCF, the values of $\bar{R}^2$ are same in all the cases.

Textiles and Textile Articles Imports and Domestic Production

In Table 7.6, results of Textiles and Textile Articles imports (TxI) highlight that Domestic Production causes Textile imports (DP → TxI) but there is no reverse causation (TxI → DP) in the case of single lag as well as in case of double lag. So there is unidirectional causality from domestic production to Textiles imports. It means

Table 7.5 : Machinery and their Parts Imports - Causality Analysis

	Single lag					Double lag				
	F_{cal}	F_{tab} (1,27)	Decision	$\bar{R}^2_r$	$\bar{R}^2_{ur}$	F_{cal}	F_{tab} (2,25)	Decision	$\bar{R}^2_r$	$\bar{R}^2_{ur}$
DP → $M_h I$	2.38	2.90(10%)	Not Rejected	0.872	0.878	2.98***	2.53(10%)	Rejected	0.867	0.884
$M_h I$ → DP	9.94*	7.68(1%)	Rejected	0.974	0.980	4.28**	3.39(5%)	Rejected	0.974	0.979
GDPFC → $M_h I$	7.29**	4.21(5%)	Rejected	0.872	0.895	5.76*	5.57(1%)	Rejected	0.867	0.902
$M_h I$ → GDPFC	2.32	2.90(10%)	Not Rejected	0.998	0.998	0.28	2.53(10%)	Not Rejected	0.998	0.998
GDCF → $M_h I$	4.24**	4.21(5%)	Rejected	0.872	0.885	3.92**	3.39(5%)	Rejected	0.867	0.891
$M_h I$ → GDCF	1.34	2.90(10%)	Not Rejected	0.969	0.969	1.16	2.53(10%)	Not Rejected	0.969	0.969

Source: Author's Calculations.

Table 7.6 : Textiles and Textiles Articles Imports - Causality Analysis

	Single lag					Double lag				
	F_{cal}	F_{tab} (1,27)	Decision	$\bar{R}^2_r$	$\bar{R}^2_{ur}$	F_{cal}	F_{tab} (2,25)	Decision	$\bar{R}^2_r$	$\bar{R}^2_{ur}$
$DP^n \rightarrow TXI$	8.88*	7.68(1%)	Rejected	0.883	0.908	7.03*	5.57(1%)	Rejected	0.903	0.933
$TXI \rightarrow DP^n$	0.58	2.90(10%)	Not Rejected	0.968	0.968	0.27	2.53(10%)	Not Rejected	0.970	0.969
$GDPFC \rightarrow TXI$	6.60**	4.21(5%)	Rejected	0.883	0.902	3.47**	3.39(5%)	Rejected	0.903	0.918
$TXI \rightarrow GDPFC$	0.03	2.90(10%)	Not Rejected	0.998	0.998	0.49	2.53(10%)	Not Rejected	0.998	0.998

Source: Author's Calculations.

imports of textiles and textile Articles supplementing the India's domestic textile industry. The calculated values of F-statistic are found to be significant at one per cent level for DP → TxI in case of both the lags. In case of DP → TxI and TXI → DP, the values of $\bar{R}^2$ both for restricted as well as unrestricted regression are found to be better in double lag case.

Textiles and Textile Articles Imports and Gross Domestic Product at Factor Cost

Results of Table 7.6 show that GDP causes textile imports (GDPFC → TxI), but there is no reverse causation, in both the cases of single and double lags. So, with the increase in national income India's textile import also show increasing trends. There exists unidirectional causality from income to textile imports. The calculated value of F-statistics for GDPFC → TxI is significant at 5 per cent level in both the cases of single lag as well as double lag. In case of GDPFC → TxI, the values of $\bar{R}^2$ are better in case of double lag whereas for TxI → GDPFC the values of $\bar{R}^2$ are almost same in both the lags.

Minerals Products Imports and Gross Domestic Product at Factor Cost

In Table 7.7, results of mineral products imports (M_nI) show that GDP causes mineral imports (GDPFC→ M_nI), in both the cases of double and single lags, but there is no reverse causation. Thus, mineral imports being a dominating category of Indian imports, increase with the increase in GDP. The calculated value of F-statistic is significant at 5 per cent in case of single lag and at one per cent level in case of double lag for GDPFC → M_nI. The values of $\bar{R}^2$ are better in double lag case for GDPFC → M_nI, whereas values are same in case of both the lags for M_nI → GDPFC.

Pearls, Precious and Semi-precious Stones Imports and Gross Domestic Product at Factor Cost

According to Table 7.8, results of Pearls, Precious and Semi-Precious

Table 7.7 : Mineral Products Imports - Causality Analysis

	Single lag					Double lag				
	F_{cal}	F_{tab} (1,27)	Decision	$\bar{R}^2_r$	$\bar{R}^2_{ur}$	F_{cal}	F_{tab} (2,25)	Decision	$\bar{R}^2_r$	$\bar{R}^2_{ur}$
GDPFC → M_nI	5.12**	4.21(5%)	Rejected	0.971	0.975	6.22*	5.57(1%)	Rejected	0.972	0.980
M_nI → GDPFC	0.77	2.90(10%)	Not Rejected	0.998	0.998	0.71	2.53(10%)	Not Rejected	0.998	0.998

Source: Author's Calculations.

Table 7.8 : Pearls, Precious and Semi Precious Stones Imports - Causality Analysis

	Single lag					Double lag				
	F_{cal}	F_{tab} (1,27)	Decision	$\bar{R}^2_r$	$\bar{R}^2_{ur}$	F_{cal}	F_{tab} (2,25)	Decision	$\bar{R}^2_r$	$\bar{R}^2_{ur}$
GDPFC → PI	9.75*	7.68(1%)	Rejected	0.969	0.976	19.14*	5.57(1%)	Rejected	0.977	0.989
PI → GDPFC	2.75	2.90(10%)	Not Rejected	0.999	0.999	16.98*	5.57(1%)	Rejected	0.999	0.999

Source: Author's Calculations.

Table 7.9 : Results of Unit Root Test

	With trend		Without trend	
	DF_τ	DF_γ	DF_τ	DF_γ
TI	-4.52*	-29.60*	-12.14*	-25.50*
AI	-9.59*	-36.57*	-13.19*	-29.69*
CI	-6.06*	-47.64*	-11.27*	-28.06*
BI	-8.99*	-45.87*	-10.72*	-35.70*
M_hI	-14.61*	-35.31*	-12.26*	-32.04*
T_xI	-8.53*	-32.25*	-12.28*	-32.72*
M_nI	-11.08*	-36.24*	-29.29*	-28.99*
FI	-14.77*	-27.92*	-22.50*	-25.65*

Source: Author's Calculations.
Note: *significant at 1% level.

Stones imports show that GDP causes pearls and semi precious stones imports (GDPFC $\rightarrow$ PI) in both the cases of single as well as double lag. The reverse causation (PI$\rightarrow$ GDPFC) is present in case of double lag case. Being export oriented item, the imports of this category increase with the increase in GDP due to growth in exports. For GDPFC $\rightarrow$ PI, the calculated value of F-statistic is found to be significant at 1 per cent level in case of both the lags. For PI$\rightarrow$ GDPFC, the calculated value of F-statistic is found to be significant at one per cent level in case of double lag only. The values of $\bar{R}^2$ have been found to be better in case of double lag for GDPFC $\rightarrow$ PI. The values of $\bar{R}^2$ are almost same in both the lags for PI$\rightarrow$ GDPFC.

On the whole, the results strongly support the unidirectional causation from income to total imports, as well as in case of other major categories of imports, which includes agricultural imports, machinery and their parts imports, textiles and articles of textile imports and minerals imports in case of both the lags. The category of chemicals and allied industries imports also experienced unidirectional causality from income but in case of single lag only. The categories of pearls, precious and semi precious stones imports and base metal articles of base metals imports also show reverse causation or feedback causality (imports causing GDP) in case of double lag only. At disaggregate level, domestic production causes products of chemical or allied industries imports, base metals and articles of base metals imports, machinery and their parts imports and textiles and textile articles imports. We can conclude from here that imports of these categories are used as raw materials in India's domestic industries In case of machinery and their parts imports and products of chemical or allied industries imports; there is feedback causality between their domestic production and imports. In case of machinery and their parts imports, gross domestic capital formation causes these imports, but there is no reverse causation. It means India's capital goods imports increase with the increase in gross domestic capital formation.

CHAPTER

8

Import Policy in India

Trade policy involves regulation of imports and exports of a country. Such a regulation can be volume wise, value wise, composition wise and direction wise. Trade policy is often guided by country's domestic economic policy and lays down policy parameters and guidelines for different categories of commodities in a country's trade basket (Mukherjee, 1998; Mathur, 2003). Trade policy directly impacts volume and composition of imports and exports of a country. However, it indirectly influences the pattern, structure and direction of development of various sectors of economy, consumption pattern, investment, competitive conditions, and efficiency in the production system and entrepreneurial and business attitude. Trade policy of a country also aims at industrial and agricultural development, stability in domestic prices and augmentation and optimum utilization of its foreign exchange resources (Cherunilam, 1999).

The trade policy may be free or restrictive in nature. Purely free trade policy is without any tariffs, quantitative restrictions and other devices, which means complete freedom for international trade with minimum interference and without any restriction. On the contrary, the trade policy which imposes restrictions on the movement of goods between the countries is considered as restrictive trade policy. Besides these, we have strategic trade policy, which intends to influence the trade policies of other countries. A trade policy has a number of instruments to control and regulate foreign trade in goods and services. The main instruments consist of tariffs, quotas and other non-tariff barriers and also exchange rate policies.

A developing country like India has the necessity to adopt a dynamic trade policy to promote its economic development for various reasons (Dikshit, 2002). During 1980s many developing countries began to recognize that restrictive trade policy can constraint growth and started reform programs to facilitate trade and integration into the world economy. The trade regime of India, before 1991, was complex and was chracterised by severe quantitative restrictions on imports and exports. It included quantitative restrictions on finished consumer goods, industrial raw material, intermediates, and even on components and capital goods. The removal of quantitative restrictions began with the 1991 reforms and since 1993 industrial raw materials, intermediates, component and capital goods could be imported freely subject to the prevailing tariff levels (Sinha and Adam, 2007).

The import policy, which is an integral part of trade policy, has a positive role to play in a country's economic development as it regulates the imports as per the internal necessities of any economy. Import policy of India is influenced by the pace of industrialization, domestic market imperfections, employment opportunities, investment for raising profit, improvement in terms of trade, smuggling practices, balance of payment position, export promotion, import substitution, self reliance etc (Singh, 1985). The basic factors which influence India's import policy are economic needs of the country, effective use of foreign exchange and industrial as well as consumer requirements. The import policy has three objectives:

(1) The easy availability of essential imported goods, including capital goods for modernizing and upgrading technology.

(2) To simplify and streamline procedures for import licensing.

(3) To promote efficient import substitution and self reliance.

(4) domestic prices stabilization is another important objective of import policy.

Import policy of India changed from time to time according to changing economic conditions, domestic requirements and international changes. After independence, India's import policy was in consonance with the broad objectives of self-reliance, industrialization, technological upgradation and modernization. During fifties and sixties, India's import policy was formulated keeping in view:

(*a*) the limited foreign exchange reserves of the country

(*b*) shortages of essential commodities in the country

(*c*) capital goods requirements for the development of basic and heavy industries in the country

(*d*) scope of import substitution and

(*e*) need of export industries. Import policy discussion in India can be divided into two parts, i.e., import policies during pre 1985 period and post 1985 period.

Import Policy during Pre-1985 Period

During First Five-year Plan (1951-56), import policy was mainly liberal with some restrictions as per the necessity of the economy from year to year. The need for liberalized imports emerged in order to cover up the gap of domestic demand and supply of large number of items. The commercial policy has following objectives during this plan:

(1) it must fulfill the production and consumption targets in the plan,

(2) maintaining high level of exports,

(3) the trade deficits must be kept within the foreign exchange resources at the disposal of the country in any period,

(4) the composition of exports as well as of imports must, as far as possible, fit in with fiscal and price policies which had to be followed for the implementation of plan and

(5) there must be, to the extent practicable, a measure of continuity in policy, so that trade relations with other countries in respect of exports and imports and the plans of domestic industry and trade are not frequently disturbed (Government of India, 1951-56).

The Second Five-year Plan's (1956-61) developmental programmes were much larger and they required considerable imports of capital goods and industrial raw materials. As rapid industrialization with particular emphasis on the development of basic and heavy industries was one of the main objectives (Government of India, 1956-61). This led to the adoption of liberal policy. A main feature of the import policy of this period was the linking of imports with domestic production. The liberal import policy led to unprecedented rise in imports during 1956-57 and 1957-58 and there was foreign exchange crisis in the country. This necessitated a reversal of import policy and drastic restrictions were placed on imports by the government particularly on consumer goods. The capital goods imports were carefully regulated in order to make reasonable provision for ensuring the utilization of plant and capacity already available or in the process of being set up and for safeguarding employment (Government of India, 1957-58). The licenses for raw materials and intermediate goods were given on the basis of estimated maintenance requirement (Government of India, 1958-59).

During Third Five-year Plan (1961-66), import policy was more restrictive because with the growth of industrial production and the development of the economy as a whole, the level of imports had risen substantially over the decade of 1951-61. Thus, the import policy continued to be stringent and only under special export promotion schemes, larger import licenses for raw materials were issued (Government of India, 1960-61). Imports of consumer good and non-essentials were reduced to the minimum. Export promotion and import substitution schemes were emphasized considerably. Import policy was affected both by the difficult foreign exchange position and necessity to give priority to the requirement of defence and development. With all this, Government appointed the export and import policy committee headed by Mr. Mudaliar in 1962 to review government's trade policy. This committee recommended that (*a*) facilities should be provided for the imports of maintenance and developmental goods which are essential for the development of industries; and (*b*) priority should be given to new industries including (*i*) power and transport which had proved a serious bottleneck, (*ii*) export oriented industries and (*iii*) industries producing raw materials and components now being imported.

Import policy during three Annual Plans (1966-69) was made liberal in order to meet the domestic necessity, i.e., it was need based and production oriented to encourage exports. The imports of essential items were liberalized with the availability of foreign exchange resources and the licensing procedure was simplified in order to provide flexibility in the utilization of import licenses. Under this, imports of 59 priority industries were liberalized. This mainly included export industries, capital building industries and the industries catering to the need of common people, i.e., sugar and textiles. The arrangements were made to meet their requirements for raw materials, components and spares in full (initially for six months). The import policy for small scale industrial units making the same products as the priority industries was also substantially liberlised. The policy for 1967-68 was made need based and production oriented and provided for the continuation of the preferential treatment for the 59 priority industries. All this, increase imports faster than exports, which led to large trade deficits. Under the severe balance of payment pressure, the government devalued the rupee in June 1966 (main reasons for devaluation were rise in imports of industrial raw materials, machinery, maintenance imports and defence equipments due to 1962 and 1965 wars and large increase in debt service burden).

The import policy during Fourth Five-year Plan (1969-73) was need based and directed towards the objective of self-reliance through export promotion and import substitution, more employment, more production and encouragement to research and development. Under the import policy for 1971-72, the role of public sector agencies in imports was further expanded and exporters were given a further preferential treatment for building up of export production and export capacity. The exporters were permitted to import banned or restricted items with a view to improve the quality and competitiveness of export production. Technical and professional people as well as hospitals, medical institutions and research bodies have been given extended facilities for import of equipment and other essential goods. Under the import policy for 1972-73, import facilities accorded to export houses were further enlarged and streamlined. For the first time, Indian nationals returning from abroad were permitted to import without restrictions, equipment and raw materials up to a value of Rs. 5 lakhs and Rs. 1 lakh respectively for settling up small scale industries. In December 1971, regulatory customs duties were imposed on all imports other than food grains, books and a few other commodities (Govt. of India, 1971-72 and 1972-73).

The import policy for Fifth Five-year Plan (1974-79) was emphasized to maintain the tempo of industrial production, to encourage export and employment and to simplify the licensing procedure. The import policy during this period can be characterized as export oriented import policy. The main features of policy of import liberalization were:

1. Dominant priority to the import of capital goods and other inputs such as petrol and petroleum products etc., for export industries and essential goods of mass consumption.
2. Special considerations were given to small scale units for licenses. This import policy expected to be helpful in securing national self-reliance and industrial development with special emphasis on small scale sector and backward regions.
3. The Open General License (OGL) Scheme was enlarged to include 570 items.
4. Administrative procedures were simplified to reduce the delay in obtaining import licenses.

Import policy for 1973-74 encouraged import substitution through restriction on imports of those commodities whose domestic production had increased. Under this policy, the Industrial Raw Materials Assistance Centre (IRMAC) set up by State Trading Corporation. The priority treatment by greater allocation of imported inputs was extended to 11 more industries in 1973-74, bringing their total number to 70. Import of machinery was now allowed on a more liberal basis against replenishment licenses. During 1973-74, a number of items (about 220) for which indigenous production had developed, were taken off the permissible list and import of 55 items was restricted. Quotas for established importers were further reduced in respect of 26 items. The import of spare parts was also liberalized (Government of India, 1973-74).

The overall import policy for 1974-75 remained fairly liberal. The salient features were simplification of import licensing procedures, liberalization of import of spare parts and components, preferential treatment to export linked industries and a widening of the role of state trading agencies. The import policy for the year 1975-76 was drawn up with a view to making it more responsive to the needs of raising industrial production and diverting it to exports, elimination of non essential imports and removal of delays in providing import licenses for raw materials and components. The new term "select industries" was introduced in place of "priority" and "non priority" terms, which included industries important to national economy and for export production. The "automatic licensing" was introduced whereby industrial unit could apply directly to import control authorities without routing their application through the sponsoring authorities (Government of India, 1974-75 and 1975-76).

Import policy of 1976-77 introduced considerable degree of liberalization, further procedural simplification and certain shifts of emphasis of the import policy to achieve faster economic growth by providing essential imported inputs for enlarging the production base for exports (Government of India, 1976-77). The import policy for 1977-78 was substantially liberalized not only to meet input requirements of industries in full but also to maintain the price level particularly in respect of mass consumption goods. The OGL was further widened and policy for banning/prohibiting imports was changed significantly (Government of India, 1977-78).

There has been gradual, selective and progressive liberalization of import policy during the years 1978-81 (rolling plans) in order to increase domestic production, efficiency and to provide incentives to exports. The liberalization continued in 1978-79 import policy also. As a part of import liberalisation, the policies were simplified and the procedures were rationalized. The system of free licensing was eliminated and merged with OGL policy. To liberalise capital goods imports for strengthening production base, the list of capital goods items permitted for imports under OGL by actual user was substantially enlarged. Under import policy of 1979-80, the coverage of OGL was further enlarged to include the items such as scientific and technical books, life saving drugs, instruments required by the blind, homeopathic and ayurvedic medicines, dry fruits, spices etc. The industries of national importance like fertilizers, power generation, basic drugs, cement etc and fully export oriented industries were allowed to import plant and equipment on a global basis. Along with liberalization, the changes were made in import duties also. The most important change in import duty was downward revision of duty from 40 per cent to 25 per cent advalorem in respect of wide ranging items of capital goods. With this the reduction in capital costs in domestic industries was expected (Government of India, 1978-79 and 1979-80).

The import policy during 1980-81 mainly aimed at liberalizing and streamlining the licensing procedures, so as to meet the requirements of actual users particularly in the export sector. The import policy of 1980-81 to 1984-85 (fall under sixth plan period), followed a liberal approach of providing necessary imported inputs for the industrial sector. Under the import policy of 1982-83 and 1983-84, import replenishment licenses (REP) issued against specified export products to enable import of essential inputs for export production at international prices were made more attractive. Imports were liberalized under OGL to actual users and the value limits for imports (to promote technological upgradation and modernization) under the technological development scheme was doubled. Additional incentives were given for export oriented production and simplification of procedure continued to be taking place (Government of India, 1982-83, 1983-84). Till 1984-85, the

Government issued its export import policy every year. Following recommendations of the Abid Hussain Committee and earlier the Alexander Committee, the Government decided to issue a trade policy for a period of three years. Three long term export-import policies were announced by the govt. The first covered the period 1985-88 and second had to cover the period 1988 to 1991. However, because of the change in the Govt. at the centre, the second policy was terminated one year earlier. The third policy covered the period April, 1990 to March, 1993. This policy also did not last for full three years as the Govt. announced a new five year export import policy on March 31, 1992 covering the period 1992-97. However, real thrust in the direction of liberalization was provided from 1985 onwards when the system of formulating long-term (three year) policies was adopted. In export import policy 1985 and three year exim policies which were announced in 1985 and 1988, quantitative restrictions were abolished and number of items to be imported under OGL was substantially increased (Tripathi, 2005).

Import Policies during Post-1985 Period

The basic aim of exim policy 1985 was to facilitate production through easier access to imported inputs, to impart continuity and stability of exim policy, to strengthen the export production base, to facilitate technological upgradation and also to help all possible savings in imports. The main features of exim policy 1985 were, import of as many as 53 items was decanalised, as many as 201 items of industrial machinery were placed in OGL under the import policy, a pass book scheme was introduced to eliminate possible delays in acquiring licenses under duty exemption scheme, imports of 67 items of raw materials and components transferred to limited permissible list from OGL and automatic permissible list, a two tier policy adopted for import of computer/computer based systems.

The second three year import export policy 1988-91 also laid greater emphasis on modernization and technological upgradation for making the industry progressively more competitive through trade liberalization. This policy terminated a year earlier than scheduled. Under the 1988-91 import export policy, with a view to containing high imports of components for final stage assembly of range of consumer durables, a number of components shifted from OGL to licensable categories. Furthermore in the budget for 1989-90 a number of excise and customs duty revisions were carried out to moderate growth of imports. In order to ensure proper absorption of foreign technology and progressive indigenization of product, the phase manufacturing programme (PMP) was required by most import intensive industries like automobiles, electronics, consumer durables etc. The PMPs indicate the import entitlement for components at different stages while the remainder of its input requirements is stipulated to be met from indigenous sources (Government of India, 1989-90).

The third three year exim policy for the period 1990-93 announced with objective to give big push to exports and a drastic cut down on procedural formalities, a move to discourage non essential and low priority imports and a continuing emphasis on reposing greater trust in exporters and importers and on liberalizing the policy. The policy facilitated availability of necessary imported inputs for sustaining growth including essential imported capital goods for modernization and technological upgradation. The policy promotes the efficient import substitution and self reliance. The key feature of the policy was the enlargement and liberalization of Import Replenishment Licensing (REP) system, which will be called as Exim Scrip. These were essentially tradable import licenses issued to exporters for 30 per cent of the value of exports. Exim Scrips could be used to import a wide range of items which were earlier importable against supplementary licenses and with the introduction of Exim Scrips, supplementary licenses were abolished (Government of India, 1992-93). The policy simplified Import Replenishment Licensing (REP) scheme endowed with greater flexibility in terms of categories of items that could be imported and all this was in line with the international marketing requirements. Under the scheme, exporters, except those in the gems and jewellery sector, could avail of the facility of REP licenses to replenish raw material, components, consumables and packing material used in manufacture of products exported, so long as such inputs were in appendices 3 (list of limited permissible items) and 5A (items of imports canalised through public sector agencies). The duty exemption scheme permits the import of raw materials, components, consumables and spares meant for export production on duty free basis (Government of India, 1990-91).

The aggregate imports of India have grown at the rate of 22.08 per cent for the period 1986-87 to 1990-91 at current prices. Under the group of capital goods imports, the imports of machinery and their parts (40.01%) have grown at higher rate as compared to the imports of transport equipments (24.60%) and project goods (11.52%) for the period 1986-87 to 1990-91. The share of imports of machinery and their parts (19.92%) in total imports was also higher than the share of imports of transport equipments (3.93%) and imports of project goods (7.03%) for the year 1986-87. Further for the year 1990-91, the share of imports of machinery and their parts (13.48%) and project goods (5.90%) declined more as compared to the share of transport equipments imports (3.86%) for the year 1990-91.

The exim policies during pre 1990 period led to 28.51 per cent growth for export oriented imports of pearls, precious and semi precious stones, metals and articles for the period 1986-87 to 1990-91. The share of this category in total imports was 7.73 per cent for the year 1986-87, which increase to 8.70 per cent for the year 1990-91. Similarly under the group of industry oriented goods, the imports of chemical and allied industries (25.42%) have grown at higher rate as compared to the imports of base metals and articles of base metals (19.42%) for the period 1986-87 to 1990-91. On the contrary, the share of base metals imports (13.05 per cent) was higher than share of chemicals imports (11.41%) for the year 1986-87. The share of both base metals imports (11.20%) and chemical imports (10.87%) in total imports declined for the year 1990-91. Under the group of food items imports, the category of animal or vegetable fats and oils and their cleavage products imports, which mainly included edible oils imports grew at a negative rate for the period 1986-87 to 1990-91. The share of this category also declined to 0.84 per cent in year 1990-91 from 3.33 per cent for the year 1986-87.

Apart from these, the category of mineral products imports which was not directly influenced by the trade policy measures, grew at the highest rate of 36.07 per cent for the period 1986-87 to 1990-91. The share of this category in total imports was 17.46 per cent for the year 1986-87, which increased to 29.65 per cent for the year 1990-91.

Trade policy reforms since 1991 have been undertaken to achieve India's transition into a globally oriented economy. For this purpose India's trade policy aims at export promotion to raise export earnings and import liberalization measures are used as pre requisites for expansion of exports. According to Das (2000), import liberalization is supposed to have two major beneficial effects. First, import liberalisation permits a greater degree of international integration through greater efficiency in the production of traded goods which also improves the position of GDP growth. Second, import liberalisation, via export competitiveness, is expected to stabilize domestic prices and narrow down the trade deficit for the domestic economy. The measures of import liberalization included withdrawal of quantitative restrictions, reductions and rationalization of tariffs, liberalization in the trade and payments regime and improved access to export incentives. In June 1992, the import and export (control) act 1947, was superseded by the Foreign Trade (Development and Regulation) Act, 1992. This act was to give effect to new liberalized export and import policy of Government For the first time in trade history the Five Year Exim Policy was announced by Government of India on 31 March, 1992, which coincided with the launching of Eighth Five-year Plan (1992-97). The direction of this policy was towards fewer restrictions, greater freedom to trade and less administrative controls. The greater freedom is allowed to stabilize the industrial production which disrupted due to severe import squeeze for controlling the crisis which began in 1991 (Mathur, 2006). The broad structural objectives of this policy have been to accelerate the country's transition to an internationally oriented economy with a view to deriving maximum benefit from the expanding global market opportunities. Specially, the policy aims at stimulating India's exports by facilitating access to imported supplies and capital goods (Bhattacharyya, 1995). The main features of import policy 1992-97 were:

(*a*) All items other than those mentioned in the negative list can be imported freely.

(*b*) Capital goods, raw materials, intermediates, components, consumables, spare parts, accessories, instruments and other goods may be imported without any restriction.

(*c*) Second hand capital goods and other second hand goods shall not be imported unless permitted by this policy or in accordance with a license issued.

(*d*) Import of certain specified capital goods or their parts may be sent abroad for repairs and reimported without a license.

(*e*) Construction machinery, equipments, related spares, tools and accessories used in overseas projects can be imported without a license.

In the budget for 1992-93, a new system of exchange rate management was introduced as a transitional arrangement towards a unified exchange rate system with current account convertibility. Meanwhile, it has simplified the trade policy regime by eliminating detailed exchange control. The foreign exchange surrendered at official exchange rate is utilized to import essential items. All other imports of raw materials, components and also capital goods have been made freely importable on OGL but foreign exchange for these imports has to be obtained from the market. There is a specified negative list of items which continued to be importable against licenses.

On March, 1992 the system of Exim Scrips was abolished and replaced by Liberalized Exchange Rate Management System (LERMS). Under this system, virtually all capital goods and raw material and components were made freely importable subject to tariff protection as long as foreign exchange to pay for these imports was obtained from the market. On 1st April, 1992 the trade policy substantially pruned the negative list of licensable imports. Three import items were banned, 71 items were restricted and 7 items were canalized. Imports of capital goods were further liberalized by lowering the customs duty from 25 per cent to 15 per cent subject to an export commitment equivalent to four times the c.i.f value of imports to be achieved over a period of five years. Further import duties on capital goods, project imports, basic feedstocks for petro chemicals etc, were brought down. The Government proposed to further reduce the average and maximum tariffs and simplify and rationalize the tariff structure.

Exim policy was further liberalized as announced on July 1992, to boost exports, modifications in policy included:

(*i*) Procedures for imports and exports made simpler.

(*ii*) Compensation for unutilized import licences for duty free license scheme and Exim Scrip holders.

(*iii*) In order to encourage the use of indigenous inputs by EOU/EPZ units, the formula of value addition was revised so as to exclude the value of indigenous inputs from the computation of value addition. The Government introduced a system of value based Advanced Licenses to export houses, trading houses and star trading houses, which permitted duty free imports of necessary raw materials as components upto a stipulated ratio of value of anticipated exports (Kalirajan, 2003).

(*iv*) The Special Import Licences to eligible category of exports were given to enable them to import specified items which were on restricted list.

Under these special licences, import of 18 consumers durable items listed in negative list, have been allowed subject to the payment of normal customs duty (Government of India, 1992-93).

The budget for 1993-94 made substantial reductions in customs duties on capital goods, ferrous and non ferrous metals and chemicals. Import duties on specified capital goods for exports such as textiles, leather, marine products, gems and jewellery, food processing, horticulture and floriculture industries were reduced, the maximum import duties rates were reduced to 85 per cent, and there was a cut in the duties on personal baggage to 150 per cent from 255 per cent (Government of India, 1993-94).

In Nov. 1993, the Government allowed duty free imports of capital goods, provided the importer undertakes to export seven times the import value. On 30th March, 1994 modifications were announced that aimed at further rationalization and streamlining of the policy. Under which the scope of items importable through special import licences (SILs) was increased and all second hand capital goods with a minimum residual life of 5 years were made fully importable by actual users (Government of India, 1994-95).

Exim policy 1992-97 was further revised in March, 1995. The revisions included measures for trade promotion, as well as further simplification of procedures. It included:

(1) under zero duty imports of capital goods scheme, which was available for imports of capital goods of at least Rs. 20 crores, there were now two windows to fulfill export obligation on f.o.b (free on board) or NFE (net foreign exchange earnings) basis.

(2) Earlier consumer goods were restricted to be imported without a license only by actual users. With changes made, any person can import part or components of consumer durables freely, without a license and without actual user condition.

(3) The list of freely importable consumer goods has been further expanded to include 78 items.

(4) The list of goods permitted to be imported against the freely transferable import licenses which were granted to export houses/trading houses/star trading houses or super star trading houses, has been further expanded.

(5) Newsprint including glazed news print has been made freely importable, by all persons.

(6) Import of mandatory spares upto 5 per cent of the c.i.f value of license has been allowed (Government of India, 1995-96).

The Exim Policy 1992-97 made various efforts to dismantle protectionist and regulatory policies and liberalise the imports of capital goods and other essential goods. Trade liberalization in India started in mid eighties whereas other liberalization measures were initiated in post-1991 period. This was particularly so in case of machinery and capital goods imports. Due to this, these imports grew at high rate. Trade liberalization got further boost in the form of removal of restrictions, tariff cuts and procedural simplifications during post, 1991 period. The total imports growth rate increased to 25.02 per cent for the period 1991-92 to 1995-96 as compared to period of 1986-87 to 1990-91 (22.08%). The import liberalization measures taken under exim policy 1992-97, led to higher growth of imports of transport equipments and project goods as compared to machinery imports in the group of capital goods. The imports of machinery and their parts have grown at the rate of 38.26 per cent for the period 1991-92 to 1995-96 (which was less than the rate was for the period 1986-87 to 1990-91). But the share of this category of imports in total imports increased to 17.21 per cent for the year 1995-96 from 11.48 per cent for the year 1991-92. The imports of transport equipment grew at the rate of 45.52 per cent for the period 1991-92 to 1995-96, (which was higher than the rate for the period 1986-87 to 1990-91). The share of transport equipment imports in total imports also increased to 3.01 per cent during the year 1995-96 from 1.91 per cent during the year 1991-92. Similarly, the imports of project goods also grew at a rate of 22.55 per cent for the period 1991-92 to 1995-96 (which doubled as compared to the rate for the period 1986-87 to 1990-91). The share of project goods imports in total imports was six per cent or higher than six per cent for the years 1991-92 to 1995-96.

Despite liberalization measures taken under exim policy 1992-97, the export oriented imports showed less growth. Further the export oriented imports of pearls, precious and semi precious stones, metals and articles thereof, have grown at the rate of 15.25 per cent for the period 1991-92 to 1995-96 (which was half of the rate for the period 1986-87 to 1990-91). The share of this category in total imports also declined to 8.23 per cent during 1995-96 from 10.61 per cent during 1991-92. The imports of base metal and metal products have grown at higher rate as compared to chemical and allied industries imports under the group of industry oriented imports. The imports of base metals and metal products have grown at the rate of 26.55 per cent for the period 1991-92 to 1995-96 (which was higher than the rate for the period 1986-87 to 1990-91). But the share of this category remained around eight per cent for the years 1991-92 to 1995-96. The imports of chemical and allied industries have grown at the rate of 25.78 per cent for the period 1991-92 and 1995-96 (almost same as for the period 1986-87 to 1990-91). The share of this category fluctuated around 13 per cent for the years 1991-92 and 1995-96.

Due to measures taken under 1992-97 exim policy, imports of animal or vegetable fats and oils have grown at the rate of 67.10 per cent for the period 1991-92 to 1995-96 (which was at very high level than the rate for 1986-87 to 1990-91). The share of this category in total imports also increased to 2.07 per cent for the year 1995-96 from 0.71 per cent for the year 1991-92. Further the imports of mineral products have grown at the rate of 16.74 per cent for the period 1991-92 to 1995-96 (which was at lower level than the rate for the period 1986-87 to 1990-91). The share of this category, (which mainly included petroleum, oils and lubricants) in total imports, also declined to 25.37 per cent for the year 1995-96 from 32.27 per cent for the year 1991-92.

The new export-import policy 1997-2002 (co-terminus with 9th Plan) was announced by commerce minister on 31st March, 1997. This policy was another important step in direction of achieving a more free trade condition and integration of Indian economy into the world economy (Dikshit, 2002). It further carried forward the process of liberalization by deregulating and simplifying procedures and removing quantitative restrictions in a phased manner. The main objectives of this policy were as under:

(*a*) To accelerate the country's transition to a globally oriented vibrant economy to derive maximum benefits from expanding global market opportunities.

(*b*) To stimulate sustained economic growth by providing access to essential raw materials, intermediate, components, consumables and capital goods required for augmenting production.

(*c*) To enhance the technological strength and efficiency of Indian agriculture, industry and services, thereby improving their competitiveness while generating new employment opportunities, and encourage the attainment of internationally accepted standard of quality.

(*d*) To provide consumer with good quality products at reasonable prices.

To achieve these objectives following steps were taken:

(*i*) The restricted list of imports was substantially pruned. Imports of 542 items had been liberalized which included about 150 items that could now be imported against Special Import License (SIL). About 60 items were moved from SIL to OGL list. Restrictions were placed on 5 items on the ground of environmental safety, strategic importance, public health and security.

(*ii*) The Export Promotion Capital Goods (EPCG) scheme was streamlined. The tariff rates for the import of capital goods were reduced from 15 per cent to 10 per cent. Zero duty imports were allowed in those cases where the c.i.f. value of imports was 20 crore or more subject to export obligations. The threshold limit is Rs.1 crore for agriculture, animal husbandry, floriculture etc. and Rs. 10 lakh for software.

(*iii*) Duty exemption scheme was an important instrument for boosting exports. It consisted of duty free license and duty entitlement pass book.

(*iv*) Deemed exports benefits were extended to oil and gas sectors in addition to power sector.

(*v*) Norms for domestic sales by EOUs and EPZs in agro and allied sectors were liberalized.

(*vi*) This policy aimed to give a boost to the software industry. Software exporters were allowed to import goods on loan for a specified period.

(*vii*) Recognizing that procedures needed to be considerably simplified, this policy aimed at making the procedures transparent and less discretionary.

(*viii*) This policy announced a 1 per cent SIL on total value of exports for export of fruit, vegetables, floriculture and horticulture produce, if such exports constitute 10 per cent of total exports.

(*ix*) The gems and jewellery units in EOU/EPZ were permitted to sell in domestic tariff area, 10 per cent of their previous year exports.

(*x*) Electronic hardware units were allowed to sell up to 50 per cent in domestic tariff area on an annual basis while exporting 50 per cent.

(*xi*) Special depreciation norms were provided for electronic goods up to 70 per cent in three years.

The Exim Policy 1997-2002 was revised on 13th April, 1998, 31st March, 1999 and 31st March, 2000. The objectives of these revisions/modifications were to meet the commitments made to the WTO, further liberalize imports and promote exports. Following were the main provisions of the modified Export-Import policy on April 13, 1998:

(1) 340 more items were shifted from the restricted list to Open General License (OGL).

(2) The revised policy set an export growth target of 20 per cent.

(3) Zero duty Export Promotion Capital Goods (EPCG) scheme was extended to all software exporters.

(4) To prevent cheap imports being dumped at unreasonable prices, the govt. set up an anti-dumping cell called Directorate General (DG) of Anti-Dumping and Allied Duties.

(5) Other provisions included delegation of powers to regional licensing officer, doing away with minimum value addition of 33 per cent under advance licensing scheme, simplified procedure for clubbing of advance licence schemes and private bonded warehouses to be set up to import, stock and sell even negative list items.

On 31st March, 1999, revised Export-Import Policy added 894 items to free list of imports and an additional 414 items were removed from restricted list and put on Special Import licence (SIL) route, and no additional customs duty on import of capital goods for marine and electronics sectors under zero duty EPCG scheme. Here it is important to mention that India's international commitments required it to remove licensing curbs on imports by the year 2003. The other revisions were:

(1) The annual advance license system introduced to take care of the entire import needs of exporters.

(2) Duty free import of consumables up to certain limits for gems and jewellery, handicrafts and leather sectors.

(3) Import of second hand goods of all kinds have been restricted and import of second hand capital goods under EPCG scheme disallowed for domestic capital goods industries in light of slowdown.

(4) Wide ranging concessions on preferential basis in customs duties on imports from SAARC countries have been effected by Ministry of Finance.

(5) In order to reduce financing cost of imports and to provide credit at reasonable terms, RBI has withdrawn the interest rate surcharge of 30 per cent on import finance. Also, the maximum interest rate of 20 per cent on overdue export bills has been withdrawn (Government of India, 1999-2000).

On 31st March 2000, further modifications were suggested:

(1) Setting up of special economic zones (SEZ) under which units would be able to import capital goods and raw material duty free and the basic rational of SEZ unit was to provide a totally free atmosphere conducive for exports.

(2) Exim policy 2000-01 announced sector specific packages for seven core areas to boost exports, viz. gems and jewellery, pharmaceutical, agrochemicals, biotechnology, silk, leather and garments.

(3) This policy also announced financial incentives to states based on their export performance.

(4) This policy removed quantitative restrictions on 714 item out of 1429 items (nearly 50 per cent items) by moving them from SIL (Special Import License) to OGL (Open General License).

This was mainly in line with India's WTO obligations, where India negotiated with large number of countries and agreed to phase out quantitative restrictions by 2003 (Government of India, 2000-01).

In 2001-02 Exim Policy, government proposed:

(*i*) Import restrictions of the remaining 715 items have been removed.

(*ii*) Imports of second hand or used-vehicles, meat and poultry products and primary agricultural products and textile and textile articles have been allowed, subject to certain criteria.

(*iii*) Import of farm products have been permitted only through state trade agencies.

(*iv*) Export promoting capital goods scheme and duty exemption scheme has been extended to agricultural exports as well.

(*v*) Agro Economic Zones will be formed and new agricultural export policy will be announced.

The Exim Policy 1997-2002 continued to liberalize imports through liberalization of import policy and lowering of import duties. The import restrictions have been phased out since 1996 along with tariff cuts but no extra ordinary growth has occurred in the imports of freed items. The total imports also have grown at relatively lower rate of 14.46 per cent for the period 1996-97 to 2000-01 as compared to the growth rate for the period 1991-92 to 1995-96, i.e., 25.02 per cent. The capital goods imports showed a decline in growth rate for the period 1996-97 to 2000-01. The growth rate of imports of machinery and their parts has declined to 9.87 per cent, whereas the imports of transport equipments and project goods showed negative growth rates for the period 1996-97 to 2000-01. The share of all these categories of capital goods also declined for the year 2000-01 as compared to the year 1996-97.

On the contrary, the imports of pearls, precious, semi precious stones, metals and articles thereof showed growth rate of 33.47 per cent (more than double as compared to 1991-92 to 1995-96) for the period 1996-97 to 2000-01. The share of this export oriented category in total imports also increased to 19.20 per cent during 2000-01 from 10.14 per cent for the year 1996-97. The industry oriented imports of chemical and allied industries products showed lower growth rate of 3.66 per cent and base metals imports showed negative growth rate for the period 1996-97 to 2000-01. The share of both of these industry oriented imports in total imports also declined for this period.

Further, the imports of animals or vegetables fats and oils under agricultural imports also grew at relatively lower rate of 29.15 per cent for the period 1996-97 to 2000-01 as compared to the period 1991-92 to 1995-96, i.e., 67.10 per cent. The share of this category in total imports increased to 2.80 per cent for the year 2000-01 from 2.20 per cent during 1996-97. The imports of mineral products in case of which India has high import dependence, grew at the rate of 20.41 per cent for the period 1996-97 to 2000-01 (higher than the rate for the period 1991-92 to 1995-96, i.e., 16.74 per cent). The share of this category in total imports also increased to 36.15 per cent for the year 2000-01 from 30.60 per cent for the year 1996-97.

The long-term Exim Policy for the period 2002-07 was unveiled on March 31, 2002 (co-terminus with Tenth Five-year Plan). The two developments have been kept in mind at the time of formulation of this policy viz., the lifting of quantitative restrictions w.e.f April, 2001 and entry of china as a member of WTO (Tripathi, 2005). This policy seeks to usher in an environment free of restrictions and controls. The principal objectives of this policy were:

1. To accelerate the country's transition to a globally oriented vibrant economy to derive maximum benefits from expanding global market opportunities through sustained growth in exports to attain a share of at least 1 per cent of global merchandise trade.
2. To stimulate sustained economic growth by providing access to essential raw materials, intermediates, components, consumables and goods required for augmenting production and providing services.
3. To enhance the technological strength and efficiency of Indian agriculture, industry and services thereby improving their competitive strength while generating new employment opportunities and to encourage the attainment of internationally accepted standards of quality.

4. To provide consumers with good quality goods and services at internationally competitive prices while at the same time creating a level of playing field for the domestic producers.

Main features of exim policy 2002-07 are:

(1) All exports and imports are free, subject to the regulations imposed by the govt. except those which were contained in the negative list appended to the policy.

(2) Capital goods, both new and second hand may be imported under the EPCG (Exports Promoting Capital Goods) scheme.

(3) Advanced license granted to a manufacture exporter for the import of inputs required for the manufacture of goods without payment of basic customs duty.

(4) It makes special mention of quality awareness.

(5) No import or export can be made by any person without an importer-exporter code number granted by a competent authority.

(6) Offshore Banking Units (OBUs) were permitted in SEZs which impart security to the returns of the unit.

(7) Electronic Hardware Technology Park (EHTP) was modified to enable the sector to face zero duty regime under Information Technology Agreement (ITA-1).

(8) Changes in gems and jewellery scheme include abolition of the licensing regime for the import of rough diamonds, reduction in value addition norms for export of jewellery and permitting personal carriage of jewellery (Government of India, 2002-03).

Exim Policy 2003-04 had the following provisions:

(1) The policy introduced duty free import facility for the service sector units having a minimum foreign exchange earning of Rs. 10 lakh.

(2) Encouragement of corporate sector with proven credential to sponsor Agricultural Export Zones for boosting exports.

(3) EPCG scheme made more flexible and attractive. So that even small sector could set up and expand its manufacturing base for exports.

(4) Simplification and codification of rules, regulations and procedures applicable to SEZs and EOUs.

(5) To increase the overall competitiveness of export clusters, a scheme for upgradation of infrastructure was introduced.

(6) Extension of Duty Free Replenish Certificate (DFRC) scheme to deemed exports and reduction in its value addition norms from 33 per cent to 25 per cent.

The mini exim policy announced on 28th January, 2004, included facilitation and simplification measures to sustain the momentum of export growth, especially of gems and jewellery. It also included provisions for encouragement to tourism and making energy generation cheaper. The main features were:

(1) Free import of gold and silver for export purposes permitted, by lifting quantitative restrictions. The gold card introduced for creditworthy exporters to make available cheaper foreign currency debt on easier terms.

(2) Duty free import facility available to star hotels extended to heritage, one and two star hotels and stand alone restaurants. They allowed duty free imports equivalent to five per cent of their export earning in three preceding years.

(3) Restrictions on import of electrical energy lifted.

(4) Online license and electronic fund transfer facility for exporters made available.

The Exim Policy 2002-07 tried to liberalise the trade through import liberalization and simplification of the procedures, as a result total imports showed an increase. Total imports at current prices grew at the rate of 28.45 per cent for the period 2001-02 to 2005-06, which was double the growth rate for the period 1996-97 to 2000-01, i.e., 14.46 per cent. The capital goods imports grew at very high rate for the period 2001-02 to 2005-06. The growth rate for the imports of machinery and their parts increased abruptly to 33.20 per cent for the period 2001-02 to 2005-06. Moreover, the share of this category in total imports also increased to 17.30 per cent in total imports for the year 2005-06 as compared to 13.68 per cent for the year 2001-02. The imports of transport equipments and project goods have also grown at high rates of 59.68 per cent and 8.44 per cent respectively, for the period 2001-02 to 2005-06, as compared to negative rates for the period 1996-97 to 1999-2000. The share of transport equipment in total imports also increased to 5.93 per cent, but share of project goods imports declined to 0.60 per cent for the year 2005-06.

The export-oriented imports of pearls, precious, semi precious stones, metals and articles thereof showed decline in growth rate, i.e., 22.75 per cent for the period 2001-02 to 2005-06 and the share in total imports also declined to 13.87 per cent during the year 2005-06. Further the industry oriented imports have increased at very high rates for the period 2001-02 to 2005-06 as compared to 1996-97 to 2000-01. The chemical and allied industries imports and base metals and metal products imports grew at the rates of 23.76 per cent and 39.65 per cent respectively, for the period 2001-02 to 2005-06. The share of chemical imports in total imports declined slightly for the year 2005-06 as compared to the year 2001-02. The share of base metals imports increased to 6.60 per cent for the year 2005-06 from 4.96 per cent for the year 2001-02.

The imports of animal or vegetable fats and oils grew at the rate of 9.95 per cent for the period 2001-02 to 2005-06 (which was one third of the rate for the period 1996-97 to 2000-01). The share of this category declined to 1.53 per cent for the year 2005-06 from 2.88 per cent for the year 2001-02. The imports of mineral products grew at rate of 30.45 per cent for the period 2001-02 to 2005-06 (higher than the rate for the period 1996-97 to 2000-01). The share of this category in total imports also increased to 35.27 per cent for the year 2005-06.

On 31st August, 2004, a new Foreign Trade Policy for the period 2004-09 was announced. The new trade policy (FTP) aimed at simplifying procedures, quality products and partnership with business and industry (Tripathi, 2005). The FTP announced new initiatives that include setting up of Board of Trade and the Service Export Promotion Council. This policy sets core objectives and identifies key strategies. It focused on sectors having prospects for export expansion and potential for employment generation. Main objectives of Foreign Trade policy were:

(1) To double India's percentage share of global merchandise trade by 2009.

(2) To act as an effective instrument of economic growth by giving a thrust to employment generation. These objectives expected to enhance international competitiveness and aid in further increasing the acceptability of Indian exports.

The key strategies to achieve these objectives included:

(1) Unshackling of controls and creating an atmosphere of trust and transparency.

(2) Simplifying procedures and bringing down transaction costs.

(3) Adopting the fundamental principle that duties and levies should not be exported.

(4) Identifying and nurturing different special focus areas to facilitate development of India as a global hub for manufacturing, trading and services.

(5) Facilitating technological and infrastructural upgradation of Indian economy, especially through import of capital goods and equipment. Besides this, it also included avoidance of inverted duty structure and ensuring that domestic sectors were not disadvantaged in trade agreements and upgrading the infrastructure network related to the entire foreign trade chain to international standards.

The special focus initiatives have been announced for agriculture, handicrafts, handlooms, gems and jewellery and leather and footwear sectors. Under this main measures related to imports are:

(1) Import of seeds, bulbs, tubers and planting material has been liberalized.

(2) Duty free import of consumables for metals other than gold and platinum allowed up to two per cent of f.o.b value of exports.

(3) Duty free re-import entitlement for rejected jewellery allowed up to two per cent of f.o.b value of exports. (4) Duty free import of commercial samples of jewellery increased to Rs. 1 lakh.

(5) Import of gold of 18 carat and above allowed under the replenishment scheme.

(6) Duty free import of trimmings and embellishments for Handlooms and Handicrafts sectors increased to five per cent of f.o.b value of exports.

(7) Import of trimmings and embellishments and samples shall be exempt from CVD.

(8) Duty free entitlements of import trimmings, embellishments and footwear components for leather industry increased to three per cent of f.o.b value of exports.

(9) Duty free import of specified items for leather sector increased to five per cent of f.o.b value of exports.

(10) Machinery and equipment for Effluent Treatment Plants for leather industry shall be exempt from customs duty.

Besides these:

(1) Free Trade and Warehousing Zones (FTWZs) has been introduced to create trade related infrastructure to facilitate the import and export of goods and services with freedom to carry out trade transactions in convertible currencies.

(2) Import of second hand capital goods without any restriction on age has been permitted.

(3) The new policy has allowed transfer of the import entitlement under Duty Free Replenishment Certificate (DFRC) scheme in respect of fuel to the marketing agencies authorized by the Ministry of Petroleum and Natural Gas to facilitate sourcing of such imports by individual exporters.

(4) Policy measures announced to further rationalization and simplification of the rules and procedures.

(5) On 31st Aug, 2004, several items were made free from restrictions. This would help to increase productivity and benefit the nation through higher yields.

The Annual Supplement 2005-06 to the Foreign Trade Policy (FTP) 2004-09, was announced on April 8, 2005. It gave boost to exports from agriculture and manufacturing sectors. The imports by hotels, other service industries were also made duty free. Besides this:

(1) policy proposed to engage the state governments in providing an enabling environment for boosting international trade, by setting up an inter State Trade Council.

(2) For agricultural sector, concessional duty imports made by agro units under the EPCG scheme shall be allowed to fulfil the export obligations over a longer period of time with reduced export obligations.

(3) To promote capacity expansion and quality upgradation in the SSI sector, import of capital goods at five per cent customs duty, allowed subject to a fulfilment of an export obligation equivalent to six times the duty saved on capital goods imported under the EPCG scheme over a period of eight years.

(4) The concessional duty benefits under EPCG scheme extended for import of capital goods required by retailers having minimum covered shopping area of 1000 sq metres. This was to create modern infrastructure in the retail sector.

(5) The requirement of submitting an installation certificate for machinery imported under EPCG scheme, now not be required for the units which were not registered with central excise.

(6) To enable the service providers to upgrade the infrastructure in their associated companies, the goods imported under the 'Served from India' scheme were transferable with in the group companies and managed hotels subject to actual user condition.

(7) Entitlement for duty free imports of gems and jewellery samples have been enhanced to Rs. 3 lakh (earlier this

limit was Rs. 1 lakh) in a financial year or 0.25 per cent of the average of the last three years exports turnover or gems and jewellery items, whichever is lower.

(8) Exporters of plain/studded/precious metal jewellery will be allowed to import plain/studded/precious metal jewellery for the purposes of exports.

(9) Duty free imports of specified specialized inputs/chemicals and flavouring oils as per a defined list were allowed to the extent of one per cent of f.o.b value of preceding financial years export. Use of these special ingredients for seafood processing will enable us to achieve a higher value addition and enter new export markets.

(10) The import of monofilament long line system for tuna fishing at a concessional rate of duty, was proposed to encourage the existing mechanized vessels and deep sea trawlers to adopt modern technology for scientific exploitation of our marine resources in an eco-friendly manner and boost marine sector exports.

(11) Transfer of duty free material imported or procured under advanced license from one unit of the company to another unit of the same company was allowed without prior intimation to the jurisdictional central excise authority.

(12) Brass scrap, additives, paper/paper board and dye stuffs were removed from the sensitive list of items prescribed for import of items under Duty Free Replenishment Certificate (DFRC).

(13) Duty free spares up to 5 per cent of the value of capital goods imported for excavation purposes in the granite sector were allowed to be removed to the quarries.

(14) A fast track mechanism for clearance, examination, testing, quarantine, packaging etc., to be set up by all agencies to facilitate import/export of perishable cargo.

(15) Laying down time limits for giving approvals/sanctions for different import and export activities by different agencies to ensure a transparent system of working in Govt. departments and also ensure continuous improvement in quality of services rendered.

(16) Online web based information made available for all export and import related policies and procedures on the DGFT (Directorate General of Foreign Trade) website to enable the international trading community to access information from a single source (Government of India, 2004-05).

The Annual Supplement 2006-07 to the Foreign Trade Policy (FTP) 2004-09 was announced on 7th April, 2006. Under this special focused initiatives were identified for employment intensive areas of agriculture handlooms, gems and jewellery, leather and marine sectors. The other initiatives include:

(1) The capital goods imported under EPCG shall be permitted to be installed anywhere in the agri export zones (AEZ).

(2) Import of restricted items, such as panels, allowed under the various export promotion schemes.

(3) Imports of inputs such as pesticides were permitted under the Advanced Authorization for agro exports.

(4) Duty free import entitlement of specified trimmings and embellishments was five per cent of f.o.b value of exports during the previous financial year.

(5) Duty free import entitlement of hand knotted carpet samples was one per cent of f.o.b value of exports during the previous financial year.

(6) Duty free imports of old pieces of hand knotted carpets on consignment basis for re-export after repair was permitted.

(7) Duty free import entitlement of trimmings and embellishments was five per cent of the f.o.b value of exports during the previous financial year. The entitlement was broad banded and extended to merchant exporters tied up with supporting manufacturers.

(8) The Handicraft Export Promotion Council was authorized to import trimmings, embellishments and consumables on behalf of those exporters for whom directly importing may not be viable.

(9) CVD was exempted on duty free import of trimmings, embellishments and consumables.

(10) Import of gold of 8k and above was allowed under the replenishment scheme subjected to the import being accompanied by an Assay Certificate specifying the purity, weight and alloy content.

(11) Duty free import entitlement of consumables for metals other than gold, platinum was two per cent of f.o.b value of exports during the previous financial year.

(12) Duty free import entitlement of commercial samples was Rs. 300,000.

(13) Duty free re-import entitlement for rejected jewellery is two per cent of the f.o.b value of exports.

(14) Duty free import entitlement of specified items was 5 per cent of f.o.b value of exports during the preceding financial year.

(15) The duty free entitlement for the import of trimmings, embellishments and footwear components for footwear, gloves, travel bags and handbags was three per cent of f.o.b value of exports of the previous financial year, it also cover packing material.

(16) Re-export of unsuitable imported materials such as raw hides and skins and wet blue leather was permitted.

(17) All imported goods were subject to domestic laws, rules, orders, regulations, technical specifications, environmental and safety norms as applicable to domestically produced goods. No import or export of rough diamonds was permitted unless the shipment parcel was accompanied by Kimberley Process (KP) certificate required under the procedure specified by the Gems and Jewellery Export Promotion Council (GJEPC).

(18) Bonafide household goods and personal effects may be imported as part of passenger baggage as per the limits,

terms and conditions thereof in the baggage rules notified by the Ministry of Finance. Samples of such items that were otherwise freely importable under this policy may also be imported as part of passenger baggage without permission/certificate /licence/authorization.

(19) The new or second hand capital goods, equipments, components, parts and accessories, containers meant for packing of goods for exports, jigs, fixture, dies and moulds may be imported for export without a licence/certificate/permission/authorization on execution of legal undertaking/bank guarantee with the customs authorities provided that the item was freely exportable without any conditionality/requirement of licence/permission as may be required under ITC (HS) Schedule II.

(20) Imported goods may be exported in same or substantially the same form without a license/certificate/permission/authorization provided item was not mentioned as restricted for import or export in the ITC (HS).

(21) The duty credit may be used for import of inputs or goods, which were otherwise freely imported under ITC (HS) classifications of import and export items, imports from the port other than the port of export was allowed under TRA facility as per the terms and conditions of the notification issued by department of revenue.

(22) Duty Free Replenishment Certificate (DFRC) is issued to a merchant exporter or manufacturer exporter for the import of inputs used in the manufacture of goods without payment of basic customs duty. However, such inputs are subject to the payment of additional customs duty equal to the excise duty at the time of import.

(23) A Duty Free Import Authorisation was issued to allow duty free import of inputs which were used in the manufacture of the export product (making normal allowance for wastage), and fuel, energy, catalyst etc. which were consumed or utilized in the course of their use to obtain the export product.

(24) Exporters of gems and jewellery can import/procure duty free inputs required for manufacture of gems and jewellery items.

(25) The gems and jewellery exporters were allowed to export cut and polished precious and semi precious stones for the treatment and re-import as per customs rules and regulations.

(26) A bank authorized by RBI was allowed to export gold scrap for refining and import in the form of standard gold bars. The detailed procedure of the import of gold will be as per the guidelines notified by RBI separately.

(27) An Export Oriented Units (EOUs)/Electronic Hardware Technology Parks (EHTPs)/ Software Technology Parks (STPs)/Bio-Technology Parks (BPTs) may import and/or procure from DTA or bonded warehouses in DTA/ international exhibition held in India without payment of duty on all types of goods, including capital goods, required for its activities, provided they were not prohibited items of import in ITC (HS). Any permission required for import under any other law was applicable.

(28) The units were also permitted to import goods including capital goods required for the approved activity, free of cost or on loan/lease from clients. The imports of capital goods were on self certification basis. Goods imported by units were utilized for export production (Government of India, 2005-06).

With a view to accelerating transition to globally oriented economy, India's import policies aimed at export promotion and facilitation of imported inputs for production. The focus of policies shifted to easing of trade restrictions, simplification of procedures, improvement of environment relating to India's export competitiveness and integrate Indian economy under the global integration process by which markets and production in different countries are becoming increasingly interdependent due to trade in goods and services and flows of capital and technology. Thus, import policy of India changed from time to time according to changing economic conditions and domestic requirements. Since Independence, the Government restricted foreign competition through judicious use of import licensing, import quotas, import duties and in extreme cases, even banning import of specific goods. But from 1985 onwards, especially 1991 onwards, import policy is in consonance with overall liberal economic policies mainly focused on liberalization, openness, transparency and globalization with main objectives of promoting industrial production and productivity to improve competitiveness of Indian industry so as to meet global market requirements, export competitiveness, foreign direct investment, technology development, moving away from quantitative restrictions, facilitating input availability besides focusing an quality and above all integration of Indian economy with changing international economic order.

CHAPTER

Summary and Conclusions

Trade began with human society as without it no society can ever be self sufficient. Trade promotes growth and economic welfare by stimulating more efficient utilization of factor endowments of different regions and by enabling people to obtain goods from efficient sources of supply. Trade also makes goods available, which cannot be produced in home country due to various reasons.

A developing country needs imports of machinery and equipment which can not be produced at home in initial stages of economic development. Such imports, which help to create new capacity in production, are called developmental imports. The imports which help to properly utilize the capacity created in the country are called maintenance imports. Besides, these imports, a developing economy also requires to import consumer goods as these imports are anti-inflationary and they reduce the scarcity of consumer goods in domestic market. Thus, for a developing country such as India, on one hand the imports fulfil the needs of development, maintenance of essential supplies and inflation control and on other imports also provide production inputs, increase investment opportunities and international goodwill. Moreover, the higher investment taking place in different sectors, creating more capacity in export and domestic industries, again leads to higher level of imports. Besides imports also promote competitive forces and prevent the emergence of monopolies in the domestic market. They also induce the domestic producers to improve quality and reduce costs and hence raise overall welfare. Structure of India's imports has changed over time as a result of changing structure of Indian economy, trade policy changes and international oil prices. As development proceeds, the raw material exports generally decline because their demand increases at home to meet the requirements of growing domestic industries. Consequently, a developing economy is required to find new commodities and new markets in which it can sell its manufactures and when export earnings increase then industrial production as well as imports increase and further broaden the industrial base of the economy and its growth.

Objectives of Study

The present study entitled as "Dynamics of India's Imports" has the following objectives:

1. To study the pattern of growth of India's total imports and its categories during the study period.
2. To study the structural changes in India's imports during the study period.
3. To study the impact of liberalization on growth and structure of India's imports during the study period.
4. To analyze the determinants of India's imports at aggregate and disaggregate levels.
5. To study the import-growth causality for total imports and also for some of its major categories.
6. To study the changing trade policy regimes and their impact on India's imports.
7. To derive the policy implications.

Plan of Study

This study consists of nine chapters. Chapter 1 deals with introduction of the study. Chapter 2 reviews the studies related to the topic of the study. Chapter 3 consists of database and methodology. Chapter 4 studies the growth pattern of India's total imports and its categories/sub-categories. Chapter 5 analyses the structure of India's imports. Chapter 6 measures the determinants of India's total imports and also for some of its major categories. Chapter 7 studies the causal behaviour of imports and growth in India. Chapter 8 studies the import policy in India. Chapter 9 consists of summary and conclusions of the study.

Database

The present study is based on secondary data and various data sources used are as follows:

1. *Annual Statements and Monthly Statistics of Foreign Trade of India*, Directorate General of Foreign Trade of India, Ministry of commerce, Government of India (various issues).
2. *Economic Survey*, Government of India (various issues).
3. *Report on Currency and Finance*, Reserve Bank of India (various issues).
4. *Reports of Centre for Monitoring Indian Economy* (CMIE) Pvt. Ltd., Mumbai (various issues).
5. *Annual Survey of industries (factory sectors),* Central Statistical Organization, Government of India (various issues).

The data for total imports and also for its categories were collected at current prices. The data were deflated by using common base, i.e., 1993-94, for studying growth pattern and structure of imports in India. To study the determinants and causal behaviour of imports, the data for different variables were also deflated by using appropriate deflators with base year 1993-94.

Methodology

1. The pattern of growth of India's total imports and its categories was examined for the period of 1986-87 to 2005-06, both at current prices and constant prices. The growth rates were calculated for whole of the study period and also for the sub periods of 1986-87 to 1990-91, 1991-92 to 1995-96, 1996-97 to 2000-01, 2001-02 to 2005-06, 1990-91 to 1999-2000 and 1996-97 to 2005-06. For analyzing immediate impact and lagged impact of liberalization policies, the sub periods of 1990-91 to 1995-96 and 1996-97 to 2005-06 were considered, respectively.
2. The structure of India's imports was analyzed for the period of 1986-87 to 2005-06, at current prices and constant prices. The shares of various categories and sub categories in total imports were calculated in the form of percentages at all points of time during 1986-87 to 2005-06. However, in discussion, the points of time considered were 1986-87, 1990-91, 1996-97, 2000-01 and 2005-06.
3. The determinants were studied for India's total imports and also for the categories of agricultural imports, chemical and allied industries imports, base metals and articles of base metals imports, machinery and their parts, textiles and articles of textiles imports, mineral products imports and pearls, precious or semi precious stones, metals and articles imports, for the period of 1986-87 to 2003-04. The determinants taken at aggregate level for total imports are Relative Prices (RP), which is the ratio of unit value indices of imports to whole sale price indices, Gross Domestic Product at Factor cost (GDPFC) as income measure, Foreign Exchange Reserves (FR) as measure of capacity to import and a Dummy (Dum) variable is included to capture the impact of liberalisation policies. In addition to these, the Domestic Production (DP) variable is also considered in case of all major categories of imports except for mineral imports and pearls, precious and semi-precious

stones imports. The variable of Gross Domestic Capital Formation (GDCF) is considered as a determinant in case of machinery and their parts imports. The Exports in previous year is also taken as determinant of imports of pearls, precious and semi precious stones. The import demand functions were measured both in linear as well as in double log forms and each form was estimated both with and without dummy variable. The dummy variable was included to capture the impact of liberalization policies. For statistical significance t-values R^2, $\bar{R}^2$, F- values and D-W statistics were also analyzed.

4. The imports-growth causality was measured for total imports and also for some of its major categories for the period 1974-75 to 2003-04. The Granger causality test was applied and for checking stationarity, unit root test was performed. In Granger causality test, $\bar{R}^2$ was used for finding out the appropriate number of lags, i.e., we had considered a particular lag if $\bar{R}^2$ improved by adding it in regression equation. The results of causality analysis were calculated both with single lag and double lag. The F-statistics calculated for all possible directions of causality, which help to decide the type of causation existing in the given variable. We have studied causal relationship in the following cases:

    1. Total imports (TI) and GDPFC.
    2. Agricultural imports (AI) and GDPFC.
    3. Products of chemical or Allied Industries imports (CI) and GDPFC.
    4. Products of chemical or Allied Industries imports (CI) and Domestic Production (DP).
    5. Base Metals and Articles of Metals imports (BI) and GDPFC.
    6. Base Metals and Articles of Metals imports (BI) and Domestic Production (DP).

7. Machinery and Their Parts imports (MhI) and GDPFC.
8. Machinery and Their Parts imports (MhI) and Domestic Production (DP).
9. Machinery and Their Parts imports (MhI) and Gross Domestic Capital Formation (GDCF).
10. Textiles and Textiles Articles imports (TxI) and GDPFC.
11. Textiles and Textiles Articles imports (TxI) and Domestic Production (DP).
12. Mineral Products Imports (MnI) and GDPFC.
13. Pearls, Precious and Semi Precious Stones Imports (PI) and GDPFC.

Findings of the Study

The main findings of the study are as follows:

Growth of India's Imports

1. At current price aggregate imports grew at the rate of 19.15 per cent and at constant prices total imports grew at the rate of 10.44 per cent for the study period taken as a whole.
2. At current prices, the imports of categories of animal or vegetable fats and oils, mineral products, hides and skins, pearls, precious and semi precious stones, machinery and their parts, arms and ammunitions, misc. manufactured products, work of arts, collector pieces and antiques and misc. goods grew at the rate which was more than 20 per cent for study period taken as whole.
3. At current prices, the categories of imports which grew between the rates of 15 per cent to 20 per cent were vegetable products, prepared food stuffs and beverages, products of chemical or allied industries, plastic and rubber

articles, wood, cork and articles, paper and paper board, textile and textile articles, foot wears, headgears and umbrellas, stone, cement and ceramic products, transport equipments and instrumental apparatus during the study period. The rest of the categories (live animals; animal products, base metals and articles of base metals and project goods) grew at the rate which was less than 15 per cent for the study period.

4. At constant prices, the categories of imports of hides and skins, instrumental apparatus, arms and ammunition, misc. manufactured articles, project goods and work of art, collector pieces and antiques, grew at the rate which was more than 20 per cent.
5. At constant prices, the categories which grew at the rate of 15 per cent to 20 per cent were wood, cork and articles, textiles and textile articles, machinery and their parts, pearls, precious and semi-precious stones. The category of mineral products, animal and vegetables oils and fats, products of chemical and allied industries, stone, cement and ceramic products, transport equipments, grew around 10 per cent rate for the study period.
6. At constant prices, the categories of live animal and animal products, base metal and articles of base metals and project goods have grown at less than five per cent rate for the study period.
7. The immediate impact (1991-92 to 1995-96) of liberalization policies was relatively stronger than lagged impact (1996-97 to 2005-06) for total imports and also for most of the categories (both at current prices and constant prices).
8. At current prices, the immediate impact was stronger for most of the categories except for the categories of imports of mineral products, pearls, precious and semi-precious stones, metals and articles and work of art, collector pieces and antiques.
9. At constant prices, except the categories of imports of stone, cement and similar material, pearls, precious and

semi-precious stones, metals and articles and transport equipments, all other categories experienced stronger immediate impact as compared to lagged impact of liberalization policies.

10. Under the group of capital goods imports, the machinery and their parts imports and project goods imports grew at higher rate during immediate impact (1991-92 to 1995-96) period, both at current prices and constant prices. The imports of transport equipments grew at higher rate during immediate impact period at current prices, whereas at constant prices, the lagged impact (1996-97 to 2005-06) was stronger one.
11. For export-oriented imports of pearls, precious and semi precious stones, metals and articles, the lagged impact period experienced higher growth rate, both at current and constant prices.
12. Under the group of industry oriented goods, the immediate impact was relatively stronger for the imports of chemical or allied industries and base metals and articles of base metals, both at current prices and constant prices.
13. Within the imports of food items, the category of animal or vegetable fats and oils (includes edible oils) imports grew at higher rate during immediate impact (1991-92 to 1995-96) period, both at current prices and constant prices.
14. The category of mineral products imports showed stronger lagged impact (1996-97 to 2005-06) at current prices, whereas the immediate impact (1991-92 to 1995-96) was stronger one at constant prices.

Structure of India's Imports

15. There were some categories which had very high share in total imports like mineral products, machinery and their parts, pearls, precious and semi precious stones, chemicals and allied industries and base metals and articles of base

metals. Whereas some of the categories had experienced relatively lower share in total imports like live animals: animal products, arms, ammunition: parts and accessories and work of art, collectors and antiques.

16. The analysis of structure of Indian imports showed that the group of low and constant imports, i.e., with less than 0.5 per cent share includes live animals: animal products, hides and skins: leather products, furskins and articles thereof, footwear, headgear, umbrellas: prepared feathers and articles thereof, stone, cement and similar materials, ceramic products, glass and glassware, arms and ammunition: parts and accessories thereof, miscellaneous manufactured articles, work of art, collectors and antiques and miscellaneous goods. The category of paper and paper board and articles thereof was under the group of low and constant imports.

17. The group of leading imports, i.e., the imports whose share increased during the study period includes the imports of mineral products, pearls, precious and semi precious stones, metals, jewellery and coins, machinery and their parts: electrical and electronic equipment parts thereof, chemicals and allied industries, transport equipment, base metals and articles of base metals and animal or vegetable oils and fats.

18. The group of lagging imports, i.e., the imports whose share decreased during the study period consists of categories of imports of vegetable products, prepared food stuffs, beverages and tobacco, wood, cork and articles thereof, textiles and textile articles, instruments and apparatus and project goods.

19. During post 2000-01 period, the share of imports of mineral products in total imports has been increasing and remained higher than 30 per cent. Similarly, the share of machinery and their parts and pearls, precious and semi-precious

stones remained more than 12 per cent. The share of chemicals and allied industries imports has been stabilized around 8 per cent and of base metals and articles of base metal imports around four per cent. Similarly, the share of categories of transport equipments and animals or vegetables fats and oils fluctuated between one per cent and five per cent. The categories of vegetable products, plastic and rubber, instruments and apparatus and textiles and textile articles had the share which fluctuated between one per cent and three per cent. The category of paper and paper board and articles thereof had the share which fluctuated between one per cent and two per cent. The categories of wood, cork and articles thereof (except year 2001-02) and project goods (except years 2000-01 and 2001-02) had the share between 0.5 per cent and one per cent. The categories for which the share was between 0.1 per cent and 0.5 per cent are prepared food stuffs, beverages and tobacco (except 2004-05), hides and skins: leather, fur skins and articles thereof, stones, cement and similar material, miscellaneous manufactured articles and miscellaneous goods. The categories of live animals: animal products, footwear, headgear, umbrellas, arms and ammunition and work of art, collectors and antiques had showed the share which was lesser than 0.1 per cent during last six years of study period.

Determinants of India's Imports

20. The total imports (TI) have been found to be income elastic as well as price elastic. The coefficients of price and income variables have also been found to be highly significant in all the models. The foreign reserves variable has been found to be non significant. The dummy variable is negative in case of linear form whereas it is positive in case of double log form. In both the forms the dummy variable (for capturing effect of liberalisation policies) has

been found to be non significant for aggregate import demand function. The values of R^2 and $\bar{R}^2$ are quite high in all the models for both the forms (linear and double log). The values of D-W statistics are also appropriate one.

21. The agricultural imports (AI) have been found to be price elastic and also income elastic. The price variable is found to be highly significant in all the models and income variable has been found to be non significant in all models except in case of linear form without dummy variable. The domestic production variable has been found to be significant in case of double log form without dummy variable only. The foreign reserves variable has been found to be significant in case of double log form. The dummy variable is positive in linear form, while negative in double log form, but non-significant in both the forms. The values of R^2 and $\bar{R}^2$ are better in case of double log form. Whereas the values of D-W statistics are better in case of linear form.

22. In case of products of chemical or allied industries imports (CI), relative price variable has been found to be significant in all the models, whereas the income variable has been found to be non significant in all the models. Imports of this category have been found to be significantly related with respect to domestic production in case of double log form without dummy variable. The positive sign of domestic production confirms about increased raw material imports of this category. Thus these imports support and supplement home industry and are not of substitute nature. The foreign reserves variable has been found to be non significant except in case of linear form with dummy variable. The dummy variable is significant in both the forms, which confirms about increased imports of chemicals with the coming up of liberalisation measures. The values of R^2 and are at appropriate level. The values of D-W statistics are $\bar{R}^2$ found to be better when dummy variable is added in both the forms.

23. In case of Base metal and articles of base metals imports (BI) the income variable is found to be non-significant in all the models. The sign of income variable is positive in case of linear form, whereas it is negative in case of double log form. The price variable has been found to be highly significant in all the models. The domestic production variable has been found to be significant in case of linear form only. The positive sign of domestic production confirms about increased industrial activity in case of this category. The foreign reserves variable has been found to be non significant in all the models and has appropriate sign only in double log form of model with dummy variable. The negative sign of dummy variable show that liberalisation policies have very less impact on this category of imports. The values of R^2 and $\bar{R}^2$ have been found to be better in case of linear form. The value of D-W statistics is appropriate in both the forms.

24. In case of machinery and their parts imports ($M\text{-}_hI$), the income variable has been found to be non significant in all the models whereas the price variable has been found to be significant in all the models. These imports are highly income elastic as well as price elastic. The domestic production variable has been found to be non significant in all the cases. The foreign reserves have been found to be significant in case of linear form only. The gross domestic capital formation has also been found to be non significant with positive sign in case of linear form and negative sign in case of double log form. The dummy variable is also non-significant in both the forms (with negative sign). The values of R^2 and $\bar{R}^2$ D-W statistics have been found to be better in case of linear form.

25. In case of textiles and textiles articles imports, the income and price variables have been found to be significant in both the forms. The imports of this category have been

found to be price elastic and also highly income elastic. These imports are more elastic with respect to income as compared to prices. The foreign reserves variables have been found to be significant in case of linear form only. The sign of domestic production is negative and variable is also non-significant in both the forms. The sign of dummy variable is positive in case of linear form, while sign is negative in case of double log form. The dummy variable is also non significant in both the forms, showing less impact of liberalization policies on imports of textiles and textiles articles imports. The values of R^2, $\bar{R}^2$ and D-W statistics have been found to at appropriate level.

26. In case of mineral imports, income variable has been found to be significant in both the forms. The price variable has been found to be significant in all the cases except in case of without dummy variable model of double log form. The mineral imports are price inelastic but income elastic in case of dummy variable model of double log form. The foreign reserve variable has been found to be significant except in dummy variable model of double log form. The dummy variable has positive sign and is highly significant in both the forms. The imports of mineral products are more responsive to income than the price variable. The values of R^2 and $\bar{R}^2$ have been found to be at appropriate level. The value of D-W statistics has been found to be better in case of linear form.

27. In case of pearls, precious and semi precious stones imports, the income variable has been found to be significant in both the forms. The foreign reserves variable has been found to be non-significant in all the models. The export in the previous year variable has been found to be non-significant in case of linear form, while found to be significant in case of double log form. This variable has negative sign in all the models. The dummy variable has

negative sign in both the forms, but found to be significant in case linear form. The imports of this category are found to be highly elastic with respect to income. The values of R^2 and $\bar{R}^2$ have been found to at appropriate level. The value of D-W statistics has been found to be better in case of double log form.

Import-Growth Causality Analysis

1. Results for total imports indicate that GDP causes total imports (GDPFC→TI) in both the cases of single lag and double lag. But there is no reverse causation (TI→GDPFC) experienced in both the cases of single lag and double lag. Thus, there is unidirectional causality between the total imports and GDP of India.
2. Results of agricultural imports show that GDP causes agricultural imports i.e., (GDPFC→AI), but there is no reverse causation (AI→ GDPFC) present in both the cases of single and double lag. So there is unidirectional causality from GDP to agricultural imports.
3. The results of chemical and allied industries imports show that domestic production causes chemical imports i.e. (DP→CI), both in single lag and double lag case. The reverse causation (CI→DP) is present in case of double lag, but not in case of single lag. Similarly chemical imports are not causing GDP in both the cases, while GDP causes chemical imports (GDPFC→CI) in single lag case only.
4. The results of base metals and articles of base metals imports indicate that there is no causation between base metal imports to domestic production in both the cases of single and double lag. The domestic production causes base metal imports in case of single lag but not in case of double lag. Similarly the results show the presence of causation from GDP to base metals and articles imports (GDPFC→BI), the reverse causation (BI→GDPFC) is

also present in case of double lag, but not in case of single lag.

5. The results of machinery and their parts imports indicate that these imports cause domestic production (DP) i.e., ($M_hI \rightarrow DP$) in both the cases of single and double lag. The reverse causation ($DP \rightarrow M_hI$) is present in case of double lag, but not in case of single lag. The causality of $GDPFC \rightarrow M_hI$ is present in case of single lag and not in case of double lag. The reverse causation, i.e., $M_hI \rightarrow GDPFC$ is absent in both the cases. The results further indicate that GDCF causes machinery imports i.e. ($GDCF \rightarrow M_hI$) in both the cases of single lag and in case of double lag, but there is no reverse causation ($M_hI \rightarrow GDCF$) present in both the cases.
6. The results of textiles and articles of textiles imports highlight that domestic production causes textile Imports ($DP \rightarrow TxI$) but there is no reverse causation ($TxI \rightarrow DP$) in the case of single lag as well as in case of double lag. Similarly GDP causes textile imports ($GDPFC \rightarrow TxI$), but there is no reverse causation, in both the cases of single and double lags.
7. Results of mineral products imports show that GDP causes mineral imports ($GDPFC \rightarrow M_nI$), in both the cases of double and single lags, but there is no reverse causation. Thus, mineral imports being a dominating category of Indian imports, increases with the increase in GDP.
8. Results of Pearls and Semi Precious Stones imports show that GDP causes pearls and semi precious stones imports in both the cases, and reverse causation is present but in case of double lag only.

Import Policy in India

1. Import policy of India changed from time to time according to changing economic conditions and domestic requirements. Since independence, the Govt. restricted foreign

competition through judicious use of import licensing, import quotas, import duties and in extreme cases, even banning import of specific goods. But from 1985 onwards, especially 1991 onwards, import policy is in consonance with overall liberal economic policies mainly focused on liberalization, openness, transparency and globalization. The main objectives of liberal import policy include promoting industrial production and productivity to improve competitiveness of Indian industry so as to meet global market requirements, export competitiveness, foreign direct investment, technology development, moving away from quantitative restrictions, facilitating input availability besides focusing on quality and above all integration of Indian economy with changing international economic order.

Conclusions and Policy Implications

1. India's imports are growing at high rate and will continue to do so in future with economy passing through the phase of rapid growth. Thus the capacity to import must also grow at a fast rate in future if 9 per cent plus growth is to be attained.
2. The total imports of India are both price and income sensitive but income elasticity coefficient is higher so in future as income will grow imports will also grow. As far as price is concerned, imports are also price sensitive which implies that wherever possible we should try to increase domestic production in order to reduce imports dependence.
3. The liberalization which is one of the principle components of economic reforms in India, affected imports through its positive impact on other sectors of economy also, which in turn leads to higher imports. The same is confirmed by the unidirectional causality from GDP to total imports.
4. The immediate impact of liberalization policies is relatively stronger than the lagged impact for total imports and also for most of the categories of imports.

5. Structure of India's imports is development oriented. Most of the imports are in the category of leading and high imports such as imports of mineral products, pearls, precious or semi precious stones, metals and aricles, machinery and their parts, products of chemical or allied industries, base metals and articles of base metals, transport equipments and animal or vegetable oils and fats.
6. The agricultural imports have very small share in total imports. India is near self sufficient in agricultural sector, however the category of animal or vegetable oils and fats (includes edible oils) show high growth and share in total imports. There is a scope of increasing domestic production of edible oils within the agricultural imports.
7. Import growth is high especially in post liberalization period as some industries like chemicals and allied industries and base metals and articles of base metals are mainly dependent on the imports for their raw materials. Imports of these categories supplement the home industry and are not of substitute nature. In case of these categories, the import dependence can be reduced by promoting their domestic production.
8. The export oriented imports of pearls, precious and semi precious stones, metals and articles experienced high growth and high share in total imports, which is mainly due to high growth of exports of this category. The same is confirmed by feedback causality between imports of this exports oriented category and GDP of India. These imports are also income elastic.
9. The category of mineral products imports is a major contributor to inflate the bill of aggregate imports of India as this category show highest share in total imports due to heavy demand and insufficiency of oil production in India. These imports are income sensitive and not price sensitive, i.e., why GDP cause these imports. These imports also

show an increase with the coming up of liberalization policies because of their essential nature.

10. The analysis of import demand function shows that the income variable is significant in case of total imports and also for the categories of imports of textiles and articles of textiles, mineral products and pearls, precious and semi precious stones, metals and articles.
11. The regression analysis indicates that price variable is found to be significant in case of total imports and for the categories of imports of agricultural products, productis of chemical or allied industries products, base metals and articles of base metals, machinery and their parts, textiles and articles of textiles and mineral products.
12. Import demand functions also show that domestic production variable has positive sign in both the forms but significant in linear form only for the imports of base metals and articles of base metals and product of chemical or allied industries.
13. Foreign reserves variable is significant in case of linear form of imports of machinery and their parts, mineral products and textiles and articles of textiles and in double log form of agricultural products.
14. The policy variable is found to be significant for imports of chemicals and allied industries products, mineral products and pearls, precious and semi precious stones, metals and articles.
15. The results of causality analysis strongly support the unidirectional causation from income to total imports, as well as in case of other major categories of imports, which includes agricultural imports, machinery and their parts imports, textiles and articles of textile imports and mineral products imports in case of both single lag and double lag. The category of product of chemical or allied industries imports also experienced unidirectional causality from income but in case of single lag only. The categories of

pearls, precious and semi precious stones imports and base metal and articles of base metals imports also show reverse causation or feedback causality (imports causing GDP) in case of double lag only.

16. At disaggregate level, domestic production causes products of chemical or allied industries imports, base metal and articles of base metal imports, machinery and their parts imports and textiles and textiles articles imports. We can conclude from here that imports of these categories are used as raw materials in India's domestic industries. In case of machinery and their parts imports and producto of chemical or allied industries imports, there is feedback causality between their domestic production and imports.

17. In case of machinery and their parts imports, gross domestic capital formation causes these imports, but there is no reverse causation. It means with ongoing global changes, India's capital goods imports increase with the increase in gross domestic capital formation due to needs of infrastructural and industrial development.

18. Import policy of India is an instrument for promoting rapid economic growth through the growth of industrial and export sectors.

Bibliography

Adiseshiah, S. Maleolm (1986). *Role of Foreign Trade in Indian Economy*, Lancer International, N. Delhi.

Afxentiou, Panos and Apostolos Serletis (2000). "Output Growth and Variability of Export and Import Growth: International Evidence from Granger Causality Test", *The Developing Economies*, Vol. XXXVIII, No.2, June, pp. 144-162.

Agarwal, A.N. et al. (1989). *India Economic Information Year*, National Publishing House, N. Delhi.

Ahluwalia, Montek S. (2002). *A Decade of Economic Reform in India: The Past, Present, Future*, ed. Raj Kapila and Uma Kapila, Academic Foundation, Delhi.

Aksoy, M. Ataman. and Helena Tang (1992). "Imports, Exports and Industrial Performance in India 1970-88", *World Bank Working Papers*, The World Bank, Aug.

Alam, Shaista and Mohammad S. Butt (2002). "Causality Between Energy and Economic Growth in Pakistan: An Application of co-integration and Error Correction Modelling Techniques", *Indian Journal of Quantitative Economics*, Vol. 17, No. 1-2, pp. 39-60.

Anant, T.C.A. (2001). "India and the WTO", *Economic & Political Weekly*, Vol. 36, No. 45, Nov.

Annual Statements and Monthly Statistics of Foreign Trade of India, DGFTI, Ministry of Commercial, Govt. of India. (Various Issues).

Apostolakis, Bobby E. (1991). "Aggregate Import Demand Functions and Their Dual Econometric Specification", *The Singapore Economic Review*, Vol.XXXVI, No.1, April, pp. 35-57.

Arize, Augustin (1986). "The Supply and Demand for Imports and Exports in a Simultaneous Model", *Indian Journal of Economics*, Vol. LXVII, No. 265, Oct, pp. 177-192.

Arora, D.S. (1977). "Indo-Ghanaian Trade-Problems and Prospects", *Foreign Trade Review*, Vol.XII, No.2, July-Sep, pp. 260-277.

Attri, V.N. (1992). "Trade Liberalisation in Developing Countries: A Literature Survey", *Indian Economic Journal*, Vol.39, No.3, pp. 41-57.

AW, Bee Yan and Mark. J. Roberts (1985). "The Role of Imports from the Newly-Industrializing Countries in U.S. Production", *The Review of Economics and Statistics*, Vol. LXVII, No.1, Feb, pp. 108-117.

Bagchi, Sanjoy (2001). "End of Quantitative Restrictors: Unfounded Fears", *Economic and Political Weekly*, Vol. XXXVI, No. 18, May 5-11, pp. 1500-1503.

Bajaj, R.K. (1991). "Dimensions of Trade Liberalisation", *Encyclopaedia of Economic Development*, Vol. 9.

Bajpai, Nirupam and Jaffery D. Sachs (1997). "India's Economic Reforms: Some Lessons From East Asia", *The Journal of International Trade and Development*, 6:2, pp. 135-164.

Balasubramanyam, V.N. (1984). *The Economy of India*, UBS Publishers Ltd., New Delhi

Banga, R. (2003). "The Nature, Pattern and Impact of Japanese and US Foreign Direct Investments in Indian Manufacturing" Unpublished PhD Dissertation, Delhi School of Economics, University of Delhi, March.

Barkar, Prabirjit and Brototi Bhattacharya (2005). "Trade Liberalization and Growth: Case Studies of India and Korea", *Economic and Political Weekly*, Vol. XL, No. 53, Dec-Jan.

Basu, Kaushik (1998). *Analytical Development Economics*, OUP, Delhi (MIT Press).

Bayes, Hussain and M. Rahman (1995). "Trends in External Sector: Trade and Aid" in *Experiences With Economic Reform: A Review of Bangladesh's Development*, Centre for Policy Dialogue and University Press Limited, Dhaka.

Bhalla, V.K. (2004). *International Economy: Liberalization Process*, Anmol Publications Pvt. Ltd., N. Delhi.

Bhargava, P.K. (2000). *Current Economic Issues in the Indian Economy*, RBSA Publishers, Jaipur.

Bhasin, Niti (2005). *External Sector Reforms in India*, New Century Publications, N. Delhi.

Bhattacharjea, Aditiya (1993). "Strategic Trade Policy and Developing Countries", *Economic and Political Weekly*, Vol. XXVIII, No. 35, Aug, pp. 1803-1810.

Bhattacharya, B and Palaha, Satinder. (1996), *Policy Impediments to Foreign Trade in India*, A.H. Wheeler & Co. Ltd., N. Delhi.

Bhattacharya, B. (1994). "Pragmatic Policy to carry Forward Liberalisation", *Yojana*, Vol. 38, No.9, May 31, pp. 15-17.

Bhattacharya, Basabi (1993). "Structural Adjustments in Trade Policy - A Theoretical Perspective of Liberalization in the Changing International Scenario" in *Structural Adjustment in Indian Economy*, Vol.1, ed. Debendra Kumar Das, Deep and Deep Pub., N. Delhi, pp. 41-53.

Bhattacharya, Manas. (1989). "Import Intensity of Exports: A Case Study of Indian Economy", *Indian Economic Journal*, Vol. 36, No. 3, pp. 94-98.

Bhattacharyya, B. (1998). "Foreign Trade: Retrospect and Prospect," *Yojana*, Vol. 42, No. 2, Feb, pp.5-8.

Biswas, Basudeb and Rati Ram (1980). "Demand Function for India's Foodgrain Imports: Some Elasticity Estimates", *Indian Economic Journal*, Vol.27, No.4, April-June, pp. 12-27.

Box, G.E.P. and D. R. Cox (1964). "An Analysis of Transformations", *Journal of the Royal Statistics Society*, Series B, No. 26, pp. 211-243.

Boylan, T.A., M.P. Cuddy and Muircheartaigh. (1980). "The Functional Form of the Aggregate Import Demand Equation", *Journal of International Economics*, Vol. 10, No. 4, pp. 561-566.

Brander, J.A. and B.J. Spencer (1984). "Trade Warfare: Tariffs and Cartels, *Journal of International Economics,* 16, pp. 227-242.

Burange, L.G. (2001). "Import-Intensity in the Registered Manufacturing Sectors of India", *Indian Economic Journal*, Vol. 49, No.3, Jan-Mar, pp.42-52.

Burgess, David F. (1974). "A Cost Minimisation Approach to Import Demand Equation", *The Review of Economics and Statistics*, No. 56, pp. 225-234.

Chand, Ramesh *et al.* (2004). "WTO and Oil Seed Sector: Challenges of Trade Liberalization", *Economic and Political Weekly*, Vol. XXXIX, No.6, Feb 7-13, pp. 533-537.

Chand, Ramesh. and S.C. Tewari (1991). "Growth and Instability of Indian Exports and Imports of Agricultural Commodities", *Indian Journal of Agricultural Economics*, Vol.46, No.2, April-June, pp. 159-165.

Chang, Tsangyao *et al.* (2005). "Exports, Imports and output in the US: What Causes What?", *The Indian Journal of Economics*, Vol. LXXXV, No. 338, Part-3, Jan, pp. 423-132.

Cherunilam, Francis (1999). *International Economics*, Tata McGraw-Hill Publishing Company Ltd., N. Delhi, 3rd Edition.

Chisti, Sumitra (2001). "India and the WTO", *Economic and Political Weekly*, Vol. 36, Nos. 14-15, April, pp. 1246-1248.

CMIE Reports, Economic Intelligence (Various Issues).

Colman, David and Fredrick Nikson (1986). *Economics of Change in LDCs*, Univ. of Manchester, 2nd Edition.

Corden, W.M. (1974). *Trade Policy and Economic Welfare*, Calarendon Press Oxford.

Costa, G.C.Da. (1988), "India's Trade Balance: 1970-71 to 1984-85 – Analysis and Policy Implications", *Artha Vijnana*, Vol. 30, No.3, Sep, pp. 221-239.

Cuevas, Mario A. (2002). "Demand for Imports in Venezuela: A Structural Time Series Approach", *Policy Research Working Paper*, The World Bank, April.

Das, D.K. (2003). "Qualifying Trade Barriers: Has Protection Declined Substantially in Indian Manufacturing" Working Paper No. 105, Indian Council for Research on International Economic Relations (ICRIER), July.

Das, R. Upendra (2000). "Import Liberalization as a Tool of Economic Policy" in *Trade and Dependence: Essays an Indian Economy* by Sunanda Sen, Sage Publications, N. Delhi, pp. 192-223.

Das, Satyal and Shabtai Donnenfeld (1987). "Trade Policy and Its Impact an Quality of Imports: A Welfare Analysis", *Journal of International Economics*, Vol.23, No.1/2, Aug, pp. 77-95.

Dash, Aruna Kumar (2005). "*An Econometric Estimation of the Aggregate Import Demand Function for India*", Department of Economics, Univ. of Hyderabad, India.

Datar, M. (1990). "Composition of Imports, Expenditure, Swithcing and Trade Policy", *Artha Vijnana*, Vol.32, Nos.3 & 4, Sep-Dec, pp.256-269.

Datta, Bhabatosh (1970). *Indian Economic Thought 20th Century Perspectives 1900-50*, Tata McGraw-Hill Publishing Co. Ltd., N. Delhi.

Derosa, Dean A. and Morris Goldstein (1981). "Import Discipline in the U.S. Manufacturing Sector" *IMF Staff Papers*, Vol.28, No.3, Sep, pp. 600-634.

Dhindsa, K. S. and Anju Sharma (2006). "External Sector Reforms in India- An Evaluation", in *Economic Reforms and Development*, ed. K. S. Dhindsa and Anju Sharma, Concept Publishing Company, N.Delhi.

Dhingra, Ishwar. C. (2003). *The Indian Economy: Environment and Policy*, 17th Edition, Sultan Chand and Sons Educational Publishers, N. Delhi.

Dholakia, Ravindera H and Kapur, Deepak. (2001), "Economic Reforms and Trade Performance: Private Corporate Sector in India", *Economic and Political Weekly*, Vol. XXXVI, No.49, Dec 8, pp. 4560-66.

Dikshit, Pratima. (2002), *Dynamics of Indian Export Trade*, Deep & Deep Publications Pvt. Ltd., N. Delhi.

Dinopoulos, Elias and Kreinin, Mordechai E. (1989), "Import Quotas and VERs", *Journal of International Economics*, Vol.26, Feb, pp. 169-178.

Donnenfeld, Shabtai, Shilomo Weber and Uri Benzion (1985). "Import Controls under unperfect information", *Journal of International Economics*, Vol.19, No. ¾, Nov, pp. 341-354.

Dunkel, Arthur (1991). "Trade Policy Issues", *Encyclopedia of Economic Development*, Vol. 13.

Dutta, Amrita (1968). "Recent Trends in India's Import Capacity", *Economic Studies*, Vol. IX, No.11, Aug, pp. 153-156.

Dutta, Dilip and Nasiruddin Ahmed (2006). "An Aggregate Import Demand Function for India: A Cointegration Analysis", *Centre for South Asian Studies*, University of Sydney.

Economic Survey, Government of India (Various Issues).

Emran, M. Shahe *et al.* (1997). "A Critical Review of the Econometric Modelling of Aggregate Imports of Bangladesh", *The Bangladesh Development Studies*, Vol. XXV, Nos. 1 & 2, March-June, pp. 159-171.

Emran, M.S. and F. Shilpi (1996). "Foreign Exchange Rationing and the Aggregate Import Demand Function" *Economics Letters*, June, pp. 315-322.

Emran, M.S. and F. Shilpi (1997). "*Nonstationary, Weak-exogenity, and Econometric Modeling of Aggregate Imports: Evidence From Bangladesh*", Stanford University and The World Bank.

Enders, Walter (2004). *Applied Econometric Time Series*, 2nd edition, Wiley Student Edition.

Faini, Richard *et. al.* (1988). "*Import Demand in Developing Country*", World Bank Working Paper, The World Bank.

Fatima, Ambreen *et al.* (2003). "International Trade and Total Factor Productivity Growth in Pakistan: A Multivariate Causality Analysis", *Indian journal of Quantitative Economics*, Vol.18, No.1-2, pp. 31-54.

Frankel, J.A. and Romer D. (1999). "Does Trade Cause Growth", *American Economic Review*, Vol. 89, No. 3, pp. 379-399.

Friedrich, Klaus (1974). *International Economics Concepts and Issues*, McGraw-Hill, Kogapush Ltd.

Gafar John. (1985). "The IMF Policies and the Developing Countries: A Third World Prespective", *Indian Journal of Economics*, Vol. LXV, No. 258, Jan, pp.277-287.

Gafar, John. (1984). "Devaluation and Its Impact on the Demand for Imports in an Open Economy: The Case of Jamaica", *Indian Economic Journal*, Vol.31, No. 3, Jan-March, pp. 34-45.

Ghatak, Subrata. (1986). *An Introduction to Development Economics*, Univ. of Leicester, London.

Ghosh, Alak. (1975). *Indian Economy, Its Nature and Problems*, The World Press Private Ltd.

Ghosh, Arun (1991). "Eight plan: Challenges and Possibilities-IV, Balance of Payments", *Economic and Political Weekly*, Vol.26, Feb, pp. 263-270.

Ghosh, B.N. and Rama Gosh (1991). *Economic Growth Development and Planning*, Deep & Deep Publications, N. Delhi.

Ghosh, Jayati (1985). "Export Optimism and Import Liberalization", *Economic and Political Weekly*, Vol. XX, No.22, June, pp. 974-976.

Goldar, Bishwanath and Anita Kumari (2003). "Import Liberalization and Productivity Growth in Indian manufacturing Industries in the 1990's", *The Developing Economies*, Vol. XLI, No.4, Dec.

Goldar, Bishwanath and Suresh Chand Aggarwal (2005). "Trade Liberalization and Price-Cost Margin in Indian Industries", *The Developing Economies*, Vol.XLIII-3, Sep, pp. 346-373.

Goldar, Bishwanath, *et al.* (2003). "Ownership and Efficiency in Engineering Firms 1990-91 to 1999-00", *Economic and Political Weekly*.

Goldin, Ian and Kenneth Reinert (2007). *Globalization for Development Trade, Finance, Aid, Migration and Policy,* Co-publication of the World Bank and Palgrave Macmillan.

Goldstein, Morris and Mohsin S.Khan (1976). "Large Versus Small Price Changes and the Demand for Imports", *IMF Staff Papers*, Vol. XXIII, No.1, March, pp. 200-225.

Gonclaves, Reinaldo (1987). "Export Expansion, Import Liberalization and Economic Growth in Latin America", *Indian Journal of Economics*, Vol. IXVIII, No. 268, Oct, pp. 169-202.

Granger, C.W.J. (1969). "Investigating Causal Relations By Econometric Models and Cross Spectral Methods", *Econometrics*, 37.

Greaney, Theresa M. (1996). "Import Now! An Analysis of Market Share Voluntary Import Expansions (VIEs)", *Journal of International Economics*, Vol. 40, No.1/2, Feb, pp. 149-163.

Greene, William H. (2003) *Econometric Analysis*, 5th edition, Pearson Education Publishers, Delhi.

Grossman, Gene M. (1982). "Import Competition From Developed and Developing Countries", *The Review of Economics and Statistics*, Vol. LXIV, No.2, May, pp. 271-281.

Gujrati, D. (2004). *Basic Econometrics*, 4th ed. New York, Mclrraw Hill.

Hargopal, Sai (2001). "Performance of External Sector - A Review", *The Indian Economic Journal*, Vol. 49, No.3, Jan-Mar, pp.55-63.

Harris and Sollis (2006). *Applied Time Series Modeling and Forecasting*, Wiley Students Edition, Replika Press, India.

Havrylyshyn, Oleh and David Tarr (1991). "Trade Liberalization and the Transition to a Market Economy", *World Bank Working Papers*, The World Bank.

Hazari, Bharat (1980). *The Structure of Indian Economy - An Analysis*, The Macmillan Company India Ltd., Bombay.

Hemphill, William L. (1974). "The Effect of Foreign Exchange Receipts on Imports of Less Developed Countries", *IMF Staff Papers*, Vol. XXI, No.3, Nov.

Hossain, Akhtar (1995), *Inflation, Economic Growth and Balance of Payments in Bangladesh*, Oxford University Press, Delhi.

Hossain, M. Manir (1995). "Devaluation in Bangladesh Conflicts Between Trade Balance Improvement and Growth", *The Bangladesh Development Studies*, Vol. XXIII, Nos 3 & 4, Sept-Dec, pp. 149-169.

Houthakker, H.S. and S.P. Magee (1969). "*Income and Price Elasticities in World Trade*", The Review of Economics and Statistics, 51.

Jalan, Bimal (1992). "Balance of Payments, 1956 to 1991", in *The Indian Economy: Problems and Prospects*, ed. By Bimal Jalan, Ananda Offset Pvt. Ltd., Calcutta.

Jayaraman, T.K. (1977). "Import Demand Function of India", *Foreign Trade Review*, Vol. XI, No.3, Jan-Mar, pp. 362-372.

Jha, Satish (1997). "Changing Pattern of Intra-regional Trade in Asia", *Indian Economic Journal*, Vol. 44, No.3, Jan-Mar, pp. 44-59.

Kabir, Rezaul. (1988). "Estimating Import and Export Demand Function: The case of Bangladesh", *The Bangladesh Development Studies*, Vol. XVI, No.44, Dec, pp.115-123.

Kalirajan, Kaliappa (2003). "The Impact of Decade of India's Trade Reforms", in *Indian Economic Reforms*, ed. Raghubindera, Canberra, Australia, pp. 241-255.

Kalyoncu, Huseyin. (2006). "An Aggregate Import Demand Function for Turkey: A Cointegration Analysis, *Indian Journal of Economics*, Vol. LXXXVI, No. 343, Part 4, April, pp. 503-511.

Kantawala, B.S. (1988). "India's Imports on Bilateral Basis: Does it Benefit", *Indian Economic Journal*, Vol. 35, No.4, April-June, pp.44-56.

Kantawala, Bhavana S. (1996). "Price and Income Elasticities of Demand for Indian Exports and Imports", *Indian Economic Journal*, Vol. 43, No.3, Jan-March, pp. 74-88.

Kapila, Raj and Kapila, Uma. (2004), *Economic Developments in India*, Academic Foundation, N. Delhi.

Katrak, H. (1977). "Multinational Monopolies and Commercial Policy, Oxford Economic Papers, 29, pp. 283-291.

Kaundal, R.K. (2005). "Impact of Economic Reforms on External Sector", *Foreign Trade Review*, vol. XL, No.3, Oct-Dec, pp.72-100.

Kee, Hiau Looi, et. al. (2004). "Import Demand Elasticities and Trade Distortions", *Policy Research Working Paper*, The World Bank, No.3452, Nov.

Khan, Mohsin S. (1974). "Import and Export Demand in Developing Countries", *IMF Staff Paper*, Vol. XXI, No.3, Nov, pp. 678-693.

Khan, Mohsin S. and Knud Z. Ross (1975). "Cyclical and Secular Income Elasticities of the Demand for Imports", *The Review of Economics and Statistics*, Vol. LVII, No.3, Aug, pp. 357-361.

Khan, Mohsin S. and Knud Z. Ross (1977). "The Functional Form of the Aggregate Import Demand Equation", *Journal of International Economics*, Vol. 7, No.1, pp. 149-160.

Krishnamoorthy, D. and V.V. Subha Reddy (2002). "Growth and Instability in India's Foreign Trade: A Comparative Analysis of Pre and Post Liberalization Periods", *Artha Vijnana*, Vol. XLIV, Nos. 3-4, Sep-Dec, pp. 349-365

Kulkarni, Kishore G. (1992). "Has International Trade Benefited LDCs-India's Care", *Margin*, Vol.24, No.3, April-June, pp. 235-244.

Kutty, P. Uneen (2001). "Demand for Coffee Imports: An Econometric Analysis", *Indian Economic Journal*, Vol. 48, No.3, Jan-March, pp. 92-95.

Lal, Deepak and Sarath Rajapatirana (1987). "Foreign Trade Regimes and Economic Growth in Developing Countries", *The World Bank Research Observer*, Vol. 2, No. 2, July, pp. 189-217.

Lee, Jaewoo (1998). "Intertemporal Substitution in Imported Durables", *Journal of International Economics*, Vol. 44, Feb, pp. 113-133.

Leela, P and G.P.Raju (1993). "Dependence of the Indian Economy on Newsprint Imports", *Indian Economic Journal*, Vol. 40, No.3, Jan-March, pp. 123-129.

Leela, P. (1980). "Import Dependence of the Non-Ferrous Metals Industry in India", *The Indian Economic Journal*, Vol. 28, No.2, Oct-Dec, pp. 1-20.

Lewis, W. Arthur (1978). *Theory of Economic Growth*, George Allen and Unwin Ltd.

Lopez, Ramon. and Dani Rodrik (1989). "Trade Restrictions with Imported Intermediate Inputs", When does the Trade Balance Improve", *Policy, Planning and Research Working Paper*, The World Bank, March.

Lopez, Ramon. and Vinod Thomas (1988). " Growth in Imports and Income Considerations for Africa", *Trade Expansion Program Ocassional Paper*, The World Bank, June.

Malhotra, Neena and P.S. Raikhy (1989). "Import Policy and Self Reliance-Indian Experience", *PSE, Economic Analyst*, Vol. X, No.2.

Mallick, Sushanta Kumar (1992). "Exports Growth and Industrial Development: Empirical Evidence from India", *Indian Journal of Quantitative Economics*, Vol. 8, No.162, pp. 99-105.

Mallick, Sushanta Kumar (1996). "Causality Between Exports and Economic Growth in India: Evidence from Cointegration Based Error Correction

Models", *Indian Journal of Economics*, Vol. LXXVI, No. 302, Jan, pp. 307-320.

Mani, Sunil (1991). "External Liberalization and Import-Dependence", *Economic and Political Weekly*, Vol. XXVI, No.27, July 6-13, pp. 1693-95.

Manjappa, H.D. and Ishwar V. Hegde (1998). "Import Led Growth Led Export: A New Trade Development Model for Developing Countries", *The Indian Economic Journal*, Vol. 45, No.3, Jan-Mar, pp. 100-118.

Mankar, V.G. et. al. (1981). *Foreign Trade and Development*, Himalaya Publication House, Bombay.

Mathur, Archand S. and Arvinder S. Sachdeva (2005). "Customs Tariff Structure in India", *Economic and Political Weekly*, Vol. XL, No.6, Feb 5-11, pp. 535-539.

Mathur, Vibha (2003), *India: Foreign Trade Policy and WTO: 1991-2003*, New Century Publications, Delhi.

Mathur, Vibha (2006). *Foreign Trade of India-1947 to 2007: Trends, Policies and Prospects*, New Century Publications, N. Delhi.

Mehta, Rajesh (1997). "Trade Policy Reforms, 1991-92 to 1995-96: Their Impact on External Trade", *Economic and Political Weekly*, Vol. XXXII, No. 15, April, pp. 779-783.

Mehta, Rajesh and Swapan K. Bhattacharya (1997). "SAPTA-I, SAPTA-II and SAFTA: Impact of India's Imports", *South Asian Survey*, Vol.4, No.2, July-Dec, pp. 259-275.

Meier, Gerald M. (1970). *Leading Issues in Economic Development Studies in International Poverty*, Oxford Univ. Press, New York, U.S.A.

Meier, Gerald. M. (1973), *Economic Development Theory, History, Policy*, Bombay, Asia.

Mellor, John W. (1976). *The New Economics of Growth- A strategy for India and the Developing World*, Ithaca Cornell Univ. Press.

Meyer, F.V. (1978). *International Trade Policy*, Croom Helm, London.

Mohabbat, Khan A. *et al.* (1984). "Import Demand for India: A Translog Cost Function Approach", *Economic Development and Cultural Change*, Vol. 32, No.3, April, pp. 593-605.

Monthly Commentary on Indian Economic Conditions, The Indian Institute of Public Opinion (Various Issues).

Moran, Cristian (1981). "Trends in Foreign Trade", *Economic Trends*, Vol. X, No.2, Jan 16.

Moran, Cristian (1998). "Imports Under a Foreign Exchange Constraint", *World Bank Working Papers*, The World Bank, March.

Morgan, Theodore (1975). *Economic Development Concept and Strategy*, Harper & Row Publishers, New York.

Morrissey, Oliver (2005). "Imports and Implementation: Neglected Aspects of Trade in the Report of the Commission for Africa", *The Journal of Development Studies*, Vol. 41, No.6, Aug, pp. 1133-1153.

Mukerjee, Suman K. (1994). *Textbook of Economic Development*, Orient Longman, Hydrabad.

Mukherjee, Neela (1998). "India's Trade Policy and Performance in the Nineties", *The Indian Economic Journal*, Vol. 45, No.3, Jan-Mar, pp. 119-133.

Mukherji, Indra Nath (1983). "Trends in International Trade - Reflection on India", *Economic Trends*, Vol. XII, No.7, April, pp. 123-131.

Mukherji, Indra Nath (1998). "India's Trade and Investment Linkages with Nepal: Some Reflections", *South Asian Survey*, Vol. 5, No.2, July-Dec, pp. 183-197.

Mukundan, M. and M. Manaka (2005). "Structural Reforms and Trends in Foreign Trade" in *World Trade Organisation and Indian Economic Reforms*, ed. V.B. Jugale, Serial Publications, N. Delhi, pp. 343-350.

Murray, Tracy and Perter J. Ginman (1976). "An Empirical Examination of the Traditional Aggregate Import Demand Model", *The Review of Economics and Statistics*, Vol. LVIII, No.1, Feb, pp. 75-80.

Nag, D.S. (1962). *Problems of under Developed Economy,* Lakshmi Narain Agarwal Educational Publishers, Agra.

Nanda, Paramjit and P.S. Raikhy (2002). "India's Performance in Foreign Trade During Post Liberalization Period", *PSE Economic Analyst*, Vol. XXII, Nos. 1 & 2, pp. 1-15.

Nandi, Sukumar and Sunil Kumar (2005). "Variability of Exports and Imports in Indian Perspective: An Empirical Study", *Asia Pacific Business Review*, Vol.1, Issue.1, Jan-June, pp. 68-75.

Nkang, N.M. et. al. (2007). "Determinants of Rice Imports Demand in Nigeria: A Cointegration and Error Correction Specification", *Indian Journal of Economics*, Vol. LXXXVIII, No. 348, Part-I, July, pp. 61-74.

Obstfeld, Maurice (1980). "Intermediate Imports, The Terms of Trade and The Dynamics of the Exchange Rate and Current Account", *Journal of International Economics*, Vol.10, No.4, pp. 461-480.

Ostry, Janathan D. (1991). "Trade Liberalization in Developing Countries", *IMF Staff Papers*, Vol. 38, No.3, Sep.

Pal, Prankrishna. (2007). "WTO and Its Impact on India's Foreign Trade" in *Economic Growth and Development: Emerging Issues* ed. Prankrishna Pal, Deep & Deep Publications Pvt. Ltd.

Panchamukhi, V.R. (1978). *Trade Policies of India*, Concept Publishing Co., Delhi.

Patel, N.M. (1991), "Gaji and Its Implications for India", *Arth Vikas*, Vol. XXVII, No. 1, Jan-Dec.

Patibandla, Murali (1994). "New Theories of International Trade: A Survey of Literature", *The Indian Economic Journal*, Vol. 41, No. 3, pp. 62-78.

Patibandla, Murali (2002). "Imports of Food Products: Need for High Tariffs", *Economic and Political Weekly*, Vol. 37, No. 19, May 11, pp. 1781-1783.

Patra, Michael, D. and Rajiv Ragan (1992). "The Structure of India's Imports", *RBI Occasional Papers*, Vol. 13, No.2, June, pp. 81-105.

Paul, Jsutin and A. Ramanathan (2004). "Impact of Globalization on Foreign Trade Indian Scenario", *Paradigm*, Vol. VIII, No.2, July-Dec, pp. 21-25.

Phansalkar, S.J. (1990). "Edible Oil Imports: Winners and Losers", *Economic and Political Weekly*, Jan, 20.

Pitre, Vidya. (1981). "A Study of Trade in India's Imports: 1960-61 to 1974-75", *Economic and Political Weekly*, Vol. XVI, No.19, May, pp. 851-862.

Prasad, K.N. (2003). *Indian Economy Before and Since the Reform*, Vol. II, Atlantic Publishers and Distributors, N. Delhi.

Rao, B. Sarveswara and K. Nagabhushanam (2000). "India's Demand for Imports of Non-Monetary Gold, Non-Monetary Silver and Merchandise During 1901-1913", *Indian Economic Journal*, Vol. 48, No.3, Jan-Mar, pp. 34-38.

Rao, K.S. Ramachandra (1996). "Import Intensity of Final Consumption", *RBI Occasional Papers*, Vol.17, No.2, June, pp. 65-78.

Rao, Sambasiva (2005). "Liberalization and Productivity", *Margin*, Vol. 37, No.2, Jan-Mar.

Ray, Debraj (1999). *Development Economics*, Oxford India Paper Back, Oxford Univ. Press, pp. 57-68.

Ray, S. (2003). "MNEs Strategic Alliances and Efficiency of Firms: Emerging Trends in Liberalising Era", *Economic and Political Weekly.*

Reserve Bank of India, *Report on Currency and Finance*, Mumbai, Government of India (Various Issues).

Roy, Jayanta and, R.K. Pattnaik (2004). "Uniform Import Duty: Next Step in Tariff Reform", *Economic and Political Weekly*, Vol. XXXIX, No.24, June 12-18, pp.2483-2489.

Salvatore, Dominick and Edward T. Doucling (1977). *Theory and Problems of Development Economics*, McGraw-Hill Book Company, New York.

Sandesara, J.C. (1974). *Indian Economy: Performance and Prospects*, Bombay Univ.

Santos-Paulino, Amelia and, A.P. Thirlwall (2004). "The Impact of Trade Liberalization on Exports, Imports and The Balance of Payments of Developing Countries", *The Indian Economic Journal*, Vol.114, No.493, Feb, pp. F-50 - F-72.

Sarkar, Prabirjit and Bratoti Bhattacharya (2005). "Trade Liberalisation and Growth: Case Studies of India and Korea", *Economic and Political Weekly*, Vol. XL, No. 53, Dec- Jan.

Sarma, T.S. (1999). *Paper and Paper Board Production, Availability and Imports of India*, Antlantic Publishers and Distributors, N. Delhi.

Sastry, D.V.S. (1990). "Expenditure on R & D and Imported Technology- A Cross Section Study", *RBI Occational Papers*, Vol.11, No.4, Dec, pp. 287-296.

Satapathy, C. (2001). "Under Valued Imports and Public Interest", *Economic and Political Weekly*, Vol.36, Nos. 5 & 6, Feb 3-10, 445-447.

Sathe, Dhanmanjiri (1993). "An Analysis of the Linkages of Foreign Trade for the Indian Economy: 1951-52 to 1978-79," *Artha Vijnana*, Vol. XXXV, No.3, Sep, pp. 287-296.

Sathe, Dhanmanjiri (1997). "Import Intensity of India's Exports: Some Fresh Evidence", *Economic and Political Weekly*, Vol. XXXII, No.8, Feb 22, pp. M-31 - M-44.

Sathe, Dhanmanjiri and Sunil Agarwal (2004). "Liberalization of Pulses Sector: Production, Prices and Imports", *Economic and Political Weekly*, Vol. XXXIX, No.3, July 24-30, pp. 3391-3397.

Sau, Ranjit (1983). "Structural Adjustment in the Indian Economy: IMF Model of Import Pushed Growth", *Economic and Political Weekly,* Annual Nos., Vol. XVIII, No.19, 20 & 21, May, pp. 779-788.

Sharma, K.K. and Sukhpal Singh (2000). *Indian Economy*, Abhishek Publications, Chandigarh.

Shirazi, Nasim Shah and Turkhan Ali Abdul Manap (2004). "Exports and Economic Growth Nexus: The case of Pakistan", *The Pakistan Development Review* 43:4 Part II (Winter), pp. 563-579.

Siddharthan, N.S. (1989). "Impact of Import Liberalization on Export Intensities: A Study of the Indian Private Corporate Sector", *Indian Economic Journal*, Vol.37, No.2, pp. 103-111.

Siddharthan, N.S. (2004). "Globalization Productivity, Efficiency and Growth: An Overview", *Economic and Political Weekly*, Vol. XXXIX, No.5, Jan-Feb, pp. 420-433.

Siddharthan, N.S. and K. Lal (2003). "Liberalization, MNEs and Productivity of Indian Enterprises" *Economic and Political Weekly.*

Singh, Ajit Kumar (1992). "Liberalization, Growth Strategy and the Present Economic Crisis" in Indian Economic Crisis, Diagnosis and Treatment ed. P.C. Jain, Concept Publishing Company, N. Delhi.

Singh, Bright. (1971), *Economics of Development with Special Reference to India*, Asia Publishing House Bombay.

Singh, M.P. (1984), "Effects of Imports Control on the Rate of Profit", *Economic Studies*, Vol. XXIV, No.111, pp. 215, 277-281.

Singh, M.P. (1985). *Import Policy for a Developing Economy*, Chug Publications, Allahabad.

Singh, Mohendra Pratap (1976). "Import Policy and Pattern of Industrialisation: A Case Study of India", *The Economic Studies*, Vol. 17, pp. 361-369.

Singh, Shrawan Kumar (2001). "Globalization and Developing Countries: Same Critical Issues" in *Liberalization in India. The Road Ahead,* ed. V.S. Jafa, New Century Publications, Delhi.

Singh, Tarlok (2000). "Balance of Trade, Exchange Rate and Trade Policy Regimes in India: Some Issues and Policy Perspective", *Indian Economic Journal*, Vol. 48, No.1, July-Sep, pp. 61-82.

Sinha, Anushree and Christopher Adam (2007). "Modelling The Informal Economy in India (An Analysis of Trade Reforms)" in *Trade Liberalisation and India's Informal Economy*, Ed. Barbara Harriss White and Anushree Sinha, Oxford University Press.

Sodersten, Bo and Geoffrey Reed (1994). *International Economics,* Macmillan Press Ltd., London.

Spence, A.M. (1975). "Monopoly, Quality and Regulation, *Bell Journal of Economics,* Autumn, pp. 417-429.

Sud, Swatantra P. and M. Sadrolashrafi (1980). "Import Elasticities for Agricultural Products in Iran", *Indian Journal of Economics*, Vol. LX, No.238, Jan, pp. 341-348.

Sundararajan, S. and L.M. Bhole (1988). "Testing The Effect of Devaluation on The Balance of Payments in India" *Journal of Quantitative Economics.*

Sundararajan, S. and L.M. Bhole (1989). "Functional form of the Import Demand Function", *Margin*, Vol.21, No.3, April-June, pp. 52-57.

Sundararajan, V. and Subhash Thakur (1976). "Input-Output Approach to Import Demand Function Experiments with Korean Data", *IMF Staff Paper*, Vol. XXIII, No.3, Nov, pp. 674-698.

Svedberg, P. (1979). "Optimal Tariff Policy on Imports From Multinationals", *Economic Record*, 55, pp.64-67.

Tang, Tuck Cheong (2002). "Aggregate Import Demand Behaviour in India: Stable or Unstable", *The Economic Challenger*, No.4, Issue.14, Jan-Mar, pp. 35-37.

Thirwall, A. P. (2003). *Growth and Development With Special Reference to Developing Economies*, 7th Edition, Palgrave Macmillan.

Thomas, Vinod and John Nash (1991). *Best Practices in Trade Policy Reform,* The World Bank, Oxford Univ. Press.

Thomas, Vinod and John Nash. (1991). "Technology Imports", *Encyclopaedia of Economic Development*, Vol. 17.

Tijani, A.A. and Ajobo, O. (1999) "Productivity Export Relationship in Nigeria's Agriculture", *Indian Journal of Economics*, Vol. LXXIX, No. 314, Jan, pp. 323-332.

Todaro, Michael P. (1981) *Economic Development in Third World Countries*, Longman Group Ltd, New York, America.

Todaro, Michael P. (2004) *Economic Development in IIIrd World*, 8th edition, Longman, New York, America.

Todaro, Michael, P. (2007) *Economic Development*, 8th Edition, Pearson Education.

Tripathi, Neela. (2005) *Foreign Trade and Investment in India: Policies and Performance,* Serial Publications, N.Delhi.

Varghese, Wilson. (1990). "Structural Problems in External Sector" in *Structural Changes and Issues of Indian Economy*, ed. Ashok Vasant Bhuleshkar and Dawood M. Mithani, Himalaya Publishing House, Bombay.

Verma, P.C. (1997). "India's International Trade in Services", *Indian Economic Journal*, Vol. 44, No. 3, Jan-Mar, pp. 103-120.

Virmani, Arvind. (1991). "Demand and Supply Factors in India's Trade", *Economic and Political Weekly*, Vol. 26, Feb.

Virmani, Arvind. (2003). "India's External Reforms: Modest Globalisation, Significant Gains", *Economic and Political Weekly*, Vol. XXXVIII, No. 32, Aug 9-15, pp. 3373-3392.

Virmani, Arvind. (2005). "Customs Tariff Reform", *Economic and Political Weekly*, Vol. XL, No.11, Mar 12-18, pp. 1006-1014.

Wickramasinghe, J.W. (1994). "Internal Contradictions in Trade Liberalization Models", *South Asian Survey*, Vol. 1, No.2, July-Dec, pp. 263-274.k

Index

H

I

S